A
RISING
THUNDER

A
RISING
THUNDER

From Lincoln's Election

to the Battle of Bull Run:

An Eyewitness History

RICHARD WHEELER

HarperCollins*Publishers*

HarperCollins books may be purchased for educational, business, or sales promotional use. For information please write: Special Markets Department, HarperCollins Publishers, Inc., 10 East 53rd Street, New York, NY 10022.

FIRST EDITION

Designed by Irving Perkins Associates

Library of Congress Cataloging-in-Publication Data

Wheeler, Richard
    A rising thunder : from Lincoln's election to the Battle of Bull Run: an eyewitness history / Richard Wheeler. — 1st ed.
        p.   cm.
    Includes bibliographical references (p.) and index.
    ISBN 0-06-016992-3
    1. United States—History—Civil War, 1861–1865. 2. United States—History—Civil War, 1861–1865—Campaigns. 3. Fort Sumter (Charleston, S.C.) —Siege, 1861. 4. Bull Run, 1st Battle of, Va., 1861.   I. Title.
E471.W47 1994
973.7'3—dc20   93-20695

94 95 96 97 98 AC/RRD 10 9 8 7 6 5 4 3 2 1

To my agent, Julie Fallowfield,
with infinite thanks and warmest regards

Contents

List of Illustrations

List of Maps

Preface

Wᴵᴛʜ ᴛʜᴇ 1992 ᴘᴜʙʟɪᴄᴀᴛɪᴏɴ of *Lee's Terrible Swift Sword,* my tenth book involving an eyewitness approach to a Civil War topic, I was at first doubtful that I could come up with another idea to continue my series. Then it occurred to me that my coverage of the war, though extensive, did not include a detailed account of its commencement. Hence the birth of *A Rising Thunder.*

The period extending from the Fort Sumter crisis through First Bull Run was abundant with significant, interesting, and exciting moments, most of them richly described by participants or observers. I believe that *A Rising Thunder* marks the first time that a selection from these materials has been woven into a chronological narrative.

Although the book, with its emphasis on the human side of events, is intended for the general reader rather than for the Civil War scholar, it does not shy from the scholar's perusal, for it is offered as a veracious study. The technical statements have been checked against the historical record, and the personal episodes have been analyzed for credibility.

Most of the book's ellipses indicate that the quoted material has been condensed, but some have been used to eliminate details that appeared to be faulty. All words of my own inserted in the quotes—for clarification or enhancement—have been enclosed in brackets.

The sources of the individual quotes are not given, for I was reluctant to clutter the narrative with numbers that the general reader would be apt to find more annoying than useful. A good portion of the quotes can be readily traced through the bibliography.

The illustrations were taken from *Battles and Leaders of the Civil*

War, Frank Leslie's Illustrated History of the Civil War, Harper's Pictorial History of the Great Rebellion, and other publications of the postwar years. Many of the illustrations are adaptations of sketches or photographs made while the book's events were in progress.

1

Seeds of the Storm

PRIOR TO ABRAHAM LINCOLN'S CAMPAIGN for the presidency, the nation's movement toward disunion had progressed slowly. There had always been hope that the North and the South would somehow resolve their political and economic differences. It was because Southern leaders considered Lincoln and his Republican party to be wholly at odds with their region's interests that the situation changed radically on Election Day in November 1860. Matters did not even wait until the new president was inaugurated.

Said the governor of Virginia, John Letcher: "The idea of permitting such a man to have the control and direction of the army and navy of the United States, and the appointment of high judicial and executive officers ... cannot be entertained by the South for a moment."

The nation's journey toward this point of no return had occupied a period of about fifty years, the trouble stemming from the fact that the two sections developed in different ways. A British writer of the time saw the nation as "practically that of two distinct communities or peoples, speaking indeed a common language and united by a federal bond, but opposed in principles and interests, alienated in feeling, and jealous rivals in the pursuit of political power."

The North, which had the larger population, was geared to industrial growth, with all its attendant hustle and bustle. The South, where aristocratic values were cherished, held to a slower pace, and its chief source of wealth was large-scale agriculture,

1

Southern plantation of prewar years

with cotton the leading crop, the system dependent upon the labor of slaves. Exclusive of the Yankee shipowners who made fortunes in the slave trade, the North had never found slavery to be very profitable. Many of the farms were small enough to be run by their owners, and large urban populations were available for industrial labor. It was therefore easy for Northerners to view slavery as an evil.

In the nation's earliest days, when cotton was still a minor crop and slave labor was only modestly consequential, even many Southerners deplored the institution. But with the invention of the cotton gin (a machine that easily removed the cotton's clinging seeds) and the consequent expansion of the crop's production, these critical voices grew weak. More and more people began to find ways to convince themselves that slavery was morally justifiable. For one thing, the reasoning went, the blacks had been rescued from African paganism and introduced to Christianity. Ministers made such statements as, "If you take slaves with the intent of conducting them to Christ, the action will not be a sin but may prove a benediction."

It was the nation's great westward expansion, which involved the formation of new states, that made slavery a critical issue. The South, in order to ensure the growth of its economy and its influence, strove to spread the practice, while the North wanted it curbed in favor of its own economic system, to which slave labor was seen as a threat.

Clear-thinking Washington legislators such as Henry Clay of Kentucky understood that the only way to avert explosive trouble was to try to keep the power of the slave states and the free states on a parity, and an early bill enacted from this viewpoint was the Missouri Compromise of 1820. Ensuing years saw the passage of other compromise bills, and each played its part in delaying a showdown.

Paramount in the long struggle was the issue of states' rights. Since the nation came into being, various political figures, Northern and Southern, had regarded the powers of the federal government as being limited to those explicitly mentioned in the Constitution, and the powers of the individual states as embracing all of those not explicitly denied them. In accord with this doctrine, the Southern states maintained that Congress had no right to regulate slavery, nor to pass any other laws that infringed upon their sovereignty.

A tariff levied by Congress in 1832 was seen by the South as benefitting the North at Southern expense, and South Carolina

Henry Clay

declared the legislation null and void within its borders and also threatened to secede from the Union. Receiving no substantial support from the other Southern states, South Carolina softened its stand after a show of military force by President Andrew Jackson, who said: "Our Federal Union—it must be preserved!"

The tariff was reenacted on terms more favorable to the South. But the region's political strength was diminishing. A degree of optimism was spurred in 1845 when Texas, after breaking free from Mexico, was admitted to the Union, for the territory teemed with slave labor. The annexation, however, led to the Mexican War (1846–1848), one of the results of which was the admission to the Union of California as a free state.

Complicating the slavery issue were the North's abolitionists, whose demands for a speedy end to the system were not balanced by practical ideas as to how this could be done without destroying the South's economy and creating social turmoil. Although the abolitionists were a minority group (most Northerners were chary of the idea of granting the slave instant and unconditional freedom), their agitations were a dominant part of the scene. Among their leading spokespeople were William Lloyd Garrison, publisher of the *Liberator,* Harriet Beecher Stowe, author of *Uncle Tom's Cabin,* and Yankee poet John Greenleaf Whittier. Some of the abolitionists went so far as to deny the validity of the Constitution, since it tolerated slavery.

There were Northern newspapers, of course, that came out against the institution. A particular practice of these organs—one that stirred resentment in the South as it influenced opinion in the North—was to give detailed coverage to slave auctions, emphasizing the fact that these proceedings often broke up families.

As Northern political ascendancy resulted in the placing of tighter limits on the growth of slavery, the South felt gravely threatened. In 1850 the venerable Senator John C. Calhoun of South Carolina warned in a speech on the Senate floor: "I have . . . believed from the first that the agitation of the subject of slavery would, if not prevented by some timely and effective measure, end in disunion. . . . The agitation has been permitted to proceed, with almost no attempt to resist it, until it has reached a period when it can no longer be disguised or denied that the Union is in danger."

The year of Calhoun's speech saw the enactment of a law addressing one Southern grievance: the abolitionist practice of wel-

Harriet Beecher Stowe

coming escaped slaves into Northern territory. These blacks were now to be seized and returned, and their abolitionist friends were to be arrested and prosecuted. But the people of the North were generally opposed to the law. In a Quaker community near Christiana in Lancaster County, Pennsylvania, a group of escaped slaves were abetted in arming themselves for defense, and a Southern planter who came to claim one of them was shot to death. A number of blacks and their Quaker friends were taken into custody, but there were no convictions. The case pointed out the fact that the fugitive slave law was largely unenforceable. As if to clinch matters in this respect, the abolitionists were achieving significant results with their Underground Railroad, a system by which escaped slaves were relayed to Canada.

There were many people, both Northerners and Southerners, who believed that the secession of the South was inevitable but that it would occur peaceably. A firm dissenter from this opinion was Daniel Webster of Massachusetts, whose association with national politics spanned a period of forty years. "Peaceable secession is an utter impossibility. . . . I see it as plainly as I see the sun in heaven—I see that disruption must produce such a war as I will not describe."

In the middle 1850s, during the settlement of the Kansas Territory, immigrants from the free states and those from the slave

A slave auction

states became involved in episodes of civil strife, with bloodshed that included about two hundred fatalities, as they maneuvered for political supremacy. The free-staters at length prevailed.

It was during the fighting in Kansas that America first heard of John Brown, perhaps the most intensely earnest abolitionist of the era. Born in Massachusetts in 1800, Brown was descended from one of the *Mayflower* Puritans. He himself had fathered twenty children by two wives, the first wife dying at the birth of his seventh child, who also died. In Kansas, Brown was the leader of a band of free-state guerrillas, among whom were several of his sons. The zealot's part in a fight that took place at the village of Osawatomie—an affair during which one of his sons was slain—earned him the sobriquet "Osawatomie Brown."

There had been no gunfire in the East since the trouble at Christiana, but tempers were rising. In Washington, Preston S. Brooks, a congressman from South Carolina, assaulted Massachusetts Senator Charles Sumner with a walking stick, knocking him

John Brown

senseless and impairing his health, after Sumner had made an antislavery speech that dealt sternly with South Carolina Senator Andrew Pickens Butler, who was Brooks's uncle. Brooks resigned his seat in the House, but his constituents reelected him at once, and he was sent approving messages from friends in various parts of the South. At a banquet given in his honor, the congressman said of the North-South dispute:

"I tell you, fellow-citizens, from the bottom of my heart, that the only mode which I can think of for meeting the issue is just to tear up the Constitution of the United States, trample it under foot, and form a Southern confederacy, every state of which shall be a slaveholding state. I believe it as I stand in the face of my Maker—I believe it on my responsibility to you as your honored representative—that the only hope of the South is in the South, and that the only available means of making that hope effective is to cut asunder the bonds that tie us together, and take our separate position in the family of nations."

There was as yet no consensus in the South for so drastic a step, and the preliminaries continued. In 1857, the North protested the Supreme Court's Dred Scott decision, which stated not only that a slave, being property, had no constitutional rights as a citizen, but also that it was unconstitutional for Congress to legislate the exclusion of slavery from new territories. The South, though encouraged by the Dred Scott decision (at least until it proved to be ineffectual), was appalled when, in the autumn of 1859, John Brown and a group of his followers made an attempt to steal federal weapons from the arsenal at Harpers Ferry, Virginia (later West Virginia), for the purpose of mounting a Negro uprising.

James Buchanan was president of the United States at this time, and it fell to him to deal with the incursion—which, even before he could act, had drawn hundreds of militia volunteers from Virginia and Maryland. Buchanan responded with a detachment of marines led by Colonel Robert E. Lee and Lieutenant James Ewell Brown "Jeb" Stuart, both of whom were Virginians and both of whom were career men in the U.S. Army presently on leave from duty on the western frontier. (Stuart bore a chest scar evidencing a brush he'd had with a party of Cheyenne Indians.)

Already bloodied by the militia, Brown and his men had fortified themselves in Harpers Ferry's fire-engine house, where Lee's marines attacked them, soon quelling the lot. Brown's raid had

James Buchanan

cost him two more sons dead, and he himself was painfully slashed by a marine's sword.

Within a matter of days, Brown was brought to trial in nearby Charlestown. His wounds, which included some severe cuts about the head, were still open, and he was weak, but his spirit remained unbroken. He said at his trial: "If it be deemed necessary that I should forfeit my life for the furtherance of the ends of justice, and mingle my blood further with the blood of my children and with the blood of millions in this slave country whose rights are disregarded by wicked, cruel, and unjust enactments—I submit. So let it be done."

Sentenced to die by hanging, Brown wrote his wife: "I can trust God with both the time and the manner of my death, believing . . . that for me at this time to seal my testimony for God and humanity with my blood will do vastly more toward advancing the cause I have earnestly endeavored to promote, than all I have done in my life before."

Brown's hanging was scheduled for December 2, 1859, only six weeks from the time of his raid, and the execution was performed in the presence of several thousand military men, both regulars and militia, who had been assembled to make sure the peace was kept. The regulars were commanded by Robert E. Lee. Among the Virginia militiamen on hand was a young actor named John Wilkes Booth. Also present was Thomas Jonathan Jackson, then a professor at the Virginia Military Institute, who had accompanied the institute's corps of cadets.

The entire South, of course, was greatly relieved to see John Brown put out of the way. A hope was harbored that the North would take a lesson from his ill-conceived raid, would reconsider its antislavery policies. Surely no civilized person wanted to see the slaves incited to insurrection! But Brown was mourned and eulogized in the North, particularly among the abolitionists, some of whom had been supporting him with money. And the zealot now became a powerful symbol. He had been right in his belief that his death would advance the cause of abolitionism more than anything he had done in life.

The impact of the Harpers Ferry incident was well understood by President Buchanan, who as a Democrat was partial to Southern interests:

"In the already excited condition of public feeling throughout the South, this raid . . . made a deeper impression on the Southern mind against the Union than all former events. Considered merely as an isolated act of a desperate fanatic, it would have had no lasting effect. It was the enthusiastic and permanent approbation of the object of his expedition by the abolitionists of the North which spread alarm and apprehension throughout the South."

Adds a member of one of Virginia's leading families, Constance Cary, then a young girl living in Fairfax County, just west of Washington:

"Our homestead was . . . at a considerable distance from the theater of [the John Brown] episode; and, belonging as we did to a family among the first in the State to manumit slaves (our grandfather having set free those that came to him by inheritance, and the people who served us being hired from their owners and remaining in our employ through years of kindliest relations), there seemed to be no special reason for us to share in the apprehension of an uprising of the blacks.

"But there was the fear . . . dark, boding, oppressive, and altogether hateful. I can remember taking it to bed with me at night, and awaking suddenly, oftentimes, to confront it through a vigil of nervous terror. . . . The notes of the whip-poor-wills in the sweet-gum swamp near the stable, the mutterings of a distant

Courthouse in Charlestown where John Brown was tried and sentenced

thunderstorm, even the rustle of the night wind in the oaks that shaded my window, filled me with nameless dread.

"In the daytime it seemed impossible to associate suspicion with those familiar tawny or sable faces that surrounded us. We had seen them for so many years smiling or saddening with the family joys or sorrows. They were so guileless, so patient, so satisfied. What subtle influence was at work that should transform them into tigers thirsting for our blood? The idea was preposterous.

"But when evening came again, and with it the hour when the colored people—who in summer and autumn weather kept astir half the night—assembled themselves together for dance or prayer-meeting, the ghost that refused to be laid was again at one's elbow. Rusty bolts were drawn, and rusty firearms loaded. A watch was set where never before had eye or ear been lent to such a service. In short, peace had flown from the borders of Virginia."

Politically, it must be noted, the South had fallen into deeper disadvantage in both houses of Congress. Of the thirty-three states now in the Union, eighteen were free states and only fifteen were slave states.

2

Lincoln Takes the Stage

ALTHOUGH ABRAHAM LINCOLN LIVED through the entire period of sectional ferment that preceded the Civil War, he played no significant part in events of the earlier decades.

"I was born February 12, 1809," he explains, "in Hardin County, Kentucky. . . . My father . . . removed from Kentucky to . . . Spencer County, Indiana, in my eighth year. We reached our new home about the time the State came into the Union. It was a wild region, with many bears and other wild animals still in the woods. There I grew up. There were some schools, so-called, but . . . absolutely nothing to excite ambition for education. Of course, when I came of age I did not know much. Still, somehow, I could read, write, and cipher. . . .

"I was raised to farm work, which I continued till I was twenty-two. At twenty-two I came to Illinois, Macon County. Then I got to New Salem . . . where I remained a year as a sort of clerk in a store. Then came the Black Hawk [Indian] War, and I was elected a captain of volunteers. . . . I went the campaign . . . [then] ran for the legislature the same year (1832), and was beaten. . . . The next and three succeeding biennial elections I was elected to the legislature. I was not a candidate afterward.

"During this legislative period I had studied law, and removed to Springfield to practice it. In 1846 I was . . . elected to the lower House of Congress. Was not a candidate for reelection. From 1849 to 1854 . . . practiced law more assiduously than ever before."

Abraham Lincoln, drawn from life

Lincoln had a partner in his practice, William H. Herndon, who left this sketch:

"Mr. Lincoln's habit was to get down to his office about 9 A.M., unless he was out on the circuit, which was about six or eight months in the year. Our office never was a headquarters for politics. Mr. Lincoln never stopped in the street to have a social chat with anyone. He was not a social man, too reflective, too abstracted [and often in a state of melancholy]. He never attended political gatherings till the thing was organized, and then he was ready to make a speech. . . .

"If a man came into our office on business he stated his case, Lincoln listening generally attentively. . . . When he had sufficiently considered, he gave his opinion of the case plainly, directly, and sharply. . . . Mr. Lincoln was not a good conversationalist, except it was in the political world. Nor was he a good listener. His great anxiety to tell a story made him burst in and consume the day in telling stories. Lincoln was not a general reader, except in politics.

"On Sundays he would come down to his office, sometimes bringing [his sons] Tad and Willie and sometimes not, would write his letters, write declarations and other law papers, write out the heads of his speeches, take notes of what he intended to say. . . .

"Lincoln would sometimes lie down in the office to rest on the sofa, his feet on two or three chairs or up against the wall. [His frame extended to a length of nearly six feet four inches.] In this position he would reflect, decide on what he was going to do and how to do it; and then he would jump up, pick up his hat and run, the good Lord knows where."

Lincoln tried many of his cases before Judge David Davis, of the Eighth Illinois Judicial Circuit. The judge relates:

"In all the elements that constitute the great lawyer, he had few equals. . . . His mind was logical and direct. . . . An unfailing vein of humor never deserted him, and he was always able to chain the attention of court and jury . . . by the appropriateness of his anecdotes. . . . In order to bring into full activity his great powers, it

Lincoln's home in Springfield

was necessary that he should be convinced of the right and justice of the matter which he advocated. When so convinced . . . he was usually successful. He read lawbooks but little. . . . He was usually self-reliant, depending on his own resources, and rarely consulting his brother lawyers. . . . He never took from a client . . . more than he thought the service was worth and the client could reasonably afford to pay. . . . His presence on the circuit was watched for with interest, and never failed to produce joy and hilarity."

These were the days that saw the birth of the Republican party, which opposed the further spread of slavery, and Lincoln became a Republican. However, in spite of a strong conviction that slavery was immoral, he felt no special fraternity toward blacks; nor was he critical of Southern whites.

"They are just what we would be in their situation. If slavery did not now exist amongst them, they would not introduce it. If it did now exist amongst us, we should not instantly give it up. . . . We know that some Southern men do free their slaves, go north and become tiptop abolitionists, while some Northern ones go south and become most cruel slave-masters."

Lincoln at this time had no fixed ideas regarding emancipation. "When it is said that the institution . . . is very difficult to get rid of . . . in any satisfactory way, I can understand and appreciate the saying. I surely will not blame [the South] for not doing what I should not know how to do myself. If all earthly power were given me, I should not know what to do as to the existing institution."

Lincoln came to national notice in 1858 when he ran for the office of U.S. senator from Illinois against the popular Democrat Stephen A. Douglas, known as the "Little Giant." The campaign centered on a series of public debates dealing with the slavery issue. Although Lincoln lost the election, the brilliance of his presentations convinced many Republicans that he was presidential timber. He had developed a viewpoint he stated as follows:

"I believe we shall not have peace upon the question until the opponents of slavery arrest the further spread of it, and place it where the public mind shall rest in the belief that it is in the course of ultimate extinction; or, on the other hand, that its advocates will push it forward until it shall become alike lawful in all the States, old as well as new, North as well as South.

"Now I believe, if we could arrest the spread . . . it would be in the course of ultimate extinction. . . . The crisis would be past, and the institution might be let alone for a hundred years—if it

Stephen A. Douglas

should live so long—in the States where it exists, yet it would [through lack of growth] be going out of existence in the way best for both the black and the white races."

Lincoln gained additional support through a speech he made at Cooper Institute, New York City, in February 1860. His closing words were meant especially for members of the Republican party:

"It is exceedingly desirable that all parts of this great confederacy shall be at peace and in harmony, one with another. Let us Republicans do our part to have it so. Even though much provoked, let us do nothing through passion and ill temper. Even though the Southern people will not so much as listen to us, let us calmly consider their demands. . . .

"If slavery is right, all words, acts, laws and constitutions against it are themselves wrong, and should be silenced and swept away. If it is right, we cannot object justly to its nationality, its universality. If it is wrong, they cannot justly insist upon its extension, its enlargement.

"All they ask we could readily grant, if we thought slavery right. All we ask they could as readily grant, if they thought it wrong. . . .

Thinking it right, as they do, they are not to blame for desiring its full recognition. . . . But thinking it wrong, as we do, can we yield to them? Can we cast our votes with their view, and against our own? . . .

"Wrong as we think slavery is, we can yet afford to let it alone where it is, because that much is due to the necessity arising from its actual presence in the nation. But can we, while our votes will prevent it, allow it to spread into the national territories, and to overrun us here in these free states?

"If our sense of duty forbids this, then let us stand by our duty, fearlessly and effectively. Let us be diverted by none of those sophistical contrivances . . . such as groping for some middle ground between the right and the wrong. . . . Neither let us be slandered from our duty by false accusations against us, nor frightened from it by menaces of destruction to the Government. . . .

"Let us have faith that right makes might, and in that faith let us, to the end, dare to do our duty as we understand it."

Where Lincoln made his first reply to Douglas: the chamber of the Illinois House of Representatives

The following day Horace Greeley's New York *Tribune* reported, "No man ever before made such an impression on his first appeal to a New York audience."

In May of that year, at a convention held in Chicago, Lincoln was made the Republican party's candidate for president. How he came to be elected is explained by a Massachusetts citizen, John D. Billings, at the time a young shopworker, who followed the campaign with avid interest.

"The autumn of [1860] witnessed the most exciting political canvass this country had ever seen. The Democratic Party, which had been in power for [two terms] in succession, split into factions and nominated two candidates. The Northern Democrats nominated Stephen A. Douglas . . . who was an advocate of the doctrine of *Squatter Sovereignty,* that is, the right of a people living in a Territory which wanted admission into the Union as a State to decide for themselves whether they would or would not have slavery.

"The southern Democrats nominated John C. Breckinridge, of Kentucky, at that time Vice President of the United States. The doctrine which he and his party advocated was the right [of South-

Republican headquarters in Chicago, scene of Lincoln's nomination

erners] to carry their slaves into every State and Territory in the Union without any hindrance whatever.

"Then there was still another party, called by some the *Peace Party,* which pointed to the Constitution of the country as its guide but had nothing to say on the great question of slavery, which was so prominent with the other parties. It took for its standard-bearer John Bell of Tennessee. . . . This party drew its membership . . . largely from the Democrats. . . .

"The Republicans did not intend to meddle with slavery where it then was, but opposed its extension into any *new* States and Territories. This latter fact was very well known to the slaveholders, and so they voted almost solidly for John C. Breckinridge. But it was very evident to them, after the Democratic party divided, that the Republicans would succeed. . . .

"As early as the 25th of October, several Southerners who were, or had been, prominent in politics met in South Carolina and decided by a unanimous vote that the State should withdraw from the Union in the event of Lincoln's election. . . . Some other States held similar meetings about the same time. . . . These men were . . . known . . . as "Fire-eaters.' "

The Fire-eaters were actually elated over Lincoln's status. They were, first and last, for *secession,* and the situation that autumn suited their plans to a tee. The entire South was aroused, and even the moderates were beginning to think in secessionist terms.

Women as well as men found encouragement and even pleasurable excitement in the thought of making the South an independent nation. An exception was Kate Bowyer, a young newlywed who lived in Bedford County, Virginia.

"It was in the fall of 1860 that I picked up a letter written to my father by one of Georgia's leading Senators, and this expression was in it: 'I think we shall bring Georgia through in a solid phalanx for secession.' Secession! It was a new word in my vocabulary, and sounded like a distant signal gun of alarm. The words I have quoted . . . haunted me. All sorts of terrible possibilities loomed up. . . . 'Georgia a solid phalanx for secession!' To what horrors might not this lead? But the subject was too fraught with dread. I put it forcibly away."

Not everyone in the South was aware that a break with Washington was actually looming. Annie E. Johns, of North Carolina, tells of her first intimation of such a possibility:

"I was walking with some friends through the woods bordering on the beautiful valley of Dan River in Rockingham County. . . . Every member of the party, excepting myself, was an owner of low grounds lying on the river, and we were all slaveholders. The conversation naturally turned on the political state of the country, when a gentleman—a lawyer and man of fine sense—exclaimed, 'If Lincoln is elected, I do not consider that my property is worth one cent!' From that moment affairs assumed a much more serious aspect in my mind."

Election Day was November 6. In Springfield, Illinois, Lincoln's victory was followed by a jubilee. Among the outsiders who came to the scene was a party that included Donn Piatt, a Cincinnati journalist.

"We found Springfield drunk with delight. On the day of our arrival we were invited to a supper at the house of the President-elect. It was a plain, comfortable frame structure, and the supper was an old-fashioned mess of indigestion, composed mainly of cakes, pies, and chickens. . . . After the supper we sat, far into the night, talking over the situation.

"Mr. Lincoln was the homeliest man I ever saw. His body seemed to me a huge skeleton in clothes. Tall as he was, his hands and feet looked out of proportion, so long and clumsy were they. Every movement was awkward in the extreme. He sat with one leg thrown over the other, and the pendant foot swung almost to the floor. And all the while two little boys, his sons, clambered over those legs, patted his cheeks, pulled his nose, and poked their fingers in his eyes, without causing reprimand or even notice.

"He had a face that defied artistic skill to soften or idealize. . . . It was capable of few expressions, but those were extremely striking. When in repose his face was dull, heavy, and repellent. It brightened like a lit lantern when animated. His dull eyes would fairly sparkle with fun, or express as kindly a look as I ever saw, when moved by some matter of human interest.

"I soon discovered that this strange and strangely gifted man, while not at all cynical, was a skeptic. His view of human nature was low, but good-natured. . . . He considered the movement in the South as a sort of political game of bluff, gotten up by politicians, and meant solely to frighten the North. He believed that when the leaders saw their efforts in that direction were unavailing, the tumult would subside. . . .

"I gathered more of this from what Mrs. Lincoln said than from the utterances of our host. This good lady injected remarks into the conversation with more force than logic, and was treated by her husband with about the same good-natured indifference with which he regarded the troublesome boys. . . .

"I found myself studying this strange, quaint, great man with keen interest. A newly-fashioned individuality had come within the circle of my observation. I saw a man of coarse, tough fibre, without culture, and yet of such force that every observation was original, incisive, and striking, while his illustrations were quaint as Aesop's fables. . . .

"It was well for us that our President proved to be what I then recognized. He was equal to the awful strain put upon him in the four years of terrible strife that followed. A man of delicate mould . . . would have broken down. . . .

"There never lived a man who could say 'no' with readier facility, and abide by his saying with more firmness than President Lincoln. His good-natured manner misled the common mind. It covered as firm a character as nature ever clad with human flesh. . . .

"With all his awkwardness . . . and utter disregard of social conventionalities that seemed to invite familiarity, there was some-

Mary Todd Lincoln, the president's wife

thing about Abraham Lincoln that enforced respect. . . . I was told at Springfield that this accompanied him through life. Among his rough associates when young he was leader, looked up to and obeyed, because they felt of his muscle and [observed] his readiness in its use. Among his companions at the bar it was attributed to his ready wit, which kept his duller associates at a distance.

"The fact was, however, that this power came from a [manifestation] of reserve force of intellectual ability. . . . Through one of those freaks of nature that produce a Shakespeare at long intervals, a giant had been born to the poor whites of Kentucky."

In the Southern states, where Lincoln was known as the "Illinois Ape," secession proceedings began at once. Lincoln, with nearly four months to go before the start of his term, could do nothing but keep apace of developments as he set about forming his cabinet and shaping the other elements of his political team.

To Donn Piatt, Lincoln seemed altogether too calm about his position.

"When I told him . . . that the Southern people were in dead earnest, meant war, and I doubted whether he would be inaugurated in Washington, he laughed. . . . I became somewhat irritated, and told him that in ninety days the land would be whitened with tents. He said in reply:

" 'Well, we won't jump that ditch until we come to it,' and then, after a pause, added, 'I must run the machine as I find it.' "

3

Secession Becomes a Fact

THE STATE MOST BELLIGERENT toward Washington was South
Carolina, and the coastal city of Charleston was the state's
hottest spot. (In this age when punning was a rampant form of
humor, a Northern newspaper said that these people really had
"no warrant for their *war rant*.")

As related by South Carolinian Claudine Rhett, who was in
Charleston that autumn:

"The very air seemed to be charged with electricity.... You
could not walk more than a few steps down any thoroughfare
without meeting young men wearing conspicuously on their
breasts blue cockades, or strips of plaited palmetto fastened to
their buttonholes, which attested that they were 'minute men,' all
ready for duty. Flags fluttered in every direction, and the adjacent
islands were converted into camping grounds. Companies drilled
and paraded daily on every open square in the city, and bands of
music nightly serenaded distinguished men, and made the old
houses echo back the strains of 'Dixie' and the 'Marseillaise.'

"In December South Carolina seceded from the Union, and I
shall never forget the evening that the Ordinance of Secession was
signed, by the delegates of each district of the state, at the large
Institute Hall on Meeting Street.... The scene was one of extraordinary impressiveness, and the enthusiasm and excitement
spirit-stirring. There was scarcely standing-room in the big hall
for the eager crowd of witnesses, and the galleries were packed
with ladies. As the districts were called out in turn by ... the
chairman of the convention, and the delegates one by one went
up on the platform and signed the Ordinance, the cheering was

Secession Hall in Charleston

vehement, and the ladies waved their handkerchiefs in token of approval. Never was an act performed with more unanimity, and never did one meet with more general and hearty approbation."

A telegram carrying the news winged its way toward Washington while President Buchanan was guest of honor at a fashionable city wedding, where one of the other guests was the wife of a Virginia congressman, Mrs. Roger A. Pryor, who relates:

"After the ceremony, the crowd waited until the President went forward to wish the bride and her husband 'a great deal of happiness.' Everybody remained standing until Mr. Buchanan returned to his seat. I stood behind his chair and observed that he had aged much since the summer. He had had much to bear. Unable to please either party, he had been accused of cowardice, imbecility, and even insanity. . . .

"The crowd in the . . . drawing room soon thinned as the guests found their way to the rooms in which the presents were displayed. The President kept his seat, and I stood behind him as one and another came forward to greet him.

"Presently he looked over his shoulder and said, 'Madam, do you suppose the house is on fire? I hear an unusual commotion in the hall.'

" 'I will inquire the cause, Mr. President,' I said. I went out at the nearest door, and there in the entrance hall I found Mr. Lawrence Keitt, member from South Carolina, leaping in the air, shaking a paper over his head, and exclaiming, 'Thank God! Oh, thank God!'

"I took hold of him and said, 'Mr. Keitt, are you crazy? The President hears you, and wants to know what's the matter.'

" 'Oh!' he cried. 'South Carolina has seceded! Here's the telegram. I feel like a boy let out from school.'

"I returned and, bending over Mr. Buchanan's chair, said in a

Lawrence M. Keitt

low voice, 'It appears, Mr. President, that South Carolina has seceded from the Union. Mr. Keitt has a telegram.'

"He looked at me, stunned for a moment. Falling back and grasping the arms of his chair, he whispered, 'Madam, might I beg you to have my carriage called?'

"I met his secretary and sent him in without explanation, and myself saw that his carriage was at the door before I reentered the room. I then found my husband, who was already cornered with Mr. Keitt, and we called our own carriage. . . .

"There was no more thought of bride, bridegroom, wedding cake, or wedding breakfast."

Adds period historian Benson J. Lossing:

"While there was calmness in Congress on the annunciation of the action of the South Carolinians, there was great excitement throughout the Capital. [I] was in Washington at the time, and was in conversation with General [Lewis] Cass, at his house . . . when a relative brought to him a bulletin concerning the act of secession.

"The venerable statesman read the few words that announced

Lewis Cass

Pennsylvania Avenue at war's beginning

the startling fact, and then, throwing up his hands while tears started from his eyes, he exclaimed with uncommon emotion, 'Can it be? Can it be? Oh . . . I had hoped to retire from the public service, and go home to die, with the happy thought that I should leave to my children, as an inheritance from patriotic men, a united and prosperous republic. But it is all over! This is but the beginning of the end. The people in the South are mad; the people in the North are asleep. The President is pale with fear, for his official household is full of traitors. . . . God only knows what is to be the fate of my poor country! To Him alone must we look in this hour of thick darkness.'

"[I] left the venerable ex-Minister of State, and went over to the War and Navy Departments. The offices were closed for the day, but the halls and lobbies were resonant with the voices of excited men. There were treasonable utterances there, shocking to the ears of loyal citizens.

"I went to the hotels on Pennsylvania Avenue . . . and found them swarming with guests, for it was then the late dinner-hour. There was wild excitement among them. Secession cockades were plentiful, and treason and sedition walked as boldly and defiantly in those hotels, and in the streets of the National Capital, as in . . . the streets of Charleston.

"I took up the newspapers, and found no word of comfort therein for the lovers of the country. 'The long-threatened result of Black Republican outrage and autocracy,' said one, 'has taken place in South Carolina. Secession is a fixed fact.' Another, the Government Gazette, praised the dignity of the South Carolina Convention. . . .

"The conspirators were so confident of the success of their schemes that one of the leading Southern Senators, then in Congress, said, 'Mr. Lincoln will not dare to come to Washington after the expiration of the term of Mr. Buchanan. This city will be seized and occupied as the capital of the Southern Confederacy, and Mr. Lincoln will be compelled to take his oath of office in Philadelphia or in New York.' "

South Carolina's example was soon followed. Explains Alice Brooks, at the time a resident of Columbus, Georgia:

"As each state seceded from the Union, casting its lot with the Confederacy for victory or defeat, another star was added to our new flag of Stars and Bars, and its accession was celebrated by a grand illumination and torchlight procession. . . . It was a beautiful sight [in Columbus when Georgia seceded] to see every house for squares in every direction ablaze with light. Skyrockets rent the face of night; tar barrels and bonfires burned their brightest; men seemed almost wild with joy, and paraded the streets with torches, tossing their hats in the air and shouting huzzah for the seceding states and infant Confederacy. At the courthouse square, speeches were made to hundreds of enthusiastic people. [The speakers'] hearts burned with patriotism, and fired their words with eloquence. Hope's finger traced a picture of an independent Confederacy with its own laws and law-givers—a picture of victory crowning our Southland a queen in her own right."

Another Georgian, Mrs. I. V. Franklin of Augusta, tells of developments she experienced as a schoolgirl:

"Well do I remember . . . the wild excitement over secession, when all fierce rebel maidens wore the badge of sympathy. My school books were never taken unless the badge adorned the left shoulder for the street. On all sides nothing was discussed but the subject of secession. There was a feverish excitement pervading the atmosphere of the schoolrooms, and I remember a rebel concert given, in which every pupil wore a distinctive costume of Confederate colors. Songs of Southern zeal and full of battle spirit were sung to the roll of a drum, which was supported by a child who was draped in a banner. The wildest enthusiasm prevailed when the two hundred girls sang in chorus of their love for the Southern land, for her brave soldiers, and for their valor yet to be proven. General T. R. R. Cobb was present on this occasion, and was at the time full of ardor in his arrangements for the active field."

The general was fated to die during the Battle of Fredericksburg in December 1862.

Among the students attending the Female Seminary at Tallahassee, Florida, during these stirring days was Florida Saxon, who gives this glimpse of one of her classmates:

"A bevy of girls was gathered . . . around a dark-haired maiden who had mounted a bench and, with flushed cheeks and shining eyes, was making what the girls called a 'secession speech,' but which was in reality a defense of her native state of South Carolina. The school was about equally divided in sentiment, part being in favor of the Union and part for disunion; and never did

Woman wearing the Stars and Bars of the Confederacy

politicians plead their cause with more impassioned earnestness than did these impulsive young creatures.

"Katie Weston was the speaker on this occasion. 'Who would be a thrall of the Yankee?' she said. 'Who in this crowd'—looking scornfully around—'dares to blame the noble old State of South Carolina for rising in her might and throwing off the oppressor's yoke? I glory in her pluck. I am glad that she was the first to shake herself free from the galling shackles of tyranny. And I am proud to know that my *adopted* state, the beautiful Land of Flowers, was not slow in stepping to her side. I have five brothers. I wish they were all old enough to fight!'

"So carried away was she by her enthusiasm, she did not notice that one of the teachers had entered and was listening with a look of intense amusement on his face, until a slight stir in that part of the hall caused her to look round; and, observing the arch smile on his lips, she sprang from her perch and covered her face with both hands to hide the burning blushes."

Few men of the South manifested more ardor for the cause of independence than twenty-eight-year-old John B. Gordon, a stranger to military experience who was destined to rise to the rank of lieutenant general before the war ended. Gordon relates:

"The outbreak of war [that is, the advent of the secession movement] found me in the mountains of Georgia, Tennessee, and Alabama, engaged in the development of coal mines. This does not mean that I was a citizen of three States; but it does mean that I lived so near the lines that my mines were in Georgia, my house in Alabama, and my post office in Tennessee. The first company of soldiers, therefore, with which I entered the service was composed of stalwart mountaineers from the three States.

"I had been educated for the bar, and for a time practiced law in Atlanta. In September, 1854, I had married Miss Fanny Haralson . . . of La Grange, Georgia. The wedding occurred on her seventeenth birthday and when I was but twenty-two. We had two children, both boys. . . .

"My spirit had been caught up by the flaming enthusiasm that swept like a prairie fire through the land, and I hastened to unite with the brave men of the mountains in organizing a company of volunteers. But what was I to do with the girl-wife and the two little boys? The wife and mother was no less taxed in her effort to settle this momentous question. But finally yielding to the promptings of her own heart and to her unerring sense of duty, she

Anti-Union woodcut from a Southern newspaper

ended doubt . . . by announcing that she intended to accompany me to the war, leaving her children with my mother and faithful 'Mammy Mary.' I rejoiced at her decision. . . .

"The mountaineers did me the honor to elect me their captain. . . . Our first decision was to mount and go as cavalry. . . . This company of mounted men was organized as soon as the conflict seemed probable, and prior to any call for volunteers. They were doomed to a disappointment. 'No cavalry now needed,' was the laconic and stunning reply to the offer of our services. What was to be done, was the perplexing question. . . .

" 'Let us dismount and go . . . as infantry.' This proposition was carried with a shout, and by an almost unanimous vote. . . . Reluctantly, therefore, we abandoned our horses, and resolved to go at once . . . as infantry, without waiting for orders, arms, or uniforms. Not a man in the company had the slightest military training. . . .

Main street of an interior Southern town

"The new government that was to be formed had no standing army as a nucleus around which the volunteers could be brought into compact order . . . and the States which were to form it had but few arms. . . . The old-fashioned squirrel rifles and double-barrelled shotguns were called into requisition.

"Governor Joseph E. Brown, of Georgia, put shops in the State to work making what were called 'Joe Brown's Pikes.' They were a sort of rude bayonet, or steel lance, fastened not to guns but to long poles or handles, and were to be given to men who had no other arms. Of course, few if any of these pikemen ever had occasion to use these warlike implements, which were worthy of the Middle Ages, but those who bore them were as gallant knights as ever levelled a lance in close quarters. . . .

"The irrepressible humor and ready rustic wit which afterward relieved the tedium of the march and broke the monotony of the camp . . . had already begun to sparkle in the intercourse of the volunteers. A woodsman who was noted as a 'crack shot' among his hunting companions felt sure that he was going to win fame as a select rifleman in the army, for he said that in killing a squirrel he always put the bullet through the head. . . . An Irishman who . . . was attentively listening to this young hunter's boast . . . said to him, 'Yes, but Dan, me boy, ye must ricollict that the squirrel had no gon in his hands to shoot back at ye.' . . .

"There was at the outbreak of the war, and just preceding it, a class of men both North and South . . . who urged the sections to the conflict . . . but who, when real war began to roll . . . nearer and nearer to them, came to the conclusion that it was better for the country, as well as for themselves, to labor in other spheres. . . .

"One of these furious leaders at the South declared that . . . we could 'whip the Yankees with children's pop-guns.'

"When, after the war, this same gentleman was addressing an audience, he was asked by an old maimed soldier, 'Say, Judge, ain't you the same man that told us before the war that we could whip the Yankees with pop-guns?'

" 'Yes,' replied the witty speaker, 'and we *could*—but, confound 'em, they wouldn't fight us that way.'

"My company, dismounted and ready for infantry service, did not wait for orders to move, but, hastily bidding adieu to home and kindred, were off for Milledgeville, then capital of Georgia. At Atlanta a telegram from the governor met us, telling us to go back home, and stay there until our services were needed. Our discomfiture can be better imagined than described. In fact, there broke out at once in my ranks a new rebellion. These rugged mountaineers resolved that they would not go home. . . .

"Finally, after much persuasion and by the cautious exercise of the authority vested in me by my office of captain, I prevailed on them to get on board the home-bound train. As the engine-bell rang and the whistle blew for the train to start, the rebellion broke loose again with double fury. The men rushed to the front of the train, uncoupled the cars from the engine, and gravely informed me that they had reconsidered, and were not going back. . . . If Governor Brown would not accept them, some other governor would. . . .

"They disembarked and left the empty cars on the track, with the trainmen looking on in utter amazement. There was no course left me but to march them through the streets of Atlanta to a camp on the outskirts. The march, or rather straggle, through that city was a sight marvellous to behold. . . . Totally undisciplined and undrilled, no two of these men marched abreast; no two kept the same step; no two wore the same colored coats or trousers. The only pretense at uniformity was the rough fur caps made of raccoon skins, with long, bushy, streaked raccoon tails hanging from behind them.

"The streets were packed with men, women, and children eager to catch a glimpse of this grotesque company. . . . Curiosity was on tiptoe, and from the crowded sidewalks there came to me the inquiry . . . 'What company is that, sir?'

"Up to this time no name had been chosen. . . . I had myself, however, selected a name which I considered both poetic and appropriate, and I replied . . . 'This company is the Mountain Rifles.'

"Instantly a tall mountaineer said . . . 'Mountain hell! We are no Mountain Rifles; we are the Raccoon Roughs.'

"It is scarcely necessary to say that my selected name was never heard of again. . . .

"Once in camp, we kept the wires hot with telegrams to governors of other States, imploring them to give us a chance. Governor [Andrew B.] Moore, of Alabama, finally responded, graciously consenting to incorporate the captain of the Raccoon Roughs and his coon-capped company into one of the regiments soon to be organized.

"The reading of this telegram evoked from my men the first wild Rebel yell it was my fortune to hear. Even then it was weird and thrilling."

As each state seceded (with the number reaching seven during this first flurry between December 20, 1860 and February 1, 1861), armed citizens set about seizing federal property within the state's bounds. Chief among the prizes were fortifications, ships, arsenals, mints, custom houses, and post offices.

In Louisiana at this time was a Northerner destined to play a major role in succeeding events: William Tecumseh Sherman, of Lancaster, Ohio, a West Point soldier returned to civilian life who, two years earlier, had moved south to help Louisiana set up a new military college and to serve as its head. Sherman had a deep affection for the South, and he was not against slavery, deeming it a practical necessity; but he was a rigid Union man. He got a stark indication of the way things were going when, in February 1861, he paid a visit to an old friend in a New Orleans quartermaster's office that he had frequented while still in the army eight years earlier. The friend was Colonel A. C. Myers, who was now in the service of the new regime.

"His office," says Sherman, "was in the same old room in the Lafayette Square building which he had in 1853 when I was there . . . with the same pictures on the wall, and the letters 'U. S.' on everything, including his desk, papers, etc. I asked him if he did

William T. Sherman

not feel funny. 'No, not at all.' The thing was inevitable, secession was a complete success; there would be no war, but the two governments would settle all matters of business in a friendly spirit, and each would go on in its allotted sphere, without further confusion.

"About this date, February 16th, General [David E.] Twiggs, Myers's father-in-law, had surrendered his entire command, in the Department of Texas, to some State troops, with all the Government property, thus consummating the first serious step in the drama of the conspiracy, which was to form a confederacy of the cotton States before working upon the other slave or border States, and before . . . the inauguration of President Lincoln.

"I walked the streets of New Orleans, and found business going along as usual. Ships were strung for miles along the lower levee, and steamboats above, all discharging or receiving cargo. The Pelican flag of Louisiana was flying over the Custom House, Mint, City Hall, and everywhere. At the levee, ships carried every flag on earth except that of the United States, and I was told that during a procession on the 22nd of February, celebrating their emancipation from the despotism of the United States Government, only one national flag was shown from a house, and that the house of Cuthbert Bullitt, on Lafayette Square. He was commanded to take it down, but he refused, and defended it with his pistol.

"The only officer of the army that I can recall as being there at the time who was faithful was Colonel C. L. Kilburn, of the Commissary Department, and he was preparing to escape north.

"Everybody regarded the change of government as final; that Louisiana, by a mere declaration, was a free and independent State, and could enter into any new alliance or combination she chose. Men were being enlisted and armed, to defend the State, and there was not the least evidence that the National Administration designed to make any effort, by force, to vindicate the national authority.

"I therefore bade adieu to all my friends. . . . I left New Orleans about the 1st of March, 1861, by rail to Jackson and Clinton, Mississippi, Jackson, Tennessee, and Columbus, Kentucky, where [I] took a boat to Cairo [Illinois], and thence by rail to Cincinnati and Lancaster.

"All the way, I heard, in the cars and boats, warm discussions about politics—to the effect that, if Mr. Lincoln should attempt coercion of the seceded States, the other slave or border States would make common cause, when, it was believed, it would be madness to attempt to reduce them to subjection.

"In the South the people were earnest, fierce, and angry, and were evidently organizing for action; whereas in Illinois, Indiana, and Ohio I saw not the least sign of preparation. It certainly looked to me as though the people of the North would submit tamely to a disruption of the Union."

Massachusetts resident John Billings claims that the people of the North "stood amazed at the rapidity with which treason against the government was spreading, and the loyal Union-loving men began to inquire where President Buchanan was at this time, whose duty it was to see that all such uprisings were crushed out. And 'Oh for one hour of Andrew Jackson in the President's chair!' was the common exclamation, because that decided and unyielding soldier-President had so promptly stamped out threatened rebellion in South Carolina when she had refused to allow the duties to be collected at Charleston.

"But that outbreak in its proportions was to this one as an infant to a giant, and it is quite doubtful if Old Hickory himself, with his promptness to act in an emergency, could have stayed the angry billows of rebellion which seemed just ready to break over the nation. But at any rate he would have attempted it, even if he had gone down in the fight—at least so thought the people.

"The very opposite of such a President was James Buchanan, who seemed anxious only for his term of office to expire, making little effort to save the country. . . . [He declared] that the South was wrong in its acts, but that he had no right . . . to coerce a sovereign state. . . .

"Never before were the people of this country in such a state of excitement. At the North there were a large number who boldly denounced the 'Long-heeled Abolitionists' and 'Black Republicans' for having stirred up this trouble.

"[Being too young,] I was not a voter at the time of Lincoln's election, but I had taken an active part in the torchlight parades of the 'Wide-awakes' and 'Rail-splitters,' as the political clubs of the Republicans were called, and so came in for a share of the abuse showered upon the followers of the new President. As fresh deeds of violence or new aggressions against the government were reported from the daily papers in the shop where I was then employed, someone who was not a Lincolnite would exclaim in an angry tone, 'I hope you fellows are satisfied now. I don't blame the South an atom. They have been driven to desperation. . . . If there is a war, I hope you and every other Black Republican will be made to go and fight for the niggers all you want to. . . . You like the niggers so well you'll marry one of them yet. . . . I want to see those hot-headed Abolitionists put into the front rank and shot first.'

"These are mild quotations from the daily conversations . . . not only where I was employed but in every other shop and factory in the North. Such wordy contests were by no means one-sided affairs; for the assailed, while not anxious for war, were not afraid of it, and were amply supplied with arguments with which they answered and engaged their antagonists. . . .

"If I were asked who these men were, I should not call them by name. They were my neighbors and friends. . . . Many of them afterwards went to the field. . . . But this was the period of the most intemperate and abusive language. . . . Nothing was too harsh to utter against Republicans. . . .

"Of course, all of these revilers were not sincere in their ill-wishes, but the effect of their utterances on the community was just as evil; and the situation of the new President, at its best a perplexing and critical one, was thus made all the harder by leading him to believe that a multitude of the citizens at the North would obstruct instead of supporting him. It also gave the slave-

holders the impression that a very considerable number of Northern men were ready to aid them in prosecuting their treasonable
schemes. But now the rapid march of events wrought a change in
the opinions of the people in both sections.

"The leading abolitionists had argued that the South was too
cowardly to fight for slavery; and the South had been told by the
Fire-eaters . . . that the North could not be kicked into fighting—
that in case war should arise she would have her hands full to
keep her enemies *at home* in check.

"Alas! How little did either party understand the temper of the
other! How much like that story of the two Irishmen:

"Meeting one day . . . one says, 'How are you, Mike?' 'How are
you, Pat?' says the other. 'But my name is not Pat,' said the first
speaker. 'Nayther is mine Mike,' said the second. 'Faix, thin,' said
the first, 'it musht be nayther of us.'

"Nothing could better illustrate the attitude of the North and
South towards each other than this anecdote. Nothing could have
been more perfect than this mutual misunderstanding each displayed of the temper of the other, as the stride of events soon
showed."

4

The Charleston Forts

SIMULTANEOUSLY WITH South Carolina's secession on December 20, 1860, the national government's coast defenses at Charleston had become objects of contention. As explained by Jefferson Davis, then in Washington as a senator from Mississippi, which was still twenty days from taking its place among the first seven states to secede:

"Of the three forts in or at the entrance of the harbor, two were unoccupied, but the third, Fort Moultrie, was held by a garrison of but little more than one hundred men—of whom only sixty-three were said to be effectives [the number was probably closer to eighty-five]—under command of Major Robert Anderson, of the First Artillery.

"About twelve days before the secession of South Carolina, the Representatives in Congress from that State had called on the President to assure him, in anticipation of the secession of the State, that no purpose was entertained by South Carolina to attack, or in any way molest the forts held by the United States in the harbor of Charleston—at least until opportunity could be had for an amicable settlement of all questions that might arise with regard to these forts and other public property—provided that no reinforcements should be sent, and the military status should be permitted to remain unchanged.

"The South Carolinians understood Mr. Buchanan as approving of this suggestion, although declining to make any formal pledge. . . .

"Immediately after the secession of the State, the Convention of

South Carolina deputed three distinguished citizens of that State—Messrs. Robert W. Barnwell, James H. Adams, and James L. Orr—to proceed to Washington 'to treat with the Government of the United States for the delivery of the forts, magazines, lighthouses, and other real estate, with their appurtenances, within the limits of South Carolina . . . and generally to negotiate as to all other measures and arrangements proper to be made . . . for the continuance of peace and amity between this Commonwealth and the Government at Washington.'

"The commissioners . . . arrived in Washington on the 26th of December. Before they could communicate with the President, however—indeed, on the morning after their arrival—they were startled, and the whole country electrified, by the news that, during the previous night, Major Anderson had secretly dismantled Fort Moultrie, spiked his guns, burned his gun-carriages, and removed his command to Fort Sumter, which occupied a more commanding position in the harbor.

"This movement changed the whole aspect of affairs. It was considered by the government and people of South Carolina as a violation of the implied pledge of a maintenance of the *status quo*.

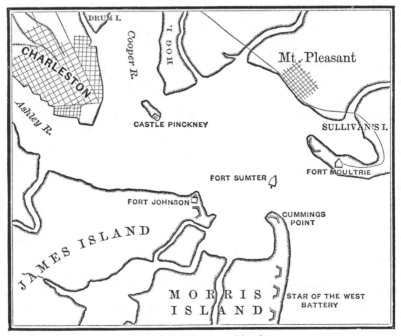

The federal forts at Charleston

Robert Anderson

The remaining forts and other public property were at once taken possession of by the State; and the condition of public feeling became greatly exacerbated.

"An interview between the President and the commissioners was followed by a sharp correspondence, which was terminated on the 1st of January, 1861, by the return to the commissioners of their final communication, with an endorsement stating that it was of such a character that the President declined to receive it. [It was strongly critical of Buchanan's refusal to intercede against Anderson.] . . .

"The kind relations, both personal and political, which had long existed between Mr. Buchanan and myself, had led him, occasionally . . . to send for me to confer with him on subjects that caused him anxiety, and warranted me in sometimes calling upon him to offer my opinion on matters of special interest or importance. Thus it was that I had communicated with him freely in regard to the threatening aspect of events in the earlier part of the winter of 1860–61. When he told me of the work that . . . was doing at Fort Moultrie—that is, the elevation of its parapet by crowning it with barrels of sand—I pointed out to him the impolicy as well as inefficiency of the measure. It seemed to me impolitic

Federals moving into Sumter in the darkness

to make ostensible preparations for defense when no attack was threatened; and the means adopted were inefficient, because any ordinary fieldpiece would knock the barrels off the parapet and thus render them only hurtful to the defenders. . . .

"After the removal of the garrison to the stronger and safer position of Fort Sumter, I called upon him again to represent, from my knowledge of the people and the circumstances of the case, how productive the movement would be of discontent, and how likely to lead to collision. . . . My opinion was that the wisest and best course would be to withdraw the garrison altogether from the harbor of Charleston.

"The President's objection to this was that it was his bounden duty to preserve and protect the property of the United States. To this I replied, with all the earnestness the occasion demanded, that I would pledge my life that, if an inventory were taken of all the stores and munitions in the fort, and an ordnance-sergeant with a few men left in charge of them, they would not be disturbed. . . .

"The President promised me to reflect upon this proposition, and to confer with his Cabinet upon the propriety of adopting it. All Cabinet consultations are secret; which is equivalent to saying that I never knew what occurred in that meeting to which my proposition was submitted. The result was not communicated to me, but the events which followed proved that the suggestion was not accepted.

"Major Anderson, who commanded the garrison, had many ties and associations that bound him to the South. He performed his part like the true soldier and man of the finest sense of honor that he was. But that it was most painful to him to be charged with the duty of holding the fort as a threat to the people of Charleston is a fact known to many others as well as myself. We had been cadets [at West Point] together. He was my first acquaintance in that corps, and the friendship then formed was never interrupted. . . .

"Mr. Buchanan, the last President of the old school, would as soon have thought of aiding in the establishment of a monarchy among us as of accepting the doctrine of coercing the States into submission. . . . If the garrison of Fort Sumter had been withdrawn . . . nothing could have operated more powerfully to quiet the apprehensions and allay the resentment of the people of South Carolina. The influence which such a measure would have exerted upon the States which had not yet seceded . . . would probably have induced further delay; and the mellowing effect of time, with a realization of the dangers to be incurred, might have wrought mutual forbearance—if, indeed, anything could have checked the madness then prevailing among the people of the Northern States."

It was at this time that the Sumter situation developed a sidelight involving Mrs. Robert Anderson, who was living in New York City. Later, she described the episode to historian Benson Lossing, and he recorded it in this way:

Mrs. Robert Anderson

"When the wife of Major Anderson . . . heard of the perilous position of her husband, she was very anxious that he should have a tried and faithful servant with him. She was then . . . an invalid, but she resolved to take an old and tried sergeant, who had served her husband in the war with Mexico, into Fort Sumter. His name was Peter Hart, and she heard that he was somewhere in New York City.

"After searching for him among all the Harts whose names were in the city directory, she found him connected with the police. At her request he called upon her, accompanied by his wife. After telling him of Major Anderson's peril, she said, 'I want you to go with me to Fort Sumter.'

"Hart looked towards his young wife, a warm-hearted Irish-woman, for a moment, and then said, 'I will go, madam.'

" 'But I want you to *stay* with the major.'

"Hart looked inquiringly towards his Margaret, and replied, 'I will go, madam.'

" 'But Margaret,' said Mrs. Anderson, 'what do *you* say?'

" 'Indade, madam, it's Margaret's sorry she can't do as much for you as Pater can,' was the reply.

" 'When will you go, Hart?' asked Mrs. Anderson.

" 'Tonight, madam, if you wish.'

" 'Tomorrow night at six o'clock I will be ready,' said Mrs. Anderson.

"In spite of the remonstrances of her physician, the devoted wife left New York [by train] on January 3, 1861, for Charleston, accompanied by Peter Hart in the character of a servant, ready at all times to do her bidding. None but her physician knew her destination.

"They travelled without intermission, and arrived at Charleston late on Saturday night. She had neither eaten, drunk, nor slept during the journey, for she was absorbed with the object of her errand. From Wilmington to Charleston she was the only woman on the train. Therein, and at the hotel in Charleston, she continually heard her husband cursed and threatened.

"She knew Governor [Francis W.] Pickens personally, and the next morning she sought from him a permit for herself and Hart to go to Fort Sumter. He could not allow a man to be added to the garrison.

Peter Hart

Francis W. Pickens

"Regarding with scorn the suggestion that the addition of one man to a garrison of seventy or eighty, when thousands of armed men were in Charleston, could imperil the 'sovereign State of South Carolina,' Mrs. Anderson sent a message to the governor, saying 'I shall take Hart with me, with or without a pass.'

"Her words of scorn and her message were repeated to the governor, and he, seeing the absurdity of his objection, gave a pass for Hart.

"At 10 A.M. on January 6, accompanied by a few personal

friends [from Charleston], Mrs. Anderson and Peter Hart went in
a boat to Fort Sumter. As she saw the banner over the fort, she
exclaimed, 'The dear old flag!' and burst into tears. It was the first
time emotion had conquered her will since she left New York.

"As her friends carried her from the boat to the sally-port, her
husband ran out, caught her in his arms, and exclaimed, in a
vehement whisper, 'My glorious wife!' and carried her into the
fort.

" 'I have brought you Peter Hart,' she said. 'The children are
well. I return tonight.'

"In her husband's quarters she took some refreshments. The
tide [cooperated] in the course of two hours, and she returned to
Charleston. She had reinforced Fort Sumter with Peter Hart . . .
the major's trusted friend. . . .

"On a bed placed in the cars, and accompanied by Major Anderson's brother, the devoted wife started for New York that evening.
She was insensible when she reached Washington. A friend carried her into Willard's Hotel. Forty-eight hours afterwards she
started for New York, and there she was for a long time threatened with brain fever."

The narrative is reassumed by Jefferson Davis:

"The little garrison of Fort Sumter served only as a menace; for
it was utterly incapable of holding the fort if attacked, and the
poor attempt soon afterward made to reinforce and provision
it . . . might, by the uncharitable, be readily construed as a scheme
to provoke hostilities. Yet from my knowledge of Mr. Buchanan,
I do not hesitate to say that he had no such wish or purpose. His
abiding hope was to avert a collision, or at least to postpone it to
a period beyond the close of his official term. The management
of the whole affair was . . . something worse than a crime—a
blunder. . . .

"The ill-advised attempt secretly to throw reinforcements and
provisions into Fort Sumter by means of the steamer *Star of the
West* [from New York] resulted in the repulsion of that vessel at
the mouth of the harbor by the authorities of South Carolina on
the morning of the 9th of January. On her refusal to heave to, she
was fired upon, and put back to sea, with her recruits and supplies.

"A telegraphic account of this event was handed to me, a few
hours afterward, when stepping into my carriage to go to the
Senate chamber. Although I had then, for some time, ceased to

visit the President, yet, under the impulse of this renewed note of danger to the country, I drove immediately to the Executive Mansion, and for the last time appealed to him to take such prompt measures as were evidently necessary to avert the impending calamity. The result was even more unsatisfactory than that of former efforts had been."

Buchanan had begun to stiffen because he was concerned about the way his administration was ending. He did not want to make his journey to his home in Pennsylvania, he said, "by the light of burning effigies."

Down in South Carolina, many people were jubilant. As reported in the Charleston *Mercury:*

"Yesterday, the 9th of January, will be remembered in history. Powder has been burnt over the [secession] decree of our State; timber has been crashed, perhaps blood spilled. [It was not.] The expulsion of the *Star of the West* from Charleston Harbor yesterday morning was the opening of the ball of revolution. We are proud that our harbor has been so honored.

"We are more proud that the State of South Carolina, so long, so bitterly, so contemptuously reviled and scoffed at, above all others, should thus proudly have thrown back the scoff of her enemies. Intrenched upon her soil, she has spoken from the mouth of her cannon. . . . Contemned, the sanctity of her waters violated with hostile purpose of reinforcing enemies in our harbor, she has not hesitated to *strike the first blow*, full in the face of her insulter. . . . We would not exchange or recall that blow for millions! It has wiped out half a century of scorn and outrage.

"Again South Carolina may be proud of her historic fame and ancestry. . . . The haughty echo of her cannon has . . . reverberated from Maine to Texas, through every hamlet of the North, and down along the great waters of the Southwest. The decree has gone forth.

"Upon each acre of the peaceful soil of the South, armed men will spring up as the sound breaks upon their ears. And it will be found that every word of our insolent foe has been . . . a dragon's tooth sown for their destruction. . . . And if that red seal of blood be still lacking to the parchment of our liberties, and blood they want—blood they shall have, and blood enough to stamp it all in red. For, by the God of our fathers, the soil of South Carolina *shall be free!*"

Besieged in Fort Sumter, Major Anderson was forbidden by

Confederates firing on Star of the West

Washington to make any aggressive moves but was told to defend himself as necessary. He was presently engaged in improving his position. As explained by one of the garrison's men, James Chester:

"Fort Sumter was unfinished, and the interior was filled with building materials, guns, carriages, shot, shell, derricks, timbers, blocks and tackle, and coils of rope in great confusion. Few guns were mounted, and these few were chiefly on the lowest tier. The work was intended for three tiers of guns, but the embrasures of the second tier were incomplete, and guns could be mounted on the first and third tiers only. . . .

"Moving such immense quantities of material, mounting guns, distributing shot, and bricking up embrasures kept us busy. . . . But order was coming out of chaos every day, and the soldiers began to feel that they were a match for their adversaries. Still, they could not shut their eyes to the fact that formidable works were growing up around them. The secessionists were busy too, and they had the advantage of unlimited labor and material. . . .

"But our preparations were more advanced than theirs; and if we had been permitted to open on them at this time, the bombardment of Fort Sumter would have had a very different termination. But our hands were tied by policy and instructions."

On the Confederate side, it was at about this time that fifteen-year-old D. Augustus Dickert, who belonged to an affluent family residing in Lexington County, South Carolina, arrived by train to join the company in which he had enlisted some weeks ago.

"The City of Charleston may be said to have been in a state of siege. . . . The headquarters of Governor Pickens and staff were in the rooms of the Charleston Hotel. . . . The city . . . was ablaze with excitement; flags waved from the housetops, the heavy tread of the embryo soldiers could be heard in the streets, the corridors of hotels, and in all the public places.

"The beautiful park on the waterfront called The Battery was thronged with people of every age and sex, straining their eyes or looking through glasses out at Sumter, whose bristling front was surmounted with cannon, her flags waving defiance. Small boats and steamers dotted the waters of the bay. Ordnance and ammunition were being hurried to the islands. The one continual talk was 'Anderson,' 'Fort Sumter,' and 'war.' . . .

"Being determined to reach my company, I boarded a steamer bound for Morris Island. . . . When I joined my company I found a few of my old school-mates; the others were strangers. Everything that met my eyes reminded me of war. Sentinels patrolled the beach; drums beat; soldiers marching and countermarching; great cannons being drawn along the beach, hundreds of men pulling them by long ropes, or drawn by mule teams.

"Across the bay we could see on Sullivan's Island men and soldiers building and digging out foundations for forts. Morris Island was lined from the lower point to the lighthouse with bat-

The Battery

teries of heavy guns. To the youthful eye of a Southerner whose mind had been fired by Southern sentiment and . . . by reading the stories of heroes and soldiers in our old *Southern Reader* . . . this sight of war was enough to dazzle and startle to an enthusiasm that scarcely knew any bounds. . . .

"My first duty as a soldier I will never forget. I went with a detail to Steven's iron battery to build embrasures for the forts there. This was done by filling cotton bags the size of 50-pound flour sacks with sand, placing them, one upon the top of the other, at the opening where the mouths of cannons projected, to prevent the loose earth from falling down and filling in the openings. The sand was first put upon common wheelbarrows and rolled up single planks in a zigzag way to the top of the fort, then placed in the sacks and laid in position.

"My turn came to use a barrow, while a comrade used the shovel for filling up. I had never worked a wheelbarrow in my life, and, like most of my companions, had done but little work of any kind. But up I went the narrow zigzag gangway, with a heavy loaded barrow of loose sand. I made the first plank all right, and the second; but when I undertook to reach the third plank on the angles, and about fifteen feet from the ground, my barrow rolled off; and down came sand, barrow, and myself to the ground below.

"I could have cried with shame and mortification, for my misfortune created much merriment for the good-natured workers. . . . It mortified me to death to think I was not man enough to fill a soldier's place. My good co-worker and brother-soldier exchanged the shovel for the barrow with me. And then began the first day's work I had ever done of that kind. Hour after hour passed, and I used the shovel with a will.

"It looked as if night would never come. At times I thought I would have to sink to the earth from pure exhaustion, but my pride and my youthful patriotism, animated by the acts of others, urged me on. Great blisters formed and bursted in my hand, beads of perspiration dripped from my brow, and, towards night, the blood began to show at the root of my fingers.

"But I was not by myself. There were many others as tender as myself. Young men with wealthy parents, school and college boys, clerks and men of leisure—some who had never done a lick of manual labor in their lives and would not have used a spade or shovel for any consideration, would have scoffed at the idea of doing the laborious work of men—were now toiling away with the farmer boys, the overseers' sons, the mechanics—all with a will, and filled with enthusiasm that nothing short of the most disinterested patriotism could have endured.

"There were men in companies raised in Columbia, Charleston, and other towns, who were as ignorant and as much strangers to manual labor as though they had been infants, toiling away with pick and shovel with as much glee as if they had been reared upon the farm or had been laborers in a mine.

"Over about midway in the harbor stood grim old Sumter, from whose parapets giant guns frowned down upon us, while around the battlements the sentinels walked to and fro upon their beats. All this preparation and labor were to reduce the fort or prevent a reinforcement. . . .

"With drill every two hours, guard duty, and working details, the soldiers had little time for rest or reflection. Bands of music enlivened the men while on drill and cheered them while at work by martial and inspiring strains of 'Lorena,' 'The Prairie Flower,' 'Dixie,' and other Southern airs.

"Pickets walked the beach every thirty paces, night and day; none were allowed to pass without a countersign or a permit.

During the day small fishing smacks, their white sails bobbing up and down over the waves, dotted the bay; some going out over the bar at night, with rockets and signals, to watch for strangers coming from the seaward.

"Days and nights passed without cessation of active operations—all waiting anxiously the orders from Montgomery to reduce the fort."

Until the end of January, the Sumter garrison included the wives and children of some of the officers. On February 1, Major Anderson decided to send them out. Charleston's authorities at once accepted them into the city and soon put them aboard a steamer for passage to New York. The vessel's route from the dock took the party back toward Sumter. As related by an unidentified observer:

"On nearing the fort, the whole garrison was seen mounted on the top of the ramparts, and, when the ship was passing, fired a gun and gave three heart-thrilling cheers as a parting farewell to the dear loved ones on board. . . . The response was weeping and waving adieus to husbands and fathers—a small band pent up in an isolated fort and completely surrounded by instruments of death, as five forts could be seen from the steamer's deck, with their guns pointing towards Sumter."

After watching the steamer out of sight, Anderson and his men turned back to their task of strengthening the fort. Again in the words of the garrison's James Chester:

"A laughable incident occurred in connection with [a ten-inch columbiad cannon altered to function as a mortar, a high-trajectory weapon] soon after it was mounted. Some of the officers were anxious to try how it would work, and perhaps to see how true its alignment was, and to advertise to the enemy the fact that we had at least one formidable mortar in Fort Sumter. At any rate, they obtained permission from Major Anderson to try the gun with a 'very small charge.'

"So, one afternoon the gun was loaded with a blind shell [one without an explosive charge inside], and what was considered a 'very small charge' of powder. The regulation charge for the gun, as a gun, was eighteen pounds. On this occasion, two pounds only were used. It was not expected that the shell would be thrown over a thousand yards, and, as the bay was clear, no danger was anticipated.

"Everything being in readiness, the gun was fired, and the eyes

Columbiad mounted as mortar

of the garrison followed the shell as it described its graceful curve in the direction of the city. By the time it reached the summit of its trajectory, the fact that the charge used was not a 'very small' one for the gun, fired as a mortar, became painfully apparent to every observer; and fears were entertained by some that the shell would reach the city, or at least the shipping near the wharves.

"But fortunately it fell short, and did no damage beyond scaring the secessionist guard boat then leaving the wharf for her nightly post of observation. . . . No more experiments for range were tried with that gun, but we knew that Charleston was within range. . . .

"The weary waiting for war or deliverance . . . developed no discontent among the men, although food and fuel were getting scarce. The latter was replenished from time to time by tearing down sheds and temporary workshops, but the former was a constantly diminishing quantity. . . . It was a favorite belief among the secessionists that the pinchings of hunger would arouse a spirit of mutiny among the soldiers, and compel Major Anderson to propose terms of evacuation. But no such spirit manifested itself."

Up in New York, the magazine *Vanity Fair* published a poem entitled "A New Song of Sixpence":

> *Sing a song of Sumter,*
> *A Fort in Charleston Bay;*
> *Eight-and-sixty brave men*
> *Watch there night and day.*
>
> *Those brave men to succor,*
> *Still no aid is sent;*
> *Isn't James Buchanan*
> *A pretty President!*
>
> *James is in his Cabinet*
> *Doubting and debating;*
> *Anderson's in Sumter,*
> *Very tired of waiting.*
>
> *Pickens is in Charleston,*
> *Blustering of blows;*
> *Thank goodness March the Fourth is near*
> *To nip Secession's nose!*

5

Two Inaugurations

By this time Jefferson Davis's status had undergone a dramatic change. He had become the South's "man of the hour."

In appearance, according to a contemporary description, Davis was "of slight, sinewy figure, rather over the middle height, and of erect, soldierlike bearing. His features are regular and well defined, but the face is thin and marked on cheek and brow with many wrinkles, and is rather careworn and haggard. One eye is apparently blind; the other is dark, piercing, and intelligent." Healthwise, Davis was no more robust than his face seemed to indicate, but he was destined for a long life.

"Jefferson Davis," says Pennsylvania journalist A. K. McClure (who knew the senator), "was of gentler birth and shared none of the desperate struggles of Lincoln in early life to advance himself. His parents moved to Mississippi in his early youth, and he was given unusual educational facilities for young men of that period. He was a student at Transylvania College, Lexington, Kentucky, then one of the foremost and most progressive Southern colleges, in 1824 when President Monroe appointed him a cadet to West Point, where he graduated in 1828 and entered the regular army.

"He had active military service in Indian campaigns for seven years, when he resigned June 30, 1835, and became a cotton planter near Vicksburg. In 1845 he was elected to Congress, but in June, 1846, he resigned to accept a colonelcy of the Mississippi regiment in the Mexican War, where he served with special distinction at the Battle of Buena Vista.

"Soon after his return from the war in 1847 he was appointed

Jefferson Davis

to fill a vacancy in the United States Senate, and in 1848 was elected for [the] full term [but interrupted a new term in 1851 to run for governor of Mississippi, a bid that failed]. . . . He was recalled to public life in 1853 by President Pierce, who made Davis his Secretary of War, and on his retirement from the Cabinet in 1857 he again entered the Senate. . . .

"Mr. Davis was a man of forceful intellect, a great student, and one of the ablest debaters in the national councils. He had the courage of his convictions, and was scrupulously honest alike in public and private life. He believed in the right of secession . . . [but] always disavowed disunion until after the election of Lincoln. . . .

"He was respected by all his associates in public life because of the sincerity that guided him in his expressions and actions. He was grave and dignified to a degree approaching austerity, but was always one of the most courteous of gentlemen, while lacking the genial and magnetic qualities of men like Lincoln."

Davis made his last trip to the Senate on January 21. He had prepared a speech that reviewed the South's grievances and was heavy with regret at the way events were progressing. According to his wife, Varina:

"Mr. Davis had been ill for more than a week, and our medical attendant thought him physically unable to make his farewell to the Senate.

"On the morning of the day he was to address his colleagues, the crowd began to move toward the Senate Chamber as early as seven o'clock. By nine there was hardly standing room within the galleries or in the passway behind the forum. The Senate's cloakroom was crowded to excess, and the bright faces of the ladies were assembled together like a mosaic of flowers in the doorway. The sofas and passways were full, and ladies sat on the floor against the wall where they could not find seats. . . . The gallery of the reporters was occupied by the Diplomatic Corps and their respective families. . . . I . . . had come from a sleepless night. . . .

"Mr. Davis, graceful, grave, and deliberate, amid profound silence, arose to address the Senate for the last time as a member of that body. Every eye was turned upon him, fearful of missing one word. . . . His voice was at first low and faltering, but soon it rang out melodiously clear. . . . Unshed tears were in it, and a plea for peace permeated every tone. Every graceful gesture seemed to invite brotherly love. . . .

"He was listened to in profound silence, broken only by repeated applause. . . . Not his wife alone, but all who sat spellbound before him knew how genuine was his grief, and entered into the spirit of his loving appeal.

"With a plea for the indulgence of his colleagues whom, in debate he might, in all the past years of heated and strenuous endeavors, have offended, he offered the hand of fellowship to each of them who might be willing to accept it.

"There was scarcely a dry eye in the multitude as he took his seat with the words, 'It only remains for me to bid you a final adieu.' "

Davis himself takes up:

"Rumors were in circulation of a purpose, on the part of the United States Government, to arrest members of Congress preparing to leave Washington on account of the secession of the States which they represented. . . . No attempt, however, was made to arrest any of the retiring members; and, after a delay of a few days in necessary preparations, I left Washington for Mississippi, passing through southwestern Virginia, East Tennessee, a small part of Georgia, and north Alabama.

"A deep interest in the events which had recently occurred was exhibited by the people of these States, and much anxiety was indicated as to the future. Many years of agitation had made them familiar with the idea of separation. . . .

"Now . . . as well in Virginia and Tennessee, neither of which had yet seceded, as in the more southern States which had already taken that step, the danger so often phrophesied was perceived to be at the door, and eager inquiries were made as to what would happen next—especially as to the probability of war between the States.

"The course which events were likely to take was shrouded in the greatest uncertainty. . . . For my own part, while believing that secession was a right, and properly a peaceable remedy, I had never believed that it would be permitted to be peaceably exercised. Very few in the South at that time agreed with me, and my answers to queries on the subject were, therefore, as unexpected as they were unwelcome.

"On my arrival at Jackson, the capital of Mississippi, I found that the Convention of the State had made provision for a State army, and had appointed me to the command, with the rank of major-general."

Davis attended to his most urgent duties at the capital, then went to his home, Brierfield, in Warren County. His narrative continues:

"The Congress of delegates from the seceding States convened at Montgomery, Alabama . . . on the 4th of February, 1861. Their first work was to prepare a provisional constitution for the new Confederacy, to be formed of the States which had withdrawn from the Union, for which the style 'Confederate States of America' was adopted. . . .

"On the . . . 9th of February an election was held for the chief executive offices, resulting . . . in my election to the Presidency, with the Hon. Alexander H. Stephens, of Georgia, as Vice-President. . . . Notice was received [by me] of my election . . . with an urgent request to proceed immediately to Montgomery for inauguration. . . .

"I was surprised, and, still more, disappointed. . . . I had not believed myself as well suited to the office as some others. I thought myself better adapted to command in the field; and Mississippi had given me the position which I preferred to any other—the highest rank in her army. . . .

"On my way to Montgomery, brief addresses were made at

various places at which there were temporary stoppages of the trains, in response to calls from the crowds assembled at such points. . . .

"The inaugural [address] was deliberately prepared . . . [as] a clear and authentic statement of the principles and purposes which actuated me."

Davis's inauguration took place on February 18, and among those in the audience was a six-year-old girl who later became Mrs. E. P. Marrisette:

"The white Capitol building loomed large on the grass-covered eminence . . . [where] a vast concourse crowded. The attending military looked stern and terrible to me, clinging to my father's hand.

Montgomery, Alabama, February 1861

"Soon the pale, resolute face of Mr. Davis appeared in the midst of the grave men on the portico, and he began his address. Rarely in all the annals of history did an audience listen as did this audience, and never to a braver, truer man.

"Clear his tones rose; chaste, simple, and fervid were his words; and at last, in expressions that even a child could comprehend, he called on God to witness the honesty of his purpose, and invoked Divine aid in the discharge of that high office to which he had been called."

Returning to Davis's personal account:

"After being inaugurated, I proceeded to the formation of my Cabinet. . . . My attention was [then] directed to preparation for military defense, for, though I, in common with others, desired to have a peaceful separation, and sent commissioners to the United States Government to effect, if possible, negotiations to that end, I , , , regarded it as an imperative duty to make all possible preparation for the contingency of war."

It was during these same days that Abraham Lincoln made his journey from Springfield to Washington. On the day before he left Springfield he paid a last visit to the law office he shared with William Herndon, his purpose to close out his unfinished business. Herndon relates:

"After these things were disposed of, he crossed to the opposite side of the room and threw himself down on the old office sofa, which, after many years of service, had been moved against the wall for support. He lay for some moments, his face towards the ceiling. . . . Presently he inquired, 'Billy . . . how long have we been together?'

" 'Over sixteen years,' I answered. . . .

"He [rose and] gathered a bundle of papers and books he wished to take with him, and started to go; but before leaving he made the strange request that the signboard which swung on its rusty hinges at the foot of the stairway should remain.

" 'Let it hang there undisturbed,' he said. . . . 'Give our clients to understand that the election of a president makes no change in the firm of Lincoln and Herndon. If I live, I am coming back sometime, and then we'll go right on practicing law as if nothing had happened.'

"He lingered for a moment, as if to take a last look at the old quarters, and then passed through the door into the narrow hallway."

During his last-minute talks with friends, Lincoln was told by one: "I believe it will do you good to get down to Washington." Lincoln responded: "I know it will. I only wish I could have got there to lock the door before the horse was stolen. But when I get to the spot, I can find the tracks."

It was about eight o'clock on the cloudy morning of February 11, 1861, that a special train lay in the Springfield station with its steam up, and with Lincoln standing on one of the open platforms for the purpose of addressing the crowd that had assembled to see him off. A Springfield newsman noted that "although it was raining fast when he began to speak, every hat was lifted and every head bent forward to catch the last words of the departing chief."

"My friends," said Lincoln, "no one not in my situation can appreciate my feeling of sadness at this parting. To this place, and the kindness of these people, I owe everything. Here I have lived a quarter of a century, and have passed from a young to an old man. Here my children have been born and one is buried. I now leave, not knowing when or whether ever I may return, with a task before me greater than that which rested upon Washington.

"Without the assistance of that Divine Being who ever attended him, I cannot succeed. With that assistance, I cannot fail. Trusting in Him who can go with me and remain with you, and be everywhere for good, let us confidently hope that all will yet be well. To His care commending you, as I hope in your prayers you will commend me, I bid you an affectionate farewell."

The details of Lincoln's trip are given as they were recorded by Northern journalist Horace Greeley:

"Immense crowds surrounded the stations at which the special train halted, wherein he, with his family and a few friends, was borne eastward through Indianapolis, Cincinnati, Columbus, Pittsburgh, Cleveland, Erie, Buffalo, Albany, New York City, Trenton, Newark, Philadelphia, Lancaster, and Harrisburg, on his way to the White House. He was everywhere received and honored as the chief of a free people; and his unstudied remarks . . . indicated his decided disbelief in any bloody issue of our domestic complications. . . .

"At Columbus, Ohio, he said, '. . . There is nothing going wrong. It is a consoling circumstance that, when we look out, there is nothing that really hurts anybody. We entertain different views upon political questions, but nobody is suffering anything. . . .'

"At Pittsburgh, Pennsylvania, on the 15th he said, '. . . There is no crisis, except such a one as may be gotten up at any time by turbulent men, aided by designing politicians. My advice to them, under the circumstances, is to keep cool. If the great American people only keep their temper both sides of the line, the trouble will come to an end. . . .'

"At Philadelphia, being required to assist at the solemn raising of the United States flag over Independence Hall, Mr. Lincoln . . . said, '. . . In my view of the present aspect of affairs, there need be no bloodshed or war. . . . I am not in favor of such a course; and I may say, in advance, that there *will* be no bloodshed, unless it be forced upon the Government, and then it will be compelled to act in self-defense.'

"Arrived at Harrisburg, however, on the 22nd, Mr. Lincoln . . . experienced suddenly a decided change in the political barometer. It had been arranged that he should next day pass through Baltimore, the center of a grand procession . . . as he had, thus far, passed through nearly all the great cities of the Free States. But Baltimore was a slaveholding city. . . . The mercantile and social aristocracy of that city had been sedulously, persistently, plied by the conspirators for disunion with artful suggestions that, in a confederacy composed exclusively of . . . Slave States, Balti-

Lincoln raising the flag at Independence Hall

more would hold the position that New York enjoys in the Union, being the great shipbuilding, shipping, importing, and commercial emporium, whitening the ocean with her sails, and gemming Maryland with the palaces reared from her ample and ever-expanding profits.

"That aristocracy had been, for the most part, thoroughly corrupted by these insidious whispers, and so were ready to rush into treason.

"At the other end of the social scale was the mob—reckless and godless, as mobs are apt to be . . . ready at all times to do the bidding of the Slave Power.

"Between these was the great middle class, loyal and peacefully inclined, as this class usually is—outnumbering both the others, but . . . as yet at no common understanding with regard to the novel circumstances of the country and the events visibly impending. . . .

"It had been proclaimed in many quarters . . . that Mr. Lincoln should never live to be inaugurated; and the Baltimore *Republican* of the 22nd had a leading article directly calculated to incite tumult and violence on the occasion of Mr. Lincoln's passage through the city. . . .

"It being considered certain that an attempt to assassinate the President would be made, under cover of mob violence, should he pass through the city as was originally intended, Mr. Lincoln was persuaded to take the cars secretly [without his family], during the evening of the 22nd, and so passed through Baltimore, unknown and unsuspected, early on the morning of the 23rd."

Pennsylvania journalist A. K. McClure adds:

"I . . . several times heard Lincoln refer to this journey, and always with regret. Indeed, he seemed to regard it as one of the grave mistakes in his public career. He was fully convinced . . . that he had fled from a danger purely imaginary, and he felt the shame and mortification natural to a brave man under such circumstances.

"Mrs. Lincoln and her suite passed through Baltimore [later] on the 23rd without any sign of turbulence. The fact that there was not even a curious crowd brought together when she passed through the city—which . . . required considerable time, as the cars were taken across Baltimore by horses—confirmed Lincoln in his belief.

"It is needless . . . to discuss the question of real or imaginary

danger in Lincoln passing through Baltimore at noonday according to the original program. It is enough to know that there were
reasonable grounds for apprehension that an attempt might be
made upon his life, even if there was not the organized band of
assassins that the detectives believed to exist. His presence in the
city would have called out an immense concourse of people, including thousands of thoroughly disloyal roughs, who could easily
have been inspired to any measure of violence. He simply acted
the part of a prudent man in his reluctant obedience to the unanimous decision of his friends in Harrisburg. . . .

"The sensational stories published, at the time, of his disguise
for the journey were wholly untrue. He was reported as having
been dressed in a Scotch cap and cloak. . . . I saw him enter the car
at the Harrisburg depot, and the only change in his dress was the
substitution of a soft slouch hat for the high one he had worn
during the day. He wore the same overcoat that he had worn
when he arrived at Harrisburg, and the only extra apparel he had
about him was the shawl that hung over his arm. . . .

"The journey to Washington was entirely uneventful, and at six
in the morning the train entered the Washington station on schedule time."

With his inauguration still nine days away, Lincoln took up
residence at Willard's Hotel, where one of the other guests was
Senator John Sherman, of Ohio. Sherman relates:

"On the evening of his arrival I called upon him, and met him
for the first time. When introduced to him, he took my hands in
both of his, drew himself up to his full height, and, looking at me
steadily, said, 'You are John Sherman! Well, I am taller than you.
Let's measure.' Thereupon we stood back to back, and someone
present announced that he was two inches taller than I. . . .

"This singular introduction was not unusual with him; but if it
lacked in dignity, it was an expression of friendliness, and so
considered by him. Our brief conversation was cheerful, and my
hearty congratulations for his escape from the Baltimore roughs
were received with a laugh."

According to period historian J. G. Holland, who became one
of Lincoln's first biographers:

"Mr. Lincoln went immediately into free conferences with his
friends, visited both houses of Congress, and . . . he was waited
upon by the Mayor and the municipal authorities, who gave him
formal welcome to the city. . . . On the second evening after his

John Sherman

arrival, the Republican Association tendered him the courtesy of a serenade, which attracted a large crowd of friends and curious spectators. . . .

"The days that preceded the inauguration were rapidly passing away. In the meantime, although General Scott [Winfield Scott, the U.S. Army's commander-in-chief] had been busy and efficient in his military preparations for the occasion, many were fearful that scenes of violence would be enacted on that day. . . .

"The leading society of Washington hated Mr. Lincoln and the principles he represented. . . . His coming and remaining would be death to the social dominance of slavery in the national capital. . . . There was probably not one man in five in Washington . . . who, in his heart, gave him welcome. It is not to be wondered at that his friends all over the country looked nervously forward to the fourth of March."

These were sad days for President Buchanan. On March 2, Colonel Erasmus D. Keyes, military secretary to General Scott, recorded in his journal:

"Today the officers of the Army, or a majority of them, in a body, paid their respects to Mr. James Buchanan, the retiring President of the United States. Mr. Buchanan made a short complimentary address and took an affectionate leave. Not a word of compliment or consolation was said to him. . . . He retires covered with obloquy, without honor, and without praise. He conceded to the South far more than he ought, but he failed, in the last days of his administration, to concede *everything,* and hence the neglect with which he is treated by *all* parties."

Returning to biographer J. G. Holland:

"The morning of the fourth of March broke beautifully clear, and it found General Scott and the Washington police in readiness for the day. The friends of Mr. Lincoln had gathered from far and near, determined that he should be inaugurated. In the hearts of the surging crowds there was anxiety; but outside, all looked as usual on such occasions, with the single exception of an extraordinary display of soldiers."

Historian Benson Lossing adds:

"The inauguration ceremonies were performed quietly and orderly, at the usual place, over the broad staircase at the eastern front of the Capitol, whose magnificent dome was only half finished. . . . Mr. Lincoln was introduced . . . and as he stepped forward, his head towering over most of those around him . . . he was greeted with vehement applause. Then, with a clear, strong voice, he read his inaugural address, during which service Senator Douglas, lately his competitor for the honors and duties he was now assuming, held the hat of the new President."

Winfield Scott

The Little Giant whispered to friends nearby: "If I can't be President, I can at least hold the President's hat."

Says Senator John Sherman:

"I have witnessed many inaugurations, but never one so impressive as this. The condition of the South already organized for war, the presence of United States troops . . . [as] preparation against threatened violence, the sober and quiet attention to the address—all united to produce a profound apprehension of evils yet to come."

The most memorable part of the inaugural address was its closing, in which Lincoln made an appeal to the South:

"In *your* hands, my dissatisfied fellow-countrymen, and not in *mine,* is the momentous issue of civil war. The government will not assail *you.* You can have no conflict without being yourselves the aggressors. *You* have no oath registered in Heaven to destroy the government, while *I* shall have the most solemn one to preserve, protect, and defend it. . . .

"We are not enemies, but friends. We must not be enemies. Though passion may have *strained,* it must not *break,* our bonds of affection. The mystic chords of memory, stretching from every battlefield and patriot grave to every living heart and hearthstone, all over this broad land, will yet swell the chorus of the Union, when again touched, as surely they will be, by the better angels of our nature."

At the conclusion of his address, according to Iowa's Senator James Harlan, Lincoln "turned partially around on his left, facing the justices of the Supreme Court, and said, 'I am now ready to take the oath prescribed by the Constitution,' which was then administered . . . the President saluting the Bible with his lips. At that moment, in response to a signal, batteries of field guns, stationed a mile or so away, commenced firing a national salute in honor of the nation's new chief. And Mr. Buchanan, now a private citizen, escorted Mr. Lincoln to the Executive Mansion, followed by a multitude of people."

Returning to the account by Benson Lossing:

"Long before sunset on that beautiful fourth of March, the brilliant pageant of the inauguration of a President had dissolved, and thousands of citizens, breathing more freely now that the first and important chapter in the history of the new Administration was closed without a tragic scene, were hastening homeward. But Washington City was to be the theater of another brilliant display

Costumes worn at Lincoln's inaugural ball

the same evening, in the character of an inauguration ball. . . .

"A large temporary building had been erected for the purpose near the City Hall. . . . [It] was decorated with red and white muslin and many shields bearing National and State arms. Several foreign ministers and their families, and heads of departments and their families, were present.

"The dancing commenced at eleven o'clock. Ten minutes later the music and the motion ceased, for it was announced that Mr. and Mrs. Lincoln, in whose honor the ball was given, were about to enter the room. The President appeared first. . . . Immediately behind him came Mrs. Lincoln, wearing a rich watered silk dress, an elegant point-lace shawl, deeply bordered, with camelias in her hair and pearl ornaments. She was leaning on the arm of Senator Douglas, the President's late political rival. The incident was accepted as a proclamation of peace and friendship between the champions. Mr. [Hannibal] Hamlin, the Vice President, was already there; and the room was crowded with many distinguished men and elegantly dressed women.

"The utmost gayety and hilarity prevailed. And every face but one was continually radiant with the unmixed joy of the hour.

That face was Abraham Lincoln's. . . . Of all that company, he was . . . the most burdened; and with the pageantry of that Inauguration Day and that Inauguration Ball, ended, for him, the poetry of his Administration."

About a week after the inauguration, William T. Sherman came to Washington to visit his brother John, the senator, feeling that the administration might offer him reinstatement in the army.

"John . . . took me with him to see Mr. Lincoln. . . . We found the room full of people, and Mr. Lincoln sat at the end of the table, talking with three or four gentlemen, who soon left. John walked up, shook hands, and took a chair near him, holding in his hand some papers referring to minor appointments in the State of Ohio, which formed the subject of conversation. Mr. Lincoln took the papers, said he would refer them to the proper heads of departments. . . .

"John then turned to me, and said, 'Mr. President, this is my brother, Colonel Sherman, who is just up from Louisiana. He may give you some information you want.'

" 'Ah!' said Mr. Lincoln, 'how are they getting along down there?'

"I said, 'They think they are getting along swimmingly—they are preparing for war.'

" 'Oh, well!' said he, 'I guess we'll manage to keep house.'

"I was silenced, said no more to him, and we soon left. I was sadly disappointed, and . . . I broke out on John, damning the politicians generally, saying, 'You have got things in a hell of a fix, and you may get them out as you best can,' adding that the country was sleeping on a volcano that might burst forth at any minute, but that I was going to St. Louis [where a civilian job offer had developed] to take care of my family, and would have no more to do with it.

"John begged me to be more patient, but I said I would not; that I had no time to wait, that I was off for St. Louis; and off I went."

In the South, according to Richmond editor Edward Pollard, Lincoln's inauguration "was generally taken as a premonition of war. . . . The Confederate States government at Montgomery . . . was anxious for peace. . . . Soon after the inauguration of Mr. Lincoln, it . . . deputed an embassy of commissioners to Washington, authorized to negotiate for the removal of the Federal garrisons from Forts Pickens and Sumter [Pickens, on the Florida coast, in a position less vulnerable than that of Sumter, would manage to stand against all Confederate threats], and to provide for the settlement of all claims of public property arising out of the separation of the States from the Union. . . .

"The commissioners were amused from week to week with verbal assurances that the government was disposed to recognize them; that to treat with them at the particular juncture might seriously embarrass the administration of Mr. Lincoln; that they should be patient and confident; and that in the meantime the military status of the United States in the South would not be disturbed. . . .

"The dalliance with the commissioners was not the only deceitful indication of peace. It was given out and confidently reported in the newspapers that Fort Sumter was to be evacuated by the Federal forces. The delusion was continued for weeks. The Black Republican Party, of course, resented this reported policy of the government; but a number of their newspapers endeavored to compose the resentment by the arguments that the evacuation

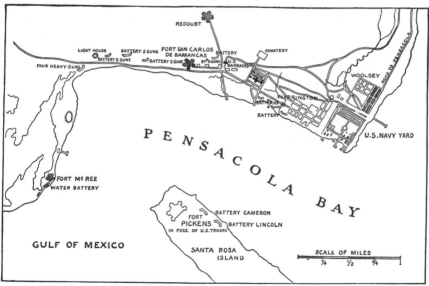

Fort Pickens, Florida, scene of a Sumter-like situation that did not explode. With the Confederates in possession of the U.S. Navy Yard and the fortifications extending to Fort McRee, Union Lieutenant Adam J. Slemmer, holding Pickens with a handful of men, stood firm against surrender demands until the fleet landed enough troops to assure the fort's retention.

would be ordered solely on the ground of military necessity, as it would be impossible to reinforce the garrison without a very extensive demonstration of force, which the government was not then prepared to make. . . .

"While a portion of the public were entertained in watching the surface of events and were imposed upon by deceitful signs of peace, discerning men saw the inevitable consequence in the significant preparations made on both sides for war. . . .

"The troops of the United States were called from the frontiers to the military centers; the Mediterranean squadron and other naval forces were ordered home; and the city of Washington itself was converted into a school where there were daily and ostentatious instructions of the soldier.

"On the other hand, the government at Montgomery was not idle. Three military bills had been passed by the Confederate Congress. The first authorized the raising of one hundred thousand volunteers when deemed necessary by the President; the second provided for the Provisional Army of the Confederate States, which was to be formed from the regular and volunteer forces of the different States; and the third provided for the organization of a Regular Army, which was to be a permanent establishment.

"But among the strongest indications of the probability of war, in the estimation of men calculated to judge of the matter—and among the most striking proofs, too, of devotion to the cause of the South—was the number of resignations from the Federal army and navy on the part of officers of Southern birth or association, and their prompt identification with the Confederate service."

On March 21, Alexander Stephens, vice president of the Confederacy, made a speech aimed at explaining the new government to the people. Later generations of Southerners would regard at least one part of the speech, with its gross vilification of the black race, as an acute embarrassment, but the point of view was widely accepted by Southerners of the time (nor was it short of adherents in the North). Stephens said:

"We are passing through one of the greatest revolutions in the annals of the world. Seven states have, within the last three months, thrown off an old Government and formed a new. . . .

"The new Constitution has put to rest forever all the agitating questions relating to our peculiar institution—African slavery as it

Alexander H. Stephens

exists among us—the proper status of the Negro in our form of civilization. This was the immediate cause of the late rupture and present revolution.

"Jefferson . . . had anticipated this as 'the rock upon which the old Union would split.' He was right. . . . But whether he fully comprehended the great truth upon which that rock stood, and stands, may be doubted. The prevailing ideas entertained by him and most of the leading statesmen at the time of the formation of the old Constitution were that the enslavement of the African was in violation of the laws of nature; that it was wrong in principle, socially, morally, and politically. It was an evil they knew not well how to deal with; but the general opinion of the men of that day was that, somehow or other, in the order of Providence, the institution would be evanescent and pass away. . . .

"Those ideas, however, were fundamentally wrong. They rested upon the assumption of the equality of races. This was an error. . . . Our new Government is founded upon exactly the opposite ideas. Its foundations are laid, its cornerstone rests, upon the great truth that the Negro is not equal to the white man; that slavery—subordination to the superior race—is his natural and moral condition. This, our new Government, is the first in the history of the world based upon this great physical, philosophical, and moral truth."

A young woman of the South (known only as "L.M.") supported the foregoing viewpoint with a graceless poem that included the following stanzas:

> *If ever I consent to be married*
> *(And who would refuse a good mate?),*
> *The man whom I give my hand to*
> *Must believe in the rights of the State.*
>
> *Should Lincoln attempt to coerce him*
> *To share with the Negro his right,*
> *Then, smiling, I'll gird on his armor,*
> *And bid him God-speed in the fight.*
>
> *We girls are all for a Union*
> *Where a marked distinction is laid*
> *Between the rights of the mistress*
> *And those of the kinky-haired maid.*

6

A Circle of Fire at Sumter

THE ADVENT OF APRIL 1861 saw the Fort Sumter issue moving toward a climax. In both North and South, the topic had been one of endless public discussion, much of it heated, and many teenage hearts were as deeply stirred as those of their elders.

Attending a Northern boarding school at the time was a boy named Jesse Bowman Young, who later recounted:

"One day at the school there was a serious commotion. Among the students were some boys and young men from Maryland and Virginia. Carter Burton, the recognized leader of these Southern students, was a handsome, graceful, hotheaded youth who had been brought up on a plantation with slaves to wait on him and plenty of money at command. He used to sneer at the abolitionists and berate the Northern people because some of them opposed slavery.

"On the day in question news had come that Fort Sumter was in danger; the very air resounded with the threats which had been made by South Carolina troops that they would destroy and take the fortress. The school was in a buzz of confusion all day long; the teachers themselves could hardly give attention to their tasks, much less keep the boys at their studies, and everybody seemed to be impressed that something dreadful was going to happen. It appeared as though a volcano was on the eve of an eruption, or as if a mine was just ready to blow up.

"In the late afternoon, as the boys were coming in to chapel

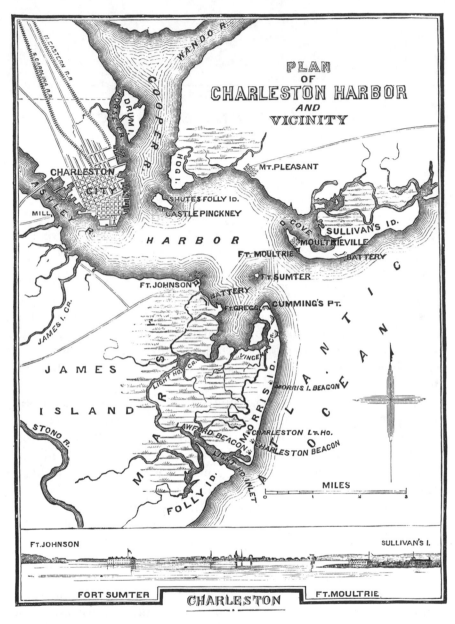

exercises, Burton was noticed in the center of an excited and noisy group of students who were arguing, threatening, quarreling, almost fighting.

"Just as they reached the chapel door, someone called out, 'Burton, what is that rosette which you have pinned on your coat?'

"The speaker was a tall, ungainly youth from the mountain

region of Pennsylvania, to whom the nickname of Lanky Jones had been given by his fellows in the school—a sturdy, quiet, hard-working lad who was earning his way through the academy by ringing the bell and sweeping the halls of the institution.

" 'None of your business, Lanky,' was the sharp retort. 'If you mind your bell rope you will have enough to do without meddling with my affairs.'

" 'Carter, that's a secession badge, isn't it?' persisted Lanky, approaching the Southerner, who, eyeing the questioner coolly, replied, 'Why do you ask me? You seem to know all about it beforehand.'

"Lanky came up gradually through the crowd nearer to Burton, his face pale and his voice trembling with excitement. He took a closer look and saw that the Southern colors were woven together in a knot of red and white ribbon on which was mounted a Confederate seal of some kind. As soon as he made the discovery, he put forth a sudden and impulsive plunge with his hand, and, snatching the offensive badge from its place on the coat, he threw it to the floor and angrily stamped upon it. Instantly Burton dealt him a heavy blow, which was partly parried; and amid increased excitement and rage the two antagonists clinched and attempted to settle their dispute with the fist.

"The confusion brought one of the teachers out of the chapel; and before either of the young combatants had received any very serious hurt they were separated, and the boys were directed to come into the service that was just commencing.

"This incident is a sample of scenes that were constantly taking place in various sections of the land."

The hottest words in the South were still being vented in Charleston itself. The Fire-eaters were urging South Carolina to "strike a blow" to cement the Confederate union. Conspicuous among the war advocates was elderly Edmund Ruffin, a tall, erect, wiry Virginian with long white hair. Ruffin's state had not yet seceded, but *he* had, with a consuming intensity, and he had been accepted as a volunteer at one of the batteries covering Sumter, where he was regarded with respect and admiration.

Now in command of the troops besieging the fort was Brigadier General Pierre Gustave Toutant Beauregard, a small, slender Louisianian whose French lineage could be traced back to the thirteenth century. He graduated second in his class at West Point and during the Mexican War won brevet promotions from lieutenant to captain and major, sustaining two wounds in the process.

According to John Esten Cooke, a Virginia author who served the Confederacy as a junior officer, variously assigned, and became acquainted with most of the army's top commanders, Beauregard was "a great soldier and a finished gentleman. . . . The nervous figure, the gaunt French, fighting, brunette countenance, deeply bronzed by sun and wind—these were the marks of the soldier. The grave, high-bred politeness; the ready, courteous smile; the kindly and simple bearing, wholly free from affectation and assumption—these were the characteristics of the *gentilhomme* by birth and habit, by nature as by breeding.

Edmund Ruffin

"Ten minutes conversation with the man convinced you that you stood in the presence of one of those men who mould events."

Beauregard was presently in the right spot to fulfill this appraisal. President Lincoln sent word to Governor Pickens at Charleston that he was dispatching a seaborne expedition to resupply Fort Sumter. This was to be a defensive act, not a hostile one, but it put the Confederates on the spot.

It is a curious fact that Major Anderson had been Beauregard's artillery instructor at West Point. Now the general had the major ringed with cannons and mortars, the deployment doubtless influenced by the major's own teachings.

Fort Sumter's surgeon, Samuel Wylie Crawford, assumes the narrative:

"On the morning of the 11th of April, the dawn of day disclosed [Confederate] activity at once unusual and significant over the entire harbor. The waters were covered with vessels hastily putting to sea. An iron-clad floating battery of four guns, the Construction of which in Charleston had been watched by the garrison for months, was towed down the bay to a point at the western end of Sullivan's Island, where its guns bore directly upon Fort Sumter. A wooden dwelling on the beach, near the end of the island, was pulled down, and unmasked a land work mounting four guns, hitherto unknown to the garrison. Its fire would enfilade the most important battery of Fort Sumter, which was upon the parapet of the right flank of the work, and whose guns were mainly relied upon to control the fire from the heavy guns on Cummings Point that would take the fort in reverse.

"Bodies of troops were landed, and the batteries on shore fully manned, and every preparation completed, when at four o'clock P.M., a boat under a white flag approached the fort. Two officials . . . Colonel [James] Chesnut and Captain S. D. Lee, were admitted to the guard room just inside the main entrance to the work. They bore a communication from the military commandant at Charleston [Beauregard], and to the following effect:

"It stated that the Government of the Confederate States had hitherto forborne from any hostile demonstration against Fort Sumter in the hope that the General Government would voluntarily evacuate it in order to avert war . . . but that the Confederate Government could no longer delay 'assuming actual possession' of a fortification so important to it. The evacuation of Fort Sumter was demanded in the name of the Government of

Pierre G. T. Beauregard

the Confederate States. All proper facilities were [to be] tendered to Major Anderson for the removal of himself and his command. He was to take with him his company and private property, and to salute his flag upon taking it down."

One of the Confederate aides, Stephen Lee, takes up: "At 4:30 P.M. [Major Anderson] handed us his reply, refusing to accede to the demand; but added, 'Gentlemen, if you do not batter the fort to pieces about us, we shall be starved out in a few days.'

"The reply of Major Anderson was put in General Beauregard's hands at 5:15 P.M., and he was also told of this informal remark. Anderson's reply and remark were communicated to the Confederate authorities at Montgomery. The Secretary of War, L. P. Walker, replied to Beauregard as follows: 'Do not desire needlessly to bombard Fort Sumter. If Major Anderson will state the time at which, as indicated by him, he will evacuate, and agree that in the meantime he will not use his guns against us, unless ours should be employed against Fort Sumter, you are authorized thus to avoid the effusion of blood. If this, or its equivalent, be refused, reduce the fort as your judgment decides to be most practicable.' . . .

"[We] aides bore a second communication to Major Anderson, based on the above instructions, which was placed in his hands at 12:45 A.M., April 12th. His [verbal] reply indicated that he would evacuate the fort on the 15th, provided he did not in the meantime receive contradictory instructions from his Government, or additional supplies; but he declined to agree not to open his guns upon the Confederate troops, in the event of any hostile demonstration on their part against his flag.

"Major Anderson made every possible effort to retain [us] . . . till daylight, making one excuse and then another for not replying [in writing]. Finally, at 3:15 A.M. he delivered his reply. In accordance with [our] instructions, [we] read it, and finding it unsatisfactory, gave Major Anderson this notification: '. . . Sir: By authority of Brigadier General Beauregard . . . we have the honor to notify you that he will open the fire of his batteries on Fort Sumter in one hour from this time. . . .'

"The above note was written in one of the casemates [one of the brick-walled gun rooms] . . . and in the presence of Major Anderson and several of his officers. On receiving it, he was much affected. He seemed to realize the full import of the consequences and the great responsibility of his position. Escorting us to the boat at the wharf, he cordially pressed our hands in farewell, remarking, 'If we never meet in this world again, God grant that we may meet in the next.' "

Adds the fort's James Chester:

"The men waited about for some time in expectation of orders, but received none. . . . Daylight [was] fully two hours off. . . . Except that the flag was hoisted, and a glimmer of light was visible at the guardhouse, the fort looked so dark and silent as to seem deserted. The morning was dark and raw."

A few of the men had been asleep during the critical parley, and they included Anderson's second-in-command, Captain Abner Doubleday, who was on a cot in one of the casemate magazines.

"About 4 A.M. on the 12th I was awakened by someone groping about my room in the dark and calling out my name. It proved to be Anderson, who came to announce to me that he had just received a dispatch from Beauregard, dated 3:20 A.M., to the effect that he should open fire upon us in an hour. Finding it was determined not to return the fire until after breakfast, I remained in bed."

Doubleday's kind of calmness was a rare thing on either side of the situation at this moment. Especially alert and anxious were many of Charleston's civilians. Mary Boykin Chesnut, wife of one of the aides who had been to the fort and a guest in a mansion overlooking the harbor, wrote in her diary: "I do not pretend to sleep. How can I? If Anderson does not accept terms at four, the orders are he shall be fired upon. I count four [as] St. Michael's bells chime out, and I begin to hope."

According to Sumter's surgeon, Samuel Wylie Crawford, "Fires were lighted in all the Confederate works, when, at 4:30 A.M., the silence was broken by the discharge of a mortar from a battery near Fort Johnson. . . . A shell rose high in the air and burst directly over Fort Sumter."

"The firing of the mortar," says Confederate officer Stephen Lee, "woke the echoes from every nook and corner of the harbor, and, in this the dead hour of night before dawn, that shot was a sound of alarm that brought every soldier in the harbor to his feet, and every man, woman and child in the city of Charleston from their beds. . . . After the second shell the different batteries opened their fire on Fort Sumter, and by 4:45 A.M. the firing was general and regular."

Confederate gun firing on Sumter

"All along the water fronts and from all the forts," adds Confederate soldier D. Augustus Dickert, "now a perfect sheet of
flame flashed out, a deafening roar, a rumbling, deadening sound,
and the war was on."

Among the men at the guns, of course, was old Edmund Ruffin,
who had been accorded the privilege of firing one of the first shots.

By this time Mary Boykin Chesnut was on her knees beside her
bed. "I prayed as I never prayed before. There was a sound of stir
all over the house, pattering of feet in the corridors. All seemed
hurrying one way. I put on my double gown and a shawl and went
too. It was to the housetop. The shells were bursting. . . . The
regular roar of the cannon—there it was. . . . The women were
wild there on the housetops. Prayers came from the women, and
imprecations from the men. And then a shell would light up the
scene. . . . We watched up there, and everybody wondered that
Fort Sumter did not fire a shot."

Most of the city's civilians were now out of doors. "The living
stream," says an unidentified resident, "poured through all the

Confederates in the floating battery

streets leading to the wharves and Battery. On reaching our beautiful promenade, we found it lined with ranks of eager spectators,
and all the wharves commanding a view of the battle were
crowded thickly with human forms. On no gala occasion have we
ever seen so large a number of ladies on our Battery as graced the
breezy walk on this eventful morning. There they stood, with
palpitating hearts and pallid faces, watching the white smoke as it
rose in wreaths . . . and breathing out fervent prayers for their
gallant kinsfolk at the guns."

"Shot and shell," says Union soldier James Chester, "went
screaming over Sumter as if an army of devils were swooping

around it. As a rule the guns were aimed too high, but all the mortar practice was good. In a few minutes the novelty [of the situation] disappeared in a realizing sense of danger, and the watchers retired to the bomb-proofs, where they discussed probabilities until reveille. . . . No serious damage was being done to the fort."

Abner Doubleday, however, had gained little rest after his decision to remain abed in the casemate magazine, which was stacked with explosives and had loose powder on its floor.

"A ball from Cummings Point lodged in the magazine wall and by the sound seemed to bury itself in the masonry about a foot from my head, in very unpleasant proximity to my right ear. . . . A shell soon struck near the ventilator, and a puff of dense smoke entered the room, giving me a strong impression that there would be an immediate explosion. Fortunately, no sparks had penetrated inside. . . .

"When it was broad daylight, I went down to breakfast. I found the officers already assembled at one of the long tables in the mess hall. Our party were calm, and even somewhat merry.

"We had retained one colored man to wait on us. He was a spruce-looking mulatto from Charleston, very active and efficient on ordinary occasions, but now completely demoralized by the thunder of the guns and crashing of the shot around us. He leaned back against the wall . . . his eyes closed, and his whole expression one of perfect despair.

"Our meal was not very sumptuous. It consisted of pork and water. But Doctor Crawford triumphantly brought forth a little farina, which he had found in a corner of the hospital.

"When this frugal repast was over, my company was told off in three details for firing purposes, to be relieved afterward by [Captain Truman] Seymour's company. As I was the ranking officer, I took the first detachment and marched them to the casemates which looked out upon the powerful iron-clad battery of Cummings Point.

"In aiming the first gun fired against the rebellion I had no feeling of self-reproach, for I fully believed that the contest was inevitable and was not of our seeking. . . .

"Our firing now became regular and was answered from the rebel guns which encircled us on four sides of the pentagon upon which the fort was built. The other side faced the open sea.

"Showers of balls from ten-inch columbiads and forty-two pounders, and shells from thirteen-inch mortars poured into the

Federals in fort firing through an embrasure

fort in one incessant stream, causing great flakes of masonry to fall in all directions. When the immense mortar shells, after sailing high in the air, came down in a vertical direction and buried themselves in the parade ground, their explosion shook the fort like an earthquake."

General Beauregard was pleased with the way things were going. "The fire of my batteries was kept up most spiritedly, the guns and mortars being worked in the coolest manner, preserving the prescribed intervals of firing."

"The battle," adds Confederate soldier D. Augustus Dickert, "is general and grand. Men spring upon ramparts and shout defiance at Sumter, to be answered by the crashing of shot against the walls of their bomb-proof forts."

Again in the words of Sumter's James Chester:

"At the end of the first four hours, Doubleday's men were relieved from the guns and had an opportunity to look about [the harbor]. Not a man was visible near any of the batteries, but a large party, apparently noncombatants, had collected on the beach of Sullivan's Island, well out of the line of fire, to witness the duel between Sumter and Moultrie.

"Doubleday's men were not in the best of temper. They were irritated at the thought that they had been unable to inflict any serious damage on their adversary, and although they had suffered no damage in return they were dissatisfied. The crowd of unsympathetic spectators was more than they could bear, and two veteran sergeants determined to stir them up a little.

"For this purpose they directed two 42-pounders on the crowd, and, when no officer was near, fired. The first shot struck about fifty yards short, and, bounding over the heads of the astonished spectators, went crashing through the Moultrie House. The second followed an almost identical course, doing no damage except to the Moultrie House, and the spectators scampered off in a rather undignified manner."

All temptation to fire upon Charleston itself was, of course, resisted. Later, New York's *Vanity Fair* would publish the following piece of light verse entitled *A Suggestion to Major Anderson:*

> *Although without question*
> *All credit is due*
> *To your courage and skill,*
> *Dear Anderson, still,*

One little suggestion
V. F. makes to you.
Why didn't you throw,
When the first bullet fell
Round your fort, a few shell,
Ten-inchers or so,
Towards the town
Where they say
All the people came down
To see, through their glasses
(The pitiful asses!)
How soon stout Fort Sumter would crumble away?
Suppose that a bomb—
Or a dozen—had come
Majestically sailing
Right over the railing
That runs round the green
(Which a delicate flattery
Has christened "The Battery"),
How many brave Southerners there had been seen?
And each beautiful lady
Of the "Five thousand fair,"
Who "held themselves ready,"
Would they have staid there?
'Twas a thing to have done,
If only for fun,
Just to show how the gallant spectators could run!

Returning to James Chester's account of affairs inside Fort Sumter:

"Major Anderson had given orders that only the casemate batteries [those with brick protection] should be manned. While this was undoubtedly prompted by a desire to save his men, it operated also, in some degree, to save the Confederates. Our most powerful batteries and all our shell guns were on the barbette tier [that is, atop the fort's wall], and, being forbidden their use, we were compelled to oppose a destructive shellfire with solid shot alone. This . . . was a great disadvantage. Had we been permitted to use our shell guns we could have set fire to the barracks and quarters in Moultrie. . . .

"This was so apparent to the men that one of them—a man named Carmody—stole up on the ramparts and deliberately fired every barbette gun in position on the Moultrie side of the work. The guns were already loaded and roughly aimed, and Carmody simply discharged them in succession; hence the effect was less than it would have been if the aim had been carefully rectified.

"But Carmody's effort aroused the enemy to a sense of his danger. He supposed, no doubt, that Major Anderson had determined to open his barbette batteries, so he directed every gun to bear on the barbette tier of Fort Sumter, and probably believed that the vigor of his fire induced Major Anderson to change his mind.

"But the contest was merely Carmody against the Confederate States; and Carmody had to back down, not because he was beaten, but because he was unable, single-handed, to reload his guns.

"Another amusing incident in this line occurred on the Morris Island side of the fort. There, in the gorge angle, a ten-inch columbiad was mounted, *en barbette,* and, as the 42-pounders of the casemate battery were making no impression on the Cummings Point iron battery, the two veteran sergeants who had surreptitiously fired upon the spectators, as already related, determined to try a shot at the iron battery from the big gun. As this was a direct violation of orders, caution was necessary.

"Making sure that the major was out of the way, and that no [other] officers were near, the two sergeants stole upstairs to the ten-inch gun. It was loaded and aimed already, they very well knew, so all they would have to do was to fire it. This was the work of a few seconds only. The gun was fired, and those in on the secret down below watched the flight of the shot in great expectations of decided results. Unfortunately the shot missed; not a bad shot—almost grazing the crest of the battery—but a miss. A little less elevation, a very little, and the battery would have been smashed: so thought the sergeants, for they had great faith in the power of their gun; and they determined to try a second shot.

"The gun was reloaded, a feat of some difficulty for two men; but to run it 'in battery' [forward], was beyond their powers. . . . The two sergeants could not budge it. Things were getting desperate around them. The secessionists had noticed the first shot, and had now turned every gun that would bear on that ten-inch gun. They were just getting the range, and it was beginning to be uncomfortable for the sergeants—who, in a fit of desperation, determined to fire the gun 'as she was.'

Gun dismounted by bombardment

"The elevating screw was given half a turn less elevation, and the primer was inserted in the vent. Then one of the sergeants ran down the spiral stairs to see if the coast were clear [that is, to make sure that no officers were near], leaving his comrade in a very uncomfortable position at the end of the lanyard and lying flat on the floor. It was getting hotter up there every second, and a perfect hurricane of shot was sweeping over the prostrate soldier. Human nature could stand it no longer. The lanyard was pulled and the gun was fired.

"The other sergeant was hastening up the stairway and had almost reached the top when he met the gun coming down, or at least trying to. . . . It had recoiled over the counter-hurters, and, turning a back somersalt, had landed across the head of the stairway. Realizing in a moment what had happened, and what would be to pay if they were found out, the second sergeant crept to the head of the stairway and called his comrade, who, scared almost to death—not at the danger he was in, but at the accident—, was still hugging the floor with the lanyard in his hand.

"Both got safely down, swearing eternal secrecy to each other; and it is doubtful if Major Anderson ever knew how that ten-inch gun came to be dismounted. It is proper to add that the shot was a capital one, striking just under the middle embrasure of the iron battery and half covering it with sand. If it had been a trifle higher it would have entered the embrasure."

Although Sumter was sufficiently supplied with shot, shell, and powder, it was short of friction primers and, in particular, of cartridge bags—containers for the individual powder charges.

"The scarcity of cartridge bags," says Chester, "drove us to some strange makeshifts. . . . Several tailors were kept busy making cartridge bags out of soldiers' flannel shirts; and we fired away several dozen pairs of woolen socks belonging to Major Anderson."

It was around noon when several vessels of the Union relief fleet appeared off the bar. Again in Chester's words:

"Orders were given to dip the flag to them. This was done, and the salute was returned, but while our flag was being hoisted after the third dip, a shell burst near the flagstaff and cut the halliards. This accident put the flag beyond our control. It ran down until the kinky halliards jammed in the pulley at the masthead, and the flag remained at about half-staff. This . . . [was later reported] as a signal of distress, but it was only an accident. There was no special distress in Sumter, and no signal to that effect was intended."

The relief fleet was hailed with joy by Sumter's men, but it was ill-prepared for an emergency of such a magnitude, so its crews did nothing more than to swell the ranks of the battle's spectators. Beauregard's men were somewhat apprehensive at the fleet's arrival, but as the afternoon wore on and it remained inactive, they began to view it with scorn.

In Charleston, Mary Boykin Chesnut was dividing her time between the housetop and her bedroom. "Boom, boom goes the cannon all the time. The nervous strain is awful."

"The firing," says Sumter's Abner Doubleday, "continued all day without any special incident of importance, and without our making much impression on the enemy's works. They had a great advantage over us, as their fire was concentrated on the fort, which was in the center of the circle, while ours was diffused over the circumference. Their missiles were exceedingly destructive to the upper exposed position of the work, but no essential injury was done to the lower casemates which sheltered us."

Several times, however, the wooden barracks in the fort were set afire by specially heated projectiles, "red-hot shot," but the flames were soon extinguished. Conspicuous in this work and in other urgent activities about the fort was Peter Hart, brought down from New York by Major Anderson's wife.

"As night approached," explains Confederate soldier D. Augustus Dickert, "the fire slackened in all directions, and at dark Sumter ceased to return our fire at all. By a preconcerted arrangement, the fire from our batteries and forts kept up at fifteen-minute intervals only."

According to Sumter's James Chester: "The first night of the bombardment was one of great anxiety. The fleet might send reinforcements; the enemy might attempt an assault. Both would come in boats; both would answer [a challenge] in English. It would be horrible to fire upon friends; it would be fatal not to fire upon enemies. The night was dark and chilly. Shells were dropping into the fort at regular intervals, and the men were tired, hungry, and out of temper. Any party that approached that night would have been rated as enemies upon general principles. Fortunately nobody appeared."

7

The Fort Is Surrendered

James Chester continues:
"The second day's bombardment began at the same hour as did the first; that is, on the Sumter side. The enemy's . . . fire . . . gradually warmed up after daylight as their batteries seemed to awaken, until its vigor was about equal to their fire of the day before.

"The fleet was still off the bar—perhaps waiting to see the end. Fire broke out once or twice in the officers' quarters, and was extinguished. It broke out again in several places at once, and we realized the truth [that the fight was unwinnable] and let the quarters burn. . . . Built [as] fireproof buildings, they were not fireproof. Neither would they burn in a cheerful way. The principal cisterns were large iron tanks immediately under the roof. These had been riddled, and the quarters below had been deluged with water. Everything was wet and burned badly, yielding . . . pungent piney smoke."

In Charleston, Mary Boykin Chesnut did not go downstairs for breakfast. She wrote in her diary:

"How gay we were last night! Reaction after the dread of all the slaughter we thought those dreadful [Union] cannon were making. Not even a battery the worse for wear. . . . Anderson has not yet silenced any of our guns. So the aides . . . with swords and red sashes by way of uniform, tell us.

"But the sound of those guns makes regular meals impossible. None of us goes to table. Tea trays pervade the corridors, going everywhere. Some of the anxious hearts lie on their beds and

moan in solitary misery. Mrs. [Louis] Wigfall and I solace ourselves with tea in my room.

"These women have all a satisfying faith. 'God is on our side,'
they say. . . .

"Mrs. Wigfall and I ask, 'Why?'

" '. . . He hates the Yankees,' we are told. 'You'll think *that* well
of him!'

"Not by one word or look can we detect any change in the
demeanor of these Negro servants. Lawrence sits at our door,
sleepy and respectful, and profoundly indifferent. So are they all,
but they carry it too far. You could not tell that they even heard
the awful roar going on in the bay, though it has been dinning in
their ears, night and day. People talk before them as if they were
chairs and tables. They make no sign. Are they stolidly stupid? Or
wiser than we are; silent and strong, biding their time?"

While Mrs. Chesnut and Mrs. Wigfall were sipping their morning tea and worrying about a slave insurrection, General Beauregard was studying Sumter through his field glasses and was
deriving strong encouragement from its columns of smoke.

"The fire of our batteries was increased, as a matter of course,
for the purpose of bringing the enemy to terms as speedily as
possible, inasmuch as his flag was still floating defiantly above him.
Fort Sumter continued to fire from time to time, but at long and
irregular intervals. . . . Our brave troops, carried away by their
naturally generous impulses, mounted the different batteries, and
at every discharge from the fort cheered the garrison for its pluck
and gallantry, and hooted the fleet lying inactive just outside the
bar."

"The scene inside the fort as the fire gained headway and
threatened the [powder] magazine," says James Chester, "was an
exciting one. It had already reached [a point near] some of our
stores of loaded shells and shell-grenades. These must be saved at
all hazard. Soldiers brought their blankets [soaked with water]
and covered the precious projectiles, and thus most of them were
saved. But the magazine itself was in danger. Already it was full of
smoke, and the flames were rapidly closing in upon it. It was
evident that [its metal door] must be closed, and . . . [that our] fire
must be maintained with such powder as we could [keep] secure
outside the magazine. A number of barrels were rolled out for
this purpose, and the magazine door—already almost too hot to
handle—was closed.

"It was the intention to store the powder taken from the magazine in several safe corners, covering it with damp soldiers' blankets. But safe corners were hard to find, and most of the blankets were already in use covering loaded shells. The fire was raging more fiercely than ever, and safety demanded that the uncovered powder be thrown overboard. This was instantly done, and if the tide had been high we should have been well rid of it. But the tide was low, and the pile of powder barrels rested on the riprapping in front of the embrasure. This was observed by the enemy, and some shell guns were turned upon the pile, producing an explosion which blew the gun at that embrasure clear out of battery, but did no further damage."

Sumter's Abner Doubleday takes up:

"By 11 A.M. the conflagration was terrible and disastrous. One fifth of the fort was on fire, and the wind drove the smoke in dense masses into the angle where we had all taken refuge. It seemed impossible to escape suffocation. Some lay down close to the ground with handkerchiefs over their mouths, and others posted themselves near the embrasures, where the smoke was somewhat lessened by the draught of air. Everyone suffered severely. . . . Had not a slight change of wind taken place, the result might have been fatal to most of us.

The bombardment at its height

"Our firing having ceased and the enemy being very jubilant, I thought it would be as well to show them that we were not all dead yet, and ordered the gunners to fire a few rounds more. . . .

"The scene at this time was really terrific. The roaring and crackling of the flames, the dense masses of whirling smoke, the bursting of the enemy's shells and our own which were exploding in the burning rooms, the crashing of the shot, and the sound of masonry falling in every direction made the fort a pandemonium. . . .

"About 12:48 P.M. the end of the flagstaff was shot down."

Confederate soldier D. Augustus Dickert was watching.

"The flag was seen to waver, then slowly bend over the staff and fall. A shout of triumph rent the air from the thousands of spectators on the islands and the mainland. Flags and handkerchiefs waved from the hands of excited throngs in the city. . . . Soldiers mount the ramparts and shout in exultation, throwing their caps in the air.

"Away to the seaward, the whitened sails of the Federal fleet were seen moving up towards the bar. Anxiety and expectation are now on tiptoe. Will the fleet attempt the succor of their struggling comrades? Will they dare to run the gauntlet of the heavy Dahlgren guns that line the channel sides? . . . No. The ships falter and stop. They cast anchor and remain a passive spectator to the exciting scenes going on, without offering aid to their friends or battle to their enemies."

Sumter's James Chester says that "the old flag was rescued and nailed to a new staff. This, with much difficulty, was carried to the ramparts and lashed to some chassis piled up there." One of the members of the party that performed this deed was Major Anderson's devoted aide, Peter Hart.

During the period while the flag was down, the Confederates decided to try to reopen talks with Anderson. Their methods were attended by confusion. The first man to seize the moment, unknown to General Beauregard, was Colonel Louis T. Wigfall (husband of Mary Boykin Chesnut's companion at morning tea, and until lately a U.S. Senator from Texas).

As reported in a letter written by an unidentified Charlestonian:

"Stationed on Morris Island, where he had been on foot or in the saddle since the commencement of the attack, he no sooner saw . . . the flagstaff shot away than he resolved to make his way

The news inflames the North

to the fort and persuade Major Anderson to desist from a resistance manifestly so unavailing. Despite the remonstrances of those around him, he embarked in a skiff, and with three Negro oarsmen and a coxswain, pulled [toward] the fort.

"He was scarce a hundred yards from shore when they hailed him to return. The Stars and Stripes were again flying. He literally turned a deaf ear to this call and pushed on, brandishing his sword, to which he had tied his white handkerchief as a flag of truce. From the [Confederate] batteries at Fort Moultrie, balls and shells were aimed at the skiff. The white flag was invisible at that distance, and the boat, only noticed when nearing the fort . . . had no business there. A thirty-two-pound ball struck the water within five yards of her, and was followed by a shell [whose explosion] came near proving fatal. The Africans strained every nerve to get under the lee of the fort. . . .

"On touching the wharf, the volunteer sprang ashore, and, finding the gate burst open by the flames, made his way round to an open port hole on the town side of the fort, through which—with the aid of a loose piece of timber which he placed beneath it—he swung himself from a protruding gun into the embrasure. He stumbled . . . upon one of the garrison, who did not know where Major Anderson was. The fire was still raging, the heat

Louis T. Wigfall

intense, and the smoke insufferable. Shells were still exploding above, and, from time to time, within the fort, from the mortars on Sullivan's Island.

"He worked his way up to a group of officers and men standing near a casemate. Was Major Anderson there? 'No!' Before the party had recovered their surprise at the apparition, Major Anderson came up. . . . He saw the sword and white handkerchief.

" 'Whom have I the honor of addressing?'

" 'Colonel Wigfall, of General Beauregard's staff.'

" 'May I inquire your business with me?'

" 'I have come to say that you must strike your colors. Your position is untenable. You have defended it gallantly. It's madness to persevere in useless resistance. You cannot be reinforced. You have no provisions. Your ammunition is nearly exhausted, and your fort is on fire.'

" 'On what terms do you summon me to surrender?'

" 'Unconditional. General Beauregard is an officer and a gentleman. He will doubtless grant you all the honors of war. . . .'

" 'Well, I have done all that was possible to defend this fort.'

" 'You have. Haul down your flag.'

" 'But your people are still firing into me.'

" 'Hoist a white one. If you won't, I will, on my own responsibility.'

"A shell burst in the ground within ten paces of them as they were speaking. Major Anderson invited the ex-Senator into a casemate. A white flag [a bedsheet] was hoisted, [and] the firing ceased."

Wigfall soon left the fort in his boat. It was now that a second Confederate expedition—one from Charleston—was maturing. Beauregard's aide, Stephen Lee, describes it from its beginning:

"As soon as General Beauregard heard that the flag was no longer flying, he sent three of his aides, William Porcher Miles, Roger A. Pryor, and myself to offer . . . Major Anderson . . . assistance in subduing the flames inside the fort. Before we reached it, we saw the United States flag again floating over it, and began to return to the city. Before going far, however, we saw the Stars and Stripes replaced by a white flag [the bedsheet]. We turned about at once and rowed rapidly to the fort.

"We were directed, from an embrasure, not to go to the wharf, as it was mined, and the fire was near it. We were assisted through an embrasure and conducted to Major Anderson. Our mission being made known to him, he replied, 'Present my compliments to General Beauregard, and say to him I thank him for his kindness, but need no assistance.' He further remarked that he hoped the worst was over, that the fire had settled over the magazine, and, as it had not exploded, he thought the real danger was about over.

"Continuing, he said, 'Gentlemen, do I understand you come direct from General Beauregard?' The reply was in the affirmative.

"He then said, 'Why, Colonel Wigfall has just been here as an aide too, and by authority of General Beauregard, and proposed the same terms of evacuation offered on the 11th instant.'

"We informed the major that we were not authorized to offer terms; that we were direct from General Beauregard, and that Colonel Wigfall, although an aide-de-camp to the general, had been detached and had not seen the general for several days.

"Major Anderson at once stated, 'There is a misunderstanding on my part, and I will at once run up my flag and open fire again.'

"After consultation [among ourselves], we requested him not to do so until the matter was explained to General Beauregard, and requested Major Anderson to reduce to writing his understanding with Colonel Wigfall, which he did. However, before we left the fort, a boat arrived from Charleston bearing Major D. R. Jones, assistant adjutant-general on General Beauregard's staff, who offered substantially the same terms to Major Anderson as those offered on the 11th, and also by Colonel Wigfall, and which were now accepted.

"Thus fell Fort Sumter, April 13th, 1861. At this time fire was still raging in the barracks and settling steadily over the magazine. All egress was cut off except through the lower embrasures. Many shells from the Confederate batteries which had fallen in the fort and had not exploded, as well as the hand-grenades used for defense, were exploding as they were reached by the fire. The wind was driving the heat and smoke down into the fort and into the casemates, almost causing suffocation.

"Major Anderson, his officers, and men were blackened by smoke and cinders, and showed signs of fatigue and exhaustion. . . . It was soon discovered, by conversation, that it was a bloodless battle. Not a man had been killed or seriously wounded on either side during the entire bombardment of nearly forty hours. Congratulations were exchanged on so happy a result."

The absence of casualties on the Union side—save for a few men with abrasions, bruises, and burns—was all the more remarkable in light of the fact that the Confederates had pummeled the fort with more than three thousand rounds of shot and shell.

Anderson had agreed to evacuate the fort the next morning. The opposing forces were now on the friendliest terms, and boatloads of Confederates began visiting Sumter. According to an unidentified member of the garrison: "Many of the South Carolina officers who came into the fort . . . who were formerly in our service, seemed to feel very badly at firing upon their old comrades and flag."

Among the citizens of Charleston, the surrender had been anticipated since the smoke had been seen to expand. Said an evening dispatch from the city: "The bells have been chiming all day, guns firing, ladies waving handkerchiefs, people cheering, and citizens making themselves generally demonstrative. It is regarded as the greatest day in the history of South Carolina."

Mary Boykin Chesnut wrote in her diary: "I did not know that one could live such days of excitement. . . . As far as I can make out, the fort surrendered to Wigfall. But it is all confusion. . . . Fire engines have been sent for, to put out the fire. Everybody tells you half of something, and then rushes off to tell something else, or hear the last news."

The crowd continued to swell as people from outlying areas streamed in. Nightfall found thousands parading the streets, many with torches. There was cheering for General Beauregard and Governor Pickens. The governor made a speech from the balcony of the Charleston Hotel.

"Thank God! Thank God! The day has come; the war is open, and we will conquer or perish. We have defeated their twenty millions, and we have humbled the proud flag of the Stars and Stripes that never before was lowered to any nation on earth. We have lowered it in humility before the Palmetto and Confederate flags, and have compelled them to raise the white flag and ask for honorable surrender. The Stars and Stripes have triumphed for seventy years, but on this 13th of April it has been humbled by the little State of South Carolina. And I pronounce here, before the civilized world, that your independence is baptized in blood. Your independence is won upon a glorious battlefield, and you are free, now and forever, in defiance of the world in arms."

While Charleston celebrated, Major Anderson and his men settled down amid Sumter's blackness, which was relieved here and there by lingering patches of flame, and enjoyed a profound sleep.

"The next morning, Sunday the 14th," relates Abner Doubleday, "we were up early, packing our baggage in readiness to go on board the transport [provided by the Confederates]. The time having arrived, I made preparations, by order of Major Anderson, to fire a national salute to the flag."

The salute was intended to be one of a hundred guns, or discharges, but it had to be limited to fifty because of an accident. Again in Doubleday's words:

"Owing to the recent conflagration, there were fire and sparks all around the cannon, and it was not easy to find a safe place of deposit for the cartridges. It happened that some flakes of fire had entered the muzzle of one of the guns. . . . Of course, when the gunner attempted to ram the cartridge down it exploded prematurely, killing Private Daniel Hough instantly and setting fire to a pile of cartridges underneath, which also exploded, seriously wounding five men."

Dr. Samuel Wylie Crawford hurried to attend to the wounded, one of whom was dying. At the same time, the new garrison sent by General Beauregard marched into the fort, and a Confederate chaplain assisted at Daniel Hough's burial, made on the rubble-cluttered parade ground. The Confederates joined the Federals in uncovering their heads during the ceremonies.

It was a little later that a writer for the Charleston *Mercury* entered Sumter.

"It were vain to attempt a detailed description of the scene. Every point and every object in the interior of the fort . . . except the outer walls and casemates . . . bore the impression of ruin. . . . Near the center of the parade ground was the hurried grave of one who had fallen from the recent casualty. To the left of the entrance was a man who seemed to be at the verge of death. . . . The shattered flagstaff . . . lay sprawling on the ground. The parade ground was strewn with fragments of shell and of the dilapidated buildings. . . . At every step, the way was impeded. . . .

"And so it was that the [Union] authorities, compelled to yield the fortress, had at least the satisfaction of leaving it in a condition calculated to inspire the least possible pleasure to its captors.

"Of all this [somberness], however, the feeling was lost when, ascending to the parapet, the brilliant panorama of the bay ap-

The fort in Confederate hands

peared; and when, from this key to the harbor . . . the flag of the Confederacy, together with the Palmetto flag, were both expanded to the breeze; and when the deafening shouts arose from the masses clustered upon boats and upon the shores; and when the batteries around the entire circuit shook the fortress with the thunders of their salutation. . . . The victory was indeed complete. . . .

"The [Union] garrison marched out and were received on board the *Isabel;* which, however, from the condition of the tide was unable to move off; and it was a somewhat unpleasant circumstance that Major Anderson and his command should have been made unwilling spectators of the exultations inspired by their defeat."

When the tide changed, the *Isabel* crossed the bar to the Union fleet. The men were transferred to the steamship *Baltic,* which soon weighed anchor to begin its trip north.

Says Dr. Crawford:

"Many an eye turned toward the disappearing fort, and as it sunk at last upon the horizon, the smoke-cloud still hung heavily over its parapet."

8

Turbulence in Baltimore

JOHN G. NICOLAY, private secretary to Abraham Lincoln, assumes the narrative:

"The news of the assault on Sumter reached Washington on Saturday, April 13th [the bombardment's second day]. On Sunday morning, the 14th, the President and Cabinet were met to discuss the surrender and evacuation. Sunday though it was, Lincoln with his own hand immediately drafted the following proclamation. . . .

" '*Whereas,* the laws of the United States have been for some time past and now are opposed, and the execution thereof obstructed in the States of South Carolina, Georgia, Alabama, Florida, Mississippi, Louisiana, and Texas, by combinations too powerful to be suppressed by the ordinary course of judicial proceedings, or by the powers vested in the marshals by law: now therefore, I, Abraham Lincoln, President of the United States, in virtue of the power in me vested by the Constitution and the laws, have thought fit to call forth, and hereby do call forth the militia of the several States of the Union, to the aggregate number of seventy-five thousand, in order to suppress said combinations and to cause the laws to be duly executed.' "

Although prepared on the Sabbath, the proclamation was not issued then. Lincoln dated it Monday, April 15, and put it aside for the day. Meanwhile, news of Sumter was sweeping both the North and the South.

Mary Ashton Livermore, a public-spirited New Englander who would soon join the U.S. Sanitary Commission, a volunteer organization dedicated to looking after the health and welfare of Union soldiers and their families, was in Boston that day.

"The pulpits thundered with denunciations of the rebellion. Congregations applauded sermons such as were never before heard in Boston. . . . Many of the clergy saw with clear vision . . . that the real contest was between slavery and freedom. . . . Some of the ministers counselled war rather than longer submission to the imperious South. Better that the land should be drenched with fraternal blood than that any further concessions should be made to the slaveocracy. . . .

"The same vigorous speech was heard on the streets, through which surged hosts of excited men. There was an end of patience, and in its stead was aroused a determination to avenge the insult offered the nation. Conservative and peaceful counsel was shrivelled in a blaze of belligerent excitement."

The arrival of the Sumter news in Richmond, Virginia, is thus described by Mrs. Sarah A. Putnam, a wartime citizen:

"It was received with the wildest demonstrations of delight. A hundred guns were fired, and, as the reverberations were heard for miles around, the people . . . knew that there was some wonderful cause for joy; and those not of the city wondered whether they commemorated the victory of the Confederates at Sumter, or whether the Convention had at last passed the ordinance of secession.

"But the intelligence of the actual event spread rapidly. Men from the adjoining country flocked to the city to hear the wonderful story. Bonfires were kindled, rockets sent up, and the most tumultuous excitement reigned. All night the bells of Richmond rang, cannons boomed, shouts of joy arose, and the strains of 'Dixie's Land,' already adopted as the national tune of the Confederates, were wafted over the seven hills of the city.

"There was little room to doubt the spirit of the people. . . . Denunciations were heaped upon the Convention because of its tardiness [in declaring for secession], and attempts were made to run up the Stars and Bars on the dome of the Capitol. Mothers, forgetful . . . of the restraint usually imposed upon their youthful sons, permitted them to join in the demonstrations of delight; and the boys shouted eagerly for the Southern Confederacy, and for Beauregard . . . and cried, 'Down with the Old Flag!' . . .

"The writer of these recollections on that day [Sunday] crossed Mayo's Bridge, and as her eye rested on the [Union] shipping that lay at anchor in the river, she saw from the mastheads of the vessels, floating in the breeze and sunshine, the Stars and Stripes,

the old flag, under whose folds . . . she had first breathed. . . . Her
pride in it had ever been intense, her love for it characterized by
the most sincere veneration. She questioned with herself whether
she had lived to see the day when that flag . . . should become the
symbol of tyranny and of oppression to the rights she held most
sacred."

Abraham Lincoln's proclamation, according to period historian
Robert Tomes, filled the North with intense enthusiasm.

"The population of the large cities became suddenly so absorbed in the excitement of the hour that all the ordinary trans-
actions of business were suspended. Flags floated from every
public building, church steeple, and private house. . . . Union devices and badges were sold at the corners of every street and
flaunted upon each patriotic waistcoat and bodice.

"Shop windows patriotically glowed with the national colors. . . .
The newspapers forgot their factious contentions and joined in a
fervid expression of Union sentiments. Their leading articles
burst forth into unusual flowers of patriotic rhetoric."

The same historian goes on to say that "the great mass of the
people were eager not only to avenge the insulted flag, but to
restore it to its former proud position throughout the wide domain of the United States. With their traditional reverence for the
Union, and faith in its power, they could not contemplate the
possibility of its disruption. And, doubting the persistence of secession and presuming on its weakness, they fondly believed that
with a single [military] effort . . . rebellion could be suppressed,
and the flag raised once more over a united land."

The narrative is taken up by John Minor Botts, a Virginian with
a long career in politics, both state and national, who had never
wavered in his support for the Union, and who had made himself
very unpopular in his state by airing his views without reservation.

"When [Lincoln's] proclamation reached Richmond on the
evening of the 15th, the city was crammed with secessionists from
all parts of the state. . . . I came down myself on the same day
from Washington, and I had scarcely set my foot upon the thresh-
old of my own door before I was visited by friends who admon-
ished me that I had better not go upon the street; that the whole
city was in a blaze of excitement, and it would be dangerous for
me, with my well-known opinions and devotion to the Union, to
be seen in public.

"I ridiculed the idea and spurned the suggestion, hastened to
get my dinner, and walked down to the governor's house, where

John Minor Botts

I found a room crowded with members of the Convention. . . . They were all in a high state of excitement, governor and all. To reason with them would be like darting straws against the wind. I soon found that my presence was not agreeable to the gentlemen assembled . . . for soon after my arrival, and upon the utterance of the first sentiment I expressed upon the subject, they began, one by one, to leave the room, until the governor and myself were left alone.

"I found all reason in vain, and I did not remain long, but extended my walk through Capitol Square and down Main Street to ascertain the extent of my danger, as predicted by my friends. Many looked askance; some seemed to avoid me; but none ventured to offer me offense.

"I never felt more proud or stepped more boldly, for I felt the most comfortable and confiding assurance that I was *in the right*. I felt that I was in the midst of a despicable set of traitors . . . and of timid, misguided men who had suffered their fears, and in some instances their prejudices and their passions . . . to get the better of their judgments.

"I walked home proudly and defiantly; but when safely pillowed under my own roof my pride and defiant spirit both forsook me, and I involuntarily burst into tears over what I too clearly saw—the calamities that were in store for my country."

Again in the words of Richmond's Sarah Putnam:

"On the 17th of April . . . the Convention of Virginia passed an ordinance of secession . . . as follows:

" 'The people of Virginia recognize the American principle that government is founded on the consent of the governed, and the right of the people of the several States of this Union, for just cause, to withdraw from their association, under the Federal Government, with the people of the other States, and to erect new governments for their better security; and they never will consent that the Federal power, which is in part their power, shall be exerted for the purpose of subjecting such States to the Federal authority.' . . .

"Suddenly—almost as if by magic—the new Confederate flag was hoisted on the Capitol; and from every hilltop, and from nearly every housetop in the city, it was soon waving. The excitement was beyond all description; the satisfaction unparalleled. All business was suspended for the time, and the work of the moment was universal congratulation.

"At last Virginia was free from the obligation that bound her to a Union that had become hateful. Cannons were fired, bells rang, shouts rent the air, the inhabitants rushed to and fro to discuss the joyful event. A stranger suddenly transported to the city without a knowledge of the preceding facts would have imagined the people in a state of intoxication or insanity."

One who was not celebrating was John Minor Botts. Nor was he thinking in terms of accepting the situation and making peace with Virginia's political machine.

"You ask me . . . what I think will be the result of this rebellion?" he wrote. "The question is . . . briefly answered. The history of the world in 6,000 years has furnished but one instance of a David and Goliath. I do not think this is likely to prove a second. Five millions of people [with blacks included, probably eight or nine] . . . without money . . . without a sufficiency of the necessaries of life, without a navy, and without commerce—to overthrow 22,000,000 of people with an abundant supply of both money and credit . . . provisions, and other appliances of war, with a most powerful navy and a commerce unrestricted with all the world, would be a miracle that could be worked out by the hand of the Almighty alone. . . . I am compelled, therefore, to conclude that the rebellion will prove in the end a most signal and disastrous failure, unless the Administration at Washington shall be guilty of some act of most absurd and stupid folly."

This was, of course, a practical view of things, but few Southerners were in a mood to listen to such warnings. Most chose to dwell upon their strong points: Their leadership was excellent, and, as a result of their agrarian culture, their men were generally adept with horses and firearms. And, paramountly, their cotton was an important part of the European economy, and they could look that way for many of the supplies they needed—might even be able to secure open intervention in their favor. Their confidence was supreme.

Not so with the administration in Washington. At the time Lincoln issued his call for troops, the capital held only a few thousand regulars and home guards. It was fearfully vulnerable. The president hoped for a speedy response by the North's militia. And he hoped the units would manage to make their way through Maryland without serious opposition from the populace.

By April 17—two days after the proclamation was issued—Pennsylvania had assembled several regiments. The National Light Infantry and the Washington Artillerists were raised in the Pottsville area of Schuylkill County. These men, however, were woefully short of weapons. They had been told that the matter would be rectified when they reached the capital.

The *Miner's Journal* of Pottsville made this report of events of the seventeenth:

"During the whole day the greatest excitement prevailed among our citizens, and the scene at the armories of the respective companies was quite lively and spirited. New recruits were rolling in at every moment, and the lists were soon swelled to above the requisite number. The Artillerists numbered one hundred and thirty rank-and-file, and the Infantry somewhat above a hundred. . . .

"The day was very cold, raw, and disagreeable; but, notwithstanding this, the people flocked in by thousands from all parts of the County, and it seemed as if its whole population had been poured forth to witness the departure of our gallant volunteers, who, with a noble spirit of self-sacrifice, have exchanged the comforts of home for the fatigue and labor of a soldier's life.

"About half past twelve o'clock, the concourse of people that had assembled about the armories of the two companies was so great that it was with difficulty that a place was cleared for them in the street. Everybody was pressing forward, and all striving to speak a parting word and take a final leave of their friends. . . .

"As the companies proceeded down Center Street to the depot of the Philadelphia and Reading Railroad, they were greeted with cheers from the thousands who lined each side of the street, and [with] a perfect ocean of handkerchiefs waved by the ladies, who had taken possession of all the windows. . . . All the stores were closed, and business entirely suspended. At the depot the crowd was immense, and it was almost impossible to force your way through it. The tops of the passenger and freight cars, the roofs of the depot and neighboring houses, were black with spectators. Never had so great a concourse assembled on any one occasion before in Pottsville.

"The Pottsville Cornet Band, which had escorted the companies to the depot . . . played 'Hail, Columbia,' and 'Yankee Doodle.'

"As the train slowly left the depot, cheer upon cheer went up from the assembled thousands. The men were in good spirits, but there were some who, though possessed of manly hearts, who could brave toil and danger without complaint or fear, who could endure suffering with stoical indifference, but who could not prevent the tear from starting from the eye when called upon to bid farewell to all their friends."

The train made for Harrisburg, Pennsylvania, where the Schuylkill County recruits were joined by companies from Reading, Allentown, and Lewistown. One of the men from Lewistown was William F. McKay, who continues the narrative:

"For some unaccountable reason we were loaded on the cars entirely unarmed to pass through the then disloyal city of Baltimore. We were accompanied by a detachment of forty regulars. . . .

"The city of Baltimore was under the control of the secessionists and an infuriated mob, frenzied with passion and liquor, who awaited our coming. As we disembarked from the cars [to march to another depot] we were surrounded by a hooting, yelling crowd. . . . A line of Marshal [George B.] Kane's police [of Baltimore] was on each side of us. The streets and sidewalks were jammed with people, and at every cross street we were met by fresh masses who hurled bricks and paving stones at us. The line of the police was nearly broken at several points. . . . Many secession flags met our gaze. . . .

"A colored servant [Nicholas Biddle] of the Pottsville companies was the first man on our side to shed his blood, north of Fort Sumter. He was knocked down by a paving stone and his head badly cut [with the mob shouting, "Nigger in uniform!"].

Northern volunteers off to Washington

"We were put into freight cars at the Washington Depot, and it was then that the mob seemed more ferocious than ever. Some mounted the decks of the cars, and by jumping on them attempted to break them through. A continual stream of missiles was flying through the openings of the cars. They attempted to tear up the track, and several times uncoupled the engine from our train. Some of our boys were hard to restrain under all these insults and abuse, and two of them jumped out and offered to fight any two men in the crowd. This seemed to please them somewhat. . . .

"After many delays, we were once more on the move, and at 7 P.M. arrived in Washington. We were silently marched to the Capitol Building, where we were reviewed by Major, afterwards General [Irvin] McDowell. We had our headquarters in the hall of the House of Representatives."

These troops from Pennsylvania were the first to report for duty at the President's call. They had entered history as the Union's "First Defenders."

On this same day, the steamship *Baltic*, bearing Major Anderson and his men from Charleston, sailed into New York Harbor. In Abner Doubleday's words:

"We had a royal reception. The streets were alive with banners. Our men and officers were seized and forced to ride on the shoulders of crowds wild with enthusiasm. When we purchased anything, merchants generally refused all compensation. Fort Hamilton, where we were [sent], was besieged with visitors, many of whom were among the most highly distinguished in all walks of life. The Chamber of Commerce of New York voted a bronze medal to each officer and soldier of the garrison."

The second set of militiamen to figure in the "on to Washington" drama were mustered in Massachusetts. As reported by Charles Carleton Coffin of the Boston *Journal:*

"Twenty companies are wanted. The soldiers are scattered far and wide, in more than twenty towns, driving teams upon their farms, making shoes, pushing the plane; some are clerks in counting-rooms, or laborers in mills where spindles are whirling and shuttles flying.

"Down by the seaside, where the waves of the Atlantic break upon the granite ledges of Marblehead, are men with sunburnt, weatherbeaten faces who have braved the storms of the sea. . . . It is four o'clock in the afternoon [on April 16] when a messenger rides up to the house of Captain Knott V. Martin. The captain has killed a pig and is ready to dress it when the messenger hands him a slip of paper. With knife in hand he reads it:

" 'You are ordered to appear with your company on Boston Common at the earliest possible moment.'

"He throws down the knife. . . .

" 'What will you do with the pig?' asks Mrs. Martin.

" 'Damn the pig!'

"Not an instant does he wait. The members of his company must be summoned, his knapsack packed. . . .

"Morning dawns, and in every village there is a beating of drums and gathering of citizens to see the soldiers take their departure. The day is dark and dreary, the wind east, the storm clouds flying in from the sea, but the streets are filled with people. There is a steady tramping of feet upon the pavement, a swinging of hats, and loud hurrahs as the companies arrive, marching to Faneuil Hall, the building where the nation in its infancy was cradled.

"The 6th Regiment is the first to leave. A great crowd assembles to witness its departure, and rend the air with their cheers.

"The next morning the troops are in New York, marching down

"Damn the pig!"

Broadway beneath a sea of banners. Hundreds of thousands of people cheer them. . . .

"April 19th. It is the anniversary of Lexington and Concord. Eighty-six years have rolled away since Major Buttrick marshalled his fifty men in the meadows of Concord . . . and now three of Major Buttrick's descendants are whirling toward Washington in response to their country's call.

"They are in Maryland, a slave state which the secessionists hope to secure for the Confederacy. They [the secessionists] have stirred up the ruffians of the city to prevent the passage of Northern troops to Washington."

It was about 10 A.M. The regiment was at Baltimore's Philadelphia Depot. (As it happened, the unit was accompanied by about a thousand unarmed Pennsylvania troops who would make no further progress, but would soon encounter a hostility that would turn them back to Philadelphia.) The 6th was nearly a mile and a half from the Camden Street Station of the Baltimore and Ohio road to Washington, and there was no through track. The cars had to be detached from the engine and drawn by horses through the city on a street railway line.

According to the regimental historian:

"The engine was unshackled and horses were at once hitched to the cars. . . . The railroad officials were making nervous haste, fearing what might happen."

Not much happened at first, since the regiment had arrived considerably earlier than expected. It took time for a crowd to

Northern volunteers marching down Broadway

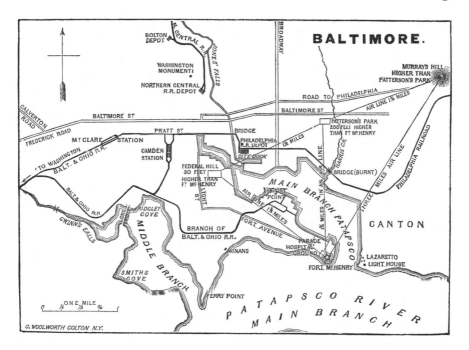

gather. The first seven cars made it to the Camden Station with-out serious trouble. Before their occupants could change to the Washington cars, however, the situation changed radically. Says an unidentified eyewitness:

"The scene . . . was indescribably fearful. Taunts, clothed in the most fearful language, were hurled at them by the panting crowd, who, almost breathless with running, passed up to the car win-dows presenting knives and revolvers, and cursed up into the faces of the soldiers. The police were thrown in between the cars, and, forming a barrier, the troops changed cars. . . .

"A wild cry was raised . . . and a dense crowd ran . . . along the railroad [ahead] . . . until the track for a mile was black with an excited, rushing mass. The crowd, as it went, placed obstructions of every description on the track. Great logs and telegraph poles requiring a dozen or more to move them were laid across the rails, and stones rolled from the embankment.

"A body of police followed after the crowd . . . and removed the obstructions as fast as they were placed on the track. Various attempts were made to tear up the track. . . . The police inter-fered on every occasion, but the crowd, growing larger and more excited, would dash off at a breakneck speed for another position farther on. . . . The police followed, running, until forced to stop from fatigue. At this point many of the throng gave up from exhaustion; but a crowd, longer-winded, dashed on for nearly a mile farther, now and then pausing to attempt to force the rails, or place some obstruction upon them. They could be distinctly seen for a mile along the track."

Meanwhile, there were two horse-drawn cars from the Philadelphia Station that hadn't been able to make it through because of barricades placed by the mob. These cars contained four companies, or about two hundred and twenty men. In the words of one of the company commanders, Captain A. S. Follansbee:

"We filed out of the cars in regular order . . . and formed in a

6th Massachusetts fighting its way through Baltimore

line on the sidewalk. The captains consulted together and decided that the command should devolve upon me. I immediately took my position at the right, wheeled into column of sections, and requested them to march in close order. Before we had started, the mob was upon us, with a secession flag attached to a pole, and told us we never could march through that city. They would kill every white nigger of us before we could reach the other depot. I paid no attention to them, but after I had wheeled the battalion, gave the order to march.

"As soon as the order was given, the brickbats began to fly into our ranks from the mob. I called a policeman and requested him to lead the way to the other depot. . . . After we had marched about a hundred yards, we came to a bridge. The rebels had torn up most of the planks. We had to play 'Scotch Hop' to get over it. As soon as we had crossed the bridge they commenced to fire upon us from the streets and houses.

"We were loaded but not capped. I ordered the men to cap their rifles and protect themselves, and then we returned their fire. . . . I saw four fall. . . . They followed us . . . [toward] the other depot. . . . The mayor of the city met us almost halfway."

The mayor, George W. Brown, assumes the narrative:

"The uproar was furious. I ran at once to the head of the column, some persons in the crowd shouting, 'Here comes the mayor.' I shook hands with the officer in command, Captain Follansbee. . . . The captain greeted me cordially. . . . I placed myself by his side and marched with him. He said, 'We have been attacked without provocation,' or words to that effect. I replied, 'You must defend yourselves.' I expected that he would face his men to the rear, and, after giving warning, would fire if necessary. . . . The safest and most humane manner of quelling a mob is to meet it, at the beginning, with armed resistance. The column [however] continued its march.

"There was neither concert of action nor organization among the rioters. They were armed only with such stones or missiles as they could pick up, and a few pistols. My presence, for a short time, had some effect, but very soon the attack was renewed with greater violence. The mob grew bolder. Stones flew thick and fast. Rioters rushed at the soldiers and attempted to snatch their muskets, and at least on two occasions succeeded. With one of these muskets a soldier was killed. Men fell on both sides. A young lawyer . . . seized a flag of one of the companies and nearly tore it from its staff. He was shot through the thigh, and was carried home."

Another eyewitness reports:

"A soldier was knocked down by a stone. He fell upon his face in the middle of the street, and endeavored to crawl towards the sidewalk. The mob made a rush towards him. One ruffian came with an axe-helve raised, shouting, 'Let me kill him!' A Boston man in the city rushed in, pushed the fellow back, and stood over him, saying, 'No, you shan't; he is a wounded man; let him alone!'

"By his efforts the soldier was protected, the crowd rushing on after the soldiers. The man then tried to get someone to open their house and take in the soldier. He called at nine doors before he could find a person with humanity enough to help the wounded man. The purport of their answers was, 'Let the Yankee die!' "

Returning to Mayor Brown:

"The soldiers fired at will. There was no firing by platoons, and I heard no order given to fire. . . . At the corner of South Street several citizens standing in a group fell, either killed or wounded. It was impossible for the troops to discriminate between the rioters and the bystanders, but the latter seemed to suffer most. . . .

"Marshal Kane, with about fifty policemen [according to Kane, it was considerably less] . . . came at a run from the direction of the Camden Street Station, and, throwing themselves in the rear of the troops, they formed a line in front of the mob, and, with drawn revolvers, kept it back. This was between Light and Charles Streets. Marshal Kane's voice shouted, 'Keep back, men, or I shoot!'

"This movement, which I saw myself, was gallantly executed, and was perfectly successful. The mob recoiled like water from a rock. One of the leading rioters . . . tried . . . to pass the line, but the marshal seized him and vowed he would shoot if the attempt was made.

"This nearly ended the fight, and the column passed on, under protection of the police . . . to Camden Station."

Shortly the four companies were aboard the Washington cars with the other units of the regiment. Says the regimental commander, Colonel Edward F. Jones:

"I caused the blinds to the cars to be closed, and took every precaution to prevent any shadow of offense to the people of Baltimore; but still the stones flew thick and fast into the train, and it was with the utmost difficulty that I could prevent the troops from leaving the cars and revenging the death of their comrades."

In reality, revenge had already been inflicted. Ten or twelve citizens had been killed, and many wounded. The 6th lost four killed and thirty-six wounded.

"After considerable delay," explains the regimental historian, "the train started, followed by an enraged crowd who piled every conceivable obstruction on the track. After frequent stops . . . the conductor reported he could go no farther, and that the regiment must march the rest of the way. Colonel Jones told him he held through tickets to Washington, and if he could not run the train through, he had men who could fill every position on the train, and could and would put the train through.

"The train was again started, and at Jackson Bridge the mob gave up the chase. After a long delay at the Relay House, the train reached Washington late in the afternoon, and the boys were received by Major McDowell, and were quartered that night in the United States Senate Chamber."

In Baltimore, the departure of the Union troops did not end the excitement. As related by one of Maryland's Union sympathizers, a lawyer named W. H. Purnell:

"Exaggerated reports were circulated. The number of citizens killed was magnified from ten to two hundred. Youths from sixteen to twenty years of age, armed to the teeth, were seen running wildly about the streets. The thoroughfares were filled with people . . . firing one another with the spirit of vengeance. An impromptu mass meeting was assembled in Monument Square. The Mayor was called out. The Governor [Thomas Hicks], who had been in the city for several days, was sent for. . . .

"A Maryland flag was hoisted over his head, and his views clamorously demanded. He responded by declaring that he would suffer his right arm to be torn from his body before he would raise it to strike a sister State [meaning that he had not sanctioned the passage through Baltimore of Northern troops on their way to coerce the South]. That night, so it is charged, the Governor agreed to an order for the destruction of the bridges on the Philadelphia, Wilmington and Baltimore, and the Northern Central Railroads in order to prevent the passage of any more troops through Maryland to Washington [by that method]. It is but justice to Governor Hicks to state that he always denied that he had

Thomas Hicks

authorized any such proceeding. However, the bridges were destroyed. . . .

"Governor Hicks . . . notwithstanding some mistakes, and despite the overawing of him on the 19th of April, was a Union man to the core. . . . In dealing with the Union question he . . . endeavored to practice in the State . . . Fabian tactics [those of extreme caution]. . . . He paid respect to the opinions and humored the prejudices of the great body of his people."

Delegations from Maryland, both political and private, hastened to approach Abraham Lincoln and urge him not to pass any more troops through their state. The President was at first diplomatic with these people, but he soon made it clear that he intended to do everything he could that promised to help save the Union. Right now his biggest concern was that Washington was very nearly defenseless. Even government officials of rank were helping to fortify the city and patrol its approaches. Many women and children were being evacuated. (Mrs. Lincoln had been advised to leave, but she chose to stay with her husband.) The Confederates massing in Virginia were threatening to march in, hang the President, and make Washington their own capital.

"What am I to do?" Lincoln asked the petitioners. "I *must* have troops. And, as they can neither crawl under Maryland nor fly over it, they must come across it."

Relates Lincoln's private secretary, John Nicolay:

"On Sunday night, April 21st, the insurrectionary authorities in [Maryland] took possession of the telegraph offices and wires, and Washington went into the condition of an isolated and blockaded

Funeral in Boston for victims of Baltimore riot

city. . . . Squads of cavalry dashed through the streets. Business practically ceased. . . .

"As the gloom increased, there began to be talk of general military impressment for the defense of the city. This had the effect of finally exposing the loyalty or disloyalty of many Washington officers, clerks, residents, and *habitués* who had maintained a dubious silence. On Monday, April 22nd, quite a stampede took place into Virginia and the South. Some hundreds of clerks from the various departments of Government, and a considerable number of officers of the army and navy, hitherto unable to decide between their treasonable inclinations and the attractions of their salaries, finally resigned and cast their fortunes with the rebellion."

The rebellion's flag, as it happened, could be seen from the windows of the Executive Mansion. It was on bold display just across the Potomac at Alexandria.

A Southern woman in Washington, relying on rumor, wrote to a friend in Louisiana:

"Old Lincoln sleeps with a hundred armed men in the East Room to protect him from the Southern army. He is expecting them to attack the city every night. He keeps a sentinel walking in front of his bedroom all night, and often gets so frightened that he leaves the White House and sleeps out, no one knows where. . . .

"Mrs. Lincoln, a few nights since, heard whispering in the hall in front of her room. She rose from bed, dressed, and sat up the remainder of the night watching for the Southern army to blow up the White House, as they are confidently expecting it."

This was exaggeration, but not of a wide margin.

9

Catastrophe at Norfolk

PRESIDENT LINCOLN'S ANXIETY was heightened by the fact that the federal government was continuing to lose valuable installations on Southern soil.

It had been realized for months that Harpers Ferry (made famous by John Brown) would be a prime target if Virginia seceded. The town's position on the Potomac at the northern end of the state's Shenandoah Valley gave it a bearing on the North's security. It was a kind of gateway to the South's backdoor route to Washington.

But there was no extra manpower available to strengthen the arsenal's garrison—and a great many troops would have been needed, since the spot, low and surrounded by hills, was a hard one to defend. And even if Lincoln had been blessed with troops aplenty he would have hesitated to strengthen Harpers for fear of further inflaming Virginia. Until the state actually seceded, he maintained at least a small hope that it would not.

The Harpers garrison numbered forty-five men, and their commander was Lieutenant Roger Jones. In his impossible position, Jones soon decided that his best course would be to prepare the arsenal for torching and abandonment.

A Confederate officer, John D. Imboden, assumes the narrative:

"The movement to capture Harpers Ferry . . . and the firearms manufactured and stored there was organized at the Exchange Hotel in Richmond on the night of April 16th, 1861 [this was the

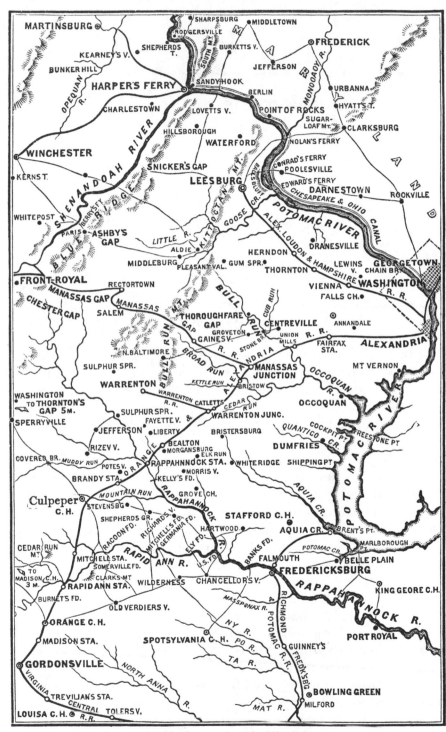

Field of operations in Virginia

night before Virginia declared for secession]. Ex-Governor Henry A. Wise was at the head of this purely impromptu affair. . . .

"The movement, it was agreed, should commence the next day, the 17th, as soon as the Convention voted to secede—provided we could get railway transportation and the concurrence of Governor Letcher. Colonel Edmund Fontaine, president of the Virginia Central Railroad, and John S. Barbour, president of the Orange and Alexandria and Manassas Gap Railroads, were sent for and joined us at the hotel near midnight. They agreed to put the necessary trains in readiness next day to obey any request of Governor Letcher for the movement of troops.

"A committee, of which I was chairman, waited on Governor Letcher after midnight, and, arousing him from his bed, laid the scheme before him. He stated that he would take no step till officially informed that the ordinance of secession was passed by the Convention. He was then asked if, contingent upon the event, he would next day order the movement. . . . He consented. We then informed him what companies would be under arms, ready to move at a moment's notice. . . . On returning to the hotel and reporting Governor Letcher's promise, it was decided to telegraph the captains of companies along the railroads mentioned to be ready next day for orders from the governor."

John Letcher

The orders were issued the following afternoon, and on the morning of April 18 there was a gathering of troops at Manassas Junction, about twenty-five miles southwest of Washington. Other units were to be met at Winchester, in the Shenandoah Valley. The Manassas troops were provided with three or four trains.

Again in the words of Confederate officer John Imboden:

"I was put in command of the foremost train. We had not gone five miles when I discovered that the engineer could not be trusted. He let his fire go down, and came to a dead standstill on a slight ascending grade. A cocked pistol induced him to fire up and go ahead. From there to Strasburg [in the Valley southwest of Winchester] I rode in the engine cab, and we made full forty miles an hour with the aid of good dry wood and a navy revolver.

"At Strasburg we left the cars."

Major General Kenton Harper was in top command of the combination of forces, perhaps a thousand in number, that began approaching Harpers Ferry during the early part of the night. The Union commander, Roger Jones, was aware they were coming. "I decided the time had arrived to carry out my determination . . . and accordingly gave the order to apply the torch."

By the time the move was begun, several Confederate officers were standing on Bolivar Heights, overlooking Harpers, making plans for their attack. Says an unidentified member of the group:

"There was seen in the direction of the armory a flash, accompanied by a report like the discharge of a cannon, followed by a number of other flashes in quick succession, and then the sky and surrounding mountains were lighted with the steady glare of ascending flames.

"Captain [Turner] Ashby, with his squad, immediately rode down into the town, and in a short time returned with the report that the troops had fired the public buildings and retreated across the Potomac Bridge, taking the mountain road toward Carlisle Barracks in Pennsylvania.

"On our way down we met a long line of men, women, and boys carrying loads of muskets, bayonets, and other military equipments [that they had stolen before the destruction had taken hold]. The streets at the confluence of the two rivers [the Shenandoah and the Potomac] were brilliantly illuminated by the flames from the old arsenal, which burned like a furnace. The enclosure around these buildings was covered with splintered glass which had been blown out by the explosion of the powder train.

Burning of the Harpers arsenal

"A few arms-boxes, open and empty [evidence of the civilian looting], lay near the entrance; but nearly all the muskets in this building . . . were destroyed.

"Of the armory buildings on Potomac Street, one large workshop was in a light blaze, and two others on fire. Alarmed by the first explosions, the citizens hesitated to approach the workshops, and warned the Virginia troops not to do so, supposing them to be mined. But presently becoming reassured on that subject, they went to work with the engines, extinguished some of the fires, and prevented their extension to the town and railroad bridges."

Confederate officer John Imboden sums up:

"Nearly twenty thousand rifles and pistols were destroyed. . . .

So we secured only the machinery and the gun and pistol barrels and locks [that remained after the stocks were burned away], which, however, were sent to Richmond and Columbia, South Carolina, and were worked over into excellent arms."

The fall of Harpers Ferry was quickly followed by another Union property loss in Virginia, one of monstrous proportions.

Lincoln's secretary of the navy, Gideon Welles, begins the story:

"The navy yard at Norfolk [Gosport], protected by no fortress or garrison, has always been a favored depot with the Government. It was filled with arms and munitions, and several ships were in the harbor, dismantled . . . and in no condition to be moved, had there been men to move them. . . . Any attempt to withdraw them [by towing] . . . would, in the then sensitive and disturbed condition of the public mind [in Virginia] have betrayed alarm and mistrust, and been likely to cause difficulty.

"Apprehensive, however, that action might be necessary, the commandant of the yard [Commodore Charles S. McCauley] was, early in April, advised of this . . . and cautioned to extreme vigilance and circumspection. . . . This commandant, whose patriotism and fidelity were not doubted, was surrounded by officers in whom he placed confidence. But most of them, as events soon proved, were faithless to the flag and the country.

"On the 10th of April, Commodore McCauley was ordered to put the shipping and public property in condition to be moved and placed beyond danger, should it become necessary; but in doing this he was warned to take no steps that could give needless alarm [to Virginia].

"The steam frigate *Merrimac* could, it was believed—were her machinery in order—be made available in this emergency, not only to extricate herself, but the other shipping in the harbor. . . . A commander and two engineers were detailed to proceed to Norfolk for that purpose. Two days after, on the 12th of April, the department [in Washington] directed that the *Merrimac* should be prepared to proceed to Philadelphia with the utmost dispatch.

"It was stated [by the engineers] that to repair the engine and put it in working condition would require four weeks. Discrediting this report, the engineer-in-chief [in Washington] was ordered to proceed forthwith in person and attend to the necessary preparations.

"On the 16th of April the commandant [McCauley] was directed to lose no time in placing armament on board the *Merri-*

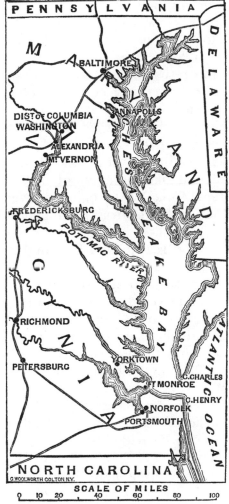

Regions of the Chesapeake

mac; to get the *Plymouth* and *Dolphin* beyond danger; to have the *Germantown* in a condition to be towed out; and to put the more valuable public property, ordnance, stores, etc., on shipboard, so that they could, at any moment, be moved beyond danger.

"Such was the energy and dispatch of the engineer-in-chief that on the 16th the department [in Washington] was advised by the commandant . . . that on the 17th the *Merrimac* would be ready for temporary service; but when, on the afternoon of that day, the engineer-in-chief reported her ready for steam, Commodore Mc-Cauley refused to have her fired up. Fires were, however, built early the next morning, and at nine o'clock the engines were working—engineers, firemen, etc., on board. But the commandant still refused to permit her to be moved, and in the afternoon gave directions to draw the fires.

"The cause of this refusal to move the *Merrimac* has no explanation other than that of misplaced confidence in his junior officers, who opposed it.

"As soon as this fatal error was reported to [Washington], orders were instantly issued to Commodore [Hiram] Paulding to proceed forthwith to Norfolk with such officers and marines as could be obtained, and take command of all the vessels afloat on that station; to repel force by force, and prevent the ships and public property, at all hazards, from passing into the hands of the insurrectionists.

"But when that officer reached Norfolk [in the warship *Pawnee*] on the evening of Saturday the 20th he found that the powder magazine [near the yard] had already been seized, and that an armed force had commenced throwing up batteries in the vicinity. The commandant of the yard, after refusing to permit the vessels to be moved on Thursday, and omitting it on Friday, ordered them to be scuttled on Saturday evening; and they were sinking when Commodore Paulding, with the force under his command, arrived at Norfolk."

The men of the yard began cheering wildly when they saw the *Pawnee*, for they believed that Paulding intended to make a fight of it. But the commodore decided he had no choice but to cooperate with McCauley's plan of destruction. In an attempt to place the sinking ships beyond salvaging by the enemy he ordered them rigged for burning. One ship, the *Cumberland*, was still fully afloat, having been saved by McCauley for the garrison's escape.

The narrative is taken up by a correspondent of the *New York Times* who accompanied Paulding's expedition:

"Many thousand stands of arms were destroyed. Carbines had their stocks broken . . . and were thrown overboard. A large lot of revolvers shared the like fate. Shot and shell by thousands went with hurried plunge to the bottom. Most of the cannon had been spiked the day and night before. There were at least fifteen hundred pieces in the yard—some elegant Dahlgren guns, and Columbiads of all sizes.

"It is impossible to describe the scene of destruction that was exhibited. Unweariedly it was continued from 9 o'clock until about

12, during which time the moon gave light to direct the operations. But when the moon sank behind the western horizon, the
barracks near the center of the yard were set on fire, that by its
illumination the work might be continued. The crackling flames
and the glare of light inspired with new energies the destroying
marines. . . . But time was not left to complete the work.

"Four o'clock of Sunday morning came, and the *Pawnee* . . .
[prepared to leave] Gosport harbor with the *Cumberland* . . . in
tow. . . . Just as they left their moorings a rocket was sent up from
the deck of the *Pawnee*. It sped high in the air, paused a second,
and burst in shivers of many-colored lights. As it did so, the well-
set trains [of powder] at the shiphouses and on the decks of the
fated vessels left behind, went off as if lit simultaneously by the
rocket."

The narrator had remained at the yard to watch the show to its
finish. As a newsman, he did not feel threatened by the Confederates. He goes on:

"I need not try to picture the scene of the grand conflagration

Burning of the Gosport Navy Yard

that now burst, like the day of judgment, on the startled citizens of Norfolk, Portsmouth, and all the surrounding country. . . . It was not thirty minutes from the time the trains were fired till the conflagration roared like a hurricane, and the flames from land and water swayed and met and mingled together and darted high, and fell, and leaped up again. . . .

"But in all this magnificent scene, the old ship *Pennsylvania* was the centerpiece. She was a very giant in death, as she had been in life. She was a sea of flame. . . . Several of her guns were left loaded, but not shotted, and as the fire reached them they sent out . . . fearful peal[s] that added greatly to the alarm that the light of the conflagration had spread through the surrounding country. . . .

"As soon as the *Pawnee* and *Cumberland* had fairly left the waters . . . the gathering crowds of Portsmouth and Norfolk burst open the gates of the navy yard and rushed in. . . . As early as six o'clock, a volunteer company [took] formal possession in the name of Virginia, and ran up her flag [on] the flagstaff.

"In another hour, several companies were on hand, and men were at work unspiking cannon. . . .

"Notwithstanding the effort to keep out persons from the yard, hundreds found their way in, and spent hours in wandering over its spacious area and inspecting its yet stupendous works, and comparing the value of that saved with that lost.

"There was general surprise expressed that so much that was valuable was spared."

The tale is completed by naval historian David D. Porter (who was himself a high-level participant in the war's naval affairs):

"The drydock was not materially injured; some of the workshops and officers' quarters were preserved, and the frigate *United States* was not much damaged. Even the *Merrimac,* though burned to the water's edge and sunk, was afterwards raised and converted into the powerful ironclad which wrought such havoc in Hampton Roads and carried consternation through the North.

"The loss of the Navy Yard at Norfolk was felt all through the North to be a great calamity. Misfortunes seemed accumulating, and people began to doubt whether the Administration had sufficient vigor to meet the emergencies that were continually arising. The destruction of the Navy Yard seems . . . to have been the result of a panic which was not justified by the facts of the case; but the actors in that scene believed they were consulting the best interests of the Government."

Less charitable in his judgment was the New York *Tribune's* Horace Greeley, who called the abandonment of the yard "the most shameful, cowardly, disastrous performance that stains the annals of the American Navy."

In the South it was believed by many that God had intervened in their behalf. Speaking before a congregation in Georgia, an Episcopal bishop declared:

"That immense navy yard, with its vast resources, with its great power of resistance . . . with its magnificent men-of-war all armed and shotted, was deserted in an unaccountable panic because of the threats of a few almost unarmed citizens. . . . And nowhere could this panic have occurred more seasonably for us, because it gave us just what we most needed, arms and ammunition and heavy ordnance in great abundance. All this is unaccountable upon any ordinary grounds."

The Union's two great losses of Harpers Ferry and Gosport were accompanied by the loss on April 22 of the arsenal at Fayetteville, North Carolina. How this came about is told by Mrs. Eliza B. Stinson, who was a schoolgirl at the time.

"All the county militia were put in requisition for the deed of daring, and . . . in every direction they were coming in. Young and old, rich and poor, flocked to the place of rendezvous. There was a company of Home Guards formed for this special occasion, comprising the citizens over age; and every man in town that could shoulder a gun, except the preachers, was under arms. There was our middle-aged physician . . . mounted on a prancing steed with a feather in his hat, on duty as a staff officer. There was a well known portly old lawyer, pompous but true-hearted, marching as a private in the ranks by the side of a white-haired merchant whose spare form held a heart beating with the resolute blood of the Scots. Bald-headed presidents of banks and grizzly bearded clerks walked side by side, resolved to do or die. Few of these old gentlemen probably had shot a squirrel in thirty years, or taken as long a walk as the distance from the rendezvous up hill to the arsenal, but they swelled the ranks of the mighty army. . . .

"But would there be any resistance on the part of the forty drilled and disciplined soldiers who comprised the garrison? That was a question which filled the hearts of the women with fear, for there was not a house that did not have one or two men in the field that day. . . . The [friendly] relations previously existing between the garrison and the townspeople had not become strained since the preparations for war set in. The officers went and came

The arsenal at Fayetteville

to the hotels as usual, where they boarded with their wives. Of course, it would be folly in a handful of men so far from their base, and in the heart of a hostile country, to resist, as eventually they would be obliged to surrender or die.

"But should they consider it their duty to destroy the arsenal or resist its capture, with their superior discipline and their artillery within the shelter of the walls, they might mow down hundreds of our raw militia before they could be overwhelmed by numbers— the artillery of [our] attacking force consisting of two old iron guns of small caliber which had been used for many years to fire salutes on the glorious [holidays] of our Republic. . . .

"The position of the arsenal, surrounded with dwellings, with the [main part of] the town close at the foot of the hills, would have necessitated fearful havoc among our houses from the use of artillery. . . . So thought and felt our women on that eventful morning. The men all professed to be confident that the place would be surrendered on demand by such a large force as we proposed to send up the hill. Nevertheless they looked serious. . . .

"I have always regretted that we did not turn out to see our band, twelve hundred strong, as they marched up the hill, but at our house the elders thought it advisable that the women should keep quiet at home, and we missed the imposing sight.

"There is a very deep cut in the road at the steepest part of the long hill, however, and from the top of the bank on either side a good view of the advancing host was had by the Hill people nearby, whose terror was overcome by their curiosity. But as we lived more than a half mile further on [in the Hill section] we saw nothing of it. Doubtless, as the Home Guard passed, irreverent girls were found to laugh. It is not often in this world that any situation of affairs can be found where schoolgirls will not find something to laugh at. 'Dear me! How much fighting can these old men do?' 'Do look at old Mr. ———. He looks as if a feather would knock him over!' 'Lawyer ——— looks as if he thought himself Napoleon himself; and I'll venture to say he's tired half to death now.' 'Don't you know some of them are scared?' 'Goodness, Lucy, let's go home. Suppose they should send a volley of shells right over here!' And so on.

"But the regiment passed on its way; and, arriving at the proper distance, halted and sent in a flag of truce . . . demanding the surrender of the arsenal to the forces of the State of North Carolina. . . .

"It was a warm day for the season, and the new soldiers were very thirsty and saw no reason why they should not refresh themselves with a drink of water while waiting to hear whether or no that hour might be their last. But one valiant captain who had worked himself up into the proper frame of mind for the stern realities of war, thought doubtless it was very unsoldierly to be complaining of thirst after so short a walk under an April sun. He sternly informed his men that they did not come there to drink water but to die.

"After much parley, and what seemed an almost interminable delay . . . it was agreed that the arsenal and all its contents were to be given up to the state troops, on condition that the garrison should be allowed to salute their flag [with cannon fire] before lowering it, and should have the liberty of returning to Washington with their baggage in safety. . . .

"In the meantime, in our little neighborhood on the very verge of the Hill settlement, half a mile from the arsenal, and half that distance from the main road, we were cut off from . . . the hill summit by groves of trees, and could not see . . . nor hear anything that was going on. We were very quiet at our house and tried to go about our usual employment, but the servants were frightened half out of their wits. With wild eyes, the middle-aged cook came in. 'Mistis,' she said with trembling lips, 'I hearn them people was gwine ter throw a bum [bomb] over dat way and one over dis 'er way befo' dey give up de ars'nal, and I jis come ter tell you I was gwine down in de holler.' We heard afterwards that the gulleys in the hillside were lined that morning with frightened Negroes.

"Our nearest neighbor was a near relation, a maiden lady, one of those persons who always look for the worst. The dear old lady was in a terrible state of mind. . . . We had all been accustomed to hear salutes fired on national festivals by our town's people in a slow and deliberate manner, with an interval of several minutes between shots; but when the United States soldiers fired off their thirty-one guns in rapid succession, with scarcely a second between, 'twas an awful sound in our ears. We thought surely it was a broadside mowing down our devoted band.

"Our excited neighbor seemed to take it for granted that her brother and son 'had rushed into the field and foremost fighting fell' . . . and she began walking up and down her front piazza, wringing her hands, screaming at the top of her voice, 'Oh, my poor brother! Oh, my poor John!' She could be heard all over the neighborhood. All the rest of us were as much frightened, but we did not scream.

"At length I remembered that the flag could be seen from the house of a neighbor, perhaps three hundred yards off. . . . 'I'll run over to Mr. W's and see if the [Union] flag is up,' said I, and away I sped . . . and when I put my foot on the high piazza—lo! the bare flagstaff greeted my delighted eyes. The lady of the house was seated on the piazza, apparently calmly sewing . . . but I had no time for a visit to our good friend that day. 'I must run right back,' I said. 'Everybody is frightened nearly to death over our way, and cousin——[the maiden lady] is almost crazy!' That was the promptest errand I ever did, and probably among the most acceptable in its results.

"So passed that eventful day. . . . Some simple souls imagined the war was over. One old lady remarked that [now] she had seen one war, and hoped never to see another.

"But the provoking part to us females was to hear, as we discussed the day with our returned braves in the evening, how it had come out that the heads on both sides had had a private consultation *beforehand,* and the terms of the surrender had been agreed upon . . . in a very friendly manner. The parade of the day had been a mere comedy to set things right at Washington [that is, to satisfy the requirements of honor], but of course the rank and file were kept in ignorance of this fact till after all was over."

The progression of events so favorable to the South prompted its newspapers to propose bold plans. Said the Eufaula, Alabama, *Express:*

"With independent Virginia on one side and the secessionists of Maryland, who are doubtless in the majority, on the other, our policy at this time should be to seize the old Federal Capital and take old Lincoln and his Cabinet prisoners of war. Once get the Head of the Government in our power and we can demand any terms we see fit, and thus, perhaps, avoid a long and bloody contest."

The Richmond *Examiner* was more venomous:

"From the mountaintops and valleys to the shores of the sea, there is one wild shout of fierce resolve to capture Washington City, at all and every human hazard. That filthy cage of unclean birds *must* and will assuredly *be* purified by fire. . . . It is not to be endured that this flight of Abolition harpies shall come down from the black North for their roosts in the heart of the South, to defile and brutalize the land. . . . The fanatical yell for the immediate subjugation of the whole South is going up hourly from the united voices of all the North; and for the purpose of making their work sure they have determined to hold Washington City as the point whence to carry on their brutal warfare.

"Our people can take it—they *will* take it. . . . The just indignation of an outraged and deeply injured people will teach the Illinois Ape to . . . retrace his journey across the borders of the Free-Negro States still more rapidly than he came. . . . Great cleansing and purification are needed and will be given to that festering sink of iniquity . . . the desecrated city of Washington; and many indeed will be the carcasses of dogs and caitiffs that will blacken the air upon the gallows before the great work is accomplished. So let it be!"

10

General Butler to the Rescue

THE FOREGOING TIRADE appeared in the *Examiner* of April 23. It was now eight days since Lincoln had issued his call for troops. So far, only the "First Defenders" from Pennsylvania and the 6th Massachusetts had reached Washington, and the city was cut off from the north by an angry Baltimore. There was a great urgency for succeeding units from the north to find an alternate route through Maryland.

Lincoln was heard to murmur, "Why don't they come? Why don't they come?"

During a review of the 6th Massachusetts, he said, "I begin to believe there is no North. . . . You are the only real thing."

Presently en route, however, were two strong regiments, the 8th Massachusetts and the 7th New York. The 8th had reached Philadelphia on April 19, the day of the great Baltimore riot, and the 7th had arrived at the same place the following morning. Both units had orders to proceed through Baltimore to Washington, but news of the riot drew them up short. In a few hours, however, their commanders made arrangements to bypass Baltimore by means of the waterways to its east.

Because the regiments were from different states, their commanders were not in cooperation, but laid out independent routes. The 8th, under Brigadier General Benjamin F. Butler, planned to go by rail to the northern end of the Chesapeake, embark there, and head down past Baltimore to the U.S. Naval Academy at Annapolis. The 7th, under Colonel Marshall Lefferts, planned to embark at Philadelphia and head down the Delaware

Bay to the open sea and on to the Chesapeake's mouth for an ascent of that waterway. Lefferts at first had some idea of trying to force a passage up the Potomac to Washington.

The 7th was an elite unit, with many of its young men belonging to New York City's most distinguished families. Among the regiment's brightest and most popular figures was Fitz James O'Brien, an established poet and essayist. O'Brien was destined to die in this tragic war, but right now his heart was high.

"On April 20 at 4:20 P.M. we left the Philadelphia dock on board the steamer *Boston*. The regiment was in entire ignorance of its destination. Some said we were going back to New York, at which suggestion there was a howl of indignation. Others presumed that we were going to steam up the Potomac—a course that was not much approved of, inasmuch that we were . . . in a kind of river steamer that a shot from the [Confederates] . . . at Alexandria might sink. . .

"The first evening, April 20, on board the *Boston* passed delightfully. We were all in first-rate spirits, and the calm, sweet evenings that stole on us as we approached the South diffused a soft and gentle influence over us. The scene on board the ship was exceedingly picturesque. Fellows fumbling in haversacks for rations. . . . Guards pacing up and down. . . . Knapsacks piled in corners. Bristling heaps of muskets . . . crowded into every available nook. . . . Groups of men lolling on deck, pipe or cigar in mouth . . . as if they were on the blue shores of Capri rather than on their way to battle. . . .

"I regret to say that all was not rose-colored. The steamer that the Colonel chartered had to get ready at three or four hours' notice. . . . The result was that she was imperfectly provisioned. . . . Notwithstanding that we found very soon that the commissariat was in a bad way, the men were as jolly as sandboys. . . . Fellows who would at Delmonico's have sent back a *turban de volaille aux truffes* because the truffles were tough, here cheerfully took their places in file between decks, tin plates and tin cups in hand, in order to get an insufficient piece of beef and a vision of coffee. . . . The scant fare was seasoned with hilarity.

"And here I say to those people in New York who have sneered at the 7th Regiment as being dandies, and guilty of the unpardonable crimes of cleanliness and kid gloves—that they would cease to scoff . . . had they beheld the square, honest, genial way in which these military Brummels roughed it. . . .

"April 21 was Sunday. A glorious, cloudless day. We had steamed all night, and about 10 o'clock were in the vicinity of Chesapeake Bay. At 11 o'clock . . . we had a service read by our chaplain, and at 1 P.M. we were seven miles from the coast. The day was calm and delicious. In spite of our troubles in regard to food . . . we drank in with delight the serenity of the scene.

"A hazy tent of blue hung over our heads. On one side the dim thread of shore hemmed in the sea. Flights of loons and ducks skimmed along the ocean. . . .

"At 5 o'clock P.M. we passed a light-ship and hailed her, our object being to discover whether any United States vessels were in the neighborhood waiting to convoy us up the Potomac River. . . . The answers we got from the light-ship and other vessels we hailed in this spot were unsatisfactory . . . and we kept on. . . .

"[In the evening] a curious phenomenon occurred. Some men in the regiment . . . had been singing—with all that delicious effect that music at sea produces—several of the finest psalms in our liturgy. . . . While we were singing, the moon swung clear into the air, and round her white disk was seen three circles, clear and distinct—*red, white, and blue!*

"The omen was caught by common instinct, and a thousand cheers went up to that heaven that seemed in its visible signs to manifest its approval of the cause in which we were about to fight.

"All this time we were entirely ignorant of where we were going. The officers kept all a secret, and our conjectures drifted like a drifting boat.

"On the morning of the 22nd, we were in sight of Annapolis."

The 8th Massachusetts, aboard the steam ferry *Maryland,* had arrived off Annapolis during the early hours of the preceding day, and General Butler was involved in a correspondence with Governor Hicks, who was there at the time, Annapolis being the state capital.

This was one of those occasions in the nation's history when exactly the right man was on hand to deal with a crucial moment. Not that Ben Butler, at age fifty-two, was a hero of the romantic mold. He had a bulky figure, a shiny pate, and a left eye that was partially hooded by a drooping lid. He was not a professional military man, but a lawyer. And, as a Democrat, he had supported Southern politicians, including Jefferson Davis. But right now Butler was fighting for the Union, and he had the talent and the will to prevail.

Benjamin F. Butler

Two years earlier, a fellow lawyer had written of Butler:

"He was born in New Hampshire. He worked his own way to college, and through it, at Waterville, Maine. . . . Through life he has cut his own way, and . . . has wrung success from men and circumstances . . . that were reluctant to concede it to him. And in so doing he has indicated his great strength.

"When he first came to the bar, the courts looked upon him as a sort of portentous phenomenon, such as never before came athwart the judicial vision. He had no family influence to aid his young steps. He had no friends to 'blow for him,' as the phrase is. His early days were spent in steady rowing upstream, with a strong wind and the current both dead against him. But he never faltered. He cleared the rapids, and up he continued to sail. He is in calmer waters now [being well established and quite wealthy]. He might anchor if he would. But his temperament will never suffer him to rest. . . . He may be safely set down as a man of irrepressible energy. . . .

"He is not a fluent nor graceful speaker. His voice is harsh and grating. . . . He makes awkward work when he undertakes to ut-

ter compliments. But he smites an adversary with the plainest of
Anglo-Saxon epithets. . . . He is a faithful and steadfast friend . . .
and . . . has a memory we think especially tenacious of friendly
acts. He is quite apt not to forget or wholly to forgive injuries, real
or fancied. . . .

"He lives in a style anything but Democratic, according to our
New England ideas. Scarcely any other lawyer . . . could maintain
such an establishment as his. But he has earned it. . . . Butler is as
able a man as walks the soil of Massachusetts. He has all the
elements necessary for the successful accomplishment of whatever he undertakes."

General Butler's first act upon reaching the Naval Academy's
waters was to keep a party of secessionists from seizing, from her
small crew, the frigate *Constitution* ("Old Ironsides"), which was at
the station as a training vessel. Butler used the *Maryland*, with the
8th Massachusetts still on board, to tow the *Constitution* beyond the
reach of those who threatened her.

The general told his command:

"The frigate *Constitution* has lain . . . substantially at the mercy

The Constitution *at Annapolis*

of the armed mob which sometimes paralyzes the otherwise loyal State of Maryland. . . . It was given to Massachusetts . . . first to man her [she was built in Boston]; it was reserved to Massachusetts to have the honor to retain her for the service of the Union and the laws. . . . By this the blood of our friends, shed by the Baltimore mob, is so far avenged. . . . The old *Constitution* . . . is now 'possessed, occupied, and enjoyed' by the Government of the United States, and is safe from all her enemies."

The narrative is taken up by Benson Lossing, the period historian whose works are well seasoned with materials gained through personal interviews:

"In assisting to get out the *Constitution*, the *Maryland* grounded on a sandbank. . . . There she lay helpless . . . to the great discomfort of her passengers. Her water casks were nearly emptied, and their provisions were almost exhausted. In the meantime, Governor Hicks . . . was urging Butler not to land 'Northern troops.'

" 'The excitement here is very great,' he said, 'and I think that you had better take your men elsewhere.'

"Butler, in his reply, spoke of his necessities and his orders, and took the occasion to correct the Governor's sectional phraseology by saying of his force, 'They are not *Northern* troops; they are a part of the whole militia of the United States obeying the call of the President.' . . .

"Butler now went ashore and had a personal conference with the Governor and the Mayor of Annapolis. 'All Maryland,' they said, 'is at the point of rushing to arms. The railway is broken up, and its line guarded by armed men. It will be a fearful thing for you to land and attempt to march on Washington.'

" 'I *must* land,' said the General, 'for my troops are hungry.'

" 'No one in Annapolis will sell them anything,' replied these authorities of State and city.

"Butler intimated that armed men were not always limited to the necessity of *purchasing* food when famishing; and he gave both magistrates to understand that the orders and demands of his Government were imperative, and that he should land and march on the Capital as speedily as possible, in spite of all opposition. At the same time he assured them that peaceable citizens should not be molested, and that the laws of the State should be respected. And more. He was ready to cooperate with the local authorities in suppressing a slave insurrection [should one arise] or any other resistance to law.

"The Governor contented himself with simply protesting against the landing of troops as unwise, and begged the General not to halt them in Annapolis."

Butler's 8th Massachusetts was still stranded on the sandbar when the 7th New York disembarked from the *Boston* during the afternoon of April 22. As explained by the literate Fitz James O'Brien:

"We were quartered in the buildings belonging to the Naval School. . . . I had a bunking place in what is there called a fort, which is a rickety structure that a lucifer match would set on fire, but furnished with imposing guns. I suppose it was merely built to practice the cadets, because as a defense it is worthless.

"The same evening boats were sent off from the yard, and . . . the Massachusetts men landed, fagged, hungry, thirsty, but indomitable. At an early hour there was a universal snore through the Naval School of Annapolis.

"The two days that we remained at Annapolis were welcome. . . . The grounds are very prettily laid out, and in the course of my experience I never saw a handsomer or better bred set of young men than the cadets. . . . Only twenty [had] left the school owing to political conviction."

By way of Annapolis Junction, on the Baltimore and Ohio Railroad to the west, the two regiments were about forty miles from Washington. The road had been damaged by the secessionists between Annapolis and the junction but was in good shape between the junction and the Capital. General Butler, now in overall command by agreement with Colonel Lefferts, decided to march the troops along the railroad bed to the junction, making repairs as he went. It had been learned that most of the missing rail sections had not been carried far from the bed. Even before the march could begin, however, a damaged locomotive had to be repaired.

"On the morning of the 24th of April," says Fitz James O'Brien, "we started on what afterwards proved to be one of the hardest marches on record. [Something of an overstatement; these men were new to marching.] The Secessionists of Annapolis and the surrounding district had threatened to cut us off in our march. . . . This, of course, was the drunken Southern ebullition. A civilian told me that he met in the streets of Annapolis two [dismounted] cavalry soldiers who came to cut our throats without delay, but as each brave warrior was endeavoring to hold the other up, my friend did not apprehend much danger. . . .

"We started at about 8 o'clock A.M., and for the first time saw the town of Annapolis, which, without any disrespect to that place, I may say looked very much as if some celestial schoolboy with a box of toys under his arm had dropped a few houses and men as he was going home from school, and that the accidental settlement was called Annapolis. Through the town we marched, the people unsympathizing but afraid. They saw the 7th for the first time, and for the first time they realized the men that they had threatened.

"The tracks had been torn up between Annapolis and the Junction, and here it was that the wonderful qualities of the Massachusetts 8th Regiment came out. . . . The rails were . . . laid . . . again. . . . These brave boys . . . were starving while they were doing this good work. . . . As we marched along the track that they had laid, they greeted us with ranks of smiling but hungry faces. One boy told me, with a laugh on his young lips, that he had not eaten anything for thirty hours. There was not, thank God, a haversack in our regiment that was not emptied into the hands of these . . . heroes, nor a flask that was not at their disposal. . . .

"Our march lay through an arid, sandy, tobacco-growing country. The sun poured on our heads like hot lava. The 6th and 2nd companies were sent on [ahead] for skirmishing duty. . . . A car, on which was placed a howitzer loaded with grape and canister, headed the column. . . . This was the rallying point of the skirmishing party, on which, in case of difficulty, they could fall back. In the center of the column came the cars laden with medical stores, and bearing our sick and [hurt], while the extreme rear was brought up with a second howitzer, loaded also with grape and canister.

"The engineer corps, of course, had to do the forwarding work. New York dandies, sir—but they built bridges, laid rails, and headed the regiment through that terrible march.

"After marching about eight miles, during which time several men caved in from exhaustion and one young gentleman was sunstruck . . . we halted; and instantly, with the Divine instinct which characterizes the hungry soldier, proceeded to forage. The worst of it was there was no foraging to be done. The only house within reach was inhabited by a lethargic person who, like most Southern men, had no idea of gaining money by labor. We offered him extravagant prices to get us fresh water, and it was with the utmost reluctance we could get him to obtain us a few pailfuls. . . .

8th Massachusetts repairing railroad bridge

"After a brief rest of about an hour, we again commenced our march—a march which lasted until the next morning. . . . I know not if I can describe that night's march. I have dim recollections of deep cuts through which we passed, gloomy and treacherous-looking, with the moon shining full on our muskets, while the banks were wrapped in shade, and each moment expecting to see the flash and hear the crack of the rifle of the Southern guerrilla.

"The tree frogs and lizards made a mournful music as we passed. The soil on which we travelled was soft and heavy. [Dodging] the sleepers lying at intervals across the track made the march terribly fatiguing. On all sides dark, lonely pine woods stretched away, and . . . over the hooting of owls or the plaintive petition of the whippoorwill rose the bass commands of 'Halt!' 'Forward, march!'—and when we came to any ticklish spot, the word would run from the head of the column along the line, 'Holes,' 'Bridge,' 'Pass it along,' etc.

"As the night wore on the monotony of the march became oppressive. Owing to our having to explore every inch of the way, we did not make more than a mile or a mile and a half an hour. We ran out of stimulants, and almost out of water. . . . I myself fell asleep walking in the ranks. Numbers . . . followed my example. But never before was there shown such indomitable pluck and perseverance as the 7th showed in that march of twenty miles.

"The country that we passed through seemed to have been entirely deserted. The inhabitants—who were going to kill us when they thought we daren't come through—now vamoosed their respective ranches, and we saw them not. . . . They, it seems, were under the impression that we came to ravage and pillage. . . . As we did at Annapolis, we did in Maryland State. We left an impression that cannot be forgotten. Everything was paid for. No discourtesy was offered to any inhabitant."

A special train was waiting at Annapolis Junction—one intended for the use of the 7th only. General Butler and his Massachusetts troops were ordered by Washington to remain at the junction and guard the repaired road to Annapolis.

Lincoln's private secretary, John Nicolay, tells of the arrival of the New Yorkers at the capital:

"Debarking from the cars amid the welcome-shouts of an assembled throng, and forming with all the ready precision of their holiday drill, they marched with exultant music and gayly fluttering banners up Pennsylvania Avenue to the Executive Mansion to receive the President's thankful salute. With their arrival, about noon of the 25th of April, all the gloom and doubt and feeling of danger to the Capital vanished. . . .

"This march of the 7th . . . marked a turning point in the national destiny, and signified the will of the people that the Capital of the Union should remain [south of the Mason-Dixon line] where George Washington planted it. . . . Following the march of the 7th Regiment, the Annapolis route remained permanently open to the Union troops from the North."

Across the Potomac at Alexandria, the Confederate flag still attested to the presence of the Confederate military, but the

South's invasion talk was diminishing, and many of Alexandria's civilians, anxious over their proximity to a girding foe, had begun fleeing southward.

On May 4, one of the hangers-on, Mrs. Judith McGuire, a mature woman with several children, recorded the following:

"I am too nervous, too wretched today to write in my diary, but . . . the employment will while away a few moments of this trying time. Our friends and neighbors have left us. Everything is broken up. The Theological Seminary is closed, the High School dismissed. Scarcely anyone is left of the many families which surrounded us. The homes all look desolate. . . .

"We [the writer and her husband] are left lonely indeed. Our children are all gone—the girls to Clarke, where they may be safer . . . and the boys, the dear, dear boys, to the camp to be drilled and prepared to meet any emergency.

"Can it be that our country is to be carried on and on to the horrors of civil war? I pray, oh how fervently I pray, that our Heavenly Father may yet avert it. I shut my eyes and hold my breath when the thought of what may come upon us obtrudes itself. . . . I cannot believe it. It *will*—I *know* the breach will be healed without the effusion of blood. The taking of Sumter without bloodshed has somewhat soothed my fears, though I am told by those who are wiser than I that men must fall on both sides by the score, by the hundred, and even by the thousand. But it is not my habit to look on the dark side, so I try hard to employ myself, and hope for the best.

"Today our house seems so deserted that I feel more sad than usual. . . . Mr. [McGuire] and myself are now the sole occupants of the house, which usually teems with life. I go from room to room, looking at first one thing, and then another, so full of sad associations. The closed piano, the locked bookcase, the nicely arranged tables, the formally placed chairs, ottomans, and sofas in the parlor! Oh, for someone to put them out of order! And then the dinner table, which has always been so well surrounded, so social, so cheerful, looked so cheerless today as we seated ourselves, one at the head, the other at the foot, with one friend—but one—at the side. I could scarcely restrain my tears, and but for the presence of that one friend, I believe I should have cried outright.

"After dinner, I did not mean to do it, but I could not help going into the girls' room, and then into C.'s [presumably that of a son]. I heard my own footsteps so plainly that I was startled by the absence of all other sounds. There the furniture looked so quiet, the beds so fixed and smooth, the wardrobes and bureaus so tightly locked, and the whole so lifeless! . . .

"I paused to ask myself what it all meant. . . . I threw open the shutters, and the answer came at once, so mournfully! I heard distinctly the drums beating in Washington. The evening was so still that I seemed to hear nothing else. As I looked at the Capitol in the distance, I could scarcely believe my senses. That Capitol of which I had always been so proud! Can it be possible that it is no longer *our* Capitol?

"And are our countrymen, under its very eaves, making mighty preparations to drain our hearts' blood? And must this Union, which I was taught to revere, be rent asunder? Once I thought such a suggestion sacrilege; but now that it is dismembered, I trust it may never, never be reunited. We must be a separate people— our nationality must be different, to insure lasting peace and good will. Why cannot we part in peace?"

A few days later, Mrs. McGuire said in another entry: "Since writing last, I have been busy. . . . We are now hoping that Alex-

Recruits from New York in a camp near Washington

andria will not be a landing-place for the enemy. . . . With the supposition that we may remain . . . I am having the grounds put in order, and they are now so beautiful! Lilacs, crocuses, the lily of the valley, and other spring flowers are in luxuriant bloom, and the roses in full bud. The greenhouse plants have been removed and grouped on the lawn; verbenas in bright bloom have been transplanted from the pit to the borders; and the grass seems unusually green after the late rains. The trees are in full leaf; everything is so fresh and lovely. . . .

"We who are left here are trying to give the soldiers who are quartered in town comfort by carrying them milk, butter, pies, cakes, etc. I went in yesterday to the barracks with the carriage well filled with such things, and found many young friends quartered there. All are taking up arms. The first young men in the country are the most zealous. . . .

"The Confederate flag waves from several points in Alexandria: from the Marshall House, the Market-house, and the several barracks. The peaceful, quiet old town looks quite warlike. I feel sometimes, when walking on King's street, meeting men in uniform, passing companies of cavalry, hearing martial music, etc., that I must be in a dream. Oh that it were a dream, and that the last ten years of our country's history were blotted out!

"Some of our old men are a little nervous, look doubtful, and talk of the impotency of the South. Oh, I feel utter scorn for such remarks. We must not admit weakness. Our soldiers do not think of weakness. . . . Their hearts feel strong when they think of the justice of their cause. In that is our hope.

"Walked down this evening to see ——. The road looked lonely and deserted. Busy life has departed from our midst. We found Mrs. —— packing up valuables. I have been doing the same. But after they are packed, where are they to be sent? Silver may be buried, but what is to be done with books, pictures, etc.? We have determined, if we are obliged to go from home, to leave everything in the care of the [Negro] servants. They have promised to be faithful, and I believe they will be. . . .

"Everything is so sad around us! We went to the chapel on Sunday as usual, but it was grievous to see the change—the organ mute, the organist gone, the seats of the students of both institutions empty; but one or two members of each family to represent the absentees; the prayer for the President [of the United States] omitted. When Dr. —— came to it, there was a slight pause, and then he went on to the next prayer—all seemed so strange!

"Tucker Conrad, one of the few students who is still here, raised the tunes. His voice seemed unusually sweet, because so sad. He was feebly supported by all who were not in tears.

"There was night service, but it rained, and I was not sorry that I could not go."

11

The Rise of Thomas Jackson

As WASHINGTON GREW STRONGER, even the fall of Harpers Ferry, which had given the Confederates a hold on the strategic "back door" route to the capital, seemed less serious. It was known, however, that the numbers there were growing. What wasn't known is that Harpers had hosted the debut of a Confederate soldier destined to become one of the Union's gravest threats.

When Sumter was taken, Thomas Jackson was at Lexington pursuing his military professorship. The thirty-seven-year-old veteran of the Mexican War was known to his students and the townspeople as an eccentric, as a man preoccupied with his health, and as a Christian of extraordinary zeal.

"At the time that the clouds of war were about to burst over the land," says Jackson's wife, Mary Anna, "the Presbytery of Lexington held its Spring meeting in the church which Major Jackson attended. These ecclesiastical gatherings ... were regarded in Virginia as seasons of special social and religious privilege and enjoyment.

"Major Jackson was entertaining some of the members of this body, but owing to the intense political excitement in the town, and the constant demands made upon him in military matters, he found but little time to give to his guests, and, still more to his disappointment, none to the services of the sanctuary. The cadets were wild with youthful ardor at the prospect of war, and the citizens were forming volunteer companies, drilling and equipping to enter the service. . . .

"While the Presbytery was still in session came the dreaded

Thomas J. Jackson, from a portrait his associates considered the best extant

news from Richmond that Virginia had seceded from the Union and cast in her lot with the Southern Confederacy. This was the death-knell of the last hope of peace. The governor of the State, 'honest John Letcher,' as he was called, notified the superintendent of the Institute that he should need the services of the more advanced classes of the cadets as drill-masters, and they must be prepared to go to Richmond at a moment's notice, under the command of Major Jackson.

"Having been almost entirely absorbed all the week with his military occupations, to the exclusion of his attendance upon a single church service, which he had so much desired, he expressed the earnest hope, on retiring late Saturday night, that the call to Richmond would not come before Monday, and that he might be permitted to spend a quiet Sabbath without any mention of politics or the impending troubles of the country, and enjoy the privilege once more of communing with God and His people in His sanctuary.

"But Heaven ordered it otherwise. About the dawn of that Sabbath morning, April 21st, our doorbell rang, and the order came that Major Jackson should bring the cadets to Richmond *immediately*. Without waiting for breakfast, he repaired at once to the Institute to make arrangements as speedily as possible for marching, but, finding that several hours of preparation would necessarily be required, he appointed the hour for starting at one o'clock P.M. He sent a message to his pastor, Dr. White, requesting him to come to the barracks and offer a prayer with the command before its departure.

"All the morning he was engaged at the Institute, allowing himself only a short time to return to his home about eleven o'clock, when he took a hurried breakfast and completed a few necessary preparations for his journey.

"Then, in the privacy of our chamber, he took his Bible and read that beautiful chapter in Corinthians beginning with the sublime hope of the resurrection . . . and then, kneeling down, he committed himself and her whom he loved to the protecting care of his Father in heaven.

"Never was a prayer more fervent, tender, and touching. His voice was so choked with emotion that he could scarcely utter the words; and one of his most earnest petitions was that, if consistent with His will, God would still avert the threatening danger and grant us peace. . . .

"Ah! How the light went out of his home when he departed from it on that beautiful Spring day! . . .

"When Dr. White went to the Institute to hold the short religious service which Major Jackson requested, the latter told him the command would march precisely at one o'clock, and the minister, knowing his punctuality, made it a point to close the service at a quarter before one. Everything was then in readiness, and, after waiting a few moments, an officer approached Major Jackson and said, 'Major, everything is now ready. May we not set out?'

"The only reply he made was to point to the dial-plate of the barracks clock; and not until the hand pointed to the hour of one was his voice heard to ring out the order, 'Forward, march!'

"From this time forth the life of my husband belonged to his beloved Southern land, and his private life becomes public history."

The narrative is taken up by Robert L. Dabney, a doctor of divinity who spent a part of the war on Jackson's staff and became one of his earliest biographers:

"The corps of cadets was conducted to Staunton, and thence by railroad to Richmond. . . . The camp of instruction near Richmond being in charge of another officer, Major Jackson had no responsible duties to perform. . . . He was exceedingly anxious for active employment; and, it must be added, distrustful of his prospects of obtaining it. For, his acute, though silent perspicacity taught him plainly enough that the estimate formed of his powers . . . was depreciatory. But he disdained to agitate or solicit for promotion; and busied himself quietly in assisting at the camp. . . .

"When the State had such urgent need of practical talent, it was impossible that an officer of Major Jackson's reputation should be wholly overlooked. . . . It was determined by the Executive War Council to employ him in the engineer department with the rank of major.

"This arrangement his advocates justly regarded as unfriendly to him, for it gave him no actual promotion, while the State was showering titles and rank on scores of men who had never seen service; and it assigned him a branch of duty for which he always professed least taste. . . . For placing a battery, an earthwork, or a line of battle, indeed, his judgment was almost infallible; but he was no draughtsman, and to set him to the drudgery of compiling maps was a sacrifice of his reputation and of his high capacities for command.

"But as soon as this purpose was made known, and before it was reported to the Convention for their approval, influential friends from Jackson's native district [Lexington was located in Rockbridge County], by whom his powers were better esteemed, remonstrated to the Council and showed them that he was the very man for a post of primary importance for which they were then seeking a commander.

"By their advice, seconded by that of Governor Letcher, this appointment was revoked, and he was commissioned colonel of the Virginia forces and ordered to take command at Harpers Ferry.

"The next day this appointment was sent to the Convention for their sanction, when someone asked, 'Who is this Major Jackson, that we are asked to commit to him so responsible a post?'

" 'He is one,' replied the member from Rockbridge, 'who, if you order him to hold a post, will never leave it alive to be occupied by the enemy.'

"The Governor accordingly handed him his commission as colonel on Saturday, April 27, and he departed at once for his command. . . . There were assembled at Harpers Ferry 2100 Virginian troops, with 400 Kentuckians. . . . The Convention had just passed a very necessary law, revoking the commissions of all the militia officers in command of volunteer forces, for their appointments, made long before . . . on every conceivable ground of political or local popularity, were no evidence whatever of fitness for actual command. . . . Of discipline there was almost none. . . . Everybody wanted a furlough, for they had come as to a frolic. There was no general staff, no hospital, nor ordnance department, and scarcely six rounds of ammunition to the man.

"To this confused mass Colonel Jackson came a stranger, having not a single acquaintance in the whole command. He brought two of his colleagues in the military school . . . who virtually composed his staff, and two young men . . . as drillmasters."

An enlisted man at the post, John N. Opie, tells of one of Jackson's first acts.

"Finding that there were great quantities of liquor in the town, he ordered it to be poured out. The barrels were brought forth, the heads knocked in, and the contents poured into the gutter. But the men dipped it up. . . . He ordered the whiskey [in the remaining barrels] to be poured into the Potomac River. But still the soldiers, particularly the Kentuckians, gathered round with buckets tied to the end of ropes and caught great quantities of the disturbing element as it poured [toward] the waters below."

In the beginning, Jackson's image was detrimental to his acceptance by his command. As explained by Southern writer John Esten Cooke, who knew Jackson, and, like Dr. Dabney, recorded his life story:

"We have a personal sketch of Jackson as he appeared at this time, which, if not very complimentary, is at least characteristic, and shows what effect he produced on strangers.

"An army correspondent of one of the Southern papers drew an outline of the newly appointed colonel. The queer apparition of the ex-professor on the field excited great merriment in this writer. The Old Dominion [Virginia] must be woefully deficient in military men, he feared, if this was the best she could do. The new colonel was not at all like a commanding officer. There was a painful want in him of all the 'pride, pomp, and circumstance of glorious war.' His dress was no better than a private soldier's, and there was not a particle of gold lace about his uniform.

"His air was abstracted; his bearing stiff and awkward. He kept his own counsels; never consulted with his officers, and had very little to say to anybody. On horseback his appearance was even less impressive. Other officers, at that early stage of the war . . . made their appearance before their troops on prancing horses with splendid trappings, and seemed desirous of showing the admiring spectators how gracefully they could sit in the saddle.

"The new colonel was a strong contrast to all this. He rode an old horse who seemed to have little of the romance of war about him, and nothing at all fine in his equipment. His seat in the saddle was far from graceful; he leaned forward awkwardly . . . and looked from side to side from beneath the low rim of his cadet cap in a manner which the risible faculties of the correspondent could not resist. A queerer figure, and one which answered less to the idea of military grace, had never before dawned on the attention of the literary gentleman who sketched it for the amusement of the Southern reader.

"The sketch . . . was not a bad description of the figure which the troops scanned curiously as he passed to and fro on duty."

According to Dr. Dabney, Jackson very soon gained his command's respect.

"His energy, impartiality, fairness, and courtesy . . . reduced the crude rabble to order and consistency. . . . Speedily the restive temper which had been provoked by the incompetent hands that essayed to guide it gave place to joy and docility. . . . His justice engaged the approbation of every man's conscience; his unaffected goodness allured their love; and, if insubordination was attempted, his sternness awed them into submission.

"Once or twice only some wilful young officer made experiment of resisting his authority; and then the snowy brow began to congeal with stony rigor, the calm blue eyes to kindle with that blaze, steady . . . and intense, before which every other eye quailed; and his penalties were so prompt and inexorable that no one desired to adventure another act of disobedience."

Captain John Imboden, one of the men who had helped to

capture Harpers Ferry and had stayed on there, had been absent on an errand to Richmond when Jackson arrived, and he got a surprise when he returned.

"What a revolution three or four days had wrought! I could scarcely realize the change. The militia generals were all gone. . . . The presence of a master mind was visible in the changed condition of the camp. Perfect order reigned everywhere.

"Instruction in the details of military duties occupied Jackson's whole time. He urged the officers to call upon him for information about even the minutest details of duties. . . .

"He was the easiest man in our army to get along with pleasantly so long as one did his duty, but as inexorable as fate in exacting the performance of it. Yet he would overlook serious faults if he saw they were the result of ignorance, and would instruct the offender in a kindly way. He was as courteous to the humblest private who sought an interview for any purpose as to the highest officer in his command. . . .

"When Jackson found we were without artillery horses, he went into no red-tape correspondence with . . . Richmond, but ordered his quartermaster, Major John A. Harman, to proceed with men to the Quaker settlements in the rich county of Loudoun, famed for its good horses, and buy or impress as many as we needed. . . .

"J. E. B. Stuart—afterward so famous as a cavalry leader—was commissioned lieutenant-colonel and reported to Colonel Jackson for assignment to duty. Jackson ordered the consolidation of all the cavalry companies into a battalion to be commanded by Stuart, who then appeared more like a well-grown manly youth than the mature man he really was.

"This order was very offensive to Captain Turner Ashby, at that time the idol of all the troopers in the field. . . . Ashby was older than Stuart, and he thought, and we all believed, that he was entitled to first promotion.

"When not absent scouting, Ashby spent his nights with me [on guard at the bridge at Point of Rocks, twelve miles down the Potomac from Harpers Ferry]. . . . He told me of Jackson's order, and that he would reply to it with his resignation. . . . I urged him to call upon Colonel Jackson that night. . . . I believed Jackson would respect his feelings and leave his company out of Stuart's battalion. . . .

"The result of his night ride was that Jackson not only relieved him from the obnoxious order but agreed to divide the companies

Jeb Stuart

between him and Stuart and to ask for his immediate promotion, forming thus the nuclei of two regiments of cavalry, to be filled as rapidly as new companies came to the front. . . .

"Ashby got back to Point of Rocks about two in the morning, as happy a man as I ever saw, and completely enraptured with Jackson."

It was while Jackson was at Harpers Ferry that he advanced a stern theory on how he believed this war should be fought. The policy of the Confederates, he said, should be to take no prisoners, but to kill every Yankee they possibly could. Dr. Dabney elaborates:

"He affirmed that this would be in the end the truest humanity because it would shorten the contest and prove economical of the blood of both parties; and that it was a measure urgently dictated by the interests of our cause, and clearly sustained by justice. . . . He affirmed this war was, in its intent and inception, different from all civilized wars, and therefore should not be brought under their rules. It was not . . . a strife for a point of honor, a diplomatic quarrel, a commercial advantage, a boundary, or a province; but an attempt on the part of the North against the very existence of the Southern States.

"It was founded in a denial to their people of the right of self-government, in virtue of which . . . the Northern States themselves existed. Its intention was a wholesale murder and piracy, the extermination of a whole people's national life.

"It was, in fact, but the 'John Brown Raid' resumed and extended, with new accessories of horror. And, as the Commonwealth of Virginia had righteously put to death every one of those cutthroats upon the gallows, why were their comrades in the same crime to claim now a more honorable treatment?

"Such a war was an offense against humanity so monstrous that it outlawed those who shared its guilt beyond the pale of forbearance."

When Jackson learned that his views were not shared by the Confederate government, he discontinued pressing them and prepared to pursue a course of treating prisoners with humanity. But he declined to say that he wasn't right.

More in line with a proper conduct of the war was another view that he held. Again in Dabney's words:

"From the beginning, he manifested that reticence and secrecy as to all military affairs for which he was afterwards so remarkable. It was his maxim that, in war, mystery was the key to success. He argued that no human shrewdness could foretell what item of information might not give some advantage to an astute adversary, and that, therefore, it was the part of wisdom to conceal everything, even those things of which it did not appear how the enemy could make use. . . .

"Not long after he took command at Harpers Ferry, a dignified and friendly committee of the Legislature of Maryland visited him to learn his plans. It was deemed important to receive them with all courtesy, for the cooperation of their State was earnestly desired, and everyone was watching to see how Colonel Jackson would reconcile his secrecy, and his extreme dislike to be questioned upon military affairs, with the demands of politeness.

"Among other questions, they asked him the number of his troops. He replied promptly, 'I should be glad if Lincoln thought I had fifteen thousand.' "

It remains for John Imboden to tell of Jackson's chief accomplishment while in command at Harpers Ferry, one that illustrated his resourcefulness.

"From the very beginning of the war the Confederacy was greatly in need of rolling-stock [of locomotives and cars] for the railroads. We were particularly short of locomotives, and were without the shops to build them. Jackson, appreciating this, hit upon a plan to obtain a good supply from the Baltimore and Ohio road [which, operated by the Union, ran through Harpers Ferry]. Its line was double-tracked, at least from Point of Rocks to Martinsburg, a distance of twenty-five or thirty miles. We had not interfered with the running of the trains. . . . [The Confederacy did not want to anger the many Southern sympathizers who were served by the line. Even now, Jackson did not intend to do it permanent harm. He knew that the locomotives and cars he appropriated for the Confederacy could be replaced by the North with little strain on its resources.]

"The coal traffic from Cumberland [Maryland] was immense, as the Washington government was accumulating supplies of coal on the seaboard. These coal trains passed Harpers Ferry at all hours of the day and night, and thus furnished Jackson with a pretext for arranging a brilliant 'scoop.'

"When he sent me to Point of Rocks [east of Harpers Ferry], he ordered . . . [Kenton] Harper with the 5th Virginia infantry to Martinsburg [the westerly limit of the double-tracking]. He then complained to President [J. W.] Garrett, of the Baltimore and Ohio, that the night trains, eastward bound, disturbed the repose of his camp, and requested a change of schedule that would pass all eastbound trains by Harpers Ferry between 11 and 1 o'clock in the daytime.

"Mr. Garrett complied, and thereafter for several days we heard the constant roar of passing trains for an hour before and an hour after noon.

"But since the 'empties' [from the seaboard] were sent up the road at night, Jackson again complained that the nuisance was as great as ever; and, as the road had two tracks, said he must insist that the westbound trains should pass during the same two hours as those going east.

"Mr. Garrett promptly complied, and we then had, for two hours every day, the liveliest railroad in America. . . .

"As soon as the schedule was working at its best, Jackson sent me an order to take a force of men . . . the next day at 11 o'clock, and, letting all westbound trains pass till 12 o'clock, to permit none to go east; and at 12 o'clock to obstruct the road so that it would require several days to repair it. He ordered the reverse to be done at Martinsburg.

"Thus he caught all the trains that were going east or west between those points, and these he ran to Winchester, thirty-two miles [southwestward] on the branch road, where they were safe. . . . [If he hadn't employed this scheme, Jackson would have been obliged to try to take the trains one by one, and the railroad people would doubtless have interrupted the runs after the first train was seized.]

"The gain to our scantily stocked Virginia roads of the same gauge was invaluable."

12

Drums Across the South

IN NEARLY ALL PARTS of the North and the South, the people had been maintaining the pace of their mobilization. The newspapers, of course, continued their salient role in fanning the flames. Most included pieces of well-written poetry based on events, and these—often read aloud at the fireside or in public places—were a powerful stimulus to the emotions.

A Southern poet wrote in the following manner of the new Confederate flag (at the same time casting a challenge at the Yankees):

> *Fling wide the dauntless banner*
> *To every Southern breeze,*
> *Baptized in flame*
> *With Sumter's name,*
> *A patriot and a hero's fame,*
> *From Moultrie to the seas,*
> *That it may cleave the morning sun,*
> *And, streaming, sweep the night—*
> *The emblem of a battle won*
> *With Yankee ships in sight.*
>
> *Come, hucksters from your markets;*
> *Come, bigots from your caves;*
> *Come, venal spies*
> *With brazen lies*
> *Bewildering your deluded eyes,*
> *That we may dig your graves.*

Come, creatures of a sordid clown
And drivelling traitor's breath—
A single blast shall blow you down
Upon the fields of Death!

As related by Miss A. C. Cooper, a resident of Atlanta, Georgia:
" 'To arms! To arms!' was the shout that woke the echoes in the sweet Southland, thrilling through the mountain heights, running like wildfire through the lowlands and dense pine forests. And, answering to the call, poured forth the Southern men—and even boys—eager for the fray. . . . There was not, at first, much serious thought about it. It was only a frolic, a playing at war, and they would soon return—those handsome, stalwart fellows, roused . . . from the dull routine of everyday life, their quick Southern blood stirred to its utmost. Only a frolic of a few weeks or months, and then they would return covered with glory . . . and again settle down. . . .

"There was much rushing to and fro . . . the masculine portion of humanity engaged in making hot speeches, much drilling, also much anxiety about the fit of their new uniforms . . . and great solicitude concerning the brightness of their arms . . . upon which Pomp, Josh, Tom, Cuffee, and a host of other . . . darkies were kept at work polishing. . . . The feminine portion busied themselves about the many needful things conducive to the comfort of these same helpless men—helpless in regard to the things which only a woman's quick intuition and deft fingers can supply. . . . There was a shimmer of bright ribbons, silk, beads, glossy satin and downy velvet; and willing fingers soon transformed these delicate materials into smoking caps, slippers, tobacco pouches, cigar cases, and portfolios [for writing paper and envelopes]."

In many sections of the South, groups of women set up small factories, with uniforms the chief product. As recalled by Mrs. James Evans of Northern Virginia:

"In our little town . . . the courthouse was the place of meeting, and thither all the ladies resorted to pass the day at work. Some would cut out garments, others work the machines, while still others would finish them off. Coats, overcoats, pantaloons, and havelocks were made in great numbers. Ladies who had never done harder work than that with a cambric needle now stitched industriously on coarse cloth, making heavy garments. They seemed to find nothing too hard for them. Besides this, they knit

Inexperienced Confederate overburdened with gear

quantities of socks of the coarsest yarn; and so engrossed were they in their work that when they went to visit their friends they would take their knitting, some even knitting as they walked or drove, and plying their needles as they discussed the all-absorbing topic, the war."

Returning to Georgia's Miss Cooper, who tells how her community's first volunteers left home:

" 'Forward, march!' With many farewells, much loud arms glittering—some dim eyes in the ranks, not from any presentiment of evil, or that the trip was aught but a frolic, but from sympathy

A departure in the South

with the fair friends and relatives, down whose cheeks streamed
the hot tears—off they marched with heads erect and much attention paid to position of the feet, keeping time, etc. Many were
the laughing promises, given with the last farewell, of the 'spoils
of war' to be brought back as keepsakes. . . .

"Thus with gay laughter and buoyant hearts, off they filed down
the dusty road, while streaming eyes looked after, till the last
fluttering pennant waved out of sight and the last strain of the
ear-piercing fife was lost in silence. Then the reaction came. All
had been done that could be, and the boys were really gone!
Suppose something should happen. Suppose they should have an
encounter and some be wounded! Suppose they should sicken
and die! Alas! dreadful thought!"

In Charleston, South Carolina, Claudine Rhett was present
when the first contingent of troops left the city by train.

"My sisters and myself drove up to the railroad depot. . . . It was
9 o'clock in the evening and the station yard was brightly lighted
up by gas lamps and pine torches. After waiting awhile the command came marching up, escorted by several other companies,

and a band cheerily played 'Dixie.' A few short speeches were made and responded to, and then the ranks were broken, and the pretty uniforms intermingled in the bustle and confusion of getting the baggage stored away and the men on board the train. They were all very gay, but *we* were saddened. . . . At last the whistle blew, and my brother ran out to say good-bye to us. One or two words were spoken; then he resumed his place amid that gallant band of heroes, and the slow-moving wheels bore them away, whilst we followed with tear-dimmed eyes the trail of the fast-fading smoke of the engine."

According to Sarah D. Eggleston, who lived in Mississippi, the days of preparation were endlessly stimulating.

"How the blood coursed through the veins of us girls! My sisters and cousins and former schoolmates gathered in the old plantation house—as with flushed cheeks and flashing eyes we talked over the battles yet to be fought and dwelt upon the speedy triumph of the Southern arms, just as if it were already an assured fact.

"In every village and hamlet companies were rapidly formed and their services eagerly offered to the Confederate Government, then recently established at Montgomery. The war spirit was so fully aroused and so general that nearly always there were more volunteers than were needed to make up the complement of the company, and many had to be rejected. . . . How serious a trial this was to many young men. 'The war will be over before I get into a fight,' are the words that were frequently heard. . . .

"These early companies were enrolled and drilled with no little ostentation—all having fancy names and flags of their own—and their departure for the seat of war or the training camp was generally attended with much ceremony. When the Fencibles of Raymond got marching orders, one of the girls in our set . . . was invited to present to the company a silk banner made by the ladies of the place. . . . She stood in her dazzling beauty, handing the flag to the captain of the company. 'The ladies of Raymond,' she said, 'feel assured that the company will bring this flag back to them untarnished by defeat.' . . .

"When they marched away, with the flag flying over their heads, there were moist eyes all along [their] line. They saw the tears and heard the sobs of mothers, wives and sweethearts who had come to take a last look at them."

An Alabama woman, Mrs. Mary Rhodes, gives this picture:

"The gentlemen of our town had formed themselves into a company, and, dressed up in their uniforms, were a goodly looking set of men. They were the flower of the county. . . . As long as it was only the dress parade, barbecues, balls, and presentations of honors, it was well enough; but when the time came to *do*—when the committee sent to the Governor with offers of service returned to say the company was accepted and must be ready to report at a moment's warning—the reality of the thing that was upon us made many a poor woman's heart stop its regular beat. . . .

"At length—all too soon—the company was ordered to Montgomery, and had only a few days' notice. . . . It was hurry-hurry to get the gray shirts and pants made up. All who did not have members of their own families going assisted those who had, and in a few hours the hurried preparations were finished, the last good-byes said; and the women turned to their lonely homes, feeling desolate indeed. We not only had the children but the Negroes and the plantations to care for and manage."

One of the most fateful occurrences of this early period was that Colonel Robert E. Lee, after his long and distinguished career in federal service, refused an offer to command Lincoln's

Robert E. Lee

new army, resigned his commission, and cast his lot with his home state of Virginia. Made a general, he was given command of the state's forces, his base in Richmond.

People who had heard of Lee but did not know what he looked like were eager to get a glimpse of him. The following story is told by a Virginia citizen, Mrs. Gilmer Breckinridge:

"When soldiers were camping at the Fair Grounds, near Richmond, where troops were daily being mustered in from every quarter, a favorite pastime of the ladies was to resort thither to witness the afternoon drill. Great was the enthusiasm. What more stirring than the sound of the drum! What more inspiring than the graceful maneuvers of the Zouaves, the Rifles, or the Rangers!

"A lady having returned from witnessing such a display congratulated herself upon having at last achieved her heart's desire—she had seen General Lee!

" 'General Lee!' exclaimed a gentleman friend. 'Surely you must be mistaken. He is not in the city.'

" 'Oh, I am quite sure I saw him,' she replied. 'He was walking in front of all the rest, wore a tall, *very* tall stiff hat, was gorgeously apparelled, and every now and then turned and waved something—a sword I suppose—which everyone else instantly obeyed.'

"It was some time before the gentleman could sufficiently recover from a fit of laughter to assure his companion the personage she had taken to be the commander-in-chief was only the drum major, and the imaginary sword was his baton, with which he was beating time for the musicians who followed him."

Among the regiments that arrived in Virginia from out of state at this time was the 6th Alabama, which included the company of Raccoon Roughs raised by John Gordon. The captain had been promoted to major, and he was commander of the regiment.

"When we reached Virginia," Gordon explains, "the military spirit was in full flood-tide. . . . Almost every young and middle-aged man was volunteering for service.

"Even the servants were becoming interested in the military positions to which the aspiring young men of the household might be assigned. . . .

"Old Simon was the trusted and devoted butler of a leading Virginia family, and was very proud of his young master, who had just enlisted as a private in the cavalry, and, dressed in his new uniform and mounted upon his blooded horse, was drilling every day with his company. He was, in old Simon's estimation, the equal, if not the superior, of any soldier that was ever booted and spurred.

"The time came for the company to start to the front, and one of them rode up and asked old Simon, 'Is Bob here, Simon, or has he gone to camp?'

" 'Is you talking about my young marster, *Colonel* Robert?'

" 'Yes, of course, I am, Simon,' replied the trooper. 'But I should like to know how in the hell Bob got to be a colonel!'

" 'Lawd, sir, he's des *born* a colonel!' said Simon."

The State of Virginia, because of its strategic location, was becoming the busiest theater of Confederate preparations. In the words of an unidentified woman of Lynchburg:

"From mountain to seaward, the excitement was immense. New companies were formed, old ones filled up. Boys of fourteen and fifteen years of age caught the infection and organized themselves into companies. Sewing societies were formed by the ladies to work for the soldiers and do whatever they could for the general good. . . . How busy our hands and how full our hearts in working for our loved ones, who seemed as if they were preparing for a fete instead of bloody graves. . . .

"I remember seeing a boy, as bright as he was beautiful, drilling, in the absence of an officer, a party of raw recruits. As it happened, one of the recruits was his teacher [of recent schooldays], a gentleman of very high culture who had . . . enlisted as a private when upwards of 40. . . . When I first saw them, the beautiful boy was double-quicking . . . his teacher, who seemed almost exhausted by the exertion. . . . The next time I saw the boy, I laughingly remonstrated with him for making his teacher run about so much. His eyes sparkled with fun as he replied: 'I am only paying him back for some of the discipline he put me through at school.' Alas! Both these gallant spirits . . . sealed their devotion to their country with their lives. . . .

"Lynchburg was an enormous camp. New companies filled with raw recruits from the mountains and adjacent counties were ordered there to be drilled. Some of the returned cadets from West Point [they had resigned from the Northern institution] and [from] the Virginia Military Institute were the drill masters.

"Soldiers from many parts of the South poured in before going to the field. The first two [were] the Oglethorpes from Savannah . . . and a company from Mobile. . . . It gave the people from Lynchburg much pleasure to do all in their power for the comfort

Recruits marching in Richmond

of the soldiers, by having them at their houses and doing for them, as far as they could, what their own mothers and sisters would have done. . . .

"A few days before a regiment from Arkansas was ordered to the field, the colonel came to one of our most prominent and active ladies . . . and requested that . . . she and the other ladies . . . make some arrangements to take care of ten or twelve men who were unable to march [because of illness]. She found she could get two rooms which had been used by a club. These were arranged as well as circumstances would admit, and this was the beginning of our 'Ladies' Hospital,' which did good service to the end."

Confederates posing for photographs to be sent home

Mrs. Roger A. Pryor, who had been in Washington with President Buchanan when he got the news of South Carolina's secession, was now at her home in Petersburg, south of Richmond. She relates:

"I am sure that no soldier enlisted under Virginia's banner could possibly be more determined than the young women of the state. They were uncompromising.

" 'You promised me my answer tonight,' said a fine young fellow, who had not yet enlisted, to his sweetheart.

" 'Well, you can't have it, Ben, until you have fought the Yankees,' said pretty Helen.

" 'What heart will I have for fighting if you give me no promise?'

" 'I'll not be engaged to any man until he has fought the Yankees,' said Helen firmly. 'You distinguish yourself in the war, and then see what I'll have to say to you.'

"This was the stand they took. . . . Engagements were postponed until they could find of what mettle a lover was.

" 'But suppose I don't come back at all!' suggested Ben.

" 'Oh, then I'll acknowledge an engagement and be good to your mother, and wear mourning . . . *provided* your wounds are all in front!' . . .

"The day came at last when our regiments were to march. They were to rendezvous at the head of Sycamore Street, and march down to the lower depot. Every old man and boy, matron, maiden, and child, every family servant, assembled to bid them God-speed.

"The reigning belles and beauties of Petersburg were all there— Alice Gregory, Tabb Bolling, Molly and Augusta Banister, Patty Hardee, Mary and Marion Meade, pretty Helen, and my own friend Agnes.

" 'We are not to cry, you know,' said Agnes, laying down the law by right of seniority.

" 'Of *course* not!' said Helen, winking away her tears and smiling.

"Just then the inspiring notes of 'Dixie,' with drum and crash of cymbal, rent the air—the first time I had heard that battle song.

" 'Forward, March!' And they were moving in solid ranks, all of us keeping step on the sidewalk, down to the depot.

"When the men were on board and the wheels began to move, Ben leaned out of his window and whispered to Helen, just below him, 'Can't I have the promise now, Helen?'

" 'Yes, yes, Ben—*dear* Ben, I promise!' And as the cars rolled away she turned and calmly announced, 'Girls, I'm engaged to Ben Shepard.'

" '*I'm* engaged to half a dozen of them,' said one.

" 'That's nothing,' said another, '*I'm* engaged to the whole regiment!' "

Kate Bowyer, of Virginia's Bedford County, the newlywed who had earlier quailed at the thought of secession, was now a stalwart supporter.

"It was appreciated that the moment for action had come. . . . My husband telegraphed Governor Letcher that he commanded a company of picked men ready to be ordered whenever and wherever the Governor might indicate. The reply summoned this company to Lynchburg. . . .

"Before this crisis arrived I had begun gradually to realize that some difficulty [of a military nature] was bound to occur, and made out in my own mind what seemed a most satisfactory and inevitable programme of the events we might look for. There would be a battle. I conceded that much—and a big one—fought near Richmond, of course [plans for defensive operations had supplanted the rash idea of an attack on Washington], where we must rout the enemy completely, when the whole misunderstanding would at once be adjusted, the war ended, and all the combatants go on their several ways, leaving the South to proceed undisturbed and prosperous to the end. . . .

"Every family now became busy with preparations for the comfort of its soldiers. My father, then a grey-haired man of 52 . . . enlisted as private in my husband's company, and our inexperienced minds invented . . . every style of camp paraphernalia: bedding which might be easily transported and yet protection against ground dampness, all sorts of head gear to shade from the sun, and foot trapping to prevent weariness on a long march. And while the Yankees had only to issue requisitions for certain dozens of complete equipment, and draw from the [commerce of the] world for their appliances, our Southern hearts were the inventors, and our homes the factories, for whatever military necessaries our gallant soldiers were furnished.

"And I must say some of these accoutrements were rare and curious in the extreme. . . . In the matter of tents, particularly, our Bedford companies were no doubt as strikingly provided as any other troops in the field. These tents consisted of small pointed sections of blue bed-ticking . . . and, while the effect of the sun streaming through the brilliant blue stripes of the ticking was perhaps novel and somewhat enlivening, it was at the same time found not conducive to the preservation of a soldier's eyesight.

"In the beginning, of course, our larders were well stored and our barns filled, so that it was hard to believe a day of scarcity could ever come to us; and no household had a higher pleasure than showering upon its soldiers every luxury in the eating department that Virginia culinary lore could suggest. In our own case, the Negro carpenter belonging to the estate was caused to build a most capacious and attractive 'mess chest' . . . with divers compartments, and stored with the choicest coffees and teas, loaf sugar, crackers, pastries, confections and condiments, with a solid foundation of old Virginia ham and beaten biscuit.

"And thus fortified we moved in a body to the camp at Lynchburg, where Cousin Robert Preston, [of] Montgomery County, as colonel, awaited the filling up and organization of the 28th Vir-

Confederate troops entraining for Manassas

ginia regiment, which he was commissioned to command. How can I ever tell what a heart of chivalry beat in that old hero's bosom, pure and true, with the gentleness of a woman and the courage of a lion combined? His devotion to the cause of right was only equalled by his iron resolution to lay down his life, if need be, to defend that right.

"And it did seem some horrible nightmare as I tried to realize, and could not, how we were all suddenly transplanted from our erewhile happy homes—where the gentlest courtesies and brightest interchangings were all we ever knew—to this desolate hillside covered with blue bed-ticking tents and men drilling for battle.

"It was simply impossible that the civil human mind could at once accommodate itself to this highly military situation; and when, after having been in camp for a week, I one evening asked Colonel Preston if he would order fresh straw for the men to sleep on. General [Jubal A.] Early, who was present, gave me a shock. He, by reason of [the war in] Mexico and other experiences, had much more developed military views than our own, and immediately piped out in his fine, incisive voice, 'What do you want with fresh straw?'

" 'The old has become broken and needs renewing,' I replied spiritedly.

"The General looked contemptuous and went on, 'Let the straw alone. The sooner the men do without it the better, for the time is coming when they will be glad to get a sharp fence rail to sleep on.'

"I burst into tears, and felt that so unfeeling a monster as General Early ought not to be permitted to live; while dear, good Cousin Robert said soothingly, and in the most unmilitary way in the world, 'Well, they shall have the straw while they can get it; shan't they, Kate? I'll have it hauled this day, my dear.' . . .

"When we had lain [at Lynchburg] for three weeks, a telegram flashed along ordering the 28th regiment to Manassas. Here was a sudden and complete revulsion of all my admirably matured plans [regarding settlement of the war in the environs of Richmond]. Manassas! Who ever heard of such a place as that? What could be the meaning of so unreasonable, so wholly inexplicable an order as that?"

Manassas, in its position twenty-five miles southwest of Washington, was a part of what the Confederacy had begun to call its "Alexandria line." Alexandria itself, however, was now only lightly occupied.

13

The North Grows Stronger

CONDITIONS IN THE NORTH at this time are described by period historian Benson Lossing:

"The enthusiasm of the people was unbounded. Money and men were offered in greater abundance than the Government seemed to need. The voluntary contributions offered to the public treasury, and for the fitting out of troops and maintaining their familes, by individuals, associations, and corporations amounted, at the beginning of May, to full *forty millions of dollars!*

"Six weeks earlier than this, that sagacious Frenchman, Count Agénor de Gasparin, one of the few foreigners who seemed to comprehend the American people and the nature and significance of the impending struggle, wrote, almost prophetically, saying:

" 'At the present hour, the Democracy of the South is about to degenerate into demagogism. But the North presents quite a different spectacle. Mark what is passing there; pierce beneath appearances. . . . You will find the firm resolution of a people uprising. Who speaks of the *end* of the United States? This end seemed approaching. . . . Honor was compromised, esteem for the country was lowered, institutions were becoming corrupted apace. . . . Now, everything has changed in aspect. The friends of America should take confidence, for its greatness is inseparable—thank God!—from the cause of justice.' . . .

"While thousands of the loyal people of New England and the other free-labor States eastward of the Alleghenies were hurrying to the field and pouring out their wealth like water in support of the Government, those of the region westward of these lofty hills and northward of the Ohio River were equally patriotic and demonstrative. They had watched with the deepest interest the development of the conspiracy for the overthrow of the Republic, and when the President's call for the militia of the country to arrest the treasonable movements reached them, they responded to it with alacrity by thousands and tens of thousands. . . .

"The Legislature of Ohio . . . pledged the resources of the State to the maintenance of the authority of the National Government. . . . Provision was also made for the defense of the State, whose peace was liable to disturbance by parties from the slave-labor States of Virginia and Kentucky. . . . The people contributed freely of their means for fitting out troops and providing for their families. . . .

"George B. McClellan, who had held the commission of captain by brevet after meritorious services in Mexico but was now in civil service as superintendent of the Ohio and Mississippi Railway,

George B. McClellan

was commissioned a major-general by the Governor and appointed commander of all the forces in the State. Camps for rendezvous and instruction were speedily formed, one of the most important of which was Camp Dennison, on the line of the Cincinnati and Columbus Railway and occupying a position on the pleasant slopes of the hills that skirt the Miami Valley, about eighteen miles from Cincinnati. . . .

"The people of Indiana moved as promptly and vigorously as those of Ohio. . . . Within four days after the President's call was promulgated from Washington, more than ten thousand Indianians were in camp. . . .

"Illinois . . . was early upon the warpath. . . . The quota of the State, six thousand, was more than filled by the 20th [of April]. . . .

"The Legislature of Illinois met at Springfield on the 23rd, and two days afterward it was addressed by the distinguished United States Senator, Stephen A. Douglas, the rival of Mr. Lincoln for the Presidency of the Republic. When treason lifted its arm to strike, Mr. Douglas instantly offered himself as a shield for his country. He abandoned all party allegiance, put away all political and personal prejudices, and, with the spirit and power of a sincere patriot, became the champion of the integrity of the Union. . . .

"Alas, his warfare was brief! He . . . [was] suffering from inflammatory rheumatism. Disease assumed various and malignant forms in his system, and . . . [he soon] died. His loss seemed to be peculiarly inauspicious . . . when such men were so few and so much needed. But his words were living and of electric power. They were oracles for thousands whose faith and hope and patriotism were strengthened thereby. His last coherent utterances were exhortations to his children and his countrymen to stand by the Constitution and the Government.

"The Legislature of Illinois appropriated three millions of dollars for war purposes, and authorized the immediate organization of the entire militia force of the State. . . .

"Michigan was equally aroused by the call of the President. He asked of her one regiment only. Ten days afterward she had five regiments ready for the field, and nine more were forming. . . . The Legislature . . . on the 7th of May . . . made liberal appropriations for war purposes. The Legislature of Wisconsin . . . was equally liberal. That of Iowa and Minnesota followed the patriotic example.

"The enthusiasm of the people everywhere was wonderful."
A poem in the Boston *Transcript* sang of the rising of the Northern states in this manner:

> *Forward! Onward! Far and forth!*
> *An earthquake shout awakes the North.*
> > *Forward!*
>
> *Massachusetts hears the cry—*
> *Hears, and gives the swift reply,*
> > *Forward!*
>
> *Pennsylvania draws her sword;*
> *Echoes from her hills the word*
> > *Forward!*
>
> *Brave New York is up and ready,*
> *With her thirty thousand steady—*
> > *Forward!*
>
> *Small Rhode Island flies to arms,*
> *Shouting at the first alarms,*
> > *Forward!*
>
> *Illinois and Indiana*
> *Shriek, as they unroll our banner,*
> > *Forward!*
>
> *Not behind the rest in zeal,*
> *Hear Ohio's thunder-peal,*
> > *Forward!*
>
> *From Vermont, New Hampshire, Maine,*
> *Comes the same awakening strain,*
> > *Forward!*
>
> *Old Connecticut is here,*
> *Ready to give back the cheer,*
> > *Forward!*
>
> *Minnesota, though remote,*
> *Swells the free, inspiring note,*
> > *Forward!*
>
> *Iowa and Michigan*
> *Both are ready to a man—*
> > *Forward!*

Not the last in honor's race,
See Wisconsin come apace—
  Forward!

Delaware, New Jersey rise
And put on their martial guise.
  Forward!

Onward! On! A common cause
Is yours—your liberties and laws.
  Forward!

Forward in your strength and pride!
God himself is on your side.
  Forward!

A mother's parting gift

A patriotic act on the part of a group of civilians was recorded as follows in the New York *Tribune:*

"The vestry of Grace Church in New York were desirous that an American flag should wave from the very apex of the spire of the church, at the height of 260 feet from the ground. Several persons offered to undertake the dangerous feat, but, on mounting by the interior staircase to the highest window in the steeple, thought they would scarcely have nerve enough to undertake it.

"At last William O'Donnell and Charles McLaughlin, two young painters in the employ of Richard B. Fosdick of Fifth Avenue, decided to make the attempt. Getting out of the little diamond-shaped window about halfway up, they climbed up the lightning rod on the east side of the spire, to the top. Here one of the men fastened the pole securely to the cross, although quite a gale was blowing at the time.

"The flag thus secured, the daring young man mounted the cross, and, taking off his hat, bowed to the immense crowd which were watching his movements from Broadway. As the flag floated freely in the air, they burst into loud and repeated cheers."

So pervasive was the war spirit that those volunteers in Northern towns who were not called at once to the theater of war lamented their status as one of deprivation.

In the words of Private A. H. Hill, of western Pennsylvania:

" 'Marching orders! Hurrah! Hurrah!'

"The sun was just sinking behind the wild old hills west of Brownsville when a glad cheer rang out on the mild evening air. It came from the throats of a company of volunteers. They stood in line in one of the principal streets of the town.

"Our company had been organized as soon as the first call for troops to crush the rebellion was made, and . . . we had been anxiously awaiting orders to go into camp . . . and the welcome order had just come.

"Early next morning we embarked for Pittsburgh, at which place we arrived after a journey of sixty miles down the beautiful Monongahela. We were ordered to Camp Wright, which was about twelve miles from the city, on the left bank of the Allegheny. On our arrival thither, we found barracks constructed of pine boards, and we . . . took possession of one of the buildings and moved in.

"Not long after, a board might have been seen swinging above, on which was inscribed in huge letters THE BROWNSVILLE GRAYS— such was our name.

"We were indeed delighted to know that we were at last *soldiers*—that we were actually *in camp*. Although we had responded to our country's call immediately after the fall of Fort Sumter, so many volunteers had flocked to Pittsburgh and offered their services that it was impossible to accept them all on the first call. . . . Our company, with many others, was compelled to wait. . . . Now our fond hopes were beginning to be realized. We were now to be armed, equipped, and organized, after which, we doubted not, we should be ordered to the seat of war. . . .

"A word as to our first night in camp. When nine o'clock came, the 'tatoo' was beaten. At ten, came the 'taps.' We were just wondering what it meant when a man who was called the 'officer of the day' came round, and, looking into our quarters, said in an authoritative tone, 'Lights out!'

"Then we understood it; no lights were to be burning in camp after taps. Our candles were at once extinguished, and we retired to our bunks. Well, you don't suppose . . . that we all dropped off quietly to sleep, do you? . . . No sooner did we find ourselves in the dark than each one discovered that he had some remark to make.

" 'Hilloa, Bill, what have you got for a pillow?' called out one to a comrade.

" 'Don't know—guess it's Tom's hat,' was the reply.

" 'Joe!' called out another. . . . 'How about those pine boards you're lying on?'

" 'Oh, they're not so soft as the bed I slept on last night.'

" 'I wonder what the old folks would say if they could see us stowed away in this manner?'

" 'Don't know. . . .'

" 'Baa!' interrupted one of our boys, imitating the cry of a sheep.

"This was all that was required to suggest a new plan of amusement. The bawl of a calf responded; the barking of a dog followed; the mewing of a cat came from a distant corner of the building; the hee-haw of a donkey was next in the order of things.

"Thus it went on—the howl of a panther, the squeal of a pig, the crow of a chicken, the hiss of a serpent; and, in fact, the voice of almost every bird and beast was represented, forming, altogether, such a confusion of sounds that it was a relief to place one's hands over one's ears.

"This highly interesting proceeding was most abruptly ended by the appearance of the officer of the day, who, as soon as he could make himself heard, informed us that such conduct was 'played out,' and that he should be obliged to arrest the whole crowd if it should be continued or repeated. This had the effect of producing a death-like stillness, and we soon fell asleep—on harder beds than we had ever before occupied.

"I was just dreaming of advancing stealthily upon a rebel masked battery when a loud report burst upon the air, shook the barracks, and caused me to spring up and strike my head against the bunk above with such force that the flash of a hundred cannon seemed to be exhibited to my startled senses. I opened my eyes and found all things bathed in the broad light of day. The report which had so suddenly interrupted my dreams of battle came from a six-pounder which was kept in camp, to be fired every morning at five o'clock.

"I arose and began to look for my inexpressibles; when lo! I discovered that I had them on. For the first time in my life I had slept a night without divesting myself of that article of apparel. It occurred to me that it was very convenient to arise without dressing, and I thought it would be still more convenient if one could get up already washed and his hair combed.

"My cogitations were interrupted by the voice of the first-sergeant, 'Fall in for roll call!'

"The reveille was now being played, and when the last tap of the drum had sounded, the roll was called. . . .

"Breakfast . . . consisted of coffee, bread, beefsteak, and potatoes. . . . [A free day followed.]

"Next day we were . . . inspected by a surgeon for the purpose

Union recruits at first muster

of ascertaining whether we were fit for the service. In order to be thoroughly examined, it was necessary that our clothes should be removed, that any defect might not remain unobserved. Then sundry gymnastic maneuvers had to be executed by each subject in turn, such as jumping upon a table or over a chair; kicking as high as the surgeon's head, and striking the backs of the hands together over the head, etc.

"When my turn came, I trembled lest the examining surgeon should detect the fact that I was affected with palpitation of the heart, for I was slightly afflicted with that disease. I executed the little maneuvers, however, with such alacrity that he observed no physical defect.

" 'You are a good, strong, active fellow,' he said, 'but . . . you are rather young. . . . Are you eighteen?'

" 'Yes, sir, indeed I am!'

" 'All right; you will pass.'

" 'Thank you!' And I sprang into my garments. . . .

"After all had been inspected, and several rejected, we were drawn up in line to be vaccinated. The surgeon passed slowly along the line, performing the operation upon the arm of each with some dispatch. He was scratching away at the arm of a slim, thin-faced young man called 'Watty' when I observed that same thin face grow, first very red, then white as a sheet; and for a few minutes he was quite sick and faint. One of our boys rallied him in the following manner—

" 'Watty, if you are so tender as that, you will never stand it to have your head lifted off by a shell. It would be the death of you.'

"A groan from Watty was the only reply. He certainly couldn't see the joke.

"The next thing administered to us was the oath. All the boys took it without the least hesitation. They had offered their services to the country, and they were in earnest. . . . We were sworn into the service of the State of Pennsylvania. . . .

"One evening it was announced to us that we were detailed for camp-guard for the following day, our captain to act as officer of the day. I was delighted at the prospect of having an opportunity of trying my hand at guard duty for the first time. . . .

"I chanced to be on the 'first relief.' Having been placed on post on the north side of the camp by the corporal of the guard, and a musket placed in my hands, I felt as proud as a king, and I remarked to myself that I certainly was a soldier now.

"Just without the camp, near my post, was our drill-ground,

and I was kept in continual merriment by observing the awkward motions of some of the companies on drill. In fact, some of the officers who acted as drill-masters were about as ignorant in the military line as the men they were endeavoring to teach.

"While I was watching the movements of a platoon which was being drilled by a youthful lieutenant, an incident occurred which struck me as being particularly ridiculous. The platoon had been standing at rest a few moments, when the lieutenant said—

" 'Now, boys, I should like to try you on a bayonet charge. Do you think you can do it up brown?'

"They all said they could. . . . They made an attempt to bring their muskets to the position of charge-bayonet, the points of their bayonets ranging from the height of the knee to the height of the head. The officer seemed to think it would do, and he said—

" 'Now for a charge. Forward! Double-quick! March!'

"The platoon made a rush right forward, placing the lieutenant . . . in imminent danger of being run through. In giving the command, it seemed he had forgotten that he was standing directly in front of his men. Now they were rushing at him with charged bayonets. He had not the presence of mind to command them to halt; so, under the impulse of the moment, he sprang backward and fell prostrate over a stump, while the men . . . rushed on, one or two . . . falling over the prostrate form of the lieutenant. That individual sprang up and cried out after his platoon—

" 'Oh . . . quit—stop! That is . . . halt!'

"But he was too late. In the excitement of the mock charge, the men either heard not, or heeded not. They kept straight on, and . . . broke up into a disorderly crowd, and . . . rushed right across the beat I was walking, and bolted into their quarters.

"The lieutenant followed presently, looking just the sheepishest mortal that I ever saw wearing shoulder straps. . . .

"Our regiment was [soon] ordered to Pittsburgh to encamp in the fairground—Camp Wilkins. . . . In Camp Wilkins . . . we had the satisfaction of drawing arms and uniforms. How nice our regiment looked standing in line with blue uniforms and bright muskets. Surely we were soldiers now, and we looked forward with eager anticipations to the time when we should be called upon to take the field."

14

Strife Invades Missouri

IN WASHINGTON, conditions had continued to improve. As explained by Lincoln's private secretary, John Nicolay:

"Day by day vessels arrived at Annapolis Harbor with volunteer regiments, with provisions and supplies for their maintenance, with war material for their equipment. These were transferred rapidly over the repaired railroad to Washington City, and it was not long before the National Capital resembled a great military camp.

"Troops found temporary lodgment in the various public buildings. Citizen recruits wrote letters home on the senators' desks, spouted bunkum for pastime from the members' seats in the House of Representatives, spread their blankets for bivouac in the ample corridors of the Patent Office. Clusters of tents filled the public squares. Regimental tactics, practice in platoon-firing and artillery-drill went on in the surrounding fields. Inspection and dress parade became fashionable entertainments. Military bands furnished unceasing open-air concerts. The city bloomed with national flags.

"The presence of an army brought an influx of civilians that at once perceptibly augmented the floating population. And this Yankee invasion of a sleepy Southern city gave Washington a baptism of Northern life, activity, business, trade, and enterprise, which, for the first time after half a century of sickly pining [the result of the dominating bickering over states' rights and slavery], made the metropolitan dreams of its founder a substantial hope and possibility."

Not all of the civilians drawn to the city were involved in improving its metropolitan status. Emma Edmonds, a woman of Canadian birth who was now a New Englander, came as a nurse.

"Soon after reaching Washington I commenced visiting the temporary hospitals which were prepared to receive the soldiers who arrived there sick. The troops came pouring in so fast, and the weather being extremely warm, all the general hospitals were soon filled, and it seemed impossible to prepare suitable, or comfortable, accommodations for all who required medical attention. . . .

"After walking through the streets . . . in search of one of those temporary hospitals, I would find a number of men there delirious with fever—others had been sunstruck and carried there—but no physician to be found in attendance. Then I would naturally come to the conclusion that the surgeons were all slack concerning their duty—but upon going to the office of the surgeon in charge of that department, would find that a certain number of surgeons were detailed every morning to visit those hospitals and were faithfully performing their duty; but that the number of hospitals and patients were increasing so fast that it required all day to make the tour. Consequently the last ones visited were obliged to wait and suffer—without any blame attaching to the surgeons.

"Then another great evil was to be remedied. There were thousands of sick men to be taken care of, but for these the Government had made no provision as regards more delicate kinds of food—nothing but hard bread, coffee, and pork, for sick and well alike. The Sanitary Commission had not yet come into operation, and the consequence was our poor sick soldiers suffered unspeakably from want of proper nourishment.

"I was speaking upon this subject one day to Chaplain B. and his wife—my constant companions in hospital labor—when Mrs. B. suggested that she and I should appeal to the sympathies of the ladies of Washington and Georgetown, and try our hand at begging. . . .

"We decided to go to Georgetown first . . . and commenced operations by calling . . . upon a clergyman's wife. . . . The lady . . . [gave] us an order on her grocer to the amount of five dollars. I gave Sister B. the credit for that, for I had introduced her as the wife of . . . [a] chaplain. . . . Then I suggested that we should separate for a few hours—she to take one street and I another, so that we might sooner get through the city.

"My next call was at a doctor's mansion, but I did not find the lady at home. However, I learned that the doctor . . . kept a drugstore nearby . . . and the consequence was half a dozen bottles of blackberry wine and two of lemon syrup, with a cordial invitation to call again.

"So prospered our mission throughout the day, and at the close of it we had a sufficient supply of groceries, brandy, ice, jellies, etc., to fill our little ambulance. And oh, what a change those little delicacies wrought upon our poor sick boys.

"We were encouraged by that day's work to continue our efforts in that direction, and finally made Dr. W.'s store a depot for the donations of those kind friends who wished to assist us in restoring to health the defenders of our beloved country."

Returning to narrator John Nicolay:

"Under the vast enlargement of military operations to which the defense and maintenance of the Government was now driven by inexorable events, the utility and employment of the three-month volunteers became necessarily limited and confined to a few local objects. The mature experience and judgment of General Scott [the commander-in-chief in Washington] decided that it would be useless, considering their very short term of service, to undertake . . . more. . . .

"Larger projects must be postponed [pending further] preparation. Ships must be improvised or built to enforce the blockade [of Southern ports declared by Lincoln]. A new army [with an enlistment period of three years] must be gathered to open the Mississippi and restore authority in the South.

"The rebels [in Maryland], though now seriously checked, were yet industriously working their local conspiracy . . . to secure the final complete insurrection and adhesion of that State. . . . But the Administration at Washington allowed them no time to gather strength . . . or draw any considerable supplies or help from Virginia. The President authorized General Scott to suspend the privilege of the writ of *habeas corpus* within certain limits [which meant that questionable Marylanders could be jailed without regard for their Constitutional rights]. . . .

"Annapolis was garrisoned and lightly fortified. A military guard was pushed along the railroad towards Baltimore simultaneously from the South and the North. And on May 13th General Butler, by a bold though entirely unauthorized movement, entered the city in the dusk of evening, while a convenient thunder-

storm was raging, with less than a thousand men, part of whom
were the now famous Massachusetts 6th [target of the Baltimore
riot], and during the night entrenched himself on Federal Hill.

"General Scott reprimanded the 'hazardous movement.' Nevertheless, the little garrison met no further molestation or attack.
And soon [it was] supported by other detachments, [and] open
resistance to the Government disappeared from the entire State.

"Independent regiments of Maryland volunteers entered the
Federal service. A sweeping political reaction also set in, demonstrating that the Union sentiment was largely predominant. . . .
The persistent secession minority and . . . local conspiracy were
effectually baffled, though not without constant vigilance."

Maryland citizen Bradley T. Johnson (destined for distin-

Raising the Stars and Stripes in Baltimore

guished service in the Confederate army) says that "social life in Baltimore was almost obliterated. Spies, male and female, of all social ranks, permeated everything. You could not tell whether the servant behind your chair at dinner, or the lady by your side whom you had taken to the table, were not in the employ of the Federal provost-marshal. But force never compels ideas, and hearts are beyond the power of bayonets. . . .

"Communication with Richmond was incessant and reliable. . . . And in one of the parlors of one of the greatest houses of the town, blazing with every luxury that wealth and culture could buy, one or two score beautiful women would meet, doors and windows sealed, to see the messenger and to hear the news from Dixie. . . .

"At one of these mystic meetings of the faithful . . . the messenger produced James R. Randall's grand war [poem], 'My Maryland.' It was read aloud, and reread, until sobs and inarticulate moans choked utterance.

"Hetty Cary was then in the prime of her first youth, with a perfect figure, exquisite complexion, the hair that Titian loved to paint, a brilliant intellect, grace personified, and a disposition the most charming. She was the most beautiful woman of the day, and perhaps the most beautiful that Maryland has ever produced. Her sister, Jenny Cary, was next to her in everything, but Hetty Cary had no peer.

"While this little coterie of beautiful women were throbbing over Randall's heroic lines, Hetty Cary said, 'That must be *sung*. Jenny, get an air for it!' And Jenny at the piano struck the chorus of the college song, '*Gaudeamus igitur*,' and the great war anthem, 'Maryland, My Maryland,' was born into the world.

"It went through the city like fire in the dry grass. The boys beat it on their toy drums, the children shrilled it at their play, and for a week all the power of the provost-marshal and the garrison and the detectives could not still the refrain—

> *The despot's heel is on thy shore,*
> *Maryland!*
> *His torch is at thy temple door,*
> *Maryland!*

for it was in the hearts of the people, and it was true!"

As for Hetty Cary, one of her friends liked to tell the story that

The despot's heel is on thy shore,
                Maryland!
His torch is at thy temple door,
                Maryland!

Avenge the patriotic gore
That flecked the streets of Baltimore,
And be the battle-queen of yore,
                Maryland! My Maryland!

Written in the Parish of Pointe Coupée,
La, April 1861 by

                James R. Randall

Facsimile of autographed copy of first stanza of Randall's poem

"on one occasion, when Federal troops were passing through Baltimore, she stood at an open window of her home and waved a Confederate flag. One of the officers of a regiment passing below noticed the demonstration and, calling it to the attention of the colonel, asked, 'Shall I have her arrested?'

"The colonel, glancing up and catching a glimpse of the vision of defiant loveliness, answered emphatically, 'No! She is beautiful enough to do as she damn pleases!' "

During the same days that Maryland was being won for the Union, the status of Missouri, another "border state," was causing special concern in Washington. The trouble had begun with the secession of South Carolina in December 1860. As related by Missourian Thomas L. Snead, a Southern sympathizer then serving as one of the state's administrative aides:

"The whole country was in the wildest excitement when the General Assembly of Missouri met at Jefferson City on the last day of the year. . . . It forthwith initiated measures for ranging Missouri with the South in the impending conflict. A State Convention was called; bills to organize, arm, and equip the militia were introduced; and the Federal Government was solemnly warned that if it sent an army into South Carolina, or into any other slaveholding State, in order to coerce it to remain in the Union, or to force its people to obey the laws of the United States, 'the people of Missouri would instantly rally on the side of such State to resist the invaders at all hazards and to the last extremity.'

"The most conspicuous leader of this movement was Claiborne F. Jackson, who had just been inaugurated Governor. . . . He was a true son of the South, warmly attached to the land that had given him birth, and to her people. . . . He was now nearly fifty-five years of age, tall, erect, and good-looking; kindhearted, brave, and courteous; a thoughtful, earnest, upright man. . . .

"In the city of St. Louis the United States had an arsenal within which were . . . 60,000 stand of arms [probably more like 40,000] and a great abundance of other munitions of war. . . . It was . . . more than a month after the inauguration of Lincoln before the Southern-rights men ventured to make any move in that direction. The Governor then came to St. Louis to concert with General D. M. Frost—who commanded a small brigade of volunteer militia—measures for seizing the arsenal in the name of the State."

It was at this time—a few days before the bombardment of Fort Sumter—that William T. Sherman arrived in St. Louis with his family to take the position of president of the Fifth Street Railroad.

"The road was well stocked and in full operation, and all I had to do was to watch the economical administration of existing affairs, which I endeavored to do with fidelity and zeal. But the whole air was full of wars and rumors of wars. The struggle was going on politically for the border States. . . . In Missouri . . . all the leading politicians were for the South in case of a war.

"The house on the northwest corner of Fifth and Pine was the rebel headquarters, where the rebel flag was hung publicly, and the crowds about the Planters' House were all more or less rebel. There was also a camp in Lindell's Grove, at the end of Olive Street, under command of General . . . Frost, a Northern man, a graduate of West Point, in open sympathy with the Southern

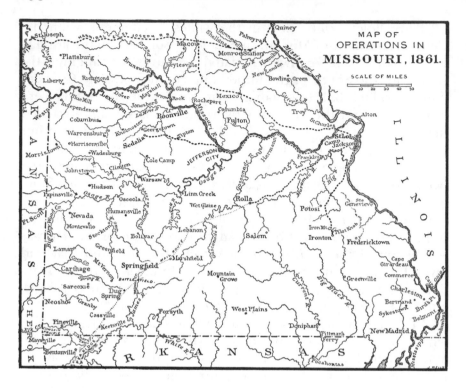

leaders. This camp was nominally a State camp of instruction, but, beyond doubt, was in the interest of the Southern cause, designed to be used against the national authority in the event of the General Government's attempting to coerce the Southern Confederacy.

"General William S. Harney was in command of the Department of Missouri, and resided in his own house, on Fourth Street, below Market; and there were five or six companies of United States troops in the arsenal, commanded by Captain [Nathaniel] Lyon. Throughout the city, there had been organized, almost exclusively out of the German part of the population, four or five regiments of Home Guards, with which movement Frank Blair . . . and others were . . . active on the part of the national authorities. Frank Blair's brother Montgomery was in the cabinet of Mr. Lincoln at Washington, and to him seemed committed the general management of affairs in Missouri.

"The newspapers fanned the public excitement to the highest pitch, and threats of attacking the arsenal, on the one hand, and the mob of damned rebels in Camp Jackson, on the other, were bandied about.

"I tried my best to keep out of the current, and only talked freely with a few men; among them Colonel John O'Fallon, a wealthy gentleman who resided above St. Louis. He daily came down to my office . . . and we walked up and down the pavement by the hour, deploring the sad condition of our country and the seeming drift toward dissolution and anarchy. I used also to go down to the arsenal occasionally to see Lyon . . . and others of my army acquaintance, and was glad to see them making preparations to defend their post. . . .

"The bombardment of Fort Sumter . . . was announced by telegraph. . . . We then knew that the war was actually begun, and though the South was openly, manifestly the aggressor, yet her friends and apologists insisted that she was simply acting on a justifiable defensive, and that in the forcible seizure of the public forts within her limits the people were acting with reasonable prudence and foresight."

When Abraham Lincoln's call for troops reached Missouri, Governor Jackson responded: "Your requisition, in my judgment, is illegal, unconstitutional, and revolutionary in its objects—inhuman and diabolical—and cannot be complied with. Not one man will the State of Missouri furnish to carry on such an unholy crusade."

Returning to Sherman's account:

"Later in that month [April] . . . a Dr. Cornyn came to our house on Locust Street one night after I had gone to bed, and told me he had been sent by Frank Blair, who . . . wanted to see me that night at his house. I dressed and walked over to his house on Washington Avenue, near Fourteenth. . . . Blair . . . told me that the Government was mistrustful of General Harney [the general was not disloyal, but he favored compromise over confrontation], that a change in the command of the department was to be made; that he held it in his power to appoint a brigadier-general and put him in command of the department, and he offered me the place. I told him I had once offered my services, and they were declined; that I had made business engagements in St. Louis which I could not throw off at pleasure; that I had long deliberated on my course of action, and must decline his offer, however tempting and complimentary. He reasoned with me, but I persisted."

Blair's next choice for the high command was Nathaniel Lyon, but the promotion was not given at once. Harney was temporarily off the scene, having been called to Washington, which left matters firmly in the hands of the Blair-Lyon team. An eager ally was found in the governor of the adjacent state of Illinois, Richard S. Yates, who was appalled at the thought of the Confederates gaining ascendancy so near his own domain.

The governor arranged to have a Mississippi steamer drop down the river from Alton, Illinois, to St. Louis, her mission to spirit away a good part of the arsenal's contents. To make things legal, the governor had armed the expedition's leader, Captain James H. Stokes, with a Washington-sanctioned requisition. Aided by Blair and Lyon and their troops, Stokes made the withdrawal during the night of April 25–26. The loaded steamer was ready to cast off by 2 A.M.

"Judge of the consternation of all hands," reported the Chicago *Tribune,* "when it was found that she would not move. The arms had been piled in great quantities around the engines . . . and the great weight had fastened the bows of the boat firmly on a rock. . . . Captain Stokes . . . called the arsenal men on board, and commenced moving the boxes to the stern. Fortunately, when about 200 boxes had been shifted, the boat fell away from the shore and floated in deep water. . . .

Nathaniel Lyon

Federals fortifying the arsenal at St. Louis

"Away they went . . . to Alton in the regular channel, where they arrived at 5 o'clock in the morning. When the boat touched the landing, Captain Stokes, fearing pursuit by some two or three of the secession military companies by which the city of St. Louis is disgraced, ran to the market-house and rang the fire-bell. The citizens came flocking pell-mell to the river in all sorts of habiliments.

"Captain Stokes informed them of the situation of things, and pointed out the [waiting railroad cars]. Instantly men, women, and children boarded the steamer, seized the freight, and clambered up the levees to the cars. Rich and poor tugged together with might and main for two hours, when the cargo was all deposited in the cars, and the train moved off, amid their enthusiastic cheers, for Springfield."

It hadn't been difficult for Blair, Lyon, and Yates to get the jump on Claiborne Jackson in his plan to seize the arsenal. The governor had been awaiting the arrival of some artillery pieces he had requisitioned from Jefferson Davis in Montgomery. These weapons—taken from a Federal arsenal in Louisiana—were only now on their way up the Mississippi (in crates labeled "Marble").

At the end of April, Blair and Lyon furthered their advantage by bolstering their arsenal troops with several thousand new volunteers. This meant that the secessionist troops under Jackson and D. M. Frost were now hopelessly outnumbered. (The spot at the edge of the city that these troops occupied was called "Camp Jackson," and it boasted a "Davis Avenue" and a "Beauregard Street.") The governor's artillery pieces reached him early in May, but they did him little good.

William T. Sherman was observing events:

"I remember going to the arsenal on the 9th of May, taking my children with me.... Within the arsenal wall were drawn up in parallel lines four regiments of the Home Guards, and I saw men distributing cartridges.... I also saw [Captain] Lyon running about with his hair in the wind, his pockets full of papers, wild and irregular.... I knew him to be a man of vehement purpose and of determined action. I saw of course that it meant business, but whether for defense or offense I did not know."

Lyon was planning to march upon Camp Jackson the following day. That afternoon he conducted a personal reconnaissance. As told by Confederate narrator Thomas Snead (who learned the story from Union sources):

"He attired himself in a dress and shawl . . . and, having completed his disguise by hiding his red beard and weather-beaten features under a thickly veiled sunbonnet, took on his arm a basket filled, not with eggs but with loaded revolvers [a precaution against discovery], got into a barouche . . . and was driven out to Camp Jackson and through it."

Lyon returned to the city with the conviction that he would have no trouble taking the camp.

Spending a few days in St. Louis at this time was Ulysses S. Grant, then working (in a civilian capacity) as a military recruiting agent. That evening Grant heard it whispered about that Lyon was preparing to take action.

"I went down to the arsenal in the morning to see the troops start out. I had known Lyon for two years at West Point, and in the old army afterwards. Blair I knew very well by sight . . . but I had never spoken to him. As the troops marched out of the enclosure around the arsenal, Blair was on his horse outside forming them into line, preparatory to their march. I introduced myself to him . . . and expressed my sympathy with his purpose."

Grant and Sherman knew each other only casually at this point, and did not meet that day. At about the time Grant was talking with Blair, Sherman was on his way to his railroad office.

"I . . . heard at every corner of the street that the 'Dutch' [Lyon's German troops] were moving on Camp Jackson. People were barricading their houses, and men were running in that direction. I hurried through my business as quickly as I could, and got back to my house on Locust Street by twelve o'clock. Charles Ewing and Hunter were there [Ewing was Sherman's brother-in-law, and John Hunter was Ewing's partner in a law firm], and insisted on going out to the camp to see 'the fun.' I tried to dissuade them, saying that in case of conflict the bystanders were more likely to be killed than the men engaged, but they would go.

"I felt as much interested as anybody else, but staid at home, took my little son Willie, who was about seven years old, and walked up and down the pavement in front of our house, listening for the sound of musketry or cannon in the direction of Camp Jackson. While so engaged, Miss Eliza Dean, who lived opposite us, called me across the street, told me that her brother-in-law, Dr. Scott, was a surgeon in Frost's camp, and she was dreadfully afraid he would be killed. I reasoned with her that [Captain] Lyon was a regular officer; that if he had gone out, as reported, to Camp Jackson, he would take with him such a force as would make resistance impossible. But she would not be comforted, saying that the camp was made up of the young men from the first and best families of St. Louis, and that they were proud, and would fight. I explained that young men of the best families did not like to be killed better than ordinary people.

"Edging gradually up the street, I was in Olive Street just about Twelfth, when I saw a man running from the direction of Camp Jackson at full speed, calling as he went, 'They've surrendered! They've surrendered!' So I turned back and rang the bell at Mrs. Dean's. Eliza came to the door, and I explained what I had heard. But she angrily slammed the door in my face! Evidently she was disappointed to find she was mistaken in her estimate of the rash courage of the best families.

"I again turned in the direction of Camp Jackson, my boy Willie with me still. At the head of Olive Street, abreast of Lindell's Grove, I found Frank Blair's regiment in the street, with ranks opened, and Camp Jackson's prisoners inside. A crowd of people was gathered around, calling to the prisoners by name, some hurrahing for Jeff Davis, and others encouraging the [Union] troops. Men, women, and children were in the crowd.

"I passed along till I found myself inside the grove, where I met

Ulysses S. Grant

Charles Ewing and John Hunter, and we stood looking at the troops on the road, [facing] toward the city. A band of music was playing at the head, and the column made one or two ineffectual starts, but for some reason was halted. [A] battalion of regulars was abreast of me, of which Major Rufus Saxton was in command, and I gave him an evening paper, which I had bought of the newsboy on my way out. He was reading from it some piece of news, sitting on his horse, when the column again began to move forward, and he resumed his place at the head of his command.

"At that part of the road, or street, was an embankment about eight feet high, and a drunken fellow tried to pass over it to the people opposite. One of the regular sergeant file-closers ordered him back, but he attempted to pass through the ranks, when the sergeant barred his progress with his musket 'a-port.' The drunken man seized his musket, when the sergeant threw him off with violence, and he rolled over and over down the bank.

"By the time this man had picked himself up and got his hat, which had fallen off, and had again mounted the embankment, the regulars had passed, and the head of Osterhaus's [German] regiment of Home Guards had come up. The man had in his hand a small pistol, which he fired off, and I heard that the ball had struck the leg of one of Osterhaus's staff. The regiment stopped; there was a moment of confusion, when the soldiers of that regiment began to fire over our heads in the grove.

"I heard the balls cutting the leaves above our heads, and saw several men and women running in all directions, some of whom were wounded. Of course, there was a general stampede.

"Charles Ewing threw Willie on the ground and covered him with his body. Hunter ran behind the hill, and I also threw myself on the ground. The fire ran back from the head of the regiment toward its rear, and as I saw the men reloading their pieces I jerked Willie up, ran back with him into a gulley which covered us, lay there until I saw that the fire had ceased and that the column was again moving on, when I took up Willie and started back for home round by way of Market Street.

"A woman and child were killed outright; two or three men were also killed, and several others were wounded. [Other accounts give the casualties in higher numbers.] The great mass of the people on that occasion were simply curious spectators, though men were sprinkled through the crowd calling out, 'Hurrah for Jeff Davis!' and others were particularly abusive of the 'damned Dutch.' "

Lyon soon began marching his prisoners toward the arsenal without interference.

As related by Ulysses S. Grant:

"Up to this time the enemies of the government in St. Louis had been bold and defiant, while the Union men were quiet but determined. . . . As soon as the news of the capture of Camp Jackson reached the city the condition of affairs was changed. . . . The Union men ordered the rebel flag taken down from the building on Pine Street . . . and it was taken down. . . . I witnessed the scene.

"I had heard . . . that the garrison [of Camp Jackson] was on its way to the arsenal. . . . I had seen the troops start out in the morning and had wished them success. I now determined to go to the arsenal and await their arrival and congratulate them.

"I stepped on a car [a horse-drawn public conveyance] standing at the corner of 4th and Pine Streets. . . . Before the car . . . had started, a dapper little fellow . . . stepped in. He was in a great state of excitement, and . . . turned to me saying, 'Things have come to a damned pretty pass when a free people can't choose their own flag. Where I come from if a man dares to say a word in favor of the Union we hang him to a limb of the first tree we come to.'

"I replied that 'after all we were not so intolerant in St. Louis as we might be; I had not seen a single rebel hung yet, nor heard of one; there were plenty of them who ought to be, however.'

"The young man subsided. He was so crestfallen that I believe if I had ordered him to leave the car he would have gone quietly out, saying to himself, 'More Yankee oppression.'

"By nightfall the late defenders of Camp Jackson were all within the walls of the St. Louis arsenal, prisoners of war."

The riot in St. Louis

But by that time, according to a writer for the St. Louis *Republican*, the city was in a turmoil:

"It is almost impossible to describe the intense exhibition of feeling which was manifested. . . . All the most frequented streets and avenues were thronged with citizens in the highest state of excitement, and loud huzzas and occasional shots were heard in various localities. Thousands upon thousands of restless human beings could be seen from almost every point on Fourth Street, all in search of the latest news.

"Imprecations loud and long were hurled into the darkening air, and the most unanimous resentment was expressed on all sides at the manner of firing into the harmless crowds near Camp Jackson. Hon. J. R. Barret, Major Uriel Wright, and other speakers addressed a large and intensely excited crowd in front of the Planters' House, and other well-known citizens were similarly engaged at various other points in the city.

"All the drinking saloons, restaurants, and other public resorts of similar character were closed by their proprietors, almost simultaneously, at dark; and the windows of private dwellings were fastened, in fear of a general riot. Theaters and other public places of amusement were entirely out of the question, and nobody went near them. Matters of graver import were occupying the minds of the citizens. . . .

"Crowds of men rushed through the principal thoroughfares, bearing banners and devices suitable to their several fancies, and by turns cheering and groaning. Some were armed and others were not armed, and all seemed anxious to be at work. A charge was made on the gun store of H. E. Dimick, on Main Street. The door was broken open, and the crowd secured fifteen or twenty guns before a sufficient number of police could be collected to arrest the proceedings. . . .

"Squads of armed policemen were stationed at several of the most public corners, and the offices of the *Missouri Democrat* and *Anzeiger des Westens* were placed under guard for protection."

The riot of May 10 was only the beginning of war-related violence in Missouri. (St. Louis, indeed, saw a similar riot on the following day.) But the prompt actions of Blair and Lyon had established a trend. Despite its strong ties with the South, the state would never succeed in making a total commitment to the Confederacy.

Three months after the St. Louis riots, however, the impetuous

Lyon, then a general, would be dead, a victim of the Battle of Wilson's Creek. (It must be noted that Lyon had said through life that it was his highest wish to die on the battlefield.)

Only three states followed Virginia during the second round of secessions: Arkansas, Tennessee, and North Carolina. Now numbering eleven states, the Confederacy had reached its greatest size. The border state of Kentucky, however, would (like Missouri) lend its partial support; and even Maryland, though firmly under Union control, would provide substantial numbers of troops.

15

Washington Takes the Offensive

O N THE EVENING of May 23, 1861, the North set in motion its first offensive against Virginia. In itself, the move was not a major one, but it had major implications. It was a clear-cut Union invasion of Confederate soil. Eight regiments and their supports—about ten thousand men—were ordered to cross the Potomac, some by bridge and some by boat, and occupy Alexandria and Arlington Heights. Only a few hundred Confederates stood in their way.

One of the Union regiments involved was the New York Fire Zouaves, made up of volunteer firemen who had marched from home with a set of colors given them by Mrs. John Jacob Astor. Their commander was Colonel Elmer E. Ellsworth, an exuberant and impulsive young man known and liked by President Lincoln himself. The unit wore a flamboyant uniform. Copied from a style in vogue in the French army, it was dominated by baggy red knickers and a red cap.

The Fire Zouaves had arrived in Washington lamenting the fact they'd been made to come by way of Annapolis. "We would have come through Baltimore," said one, "like a dose of salts." Another demanded to know the quickest route to the home of the Southern president. The regiment, he boasted, planned to secure Davis's scalp and tack it up in the White House. During their march through Washington to their quarters, the Zouaves passed a local fire company on the run to a fire, and they set up a great howl of recognition. The regiment was given a temporary berth on the third floor of a public building, and some of the men declined to

Zouave recruits in full regalia

make their egress by way of the staircase, preferring to fasten a rope at one of the windows and let themselves down in fireman fashion, or, according to an eyewitness, "like so many monkeys."

The Zouaves were soon assigned to a camp. Through a brash act of their commander, they came to great fame that night of May 23–24. As related by a special correspondent of the New York *Tribune:*

"It was generally understood in Washington on Thursday evening that an advance of some sort was contemplated, though the rumors fixed no exact time or point of assault. . . . As the night advanced, the slight fever of excitement which the half-authorized intelligence created wore away, and the city fell into its usual tranquillity. The contrast between its extreme quiet and the bustle which pervaded some of the expectant camps was very remarkable. . . .

"In . . . the Zouave camp [there were] unusual indications of busy preparation. . . . The night was peculiarly still and clear, and the moon . . . full and lustrous. . . . Above the slight murmur caused by the rustle of arms and the marching, a song would occasionally be heard, and once the whole regiment burst out into 'Columbia, the Gem of the Ocean' with all the fervor they could bring to it.

"It was not early when I reached the camp, but the exercise was still progressing under the vigilance of the colonel, who threw in now and then clear and energetic counsels for the guidance of his men. . . . Before midnight everything needful had been done, and the troops were scattered to their tents for two hours of rest.

"The colonel did not sleep until much later. He sat at his table completing the official arrangements which remained to him, and setting carefully before his subordinates the precise character of the duties they were to be charged with. After this he was alone, and I thought, as I entered his tent a little before he turned to his straw and blankets, that his pen was fulfilling a tenderer task than the rough planning of a dangerous exploit."

Ellsworth was writing a letter to his parents.

"The regiment is ordered to move across the river tonight. We have no means of knowing what reception we are to meet with. I am inclined to the opinion that our entrance into the city of Alexandria will be hotly contested. . . . Should this happen, my dear parents, it may be my lot to be injured in some manner. Whatever may happen, cherish the consolation that I was engaged in the performance of a sacred duty. . . . I am perfectly content to accept whatever my fortune may be, confident that He who noteth even the fall of a sparrow will have some purpose even in the fate of one like me. My darling and ever-loved parents, good-bye. God bless, protect, and care for you."

As continued by the *Tribune* correspondent:

"For more than an hour the encampment was silent. Then it began to stir again, and presently was all alive with action. At 2 o'clock, steamboats appeared off the shore, from one of which Captain [John A.] Dahlgren, the commander of the Navy Yard,

Elmer E. Ellsworth

came to announce that all was ready for the transportation. The men marched . . . to the beach. At this time the scene was animated in the highest degree. The vivid costumes of the men . . . the glittering rows of rifles and sabers, the woods and hills and the placid river . . . all . . . suffused with the broad moonlight, were blended in . . . novel picturesqueness. . . .

"The embarkation . . . was completed in less than two hours. The entire regiment, excepting the small guard necessarily left behind, nearly one thousand men, were . . . on their way down the river by 4 o'clock, just as the dawn began to shine over the hills and through the trees. . . .

"It had been thought possible that the rebels . . . might fire the bridge by which other regiments were to advance upon them. . . .

Nothing of this kind, however, had been attempted, and as we steamed down the river . . . there was no sign . . . that any inroad was provided against. . . . It was not until our boats were about to draw up to the wharf that our approach was noted in any way. . . . A few sentinels . . . fired their muskets in the air as a warning, and, running rapidly into the town, disappeared. Two or three of the Zouaves . . . discharged their rifles after the retreating forms, but no injury to anybody followed. . . . When we landed, about half-past 5 o'clock, the streets were . . . deserted. . . .

"Before our troops disembarked, a boat filled with armed marines and carrying a flag of truce put off from the *Pawnee* and landed ahead of us. From the officer in charge we learned that . . . the Rebels had consented to vacate. . . . This seemed to settle the question of a contest in the negative. . . .

"It certainly did not enter our minds . . . that a town half-waked, half-terrified, and under truce could harbor any peril for us. So the colonel gave some rapid directions for the interruption of the railway course by displacing a few rails near the depot, and then turned toward the center of the town to destroy the means of communication southward by the telegraph. . . . He was accompanied by Mr. H. J. Winser, military secretary to the regiment, the chaplain, the Rev. E. W. Dodge, and myself.

"At first he summoned no guard to follow him, but he afterward turned and called forward a single squad, with a sergeant, from the first company. We passed quickly through the streets, meeting a few bewildered travellers issuing from the principal hotel, which seemed to be slowly coming to its daily senses, and were about to turn toward the telegraph office when the colonel, first of all, caught sight of the secession flag which has so long swung insolently in full view of the President's house.

"He immediately sent back the sergeant with an order for the advance of the entire first company, and, leaving the matter of the telegraph office for a while, pushed on to the hotel, which proved to be the Marshall House, a second-class inn. On entering the open door the colonel met a man in his shirt and trousers, of whom he demanded what sort of flag it was that hung above the roof. The stranger, who seemed greatly alarmed, declared he knew nothing of it, and that he was only a boarder there.

"Without questioning him further, the colonel sprang up the stairs, and we all followed to the topmost story, whence, by means of a ladder, he clambered to the roof, cut down the flag with

Winser's knife, and brought it from its staff. There were two men in bed in the garret whom we had not observed at all when we entered, their position being somewhat concealed, but who now rose in great apparent amazement. . . .

"We at once turned to descend, Private [Francis E.] Brownell leading the way, and Colonel Ellsworth immediately following him with the flag. As Brownell reached the first landing-place [below the garret] . . . after a descent of some dozen steps, a man jumped from a dark passage, and, hardly noticing the private, levelled a double-barrelled gun square at the colonel's breast. Brownell made a quick pass to turn the weapon aside, but the fellow's hand was firm, and he discharged one barrel straight to its aim, the slugs or buckshot with which it was loaded entering the colonel's heart and killing him at the instant.

"I think my arm was resting on poor Ellsworth's shoulder at the moment. At any rate, he seemed to fall almost from my own grasp. He was on the second or third step from the landing, and he dropped forward with that heavy, horrible, headlong weight which always comes of sudden death inflicted in this manner.

"His assailant had turned like a flash to give the contents of the other barrel to Brownell, but either he could not command his aim or the Zouave was too quick with him, for the slugs went over his head and passed through the panels and wainscot of a door which sheltered some sleeping lodgers. Simultaneously with this second shot, and sounding like the echo of the first, Brownell's rifle was heard, and the assassin staggered backward.

"He was hit exactly in the middle of the face, and the wound . . . was the most frightful I ever witnessed. Of course Brownell did not know how fatal his shot had been, and so, before the man dropped, he thrust his saber-bayonet through and through the body, the force of the blow sending the dead man violently down the upper section of the second flight of stairs, at the foot of which he lay, with his face to the floor.

"Winser ran from above crying 'Who is hit?' but, as he glanced downward by our feet, he needed no answer.

"Bewildered for an instant by the suddenness of this attack, and not knowing what more might be in store, we . . . gathered together defensively. There were but seven of us altogether, and one was without a weapon of any kind.

"Brownell instantly reloaded, and while doing so, perceived the door through which the assailant's [second] shot had passed be-

Shooting of Ellsworth by Jackson

ginning to open. He brought his rifle to the shoulder and men-aced the occupants, two travellers, with immediate death if they stirred. The three other privates guarded the passages, of which there were quite a number converging to the point where we stood, while the chaplain and Winser looked to the staircase by which we had descended and the adjoining chambers. I ran down-stairs to see if anything was threatening from the story below, but it soon appeared there was no danger from that quarter.

"However, we were not at all disposed to move from our posi-tion. From the opening doors and through the passages, we dis-cerned a sufficient number of forms to assure us that we were dreadfully in the minority. I think now there was no danger, and that the single assailant acted without concert with anybody; but . . . it was certainly a doubtful question then.

"The first thing to be done was to look to our dead friend and leader. He had fallen on his face, and the streams of blood that flowed from his wound had literally flooded the way. The chaplain turned him gently over. . . . Winser and I lifted the body with all the care we could apply, and laid it upon a bed in a room nearby. The rebel flag, stained with his blood . . . we laid about his feet. It was at first difficult to discover the precise locality of his wound, for all parts of his coat were equally saturated with blood. By cautiously loosening his belt and unbuttoning his coat we found where the shot had penetrated. None of us had any medical knowledge, but we saw that all hope must be resigned.

"Nevertheless, it seemed proper to summon the surgeon as speedily as possible. This could not easily be done; for, secluded as we were in that part of the town, and uncertain whether an ambush might not be awaiting us also, no man could volunteer to venture forth alone; and to go together, and leave the colonel's body behind, was out of the question.

"We wondered at the long delay of the first company, for the advance of which the colonel had sent back before approaching the hotel; but we subsequently learned that they had mistaken a street and gone a little out of their way. Before they arrived we had removed some of the unsightly stains from the colonel's features, and composed his limbs. His expression in death was beautifully natural. . . .

"The detachment was heard approaching at last, [and] a reinforcement was easily called up, and the surgeon was sent for. His arrival, not long after, of course sealed our own unhappy belief.

"A sufficient guard was presently distributed over the house, but meanwhile I had remembered the colonel's earnestness about the telegraph seizure, and obtained permission to guide a squad of Zouaves to the office, which was found to be . . . deserted. . . . The men . . . [took] charge. I presume it was not wholly in order for me, a civilian, to start upon this mission; but I was the only person who knew the whereabouts of the office; and the colonel had been very positive about the matter.

"When I returned to the hotel, there was a terrible scene enacting. A woman had run from a lower room to the stairway where the body of the defender of the secession flag lay, and, recognizing it, cried aloud with an agony so heartrending that no person could witness it without emotion. She flung her arms in the air, struck her brow madly, and seemed in every way utterly abandoned to desolation and frenzy. . . . It was her husband that had been shot. He was the proprietor of the hotel. His name was James T. Jackson. . . .

"As the morning advanced, the townspeople began to gather in the vicinity, and a guard was fixed, preventing ingress and egress. This was done to keep all parties from knowing what had occurred, for the Zouaves were so devoted to their colonel that it was feared if they all were made acquainted with the real fact, they would sack the house. On the other hand, it was not thought wise to let the Alexandrians know, thus early, the fate of their townsman. The Zouaves were the only regiment that had arrived, and their head and soul was gone. Besides, the duties which the colonel had hurriedly assigned them . . . had scattered some companies in various quarters of the town.

"Several persons sought admission to the Marshall House, among them a sister of the dead man, who had heard the rumor but who was not allowed to know the true state of the case. It was painful to hear her remark, as she went away [believing her brother to be safe], that 'of course they wouldn't shoot a man dead in his own house about a bit of old bunting.'

"Many of the lodgers were anxious to go forth, but they were all detained. . . . All sorts of arguments and persuasions were employed, but the Zouave guards were inexorable.

"At about 7 o'clock a mounted officer rode up and informed us that the Michigan 1st had arrived and had captured a troop of rebels. . . . Not long after this, the surgeon made arrangements for the conveyance of Colonel Ellsworth's body to Washington. It was properly veiled from sight, and, with great tenderness, taken by a detachment of the Zouaves and the 71st New York Regiment—a small number of whom, I neglected to state, embarked in the morning at the Navy Yard and came down with us—to the steamboat, by which it was [taken] to the Navy Yard."

Even while the body was crossing to Washington, troops with entrenching tools were crossing from Washington to Virginia, their mission to fortify the captured approaches to the city. This work was important to the Northern cause, but the public's interest was centered on the death of Ellsworth.

As reported in the *New York Times* on May 26:

"Funeral ceremonies over the body of Colonel Ellsworth took place in Washington. The remains lay in state in the East Room of the President's house for several hours. Owing to the immense throng of anxious gazers on the remains of the deceased, the funeral cortege delayed moving from the Executive Mansion till near 1 o'clock.

"All along the line of Pennsylvania Avenue flags were displayed at half-mast and draped in mourning. Every available point, including the windows, balconies, and housetops, was thronged with anxious and sorrowful gazers. Various testimonials of respect were paid. All the bells of the city were tolled, and the heads of the soldiers . . . uncovered.

"Several companies of the City Corps, followed by the New York 71st Regiment Marines, and the local Cavalry Corps, formed the military escort, with their arms reversed and colors shrouded. The hearse was followed by a detachment of Zouaves, one of whom, the avenger of Colonel Ellsworth, carried the identical secession flag torn down by the deceased. Then followed the President [and his party]. . . . The rest of the procession was composed of carriages containing the captains of the Zouave regiment."

The body was taken to New York City, where it lay in state in the City Hall before being carried through the streets as part of another large, massively viewed procession. Interment was made at Mechanicville, a town on the upper Hudson.

The Ellsworth incident, of course, provided the North an excellent topic for patriotic versifying. These two stanzas appeared in one of the poems:

> *Columbia bends in sadness now*
> *　Above her gallant soldier's grave;*
> *Laurel and cypress deck the brow*
> *　Of the dead Zouave—so young, so brave.*
> *Cut down in manhood's brightest bloom—*
> *　Of his dear friends the hope and pride—*
> *He sleeps within an honored tomb*
> *　Who for his country bravely died.*
>
> *Brave Fire Zouaves! Your leader's name*
> *　Is left you for a battle cry;*
> *Let Ellsworth's pure and spotless fame*
> *　Lead you to conquer or to die.*
> *Strike bravely when the* rebel rag
> *　Shall meet your eyes on Southern plain.*
> *Strike till Columbia's starry flag*
> *　O'er this whole land shall wave again!*

For a Southern view of the North's first offensive, we'll turn to the Richmond *Examiner:*

"Virginia is invaded. That horde of thieves, robbers, and assassins in the pay of Abraham Lincoln, commonly known as the army of the United States, have rushed into the peaceful streets of a quiet city of the State and stained the hearth of Virginia homes with the blood of her sons. Alexandria has been captured without resistance, for none had been prepared.

"The city was left—perhaps with strategic reason—without a picket guard, and no attempt has ever been made to blow up or batter down the bridge across the Potomac River over which the troops of Lincoln marched to it.

"One trait of true heroism has signalized this unhappy affair. A citizen of Alexandria named Jackson lacked the prudence to haul down the flag of his country, which streamed over his dwelling. That band of execrable cutthroats and jailbirds known as the Zouaves of New York, under the chief of all scoundrels called Colonel Ellsworth, surrounded the house of this Virginian and broke open the door to tear down the flag of the South.

"The courageous owner of that house neither fled nor submitted. He met the favorite hero of every Yankee there in his hall, he alone against thousands, and shot him through the heart!

"As a matter of course, the magnanimous soldiery surrounded him and hacked him to pieces with sword-bayonets—on the spot, in his own violated home. But he died a death which emperors might envy, and his memory will live in history and in the hearts of his countrymen, through endless generations.

"Here, indeed, was courage! He stood by his flag, he fell alone in defense of his hearth, and taught the invader what soil he trod on.

"Apart from the sufferings of our devoted countrymen in Alexandria, the capture of the city in itself is not important."

A correspondent writing in Montgomery, Alabama, then still the Confederate capital, found a deeper meaning in the Northern act.

"The mere taking of a deserted and exposed village is in itself nothing; but when regarded as indicative of the future policy of the old Government it at once becomes a question pregnant with great importance. Mr. Lincoln has declared in his proclamation, and at various other times reiterated the expression that the only object his Government had in view was the retaking and the reoccupation of what he asserted to be Government property; but now, in the face of his promise, which has gone before the world, he converts his Abolition horde into an army of invasion, and now occupies a city within the boundaries of our Republic.

"This Government [that of the South] has no longer an election. Its duty is now manifest to all. The nation must rise as a man and drive the hireling miscreants from a soil polluted by the foulness of their tramp."

Alexandria diarist Judith McGuire and her husband (residents of a suburban area) had remained in their home until the day the town was occupied. On the following day, May 25, Judith wrote:

"The . . . suspense is at an end. Alexandria and its environs, including, I greatly fear, our home, is in the hands of the enemy. Yesterday morning, at an early hour, as I was in my pantry putting up refreshments for the barracks preparatory to a ride to Alexandria, the door was suddenly thrown open by a servant, looking wild with excitement, exclaiming, 'Oh, madam . . . Alexandria is filled with Yankees!'

" 'Are you sure, Henry?' said I, trembling in every limb.

" 'Sure, madam! I saw them myself . . . and saw our men going to the cars.'

" 'Did they get off?' I asked, afraid to hear the answer.

" 'Oh, yes. The cars went off full of them, and some marched out. And then I went to King Street, and saw such crowds of Yankees coming in! They came down the turnpike, and some came down the river. . . . I came home as fast as I could.'

"I lost no time in seeking Mr. [McGuire], who hurried out to hear the truth of the story. He soon met Dr. ——, who . . . more than confirmed Henry's report, and gave an account of the tragedy at the Marshall House. Poor Jackson, the proprietor, had always said that the Confederate flag which floated from the top of his house should never be taken down but over his dead body. . . . Jackson leaves a wife and children. I know the country will take care of them. He is the first martyr. I shudder to think how many more there may be.

"The question with us was, what was next to be done? Mr. [McGuire] had voted for secession, and there were Union people enough around us to communicate everything of the sort to the Federals. The few neighbors who were left were preparing to be off, and we thought it most prudent to come off too. Pickets were already thrown out . . . and they were threatening to arrest all secessionists.

"With a heavy heart I packed trunks and boxes, as many as our little carriage would hold . . . locked up everything; gave the keys to the cook, enjoining upon the servants to take care of the cows, Old Rock [a horse], the garden, the flowers, and . . . J——'s splendid Newfoundland [presumably the pet of an absent son]. Poor dog, as we got into the carriage, how I did long to take him!

"When we took leave of the servants, they looked sorrowful, and we felt so. . . . Mr. [McGuire] said, as he looked out upon the green lawn just before we set off, that he thought he had never seen the place so attractive. . . . The bright flowers we had planted seemed in full glory. . . . In bitterness of heart I exclaimed, 'Why must we leave thee, Paradise?' And for the first time my tears streamed.

"As we drove by the Seminary, the few students who remained came out to say good-bye. . . . When we got to Bailey's Crossroads, Mr. [McGuire] said to me that we were obliged to leave our home, and as far as we have a *right* to any other, it makes not the slightest difference which road we take—we might as well drive to the right hand as to the left; nothing remains to us but the barren, beaten

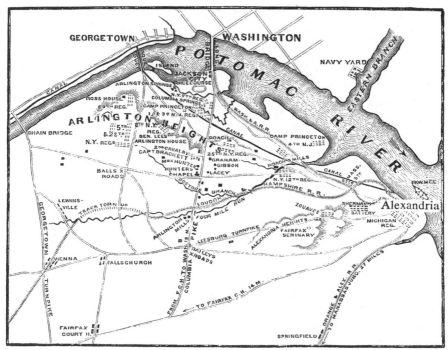

Washington's first defenses on Virginia side of Potomac

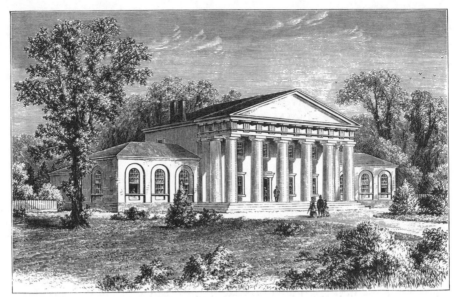

Arlington House

track. It was a sorrowful thought. But we have kind relations and friends whose doors are open to us. . . . The South did not bring on the war, and I believe that God will provide for the homeless.

"About sunset we drove up to the door of . . . the house of our relative [in Fairfax Courthouse], the Rev. Mr. B., and were received with the warmest welcome."

In the same area at this time was Mrs. Robert E. Lee, who had abandoned historic Arlington House, the Lee property up the Potomac from Alexandria. Mrs. Lee was now at Ravensworth, the home of an aunt. From Richmond, Robert E. Lee wrote his wife: "I sympathize deeply in your feelings at leaving your dear home. . . . I do not think it prudent or right for you to return there while the United States troops occupy that country." Arlington House, in truth, had been lost to the Lees forever.

Among the residents of the Alexandria region who had chosen to remain in their homes was Miss E. V. Mason, who recounts:

"No Virginian thought it possible . . . that the brothers with whom we had always held affectionate intercourse, with whom we had married and intermarried, could invade our quiet homes. . . . [We became] prisoners in these homes and must have permission to pass in and out of them. There must be a pass for the cow to go to pasture, another for the horse to be shod, a third to go to the postoffice, a fourth to go to church, another for town, and so on interminably. . . .

"But though we were forced to have passes to get out, there needed no permission for those who wished to get in to us. Half a dozen soldiers would enter while we were at breakfast, clear off the table, drink all the milk in the cellar, dig our potatoes from the garden and cook them with the wood from our fences or out-houses. We were never safe from these intruders. . . . They helped themselves to our gold thimbles and earrings, rummaged our drawers under pretense of looking for arms (we were four un-protected females), and took what they liked. Our days were spent in hiding from these wretches, and our nights were passed in hopeless terror behind barricades of tables, chairs, wardrobe and piano, which were piled before doors and windows."

Not all of the region's females held the Yankees in dread. An unidentified observer, "A Virginian," tells this story:

"There lived on the turnpike, a short distance from town, two large, raw-boned young women who supported themselves by taking in washing. They were very pronounced in their Southern sentiments, and shared in the irritable feeling of the community at the presence of the Federal troops. One of them had occasion one day to go into Alexandria, but she had neglected to provide herself with a pass. The sentinel stopped her and told her she could not go on. She declared that go she would; and when he, with perhaps unnecessary roughness, reiterated his negative, she indignantly seized his gun (the sentinel being about half her size), threw it over the fence, knocked him down, and, after scratching him vigorously, took her triumphant way into the town. She went straight to the colonel there, and reported the unfortunate delin-quent; and this officer, doubtless entering into the humor of the situation, declared if she did not think the soldier sufficiently punished he would inflict some penalty on him himself."

16

A New Role for Richmond

DURING THE SAME DAYS in May that saw the Federals take possession of the Alexandria-Arlington line, Virginia was made to feel the beginnings of pressure at another spot, about a hundred and fifty miles to the southeast. Here, at the tip of her "peninsula" (the region between her York and James rivers), lay Fort Monroe, a federal installation overlooking the waters of Hampton Roads at the mouth of the Chesapeake.

Union land and naval forces had managed to take a firm grip on this highly strategic fort, and on May 22 General Benjamin Butler, recently of Maryland, was made its commander. Butler's first act was to order a reconnaissance out about three miles to the village of Hampton, held by two hundred loosely organized and poorly equipped militiamen.

One of the civilian residents was a woman named Lee Hampton, who relates:

"Upon the evening of the 23rd of May ... [the town] was thrown into a state of tumult by the announcement of the picket on duty that a regiment of United States troops was approaching, supported by a battery of six field pieces! The citizens rushed forward en masse, armed with any weapon they could find to repel the invaders. . . .

"At length the matter was compromised by mutual pledges that no violence should be committed on either side, and . . . the Federal troops marched into town. . . . Murmurs, not loud but deep, were heard on every side, and the excited citizens could with difficulty restrain their wrath, but . . . the excitement was soon quelled by the countermarching of the troops."

Fort Monroe

Butler's reconnaissance was only a prelude to his inflammation of the Virginians of the region. His next offense—the result of happenstance rather than of plan—involved their slaves.

As explained by the Boston *Journal*'s man in the field, Charles Carleton Coffin:

" 'The cornerstone of the Confederacy is African slavery,' said Alexander H. Stephens, Vice President of the Confederacy.

" 'Our Negroes will do the shoveling while our brave cavaliers will do the fighting,' said one of the Richmond newspapers.

"But before a battle had been fought the cornerstone began to crumble.

"The slaveholders around Norfolk and Hampton . . . sent their slaves with shovels to throw up fortifications. Some of the slaves, watching their opportunity when night came, crept through the woods, swam rivers, and made their way to Fortress Monroe. . . . The slaves knew instinctively that the Union soldiers were their friends. . . . They comprehended the meaning of this gathering of armies—that it was a war between slavery and freedom.

"One slave named Luke made his way to Fortress Monroe and became a servant to [a] Captain Tyler. Luke's owner . . . came to get him. . . . The Negroes in the camp heard of it, and were much excited. Luke, with tears upon his cheeks, came to Captain Tyler. [The captain said,] 'I don't think that you will be sent back, for General Butler has not any authority to send you.'

"A moment ago the Negroes were weeping and moaning, but now they were wild with joy. The news spread. General Butler heard of it, and ordered Captain Tyler to appear before him.

" 'I understand, sir,' said the general, 'that you have been telling the Negroes that they can't be sent back to their masters. Now, sir, I want to know by what authority you have told them so.'

" 'By the authority of common sense.'

" 'What do you mean by that, sir?'

" 'The case is this: Luke's former master sent him to work on the Confederate fortifications. That act made Luke contraband of war, and liable to be confiscated to the United States in case he should ever be found within our lines, either by his own act or by the advance of our troops. While thus employed, he escaped to our lines. . . . His master cannot demand him, for he held him only as property, and employed that property in acts of war against the United States. . . . Luke, as property, is contraband of war, and confiscated to the United States. . . .'

" 'Slaves are contraband of war' was the proclamation made by General Butler [who, it seems, had been thinking in these terms on his own, the interview merely reinforcing his conclusions], and sent out from Fortress Monroe.

"Never had the men who laid their plans to build the Confederacy and perpetuate slavery dreamed that the institution, before a battle had been fought, would begin to settle from its foundations. They began to see that military law was far different from civil law. . . . The . . . planters went sadly back to their homes. Thousands of dollars' worth of property had walked away, nor was there any law by which they could recover it."

General Butler soon had several hundred "contrabands" at Fort Monroe. As an experiment, a party of sixty-four, promised a modest wage, was assigned to help with the construction of earthworks. According to the Union officer in charge of the experiment:

"The contrabands worked well, and in no instance was it found necessary . . . to urge them. . . . Some days they worked with our soldiers, and it was found that they did more work, and did the nicer parts—the facings and dressings—better. There was one striking feature in the contrabands which must not be omitted. I did not hear a profane or vulgar word spoken by them during my superintendence, a remark which it will be difficult to make of any sixty-four white men, taken anywhere in our army."

Though not written into Union law, the policy that Ben Butler adopted toward fugitive slaves was to be widely followed through-out the war. And these blacks would ever be known as "contra-bands."

On May 27, in order to expand the Union's staging area at the tip of the peninsula, Butler sent troops by boat from Fort Monroe to Newport News, about eight miles up the coast. The village of Hampton lay between the fort and Newport News, and the Yan-kee move, according to Lee Hampton, "rendered Hampton un-tenable and made it necessary to evacuate the town before all chance of retreat was cut off. . . .

"The exodus was universal. Every available means of trans-portation was seized upon to convey the distressed women and children to the neighboring towns of York and Williamsburg. Their altars and firesides were deserted, and the homesteads of . . . centuries abandoned. They stopped not to save their most precious relics. The old portraits were left hanging on the walls—afterwards to be hacked by ruthless swords; the family china was not taken from the closet, nor even the sweetmeats from the pantry.

"And this recalls a letter written by a dainty old maiden lady [a

General Butler defining blacks as "contraband of war"

Contrabands on their way to work

refugee from Hampton who learned what had happened to her house]. . . . After describing the vandalism, which broke up all the furniture, cut the piano into pieces with an axe, and shattered the cut-glass, she adds, waxing yet more indignant as she reaches what she considers the climax of all this iniquity, 'and God forgive them! They smeared preserves all over the carpets!' "

According to one of Ben Butler's regimental commanders, Joseph B. Carr of the 2nd New York, the controversial general was growing quite comfortable in his new job:

"He developed remarkable ability in civil organization, and showed courage and determination in any project in which he was interested. While just and even generous in dealing with the men in his department, his manner was decidedly autocratic. He rarely tolerated conduct savoring of insubordination, and yet under peculiar circumstances he overlooked it.

"On one occasion, when residents were complaining of acts of vandalism, Butler was informed that a certain regiment was guilty. Lieutenant Butler, the general's nephew, then quite young, was sent to summon the colonel of the regiment. Entering the colonel's tent, he said, 'Colonel, Uncle Ben wants you, and is going to give you hell!'

" 'Who is Uncle Ben?' inquired the colonel.

" 'Why, General Butler!'

" 'Very well, I will attend; but not to *get hell,* young man. I did not come here for that purpose.'

" 'That's right!' said the lieutenant. 'I like to see men who are not afraid of Uncle Ben!'

"Entering General Butler's quarters, the colonel saluted and said, 'You sent for me, General?'

" 'Sit down, sir!' roared the exasperated chief. Then, wheeling in his chair, the general recited the crimes charged, and, concluding, said, 'I'll send your whole regiment to the Rip-Raps [a lonely isle in the waters of Hampton Roads]. What have you to say, sir, in your defense?'

"The colonel, now as angry as his chief, rose and said, 'I have this to say: Any man who says that my men are guilty of the crimes you enumerate, lies, sir!'

" 'Do you dare to tell *me* that I lie?' roared the general.

" 'I tell you or any man uttering the charges that he lies,' was the reply.

"General Butler stared at the colonel for a few seconds. Then, taking a cigar from his pocket, tendered it to the colonel, saying, 'Smoke, Colonel, and we will talk of this matter later.'

"General Butler showed no further resentment, but thereafter favored the colonel. Events proved that the regiment was innocent of the crimes charged."

The Union movements inside Virginia's borders were of particular concern to Robert E. Lee, in his position as the state's top military commander. His job had assumed a new dimension on May 20, when word came from Montgomery that the Confederacy's capital was to be transferred to Richmond.

According to the general's nephew, Fitzhugh Lee (who not only fought through the war under his illustrious uncle but also became one of his biographers):

"The sagacity, skill, and experience of Lee were taxed to the uttermost equipping and sending to threatened points the troops rapidly arriving from the South. There was no regular army to serve as a nucleus, or navy, commissary, quartermaster's, or ordnance departments. Everything had to be provided. . . . Raw re-

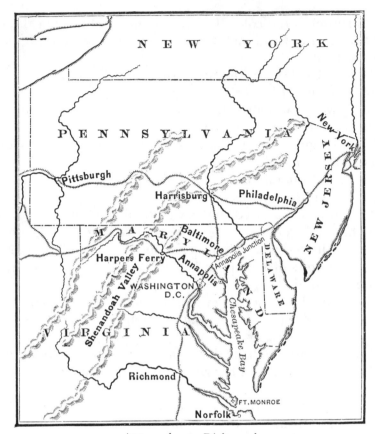

Approaches to Richmond

cruits had to be drilled and disciplined, companies assigned to regiments, regiments to brigades, brigades to divisions.

"With the map of Virginia before him, Lee studied to make a successful defensive campaign. He knew that the object of the greatest importance to his enemy was the capture of Richmond, and that the fall of that city early in the contest might terminate the war. His genius for grand tactics and strategy taught him at once that the most natural advance to Richmond from Washington would be along the Orange and Alexandria Railroad. . . . It was the only railway running into the State at that time from Washington, and troops moving along its line could be so directed as not to uncover their capital, while prompt facilities could be obtained for transportation of supplies from the base established at Alexandria. . . .

"Another route lay up the peninsula lying between the James

and York Rivers, with Fort Monroe and its vicinity as a base for operations. Another way to enter the State was by crossing the upper Potomac at Harpers Ferry and Williamsport, and then on through the great valley of Virginia between the Blue Ridge and Shenandoah Mountains; and still another entrance might be effected through the mountain ranges of West Virginia. Norfolk, too, by the sea, had to be watched and protected.

"Troops, therefore, as fast as they arrived in Richmond and could be prepared for the campaign, were sent principally to these points. It was necessary that organized forces should be in such position as to check any forward movements by any of these routes.

"General Lee early had predicted the march of the Army of the Potomac, as the Washington army was called, and pointed out what would in all probability be the battlefield. He ordered the largest number of troops to Manassas Junction, that being the point of union of the railroad coming into Virginia from Washington with a branch road leading into the Valley of Virginia. It was a strategic point because [a Confederate] army in position there would be able to resist the further progress of the opposing hosts, and could, if necessary, reinforce the troops in the Valley [or could, if severely threatened itself, request assistance from these troops]."

There had been a change of command in the Valley—or, more precisely, at Harpers Ferry. Colonel Thomas Jackson was replaced by an officer of higher rank, a fifty-two-year-old brigadier general named Joseph Eggleston Johnston, who had seen wide service in

Joseph E. Johnston

the federal military before his defection. Short, slim, and dapper, Johnston was a Virginian of distinguished lineage. He was a grandnephew of Patrick Henry, and the sword he wore had been carried by his father in the American Revolution. Johnston was an officer of superior ability, but he usually opted for caution over boldness.

As for Thomas Jackson, he was kept at Harpers and given command of a brigade.

There was a battalion of Marylanders with the Harpers troops, and they found their situation to be different from that of the others. One of their leaders (a captain at the time) was the dedicated Bradley T. Johnson, who explains:

"They had rushed off from home, fired by the enthusiasm of those days in Baltimore, had stolen rides on the cars or had walked to Point of Rocks and to Harpers Ferry, where they were fed. Provisions were plenty, but they had no clothes, blankets, tents, cooking utensils—nothing that soldiers need and must have to be of any service. They had no government to appeal to for arms. In fact, they were outlaws from their own State government. They were too proud to go back home; stay and fight they would and must. All around them were warmhearted comrades who shared their blankets with them at night and their rations by day.

"Unless something could be done to keep them together, unless they could be armed, equipped, and legally organized, they must inevitably dissolve, be absorbed in surrounding commands, and thus Maryland lose her main hope and best chance to be represented by her own sons, bearing her flag in the army of the Confederate States.

"At this crisis Mrs. Bradley T. Johnson [wife of the narrator] came forward and offered to go to North Carolina and apply there for arms and equipment. She was the daughter of the Hon. Romulus M. Saunders, for a generation a leading and distinguished member of Congress from North Carolina, and . . . minister plenipotentiary and envoy extraordinary to Spain. . . . His young daughters were with him and were introduced to court and presented to the queen. . . .

"Mrs. Johnson was then in the prime of her youth, handsome, graceful, accomplished. She had left her comfortable home in Frederick with her little boy, a lad five years old, to follow her husband. She now volunteered to serve him. She was the only hope of Maryland. . . .

"On May 24, 1861, she left the camp . . . escorted by Capt. Wilson Carey Nicholas . . . and Second-Lieut. G. M. E. Shearen . . . to go to Raleigh via Richmond. At Leesburg they found that Alexandria had that day been occupied by the Federals and thus communication southward cut. Returning, she and her staff went up to Harpers Ferry and thence by Winchester and Strasburg and Manassas Junction to Richmond and Raleigh, where she arrived on the night of the 27th.

"The next morning, accompanied by her father and her escort, she applied to Gov. Thomas H. Ellis and the Council of State for arms for her husband and his men. There were on that council some plain countrymen, in their homespun, but they bore hearts of gold.

"It was a picturesque incident. Here this elegant, graceful, refined young lady, whose family was known to every man of them, and to some of whom she was personally known—there the circle of grave, plain old men taking in every word she uttered, watching every movement. . . .

"She said, 'Governor and gentlemen, I left my husband and his comrades in Virginia. They have left their homes in Maryland to fight for the South, but they have no arms, and I have come to my native State to beg my own people to help us. Give arms to my husband and his comrades, so that he can help you!'

" 'Madam,' said one of the council, old, venerable, and gray-haired, slapping his thigh with a resounding blow, 'Madam, you shall have everything that this State can give.'

"And the order was made then and there . . . that she should be supplied with five hundred Mississippi rifles and ten thousand cartridges, with necessary equipments. This at the time when, in the language of the day, every cartridge was worth a dollar.

"But her visit and her errand lighted the greatest enthusiasm among her fellow countrymen. The Constitutional Convention of North Carolina was then in session. . . . The members of it called a meeting at night in the capitol. . . . The meeting was held in the hall of the House of Commons . . . and was attended with great enthusiasm. The cause of the Marylanders was espoused with ardor, the meeting making a liberal contribution of money on the spot. Hon. Kenneth Raynor, ex-member of Congress, addressing the meeting, said:

" 'If great events produce great men—so, in the scene before us, we have proof that great events produce great women. . . .

One of our own daughters, raised in the lap of luxury, blessed with the enjoyment of all the elements of elegance and ease, had quit her peaceful home, followed her husband to the camp, and, leaving him in that camp, has come to the home of her childhood to seek aid for him and his comrades, not because he is her husband, but because he is fighting the battles of his country against a tyrant.'

"He paid a high tribute to the patriotism and love of liberty which eminently characterized the people of Maryland.

" 'They are fighting our battles,' he said, 'with halters round their necks.'

"On the 29th Mrs. Johnson left Raleigh with her escort and her arms, and her route was a continued ovation. At every town, at every station, the people had gathered to see the woman who was arming her husband's regiment, and they overwhelmed her with enthusiasm. . . .

"At Petersburg a substantial sum of money was handed to her, and, stopping at Richmond, she procured from John Letcher, governor of Virginia, a supply of camp kettles, hatchets, axes, etc., and, with money in her hands, ordered forty-one wall tents made at once.

"On the 31st of May she left Richmond with her arms, ammunition, and supplies. At Manassas . . . [she received] an order to take any train she might find necessary for transportation. . . . She rode in the freight car on her boxes of rifles . . . and . . . after an absence of ten days from camp she returned and delivered to her husband the results of her energy, devotion, and enthusiasm. . . . [The] incident . . . thrilled that army through every rank and fiber."

By this time the capital of the Confederacy had been transferred to Richmond. Jefferson Davis left Montgomery by special train during the last week in May. In a state of exhaustion from anxiety and overwork, he spent most of the trip in bed; but he rallied by the time he reached the new capital.

"He was received with an outburst of enthusiasm," says Richmond citizen Sarah Putnam. "A suite of handsome apartments had been provided for him at the Spotswood Hotel until arrangements could be made for supplying him with more elegant and suitable accommodations. Over the hotel, and from the various windows of the guests, waved numerous Confederate flags; and the rooms destined for his use were gorgeously draped in the

The Capitol at Richmond

Confederate colors. In honor of his arrival, almost every house in the city was decorated with the Stars and Bars.

"An elegant residence for the use of Mr. Davis was soon procured. It was situated in the western part of the city, on a hill overlooking a landscape of romantic beauty. This establishment was luxuriously furnished, and there Mr. and Mrs. Davis dispensed the elegant hospitalities for which they were ever distinguished. . . .

"Mrs. Davis is a tall, commanding figure, with dark hair, eyes, and complexion, and strongly marked expression, which lies chiefly in the mouth. With firmly set yet flexible lips, there is indicated much energy of purpose and will, but beautifully softened by the usually sad expression in her dark, earnest eyes. She may justly be considered a handsome woman, of noble mien and bearing, but by no means coming under the description of the feminine adjective 'pretty.' Her manners are kind, graceful, easy, and affable, and her receptions were characterized by the dignity and suavity which should very properly distinguish the drawing-room entertainments of the Chief Magistrate of a republic.

"There was now work for everyone to do. The effects of the blockade of our ports was very early felt. The numberless and

Mrs. Jefferson Davis

nameless articles for which we depended upon foreign markets were either to be dispensed with or to be manufactured from our own industry and ingenuity. With a zeal as commendable as that which answered the call to arms . . . the people set themselves to work to meet the demands made by the exigencies of the times.

"Troops continued to pour into Richmond . . . without the necessary uniform or equipments to send them to the field. Our ladies engaged to prepare them properly for the work upon which they were committed to enter. Sewing societies were multiplied, and those who had formerly devoted themselves to gaiety and fashionable amusement found their only real pleasure in obedience to the demands made upon their time and talents in providing proper habiliments for the soldiers. . . .

"They very soon became adepts in the manufacture of the different articles which compose the rough and simple wardrobe of the soldier. To these . . . they took delight in adding various other articles. . . . There were very few of the soldiers who were not furnished with a neat thread-case supplied with everything necessary to repair his clothing when absent from a friendly pair of hands which would do it for him; a visor to shield his face from the too fierce heat of the summer sun or to protect him from the cold of winter; a warm scarf and a Havelock.

"The sewing operations were varied by the scraping of lint [the preparation of cotton], the rolling of bandages, and the manufacture of cartridges, and many things unnecessary to mention, but which were the work of the women. . . . They employed themselves cheerfully upon anything necessary to be done. Heavy tents of cumbrous sailcloth, overcoats, jackets, and pantaloons of stiff, heavy material, from the sewing on which they were frequently found with stiff, swollen, bleeding fingers, were nevertheless perseveringly undertaken. . . .

"The usual routine of social life in Richmond had undergone a complete change. It had become a very rare occurrence to meet a young man of the usual age for military duty in the garb of a citizen. Indeed, it became remarkable; and for the sake of their reputation, if for no other or higher motive, it grew into a necessity for our young men to attach themselves in some capacity to the army.

"We were awakened in the morning by the reveille of the drum, which called the soldiers to duty, and the evening 'taps' reminded us of the hour for rest. At all hours of the day, the sounds of martial music fell upon our ears, and the 'tramp, tramp' of the soldiers through the streets was the accompaniment. Nothing was seen, nothing talked of, nothing thought of, but the war in which we had become involved. . . .

"As regiment after regiment passed through our streets, on their way to the theaters of active engagement, cheerful adieus were waved from every window . . . and bright smiling faces beamed in blessing on the soldier—but heavy hearts were masked beneath those smiles. . . .

"An old lady, the mother of several dearly loved sons, but echoed the almost universal sentiment when she said . . . 'War, I know, is very dreadful, but if, by the raising of my finger, I could prevent my sons from doing their duty to their country now, though I love them as my life, I could not do it. . . . They must go if their country needs them.' . . .

"The change wrought in the appearance of Richmond can only be understood by those who daily witnessed the stirring scenes which were occurring. One excitement had not time to subside before a fresh cause presented itself.

"The arrival [from Charleston] of General Beauregard, who had become the prominent hero of the people, called forth the most hilarious demonstrations of admiration for his bravery, and the most profound respect for his acknowledged genius. For a long distance, before the train of cars which bore him reached the depot in Richmond, the road was lined with crowds who pressed forward to get a look at the wonderful man of Fort Sumter.

"Loud cheers greeted him, bands of music discoursed the popular and now national air, 'Dixie,' and a speech was loudly called for as he descended from the cars. But, taking a carriage in readiness, he was borne off to his hotel, followed by the crowd, keenly anxious to get a better sight of Richmond's illustrious guest. No speech could be obtained from him. His modesty equalled his bravery."

Beauregard was sent to Camp Pickens, at Manassas Junction, where he took command of Virginia's main army. He soon issued a proclamation in which he urged the troops to use every means in their power to drive back Abraham Lincoln's "abolition hosts," whom he accused of abandoning all rules of civilized warfare. "They proclaim by their acts, if not on their banners, that their war cry is 'Beauty and Booty.' "

Edward Pollard of the Richmond *Examiner* says that "General Beauregard was singularly impassioned in defense of the cause which he served. He hated and despised the Yankee. . . . That the South would easily whip the North was his constant assertion. . . . He had ardor, a ceaseless activity, and an indomitable power of will. . . .

"It is not to be wondered that General Beauregard, with the éclat of the first victory of the war, and the attractions of a foreign name and manners, should have been the ladies' favorite among the early Southern generals. He was constantly receiving attentions from them, in letters, in flags, and in hundreds of pretty missives. His camp table was often adorned with presents of rare flowers which flanked his maps and plans, and a bouquet [in a vase] frequently served him for a paper weight.

"There was perhaps a little tawdriness about these displays in a military camp. But General Beauregard had too much force of character to be spoiled by hero-worship, or by that part of popular admiration—the most dangerous to men intent on great and grave purposes—the flattery and pursuit of women."

17

Blunder at Big Bethel

T HE SOUTH had been quick to draw upon its greatest re-
source: its pool of accomplished military commanders. Jefferson Davis, himself an experienced soldier, had Robert E. Lee
in Richmond, Pierre Beauregard at Manassas, and Joe Johnston
in the Shenandoah Valley, and under Johnston were Tom Jackson and Jeb Stuart. Down the Virginia peninsula, facing Fort
Monroe and Ben Butler, was John Bankhead "Prince John" Magruder, known for his dramatic posturing and his passion for
high living, who had achieved a brilliant record as an artillerist in
the war with Mexico.

Unlike Jefferson Davis, Abraham Lincoln was not versed in
things military (the Black Hawk War had provided him nothing
but a few exercises in marching); nor did he have a wide range of
lustrous officers from whom to choose the combat commanders
he needed.

The greatest soldier in the North was a Virginian who had not
defected (and therefore had become a traitor in Southern eyes),
Lincoln's commanding general, Winfield Scott. A twice-wounded
hero of the War of 1812, Scott had gone on to serve against the
Indians of the Southeast (the Seminoles and the Creeks), and,
made the army's top commander in 1841, had led the operations
in Mexico. But the general was now seventy-five years old, obese,
and feeble. His duties in Washington were performed from a
couch or a chair, and he needed assistance to rise.

Selected to lead Lincoln's main army—the one mustering along
the banks of the Potomac at Washington and Alexandria—was

Irvin McDowell

Brigadier General Irvin McDowell. A career soldier from Ohio, McDowell had served in Mexico as a staff officer and continued in staff jobs afterward. He had never led troops in the field, nor was he endowed with any of the special sparks of military leadership that kindle fighting spirit. He was, however, able, hardworking, and dedicated, and he now established his headquarters at Arlington House, recently vacated by Mrs. Robert E. Lee, where he began to prepare a march against Richmond.

Neither side was ready for a major confrontation, but small affairs had begun to occur. Federal naval vessels were exchanging fire with batteries on the Virginia side of the Potomac and at an earthen fort at Sewell's Point in Hampton Roads, a spot commanding the Elizabeth River route to the Gosport Navy Yard. There were also light encounters on land as the belligerents scouted each other.

In the darkness of the earliest hours of June 1, a company of Union cavalry made a scout to Fairfax Courthouse, the refuge of Mrs. Judith McGuire after her flight from Alexandria a few days before. She had felt secure at the home of "the Rev. Mr. B.," and was peacefully asleep when the Yankees, unaware that the town's defenders had been mustered to meet them, made their entry.

"About three o'clock in the night we were aroused by a volley of musketry not far from our windows. Every human being in the house sprang up at once. We soon saw by the moonlight a body of cavalry moving up the street [the Yankees had recoiled from a fusillade delivered from behind fences, from windows, and from rooftops]; and, as they passed below our window . . . we distinctly heard the commander's order, 'Halt.'

"They . . . turned and approached [the defenders] slowly, and as softly as though every horse were shod with velvet. In a few moments there was another volley. . . . Then [again in retreat] came the same body of cavalry rushing by in wild disorder. Oaths loud and deep were heard from the commander.

"They again formed, and rode quite rapidly into the village. [This time the Yankees scattered some mounted troops, but the foot troops remained a frustration.] Another volley, and another, then such a rushing as I never witnessed. The cavalry strained by, the commander calling out 'Halt! Halt!' with curses and imprecations. On, on they went, nor did they stop. . . .

"Then came the terrible suspense. All was confusion on the street, and it was not yet quite light. One of our gentlemen soon came in with the sad report that Captain [John Q.] Marr of the Warrenton Rifles, a young officer of great promise, was found dead. The gallant Rifles [had been] exulting in their success, until it was whispered that their captain was missing. Had he been captured? Too soon the uncertainty was ended, and their exultant shouts hushed. His body was found in the high grass. . . .

"Two of our men received slight flesh wounds. The enemy carried off their dead and wounded [plus several prisoners]. We captured four men and three horses. Seven of their horses were left dead on the roadside. They also dropped a number of arms, which were picked up by our men.

"After having talked the matter over, we were getting quite composed, and thought we had nothing more to fear, when we observed them placing sentinels in Mr. B.'s porch [that of the narrator's refuge], saying that it was a high point, and another raid was expected.

"The gentlemen immediately ordered the carriages, and in half an hour Mr. B.'s family and ourselves were on our way to [Chantilly]. As we approached the house [of a friend, "Mrs. S."] after a ride of six miles, the whole family came out to receive us. . . . We were soon seated in the parlor, surrounded by everything that was delightful. . . . It was indeed a haven of rest to us after the noise and tumult of the court house.

"They were, of course, in great excitement, having heard wild stories of the fight. We all rejoiced, and returned thanks to God that He had enabled our men to drive off the invaders."

The first confrontation in Virginia that rose to the status of a battle (though barely so) occurred in the Butler-Magruder theater on the peninsula. Magruder was headquartered at Yorktown, some twenty miles up the peninsula from Fort Monroe. Butler's patrols were ranging over the intervening territory, and some of the men, in spite of orders to respect private property, spent more time plundering abandoned homes than they spent scouting. Magruder decided to move against the practice by sending a part of his force to establish itself about a dozen miles down the peninsula.

The detachment was placed under the command of Colonel

The skirmish at Fairfax Courthouse

D. H. Hill, until lately a professor of mathematics (following a tour at West Point and service in the Mexican War), and now beginning a notable role as a Confederate. One of Hill's subordinates was Major James H. Lane, also an officer of special promise. (Though a young man, Lane was shiny bald, a circumstance he passed off by saying that he dwelt on a higher plane than his well-thatched associates, for there wasn't a hair between him and heaven.)

Hill's detachment made its main camp at Big Bethel and set up an advanced post at Little Bethel, only about five miles from Hampton and Newport News and eight from Butler's headquarters at Fort Monroe. Hill did not confine himself to chasing the marauders from the abandoned estates. He attached some of the male slaves left as caretakers and sent them up to Yorktown and Williamsburg to work on the fortifications being developed there. He also dispatched night patrols to harass the Yankee pickets at Hampton and Newport News.

Colonel Magruder himself soon came down from Yorktown to confer with Hill on plans for even bolder operations in the face of the superior foe. Young Lieutenant J. W. Ratchford found himself wondering what Ben Butler's reaction would be. Ratchford had been filled with eagerness for combat at the time of his enlistment, but the feeling had subsided.

"A battle now seemed imminent, and the prospect had now none of its hazy fascination of a month before. All my previous experience of the use of firearms had been in hunting small game. . . . I felt sure my hours on earth were numbered. However . . . I heard a conversation between Colonels Hill and Magruder which was very comforting. They agreed that for one-fourth of the men engaged in a fight to be hit was a very heavy loss, and for one-fourth of those hit to be killed was a heavy mortality.

"The rapidity of my mental calculation on my chances of life would have been the delight of Professor Hill in classroom days."

Ben Butler's preparations to counter Magruder's audacity were made in conference with his thirty-two-year-old aide and military secretary, Major Theodore Winthrop, whose prewar years, thanks to a restless nature, had been remarkably diverse. A Yale graduate, Winthrop had first traveled in Europe; then, after a stint as a private tutor, he accepted employment with a shipping concern in Panama. Following a work-related trip to California, Oregon, and Vancouver, he returned to Panama and volunteered for a jungle

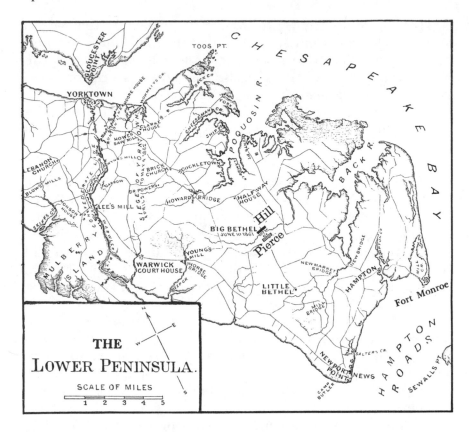

THE
LOWER PENINSULA.

SCALE OF MILES
1 2 3 4 5

expedition of an exploratory nature, and its rigors impaired his health. Turning to the study of law, Winthrop won admittance to the bar, at the same time beginning a career in political speaking. During these years of varied activities, he had also been writing novels, but publication had eluded him. Since his induction into Lincoln's army, however, he had placed some impressions of the experience with the *Atlantic* magazine.

Winthrop had this to say about the war itself:

"I see no present end to this business. We must conquer the South. Afterward we must be prepared to do its police in its own behalf, and in behalf of its black population, whom this war must, without precipitation, emancipate. . . . We must think of these things, and prepare for them."

The plan against Magruder developed by Winthrop and Butler called for two columns to advance under cover of darkness, the right column leaving from the camp near Fort Monroe, the left from Newport News. Converging at a point along the route to

Little Bethel, the troops were to press forward and take that place; then, if conditions were right, they were to advance and attack Big Bethel. Command of the expedition was assigned to a militia brigadier from Massachusetts, Ebenezer W. Pierce, whose prewar military experience had been limited to leading troops in holiday parades.

A memorandum covering the planned expedition contained the line: "George Scott—colored guide—to have a shooting iron." This seems to be the first time in the war that thought was given to arming a Negro.

Major Winthrop won Butler's permission to go along as a free agent. A newsman who was present while Butler and Winthrop were completing their plans reported:

"The last instruction given by General Butler to Major Winthrop was 'Be brave as you please, but run no risk.'

" 'Be bold! Be bold! But not too bold! shall be our motto,' responded Winthrop."

The columns began their respective marches during the night of June 9–10. Questions of identification as the columns merged were intended to be resolved by white armbands and the shouting of the word *Boston,* but not all of the units had been notified of the scheme. Mismanagement marked the convergence. The left col-

Theodore Winthrop

umn was tardy in its march, and the head of the right column continued past the assigned meeting place toward Little Bethel. One of the regiments of the left column, as it approached the meeting place and spotted the dim forms of the rearward troops of the right column, mistook them for enemy forces, and the result was an exchange of fire that downed about thirty men before the mistake was realized.

The sounds of the exchange puzzled the troops of the right column who had gone ahead: Colonel Abram Duryea's New York Zouaves and elements of Colonel Peter Washburn's 1st Vermont. As related by the latter unit's adjutant:

"Just as we halted to start to the rear on hearing firing, a rebel scoundrel came out of a house and deliberately fired his gun at us. The ball passed so close to me that I heard it whiz—on its way going through the coat and pants, and just grazing the skin of Orderly Sergeant Sweet of the Woodstock company. The rascal was secured . . . [as] a prisoner. . . . I then—as the firing in the rear had ceased—with revolver in hand, accompanied by Fifer [another Vermonter], approached the fellow's house. . . .

"Some Negroes came from the house. . . . On inquiry, the slaves told me that . . . we had just taken prisoner . . . the owner, that he belonged to the secession army, and that no white folks were in the house, all having left.

"Without the ceremony of ringing, I entered and surveyed the premises, and found a most elegantly furnished house. I took a hasty survey in search of arms, but, finding none, left the house and started to overtake our column [that of the Vermont units, now in full march to the rear; Duryea's Zouaves were still at the front, only now beginning to turn to follow the Vermonters].

"On reaching the bend in the road, I took a survey of the rear . . . and . . . observed a horseman coming at full speed. . . . On reaching the house, he turned in, which induced me to think him a secessionist. . . . Revolver in hand, [I] ordered him to dismount and surrender.

"He cried out, 'Who are you?'

"Answer: 'Vermont!'

" 'Then raise your piece, Vermont. I am Colonel Duryea of the Zouaves.'

"And so it was. His gay-looking red boys just appeared, turning the corner of the road, coming towards us. He asked me the cause of the firing in the rear, and whose premises we were on. I told him he knew the first as well as I did; but, as to the last, I could give full information; that the house belonged to one . . . who, just before, had sent a bullet whizzing by me . . . and that my greatest pleasure would be to burn the rascal's house in payment.

" 'Your wish will be gratified at once,' said the Colonel. 'I am ordered by General Butler to burn every house whose occupant or owner fires upon our troops. Burn it!'

"He leaped from his horse, and I upon the steps; and by that time three Zouaves were with me. I ordered them to try the door with the butts of their guns. Down went the door, and in went we. A well-packed travelling bag lay upon a mahogany table. I tore it open with the hope of finding a revolver, but did not.

"The first thing I took out was a white linen coat. I laid it on the table, and Colonel Duryea put a lighted match to it. Other clothing was added to the pile, and soon we had a rousing fire.

"Before leaving, I went into the large parlor in the right wing of the house. It was perfectly splendid. A large room with a tapestry carpet, a nice piano, a fine library of miscellaneous books, rich sofas, elegant chairs with superior needlework wrought bottoms, whatnots in the corners loaded with articles of luxury, taste, and refinement—and upon a mahogany center-table lay a Bible and a lady's portrait. The last two articles I took. . . . I also took a decanter of most excellent old brandy from the sideboard, and left the burning house.

"By this time the [entire] Zouave regiment had come up. I joined them [in their rearward march], and in a short time . . . saw a sight the like of which I wish never to see again—viz.: nine of Colonel [Frederick] Townsend's Albany regiment stretched on the floor of a house where they had just been carried . . . wounded *by our own men.* Oh, the sight was dreadful! I cried like a boy, and so did many others.

"I immediately thought of my decanter of brandy, took a tin cup from a soldier and poured into it the brandy, and filled the cup with water from a canteen; and from one poor boy to another I passed and poured into their pale and quivering lips the invigorating fluid, and with my hand wiped the sweat drops . . . from their foreheads. Oh, how gratefully the poor fellows looked at me."

The wounds of two of the men were mortal.

Daylight had come, and General Pierce, with his forces now united, gave orders for a march upon Little Bethel. The outpost, however, was found to be unmanned. The Confederates had been forewarned by the firing between the federal columns, and their entire body was now at Big Bethel, which had been well fortified for defense. Pierce decided to make an attack.

As related by an unidentified Confederate soldier:

"The guns were placed in battery, and the infantry took their places behind their breastwork. Everybody was cool, and all were anxious to give the invaders a good reception. About 9 o'clock the glittering bayonets of the enemy appeared on the hill opposite, and above them waved the Star-Spangled Banner. The moment the head of the column advanced far enough to show one or two companies, the Parrott gun of the Howitzer Battery opened on them, throwing a shell right into their midst. Their ranks broke in confusion, and the column—or as much of it as we could see—retreated behind two small farmhouses. From their position a fire was opened on us."

Adds Confederate Lieutenant J. W. Ratchford, the man who had learned from experienced soldiers D. H. Hill and John Magruder that his mathematical chances of surving a battle were excellent:

"As the firing began, all the assurance I had drawn from the conversation of the colonels . . . vanished as thin air, and when one of the first shells fired from the Federal batteries burst a few yards from me, literally tearing a mule to pieces, the one chance of being killed seemed much more imminent than the fifteen of escape.

"When the enemy had driven our skirmishers in, and were feeling for the weak places in our line, Colonel Hill sent me several hundred yards to the left of our line to call in a company of pickets who were in danger of being cut off from the main body of the army. . . .

"When I returned, [Hill and his staff] were nowhere to be found. I now began to have a wild longing for the solitude of the woods, and I remember thinking that if only it were dark I should lose no time in satisfying that longing; but stronger even than my fears was my knowledge of the fate that awaited cowards and shirkers at the hands of those at home, and, feeling half-thankful, half regretful for my regard for public opinion, I went about my duty with a great show of calmness. . . .

"I was the only man on horseback in sight, and the enemy, probably thinking me an officer of high rank, turned loose on me

Federals attacking Big Bethel defenses

with grape and canister, until the sound of the missiles coming through the air was like a covey of flying quail rising from the ground. A shot grazed my temple. I felt very much as if it had taken half my head with it, and I remember raising my hand to feel how much was gone, and thinking how horrible I should look as a corpse. Then consciousness left me, and I fell from my horse. The animal, fully sharing my longing for solitude, and not having my restraints, took to the woods.

"The last of the fight which I saw was the charge of the Federals led by the gallant Major Winthrop."

Another witness to this charge was a Virginia soldier named J. B. Moore.

"Major Winthrop headed a force intending to turn our left flank. On our left was a slight earthwork. About 75 yards in front of this was a rail fence. Our attention was called by cheering to his advance. Looking up, we saw the major and two privates on the fence. His sword was drawn, and he was calling on his troops to follow him. Our first volley killed these three. Those following . . . beat a precipitate retreat. . . . Major Winthrop was shot in the breast. . . . Among the incidents of this skirmish, none is more indelibly impressed on my mind than the gallant bearing of this unfortunate young man."

Returning to the account by the unidentified Confederate soldier:

"At the redoubt on the right, a company . . . charged one of our guns but could not stand the fire of the infantry, and retreated. . . . During these charges the main body of the enemy on the hill were attempting to concentrate for a general assault, but the shells from the Howitzer Battery prevented them. As one regiment would give up the effort, another would be marched to the position, but with no better success, for a shell would scatter them like chaff. The men did not seem able to stand fire at all."

The inexperienced General Pierce, in spite of some apt suggestions on the part of a young West Pointer named Gouverneur K. Warren (then with Duryea's Zouaves), failed to get his effort in hand, and by 11 A.M. the fight was winding down. Completing a march from Fort Monroe at this time were some reserves under Colonel Joseph Carr.

"On approaching, we were surprised and puzzled at the condition of the troops. For at least one mile from the scene of action the men and officers were scattered singly and in groups, without form or organization, looking far more like men enjoying a huge picnic than soldiers awaiting battle. I reported my regiment to General Pierce, who consented to give me support for a charge on the Confederate works. Colonel Townsend promptly volunteered to support me with his regiment, and departed to make the necessary preparations.

"Having placed the 2d New York on the right and left of the road, I was preparing for the charge when a message reached me from General Pierce, stating that, after consultation with the colonel [Townsend] he found that troops could not be formed to make the charge effective, and that during the consultation an order had been received from General Butler ordering a retreat. . . .

"The only firing occurring after 12 o'clock . . . was from the gun brought up by my regiment, and in command of Lieutenant [John T.] Greble. About one dozen shots had been fired when Greble was killed. The gun was abandoned on the field and Greble's body was left beside it. I called for volunteers to rescue the gun, and . . . [a] company of the 2d New York responded, and, in the face of the enemy, gallantly rescued the gun, bringing it in with Greble's body lying on it."

The retreat was begun at about one in the afternoon. Some Confederate cavalry followed, but did little harm. These men, however, grew rich with booty, for the roadside was strewn with discarded muskets, overcoats, blankets, haversacks, canteens, and other accoutrements.

Back on the battlefield, Confederate Lieutenant J. W. Ratchford had awakened from his grapeshot-induced sleep.

"When I recovered consciousness, I was lying in the breastworks, a few yards from the spot where Major Winthrop had fallen. The enemy were gone, and there was no sound to be heard save the voice of the Negro cook offering me coffee."

Withdrawing with Greble's body

The unidentified Confederate quoted earlier now left the breastworks for a tour of the ground the Federals had occupied.

"The houses behind which they had been hid had been burnt by our troops [presumably by means of shellfire]. Around the yard were the dead bodies of the men who had been killed by our cannon, mangled in the most frightful manner. . . . A little further on we came to the point to which they had carried some of their wounded, who had since died. The gay-looking uniforms of the New York Zouaves contrasted greatly with the paled, fixed faces of their dead owners.

"Going to the swamp through which they attempted to pass to assault our lines . . . I saw one boyish, delicate-looking fellow lying on the mud with a bullet hole through his breast. His hand was pressed on the wound from which his life-blood had poured, and the other was clenched in the grass that grew near him. Lying on the ground was a Testament which had fallen from his pocket, dabbed with blood. On opening the cover, I found the printed inscription, 'Presented to the Defenders of their Country by the New York Bible Society.' A United States flag was also stamped on the title page.

"Among the haversacks picked up . . . were many letters from the Northern States asking if they liked the Southern farms, and if the Southern barbarians had been whipped out yet.

"The force of the enemy brought against us was 4,000, accord-

A grave at Newport News

ing to the statements of the six prisoners we took. Ours was 1,100."

These figures are about correct. As for casualties, the Confederates lost but a handful of men in killed and wounded, the Federals nearly a hundred. The only plus for the Federals was that Magruder gave up his advanced posts and returned to Yorktown.

Big Bethel had no significant strategic effect on the developing war, but it caused a great stir among the residents of North and South alike. To the South it was a victory that illustrated the superiority of the Confederate soldier. (Some of the accoutrements cast aside by the retreating Federals were proudly displayed in Richmond store windows.) To the North, Big Bethel was another maddening humiliation. Ben Butler was severely criticized.

A curious result of Big Bethel was that the publicity given Major Winthrop's death generated a market for his unpublished novels, which were well received. The writings, according to one source, were found to be "fresh, rapid, vigorous, inspiring sketches of life and manners."

For young Mrs. Fannie Beers, a Southern sympathizer living in a Northern village, Big Bethel was a source of serious personal trouble. Fannie had been born and raised in this village, but a few years before the war she had married a Southerner and moved to Louisiana, soon becoming an impassioned supporter of Southern principles. Upon the secession of Louisiana, Fannie's husband had joined the military. Fannie, who was pregnant and in poor health, returned to her mother's home in the North.

"From my house of refuge I watched eagerly the course of events, until at last all mail facilities were cut off and I was left to endure the horrors of suspense as well as the irritating consciousness that, although sojourning in the home of my childhood, I was an alien, an acknowledged 'rebel,' and as such an object of suspicion and dislike to all save my immediate family. Even these, with the exception of my precious mother, were bitterly opposed to the South and secession. From mother I received unceasing care, thorough sympathy, surpassing love.

"During this troubled time a little babe was born to me . . . who only just opened its dark eyes upon the troubled face of its mother to close them forever. . . .

"One day I received a kindly warning from an old friend concerning a small Confederate flag which had been sent to me by my husband. It was a tiny silken affair which I kept in my prayer book. This harmless possession was magnified by the people of the town into an immense rebel banner which would eventually float over my mother's house. I had still a few friends whose temperate counsel [with the townspeople] had hitherto protected me. The note referred to warned me that while I retained possession of the flag I might at any time expect the presence of a mob.

"I would not have destroyed my treasure for worlds—and how to conceal it became a subject of constant thought. The discovery one day of a jar of 'perpetual paste' in mother's secretary suggested an idea which was at once carried out. Applying this strongly adhesive mixture to one side of the flag, I pasted it upon the naked flesh just over my heart.

"One morning the mail brought certain news of a Confederate victory at Big Bethel. This so exasperated the people that . . . an excited crowd halted under my window, crying out, 'Where's that rebel woman?' 'Let's have that flag.' 'Show your colors,' etc.

"Carried away by intense excitement, I threw open the blinds, and, waving the newspaper above my head, shouted, 'Hurrah! Hurrah for Big Bethel! Hurrah for the brave rebels!'

"A perfect howl of rage arose from below, and greater evil might have befallen but for the timely appearance of the venerable village doctor, who now rode hastily in among the excited men, and, standing up in his buggy, cried out, 'Friends, she is but a frail, defenseless woman. Be thankful if your morning's work be not her death.'

"Slowly and sullenly the crowd dispersed, while the good doctor hastily ascended to my chamber. I lay with fevered cheeks and burning eyes among the pillows where my mother had placed me. The terrible excitement under which I labored forbade all blame or any illusion to my act of imprudence. I was soothed and tenderly cared for until, under the influence of a sedative, I fell asleep.

"Early next morning the doctor appeared at my bedside. . . . 'Ah! Better this morning? That's my brave girl.'

"Meeting his gaze fully, I replied, 'I shall try henceforth to be brave, as befits the wife of a soldier.'

"A frown appeared upon the doctor's brow. Tenderly placing his hand upon my head, he said, 'My child, I fear your courage will soon be put to the test. Your own imprudence has greatly incensed the town people. Danger menaces you, and, through you, your mother. Fortunately, the friends of your childhood still desire to protect you. But your only safety lies in giving up the rebel flag which it is said you possess. Give it to me, Fannie, and I will destroy it before their eyes, and thus avert the threatened danger.'

"I only smiled as I replied, 'Doctor . . . since the rebel flag has existed I have cherished it in my heart of hearts. You may search the house over. You will find no flag but the one I have here,' placing my hand on my heart.

"The good man had known me from childhood, and he could not doubt me. He questioned no further, but took his leave, promising to use his influence with the incensed villagers. They, however, were not so easily convinced. They had been wrought up to a state of frenzied patriotism, and declared they would search the house where the obnoxious flag was supposed to be. Dire threats of vengeance were heard on every side.

"At last a committee was appointed to wait upon *the traitress* and again demand the surrender of the flag. It was composed of gentlemen who, though . . . uncompromising 'Union men,' were yet well known to me and were anxious, if possible, to shield me. They were admitted to the room, where I calmly awaited them. I reiterated the assertion made to the doctor . . . with such apparent truth that they were staggered. But they had come to perform a duty, and they meant to succeed. They convinced me that the danger to myself and to the house of my mother was real and imminent. But I only repeated my assertions, though my heart throbbed painfully as I saw the anxiety and trouble in mother's face.

"Suddenly I remembered that I had in my possession a paper which, just before all mail communication had ceased between the North and the South, had been sent to me for the purpose of protection. It was simply a certificate of my husband's membership and good standing in a Masonic lodge, and had a seal affixed.

"As I called for the portfolio, all eyes brightened with expectation of seeing at last the 'rebel flag.' Drawing forth from its envelope the fateful document, I said, 'I was told to use this only in dire extremity. It seems to me that such a time is at hand. . . .'

"Thus speaking, I handed the paper to one whom I knew to be a prominent Mason. The certificate was duly examined, and, after a short conference, returned.

" 'We will do our best,' said the spokesman of the party, and all withdrew.

"The day passed without further trouble, and as I sank to sleep

Fannie Beers in a postwar pose. Mnemosyne was the Greek goddess of memory.

that night there came to me a feeling of safety and protection which was indeed comforting."

As soon as her health permitted, Fannie left her mother's home and made her way to Baltimore, and from there into Virginia. Becoming a hospital matron, she spent the entire war in the Confederate states, ministering to the sick and wounded soldiers with a capability and a dedication that won her an almost reverential renown. Many called her the "Florence Nightingale of the South."

18

Johnston Abandons Harpers Ferry

THE BATTLE at Big Bethel was quickly followed by new de velopments at Harpers Ferry. Perhaps fifteen thousand Federals had been assembled in south-central Pennsylvania, their mission to put pressure on Joe Johnston's Confederates, then numbering about nine thousand. Commander of the federal army was sixty-nine-year-old Major General Robert Patterson, a veteran of the War of 1812 and the war with Mexico. A militia officer, Patterson had spent most of his years in civilian life and had grown wealthy in business pursuits that included the production of textiles and investments in agriculture and transportation. The general was known to his men as "Granny Patterson," but his powers were still intact.

Unfortunately, Patterson and his superior in Washington, Winfield Scott, had trouble communicating. Primarily, Scott's orders lacked directness, perhaps because he wasn't sure what Patterson ought to do. Patterson was left to wonder whether he should pursue a course based on boldness or on caution. His problem was solved, at least temporarily, by Joe Johnston himself.

The Confederate general had decided to abandon Harpers Ferry and withdraw into the Shenandoah Valley to Winchester, about twenty-five miles from Harpers. This was in opposition to the wishes of Jefferson Davis and Robert E. Lee, who felt that Harpers ought to be maintained as a fortress. Johnston, however, had concluded that the town—low-lying, overlooked by mountains, and also easy to flank—did not lend itself to such a concept. Moreover, the commander feared that Union General George

Robert Patterson

McClellan, who was building an army in Ohio and western Virginia, and was already active on west Virginia soil, might menace him from the rear. Johnston had no way of knowing that McClellan had no immediate plans for operations that far eastward.

A notable sidelight to Robert Patterson's campaign is that, at the outset, the general's staff included Senator John Sherman (brother of William T.). The senator's story had its beginnings during the period immediately following Lincoln's first call for volunteers.

"I remained in Washington a few days and then started for my home at Mansfield [Ohio] to encourage enlistments, but found that no help was needed; that companies were enlisted in a day. One was recruited by William McLaughlin, a gallant soldier in the war in Mexico, a major general of Ohio militia who had [reached] the age of sixty years. He dropped his law books, and in twelve hours had a company of one hundred men ready to move at the command of the governor. A like patriotism was aroused in all parts of the state, so that in a very short time two full regiments, numbering 2,000 men, were organized under the command of Colonel A. McD. McCook of the United States Army, and were on the way to Washington, then blockaded by the roughs of Baltimore. I met them at Harrisburg [Pennsylvania] and went with them to Philadelphia. They were camped at Fairmont Park, and were drilled with other regiments by Colonel Fitz-John Porter, the entire force being under the command of General Patterson.

"When the blockade was opened by the skill and audacity of General Benjamin F. Butler, the two Ohio regiments were ordered to Washington and were there received by President Lincoln, at which time a pleasant incident occurred which may be worthy of mention.

"I accompanied the President to the parade, and passed with him down the line. He noticed a venerable man with long white hair and military bearing, standing in position at the head of his company with arms presented ["arms" meaning his sword], and inquired his name. I said it was General McLaughlin and hurriedly told him his history, his politics, and patriotism.

"The President, as he came opposite him, stopped, and, leaving his party, advanced to McLaughlin and extended his hand. McLaughlin, surprised, had some difficulty in putting his sword under his left arm. They shook hands and Lincoln thanked him, saying when men of his age and standing came to the rescue of their country there could be no doubt of our success. McLaughlin highly appreciated this compliment. He afterwards enlisted for the war and died in the service of his country.

"These two regiments were subsequently ordered to Harrisburg, to which place they went accompanied by me, and there they formed a part of the command of General Patterson. . . . I was serving on the staff of General Patterson as a volunteer aide without pay.

"While at Harrisburg it was suggested to me that ex-president Buchanan, then at his country home near that city, had expressed a wish to see me. As our personal relations had always been pleasant, though our political opinions were widely different, I called upon him. . . . I was surprised at the frankness and apparent sincerity of the opinions expressed by him in relation to the war. He said he had done all he could to prevent the war, but now that it was upon us it was the duty of all patriotic people to make it a success, that he approved all that had been done by Mr. Lincoln, of whom he spoke in high terms of praise. I believe he was sincere. . . .

"The command of General Patterson moved slowly to Chambersburg [Pennsylvania], where it remained several days under constant drill, then to Hagerstown [Maryland] and to the village of Williamsport on the Potomac. While at the latter place, [William T.] Sherman, who had been at Washington and received his commission as colonel of the 13th United States Infantry, then being recruited, came to visit me at my lodgings in a country tavern. He then met for the first time in many years his old classmate, Colonel—afterwards, Major General—George H. Thomas, who then commanded a regular regiment of the United States Army in the force under the command of General Patterson.

"The conversation of these two officers, who were to be so intimately associated in great events in the future, was very interesting. They got a big map of the United States, spread it on the floor, and, on their hands and knees, discussed the probable salient strategic places of the war. They singled out Richmond, Vicksburg, Nashville, Knoxville, and Chattanooga. To me it has always appeared strange that they were able confidently and correctly to designate the lines of operations and strategic points of a war not yet commenced, and more strange still that they should be leading actors in great battles at the places designated by them at this country tavern."

Neither John nor William T. Sherman stayed long at Williamsport. The senator was needed in Washington for attendance at a special war-related session of Congress, and the colonel went to the same place to drill his raw regiment.

During the final days of Joe Johnston's occupation of Harpers Ferry, cavalry commander Jeb Stuart was kept busy picketing the river above and below. According to Virginia's novelist-soldier John Esten Cooke, who knew Stuart and spent a part of the war on his staff:

"This officer, styled by Johnston 'the indefatigable Stuart,' here

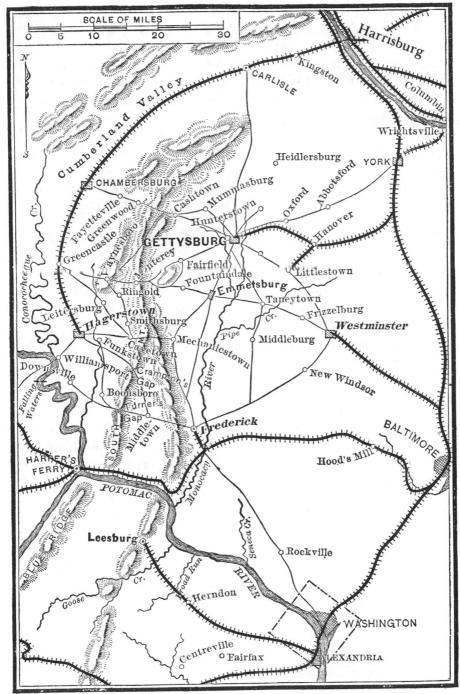

Regions between Harrisburg and Washington

inaugurated that energetic system of cavalry tactics which afterwards on a wider field accomplished so much and secured for its
originator his great and justly earned reputation. Bold, ardent,
and 'indefatigable,' by mental and physical organization, the
young Virginian—for he was [only] twenty-eight years of age—
concentrated all his faculties upon the task before him, of watching for the enemy's approach and penetrating his designs.

"Educated at West Point and trained in Indian fighting on the
prairie, he brought to the great struggle upon which he had now
entered a thorough knowledge of arms, a bold and fertile conception, and a constitution of body which enabled him to bear up
against fatigues which would have prostrated the strength of other
men.

"Those who saw him at this time are eloquent in their description of his energy and the habits of the man. They tell how he
remained almost constantly in the saddle; how he never failed to
take to one side and specially instruct every squad which went out
on picket; how he was everywhere present, at all hours of the day
and night, along the line which he guarded; and how, by thus
infusing into the raw cavalry his own untiring activity and watchfulness, he was enabled, in spite of the small force which he commanded—about three hundred men—to observe the whole front
of the Potomac from the Point of Rocks east of the Blue Ridge to
the western part of Berkeley.

"His personal traits made him a great favorite with all who
knew him, and contributed to his success with volunteers. His
animal spirits were unconquerable, his gayety and humor unfailing. He had a ready jest for all, and made the forest ring with his
songs as he marched at the head of his column. So great was his
activity that General Johnston compared him to that species of
hornet called a 'yellow jacket,' and said that 'he was no sooner
brushed off than he lit back again.'"

Johnston began his movement from Harpers Ferry on Thursday, June 13, which happened to be a day that Jefferson Davis
had set aside for fasting throughout the Confederacy, his purpose
to heighten religious zeal for the war effort.

As related by an unidentified member of Johnston's command:

"Just as the troops were in a fair way for the enjoyment of the
holiday from military duty consequent upon the fast day, an order was circulated among the different regiments for immediate
preparations for march. This was the first intimation we had of

General Johnston's purpose to evacuate Harpers Ferry. Instantly the whole place was in a stir. Hundreds of baggage wagons were laden . . . and stuffed with provision stores, while ammunition was carefully deposited in safe trains [that is, wagon trains]; and from every side arose the swelling strains of music. . . .

"A large number of men left by railway for Winchester, and others . . . marched afoot [while still others lingered at Harpers to deal with the last-minute tasks]. During the day there was an indescribable scene of excitement. Broadway . . . never witnessed such a jam as this little town. The business houses were closed, families were attempting to move their effects, and every street and avenue was crowded with loaded wagons. Officers [on horseback] were dashing hither and thither, and soldiers were on the *qui vive* [on the alert] for movement.

"Loads of provisions that it was found impossible to transport were dumped in the river. There was a general rush by the boys for sugar and bread. It was, indeed, in more senses than one, a *fast* day. In the first place, we had no regular meal, and every movement was made at the most accelerated rate of speed. . . .

"Just after dark, Captain Desha's company [to which the narrator belonged] was ordered to accompany . . . the chief engineer across the Potomac and make preparations for blowing up the bridge. . . . I have slept in many places and under many disadvantages, but never before above a foaming, turbulent river and just above a terrible mine that in an instant could flash the structure into a myriad of fragments. The night, however, passed quietly, and in the early gray of the morning . . . the immense bridge, over three quarters of a mile in length, was thoroughly saturated, the torch lit, and just as we reached the Virginia shore the magnificent structure was hurried into mid-air, falling a shapeless mass of ruins into the rapid stream. The burning debris, with the clouds of lurid flame, presented a picture worthy an artist's study.

"In an hour or two the massive and extensive armory buildings were ignited, and the conflagration that ensued was of the most terrific and impressive character. In order to prevent the flames extending to private property . . . troops were detailed to act as firemen . . . and right manfully did they discharge their arduous duty. Not a penny's worth of that which did not belong to the Government was destroyed."

Union General Patterson chose to respond to Johnston's retreat by sending a major part of his army across the Potomac. The story of the crossing is told by one of Patterson's regimental chaplains, the Reverend A. M. Stewart, a keen observer who, on June 16, wrote the following letter for publication in a Pennsylvania newspaper:

"Never has it been my lot to witness so general a display of order and strength, beauty and romance, as today. Without any of the soldiers knowing the destination, the immense columns com-

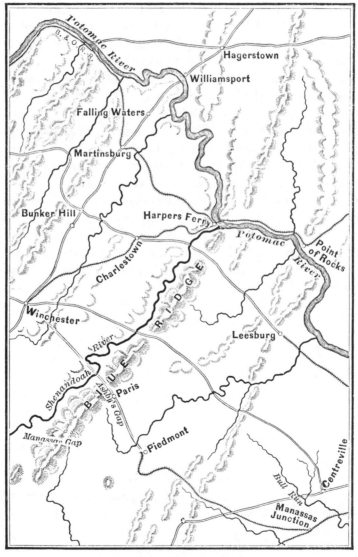

Regions of Harpers Ferry

menced filing into the road leading down to Williamsport nearby [some twenty miles up the river from Harpers Ferry]. Cavalry and infantry, artillery and baggage wagons, followed each other. Down through the town, over the long, sloping banks of the beautiful river, and to the water's edge of the Potomac, which divides Virginia from Maryland. No halt was ordered, but on went the grand cavalcade, straight into the river. Skiffs, boats, and bridges had all been destroyed by the enemy.

"With tremendous shouts and cheering the soldiers waded into the river—to the ankle, to the knees, to the loins, and to the waist—on they waded and shouted through the clear flowing stream. On they went in a seemingly endless stream of four men deep. Our 13th Regiment [the narrator's unit] had the honor of being near the front of the column. Walking in its front rank, I stepped into the famous old river with boots and clothes on, and hugely enjoyed a splashing and dabbling, waist deep, to the opposite shore, and invaded Old Virginia.

"On and up the steep bank and away over the rising, swelling ground advanced the invading army. Not a secessionist appeared to stop its progress, not a dog moved his tongue. When nearly a mile up the rising ground I stopped to rest under the shade of a tree and look on the panorama behind. What a vision!

"For three miles, down to the river, across, up the opposite bluffs, and away over into Maryland, could be distinctly seen that moving mass of men four deep. As it faded away in the distance, the column seemed like an enormous serpent, twisting round the bends of the road across the river, up and down the various ridges of hills, as they sank and swelled away into the distance. More than a dozen large bands rolled up inspiring music at the head of each regiment. Had the eye of Jeff Davis, or any other intelligent secessionist, rested on this vision, the idea of physical resistance against it must have at once died within him.

"About two o'clock the head of the column, in which our regiment is, halted and pitched tents on rising ground some two miles west of the river. For four hours the column has been coming on and encamping; and still, as I write, it comes. Never before were these quiet old fields and woods of Virginia waked up with such a living excitement.

"Whither we are to move on tomorrow, I have neither asked nor have any information. The news in camp is that Harpers Ferry has been burnt and abandoned."

Virginia trooper of 1861

At this significant moment, some of Patterson's regulars—his most experienced troops—were called to Washington as the result of a rumor that the city's secessionist element was plotting mischief in cooperation with Beauregard at Manassas. It was believed that the Government was in danger. If any such plot existed, it never matured; but Patterson's loss of troops was the ruin of his advance. Nothing developed but a little sparring with Jeb Stuart's cavalry.

It was at this time that Stuart's small command was reinforced by a company of horsemen that included twenty-one-year-old George Cary Eggleston, until recently a Virginia law student who was equally interested in literature and had already gained a reputation as an essayist. Eggleston relates:

"General Johnston's army was at Winchester, and the Federal force under General Patterson lay around Martinsburg. Stuart, with his three or four hundred men, was encamped at Bunker Hill, about midway between the two, and thirteen miles from support of any kind. He had chosen this position as a convenient one from which to observe the movements of the enemy. . . .

"My company arrived at the camp about noon [the date was probably June 16], after a march of three or four days, having traveled twenty miles that morning. Stuart, whom we encountered as we entered the camp, assigned us our position and ordered our tents pitched. Our captain, who was even worse-disciplined than we were, seeing a much more comfortable camping place than the muddy one assigned to us, and being a comfort-loving gentleman, proceeded to pay out a model camp at a distance of fifty yards from the spot indicated. It was not long before the colonel particularly wished to consult with that captain, and after the consultation the volunteer officer was firmly convinced that all West Point graduates were martinets, with no knowledge whatever of the courtesies due from one gentleman to another.

"We were weary after our long journey, and disposed to welcome the prospect of rest which our arrival in the camp held out. But resting, as we soon learned, had small place in our colonel's tactics. We had been in camp perhaps an hour when an order came directing that the company be divided into three parts, each under command of a lieutenant, and that these report immediately for duty. Reporting, we were directed to scout through the country around Martinsburg, going as near the town as possible, and to give battle to any cavalry force we might meet.

"Here was a pretty lookout, certainly! Our officers knew not one inch of the country, and might fall into all sorts of traps and ambuscades; and what if we should meet a cavalry force greatly superior to our own? This West Point colonel was rapidly forfeiting our good opinion. Our lieutenants were brave fellows, however, and they led us boldly if ignorantly, almost up to the very gates of the town occupied by the enemy. We saw some cavalry but met none, their orders not being so peremptorily belligerent, perhaps, as ours were; wherefore they gave us no chance to fight them.

"The next morning our unreasonable colonel again ordered us to mount, in spite of the fact that there were companies in the camp which had done nothing at all the day before. This time he led us himself, taking pains to get us as nearly as possible surrounded by infantry, and then laughingly telling us that our chance for getting out of the difficulty, except by cutting our way through, was an exceedingly small one.

"I think we began about this time to suspect that we were learning something, and that this reckless colonel was trying to teach us. But that he was a hare-brained fellow, lacking the caution belonging to a commander, we were unanimously agreed. He led us out of the place at a rapid gait before the one gap in the enemy's lines could be closed, and then jauntily led us into one or two more traps before taking us back to camp."

Stuart's fun was interrupted by Patterson's return across the Potomac to Maryland. Watching the retreat was Thomas Jackson, whom Joe Johnston had sent forward on a scout. Jackson and his men were disappointed at being cheated out of a chance to try their arms, but they had other things to do. As explained by Jackson's associate and biographer, Dr. Dabney:

"On this expedition Colonel Jackson was ordered by General Johnston to destroy the locomotives and cars of the Baltimore Railroad at Martinsburg. At this village there were vast workshops and depots for the construction and repair of these cars; and more than forty of the finest locomotives, with three hundred burden-cars, were now destroyed. Concerning this he writes: 'It was a sad work; but I had my orders, and my duty was to obey. If the cost of the property could only have been expended in disseminating the gospel of the Prince of Peace, how much good might have been expected!' "

As for Union General Patterson, the retreat cost him dearly in reputation, though he was helped to a degree by the support of Senator John Sherman. The senator wrote him from Washington:

"Great injustice is done you and your command here, and by persons in the highest military positions. I have been asked, over and over again, why you did not push on. . . . I have been restrained, by my being [lately] on your staff, from saying more than simply that you had executed your orders, and that, when you were prepared to advance, your best troops were recalled to Washington."

During Patterson's abortive invasion of Virginia, Washington had known a moment of novel interest. The war's first hydrogen-filled observation balloon was sent up. By means of a telegraph wire leading from the basket to the War Department, the balloon's designer, Professor Thaddeus S. C. Lowe, sent a message to President Lincoln:

"This point of observation commands an area nearly fifty miles in diameter. The city, with its girdle of encampments, presents a superb scene. I take great pleasure in sending you this first dispatch ever telegraphed from an aerial station, and in acknowledging my indebtedness to your encouragement for the opportunity of demonstrating the availability of the science of aeronautics in the military service of the country."

Later in June, the South saw a nautical development of consid-

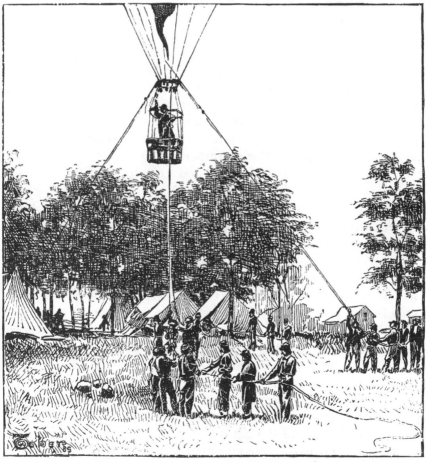

Professor Lowe in car of observation balloon

erable importance to its war effort. As reported in the New Orleans *Picayune:*

"The C.S. steamer-of-war Sumter sailed on Saturday last [June
29] on a cruise, having run the paper blockade of the Lincoln
abolition war steamers off the mouth of the Mississippi. She has a
picked crew, and her commander [Raphael Semmes] is known to
be a most brave and chivalrous sailor, and he has under him a
most gallant set of officers . . . [and] a crew of sixty-five men and
twenty marines."

Semmes became a commerce raider, and he took a heavy toll of
federal merchantmen.

In Maryland, the first of July found Union General Patterson
reinforced and ready for another move into Virginia. As recorded
in one of Chaplain Stewart's letters:

"On Tuesday morning, the 2nd instant, at three o'clock, the
advance column commenced fording the Potomac opposite Williamsport. Twenty thousand men—cavalry, infantry, and artillery, with five hundred large baggage wagons, were ready to
invade the Old Dominion. For six long hours the magnificent
parade moved down to the river, across the ford, up the opposite
banks, and . . . away among the woods and valleys of Virginia. . . .
The regiments which had crossed . . . twenty days since—and returned—went back with their bands playing, 'O, carry me back to
Old Virginny.' The others marched to the sound of 'Dixie's
Land.' "

Setting out on the road to Martinsburg, Patterson's column
soon encountered Jeb Stuart's cavalry. As related by Confederate
trooper George Cary Eggleston:

"When . . . our pickets were driven in, the most natural thing to
do . . . was to fall back upon our infantry supports at Winchester,
and I remember hearing various expressions of doubt as to the
colonel's sanity when, instead of falling back, he marched his
handful of men right up to the advancing lines and ordered us to
dismount. The Federal skirmish line was coming toward us at a
double-quick, and we were set going toward it at a like rate of
speed, leaving our horses hundreds of yards to the rear.

"We could see that the skirmishers alone outnumbered us three
or four times, and it really seemed that our colonel meant to
sacrifice his command deliberately. He waited until the infantry
was within about two hundred yards of us, we being in the edge
of a little grove, and they on the other side of an open field.

"Then Stuart cried out, 'Backwards, march! Steady, men—keep

your faces to the enemy.' And we marched in that way through the timber, delivering our shot-gun fire slowly as we fell back toward our horses. Then mounting, with the skirmishers almost upon us, we retreated, not hurriedly but at a slow trot, which the colonel would on no account permit us to change into a gallop. Taking us out into the main road, he halted us in a column with our backs to the enemy.

" 'Attention!' he cried. 'Now I want to talk to you, men. You are brave fellows, and patriotic ones too, but you are ignorant of this kind of work, and I am teaching you. I want you to observe that a good man on a horse can never be caught. Another thing: cavalry can *trot* away from anything, and a gallop is a gait unbecoming a soldier, unless he is going toward the enemy. Remember that. We gallop toward the enemy, and trot away, *always*—

" 'Steady now! Don't break ranks!' And as the words left his lips, a shell from a battery half a mile to the rear hissed over our heads.

" 'There,' he resumed. 'I've been waiting for that, and watching those fellows. I knew they'd shoot too high, and I wanted you to learn how shells sound.' "

Stuart was now willing to yield at least a part of the fighting to Joe Johnston's advance brigade, that of Thomas Jackson. One of Jackson's private soldiers was seventeen-year-old John N. Opie, whose home was farther southward in the great valley he was helping to defend. Opie recounts:

"So little did our men realize that we were going into battle that they broke ranks and climbed upon the fences, that they might thereby obtain a better view. On they came in battle array, the first army we had ever beheld; and a grand sight it was—infantry, artillery, and mounted men; their arms and accoutrements glittering in the sunlight, their colors unfurled to the breeze, their bands playing and drums beating, the officers shouting the commands as regiments, battalions, and companies marched up and wheeled into position.

"Then a battery took position and commenced firing at us, when [one] of our guns, unlimbering, immediately returned their fire. The officer in command of our artillery was a pious old gentleman, an Episcopal preacher, [William N.] Pendleton, who subsequently became general of artillery. He named his cannon Matthew, Mark, Luke, and John. When he wished a gun to be fired, he raised his hands towards the heavens and exclaimed aloud, 'May the Lord have mercy on their wicked souls! Fire!'

"Our regiment, the 5th Virginia, was deployed, and a fight

immediately commenced with the enemy's sharpshooters. . . . When the first shell exploded over us, one of our company threw away his gun and fled down the pike at breakneck speed. . . . I saw a soldier fall, slightly wounded in the neck and begging to be helped up, who, when assisted to his feet, made for the rear with lightning-like rapidity, although he would not rise until assisted."

Most of the troops took the fire well. Jackson withstood a near miss from a cannonball without a twitch. He relates:

"The advance of the enemy was driven back. They again advanced, and were repulsed. My men got possession of a house and barn, which gave them a covered position and an effective fire. But finding that the enemy were endeavoring to get in my rear and that my men were being endangered, I gave the order to their colonel that, if pressed, he must fall back. He obeyed, and fell back. . . .

"Besides my cavalry [that of Stuart], I had only one regiment engaged. . . . My orders from General Johnston required me to retreat in the event of the advance in force of the enemy, so as soon as I ascertained that he was in force I obeyed my instructions. I had twelve wounded and thirteen killed and missing. My cavalry took forty-nine prisoners [Stuart had made a dash that took a company by surprise]. A number of the enemy were killed."

Adds Confederate narrator Dr. Dabney:

"In this combat, known as that of Haines' Farm [or Falling Waters], Colonel Jackson . . . was probably the only man in the detachment of infantry who had ever been under fire. . . . His coolness, skill, care for the lives of his men, and happy audacity, filled them with enthusiasm. Henceforward, his influence over them was established."

On the Union side, Chaplain Stewart made an examination of the battlefield.

"Brief and limited as was the strife, yet were sad and too evident traces left of war's desolating scourge. A fine farm was left a ruin. Barns, sheds, fences, all burned. House riddled with cannon balls. Wheat fields, ripe for the sickle, level as a floor from the passage of regiments of horse, foot, and artillery. Articles of clothing, knapsacks, canteens, all manner of camp articles lay scattered over the ground. . . . Such is war."

The Union army had begun moving toward Martinsburg. There was no opposition except for the little band under Jeb Stuart. According to Stuart's man George Cary Eggleston, the troopers operated "literally within the Federal lines. We were shelled, skirmished with, charged, and surrounded . . . until we learned to hold in high regard our colonel's masterly skill in getting into and out of perilous positions. He seemed to blunder into them in sheer recklessness, but in getting out he showed us the quality of his genius; and . . . we . . . learned, among other things, to entertain a feeling closely akin to worship for our brilliant and daring leader. We had begun to understand, too, how much force he meant to give to his favorite dictum that the cavalry is the eye of the army."

Independence Day found Patterson setting up camp just north of Martinsburg, with Johnston on the alert a few miles to the southwest.

On that day, Colonel Jackson wrote his wife: "The enemy are celebrating the 4th of July in Martinsburg, but we are not observing the day."

On its way to Jackson at this time was a letter from Robert E. Lee. "I have the pleasure of sending you a commission of brigadier-general in the Provisional Army, and to feel that you merit it. May your advancement increase your usefulness to the State."

Delighted at the promotion, Jackson wrote his wife: "One of my greatest desires for advancement is the gratification it will give my darling, and [the opportunity it will give me] of serving my country more efficiently. I have had all that I ought to desire in the line of promotion. I should be very ungrateful if I were not contented, and exceedingly thankful to our kind Heavenly Father."

Patterson remained at Martinsburg, while Johnston returned to Winchester. This placed the armies some twenty miles apart. Neither commander was eager for battle at this time, so neither made any aggressive moves. Each camp, however, experienced its share of false alarms.

As told in a letter by the Union's Chaplain Stewart:

"A town has no very enviable situation when lying between two hostile armies, ready to open fire on each other at any hour of the day or night. Such is Martinsburg at present. Our encampment is on the Potomac side, and that of the enemy some miles on the other. Twenty-five hundred [of our] pickets and sentinels each night watch our encampment for miles around. The soldiers are watchful, excitable, and inexperienced. At night, the horse, cow, dog, or even shaking bush that will not respond to the challenge of the sentinel is sure to get a Minnie bullet whizzed at it. One gun discharged causes the neighboring sentry to fire—then bang, bang, crash, crash go the sentinels and squads of pickets for a circuit of long miles through woods and fields.

"Up bounds the whole army from thousands of tents and bivouacs, and, in less time than it takes to write of it, all are arrayed in order of battle. Such an alarm in the darkness is truly grand. . . . I have a renewed enjoyment at each recurrence.

"Not so, however, the poor townsfolk. Women and children spring from their beds . . . startled from uneasy slumbers, rush into cellars and other hiding places, or run into the streets with frantic cries, vainly looking for some place of supposed safety. . . .

"Why have not all the inhabitants long since fled away? How, and where could they? Ere our coming, the rebels effectually destroyed their only railroad. For long miles, every other way is effectually blocked or guarded, this hindering ingress or egress. With all their dangers [here], the people are about as safe at home as though they made an effort to run away. . . .

"After such a night's alarm, I lately called on a family in the suburb with whom an acquaintance had been formed. A mother with a large squad of little hopefuls, and a grandmother graced the household. During the . . . night's alarm, Granny had seized a little youngster under each arm, ran out into a little quiet cranny, and staid all night.

"At my coming, the old Methodist grand-dame had but lately come in with her hopefuls.

" 'Ah, Brother Stewart,' said the old lady, with a lugubrious but, to me, rather comic air, 'laws me, I wish I was in heaven.'

"Looking at her with all the gravity that could be summoned [when a smile was threatening], my response was, 'Dear old mother, I do wish you were.'

"With a sudden start, her answer hardly seemed to appreciate my pious wish. 'But laws me, what then would become of these poor grandchildren?'

"This was simple nature. . . . We parted with mutual wishes for a return of peace to our beloved but distracted country.

"Such scenes would reconcile to the most tender and benevolent of hearts a desire to see Henry A. Wise [Virginia's governor just prior to the war], with a hundred other such arch-traitors, *hung*. Thousands of such lives could not atone for the numberless calamities they have needlessly brought upon poor old Virginia."

Both General Patterson and General Johnston knew, of course, that their efforts were to be tied in with the campaign that was simmering between Washington and Manassas. It would be Patterson's job to keep Johnston from reinforcing Beauregard, and Johnston's job to keep Patterson from reinforcing McDowell.

McDowell was presently under great pressure from both the Northern public and official Washington to begin advancing. It was believed he might be able to storm through Beauregard at Manassas and go on to seize the Confederate capital, thus ending the war with a single blow. "On to Richmond!" was the Northern battle cry. Although McDowell protested his unreadiness for such a move, he had no choice but to mature a plan.

Not among McDowell's prodders was Winfield Scott, who favored a different approach to the war. His "Anaconda Plan" called for a tightening of the blockade of the Confederacy's eastern and southern coasts and the seizure of the Mississippi River to the Gulf of Mexico. Once surrounded (as if by a constricting snake), the Confederacy might be expected to submit. Aside from the uncertainty of its merit, Scott's proposal had a heavy aura of slowness about it. President Lincoln himself was urging a speedy thrust by McDowell.

For a few days toward the middle of July, however, the spotlight shifted from McDowell and his preparations. Union General George McClellan had begun making big news in western Virginia.

19

McClellan and the Pinkertons

N O FIGURE of the Civil War, North or South, became more of a subject of controversy than George McClellan. Nor did any figure begin his career with more promise. A West Point honor graduate who distinguished himself in the Mexican War, McClellan spent the immediate afteryears in special military offices, at home and abroad, then left the service for the business world and was a railroad president when the Civil War began. Thirty-five years old, he was of medium height, uncommonly strong, graceful of carriage, facially attractive, and charming of manner. He was a studious reader and was brilliantly versed in a variety of topics. On the deficit side, McClellan regarded himself as a man of rare destiny who was superior to his contemporaries— and this included Abraham Lincoln, whom he saw as a backwoods incompetent.

But there is no denying that McClellan had a genius for military organization, a ready knowledge of strategy and tactics, a solid courage, and a style of leadership that stirred idolatry in his troops. He might well have entered military history as one of the all-time greats, but he had one serious failing: he was overcautious. To achieve greatness, a general must take some calculated risks. McClellan took none. He had the bearing of a bold leader and he talked like one, but caution was ever his watchword.

To be sure, no one was criticizing McClellan at the outset of the war. From his headquarters at Cincinnati, he had taken efficient charge of his Department of the Ohio, which consisted of the states of Ohio, Indiana, Illinois, a small part of western Pennsyl-

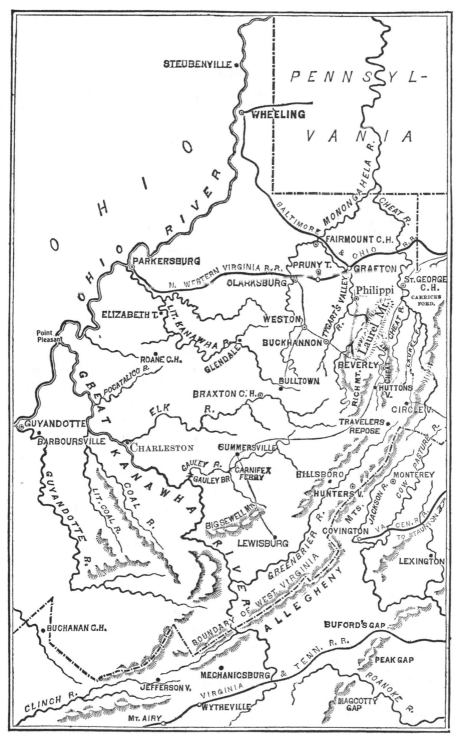

Western Virginia (now West Virginia)

vania, and that part of western Virginia (now West Virginia) lying north of the Great Kanawha River and west of the Allegheny Mountains. The general organized his accumulating troops with great care, using praise to stimulate their morale; he issued stirring public proclamations in which he vowed to protect the region's Unionist residents; and he made showy tours of inspection by rail.

Western Virginia was soon the focus of McClellan's attention. He said later: "My movements . . . were, from first to last, undertaken upon my own authority and of my own volition, and without any advice, orders, or instructions from Washington or elsewhere."

McClellan did, however, have the aid of "E. J. Allen," chief of the Government's secret service, who was really Allan Pinkerton of the Pinkerton Detective Agency, based in Chicago. (The agency's symbol was a bright-looking human eye over the motto "We Never Sleep.") A short, stocky man with a lively imagination and a flare for dramatic action, Pinkerton had been associated with the Underground Railroad and had counted John Brown as a bosom friend. The detective and his operatives had tried to rescue Brown from jail. "Had it not been for the excessive watchfulness of those having him in charge, the pages of American history would never have been stained with a record of his execution."

It had been Pinkerton who had investigated the rumored plot against Lincoln at the time of his trip from Springfield to Washington, the detective declaring the plot to be a very real one, and ever afterward claiming he had saved the president's life. "I cannot repress a sense of pride in the fact that at the commencement of his glorious career I had averted the blow that was aimed at his honest, manly heart."

Pinkerton worked with McClellan from the start to the finish of the general's Civil War career. It was partly Pinkerton's fault that McClellan was relieved of his command of the Army of the Potomac in November 1862 for a lack of aggressive action. Inexplicably, Pinkerton's spies developed a habit of returning from their errands with gross overestimates of the enemy's numbers, and the reports, of course, contributed to McClellan's timidity. In the early days, however, Pinkerton's operations were largely reliable, and the detective, headquartered in Cincinnati, helped significantly with McClellan's work in western Virginia.

As Pinkerton tells it:

Pinkerton conferring with McClellan

"At this time the condition of affairs in the State of Virginia . . . presented a most perplexing and vexatious problem. The antagonistic position of the two sections of that state demanded early consideration and prompt action on the part of the Federal Government, both in protecting the loyal people in the western section and of preserving their territory to the Union cause. . . .

"From the nature of its earlier settlement, and by reason of climate, soil, and situation, eastern Virginia remained the region of large plantations, with a heavy slave population. . . . West Virginia, on the contrary, having been first settled by hunters, pioneers, lumbermen, and miners, possessed little in common with her more wealthy and aristocratic neighbors beyond the mountains. . . . It was not a matter of surprise, therefore, that secessionism should be rampant in the east, and that a Union sentiment should almost universally prevail in the west. . . .

"Governor Letcher of Virginia, ignoring the attitude assumed by the people of the west . . . issued his proclamation calling for the organization of the state militia, and [included] western Virginia in the call. . . . He at an early date dispatched officers to that locality. . . . The rebel emmissaries found . . . that while fragments of rebel companies were here and there springing up, it was very evident that no local force sufficient to hold the country would respond to the Confederate appeal, while the close proximity of Union forces at several points along the Ohio [River] pointed to a short tenure of Confederate authority. . . .

"On the 23d day of May the State voted upon the ordinance of secession, and East Virginia, under complete military domination, accepted the ordinance, while West Virginia, comparatively free, voted to reject the idea of secession.

"Immediately after the result was ascertained, the rebel troops [in the west] became aggressive. . . . The appearance of these troops was quickly brought to the notice of the Federal authorities at Washington. On the 24th of May the Secretary of War and General Scott telegraphed this information to General McClellan and inquired whether its influence could not be counteracted.

"General McClellan at once replied in the affirmative, and this was the sole [communication] he received from Washington regarding a campaign in Virginia.

"On the 26th, the General ordered two regiments to cross the river at Wheeling, and two others at Parkersburg. . . . After a most brilliant strategic movement [that climaxed at the village of Philippi] . . . the rebels were forced to disperse in utter rout and confusion. This complete success of the first dash at the enemy had the most inspiriting effect upon the Union troops, and also encouraged . . . the western Virginia unionists in their determination to break away from the east and to form a new State. . . . General McClellan, in furtherance of this object, ordered additional forces into the State from his department.

"In order to act intelligently in the matter, it was necessary that some definite information should be derived respecting the country which was now to be protected, and from which it was necessary the invading rebels should be driven. For this purpose the General desired that I should dispatch several of my men, who, by assuming various and unsuspicious characters, would be able to travel over the country, obtain a correct idea of its topography [and] ascertain the exact position and designs of the secessionists.

"For this duty I selected a man named Price Lewis, who had just returned from a trip to the South, and whom I had reason to be satisfied was equal to the task . . . together with several others. . . . In order to afford variety to the professions of my operatives, and because of his fitness for the character, I decided that Price Lewis should represent himself as an Englishman traveling for pleasure, believing that he would thus escape a close scrutiny or a rigid examination, should he, by any accident, fall into the hands of the rebels [who were on friendly terms with England].

"Procuring a comfortable-looking road-wagon and a pair of strong gray horses . . . I stocked the vehicle with such articles of necessity and luxury as would . . . give the appearance of truth to such professions as the sight-seeing Englishman might feel authorized to make. I provided him also with a number of English certificates of various kinds, and I also supplied him with English money which could be readily exchanged for such currency that would best suit his purposes in the several localities which he would be required to visit.

"Lewis wore a full beard, and this was trimmed in the most approved English fashion; and when fully equipped for his journey he presented the appearance of a thorough well-to-do Englishman who might even be suspected of having 'blue blood' in his veins. In order that he might the more fully sustain the new character he was about to assume, and to give an added dignity to his position, I concluded to send with him a member of my force who would act in the capacity of coachman, groom, and body servant, as occasion should demand.

"The man whom I selected for this role was a jolly, good-natured, and fearless Yankee named Samuel Bridgeman, a quick, sharp-witted young man who had been in my employment for some time, and who had on several occasions proved himself worthy of trust and confidence in matters that required tact as well as boldness, and good sense as well as keen wit. Calling Sam into my office, I explained to him fully the nature of the duties he would be required to perform, and when I had concluded I saw by the merry twinkle in this eyes, and from the readiness with which he caught at my suggestions, that he thoroughly understood and had decided to carry out his part of the program to the very letter.

"In addition to these, I arranged a route for two other men of my force. They were to travel through the valley of the Great Kanawha River, and to observe carefully everything that came under their notice which might be of importance in perfecting a military campaign, in case the rebels should attempt hostile measures, or that General McClellan might find it necessary to promptly clear that portion of Virginia from the presence of secession troops. These two men were to travel ostensibly as farm laborers, and their verdant appearance was made to fully conform to such avocations.

"Everything being in readiness, the two parties were started, and we will follow their movements separately, as they were to travel by different routes.

"Price Lewis, the pseudo-Englishman, and Sam Bridgeman, who made quite a smart-looking valet in his new costume, transferred their horses, wagon, and stores on board the trim little steamer *Cricket* at Cincinnati, intending to travel along the Ohio River and effect a landing at Guyandotte, in western Virginia, at which point they were to disembark and pursue their journey overland through the country.

"I accompanied Lewis to the wharf, and, after everything had been satisfactorily arranged, I bade him good-bye, and the little steamer sailed away up the river.

"There were the usual number of miscellaneous passengers upon the boat; and added to these were a number of Union officers who had been dispatched upon various missions throughout that portion of the State of Ohio. These men left the steamer as their points of destination were reached, and, after they had departed, several of the passengers who had hitherto remained silent became very talkative. They began in a cautious manner to express their opinions, with a view of eliciting some knowledge of the sympathies of their fellow-travelers in the important struggle that was now impending.

"Lewis had maintained a quiet, dignified reserve which, while it did not forbid any friendly approaches from his fellow-passengers, at the same time rendered them more respectful and prevented undue familiarity.

"Sam Bridgeman contributed materially to this result. His deference to 'my lord' was very natural, and the respect with which he received his commands convinced the passengers at once that the English-looking gentleman was a man of some importance.

"The passengers all appeared to be Union men, and, while they expressed their regrets that the war had commenced, they regarded their separation from eastern Virginia with undisguised satisfaction.

"At midnight on the second evening, the boat landed at Guyandotte, and Samuel . . . attended to the transfer of his master and the equipage from the boat to the wharf. . . . Stopping at [a] hotel overnight, they continued their journey on the following morning. . . . In the afternoon . . . [they] reached the little village of Colemouth, where there was a rebel encampment. . . . They

were halted by the guard, who inquired their business and destination.

"Lewis told him he was an Englishman, accompanied only by
his servant, and that he was traveling through the country for
pleasure. The guard . . . asked Lewis to go with him to the captain's headquarters, which was located in a large stone house a few
hundred yards distant. My operative willingly consented, and,
leaving Sam in charge of his carriage, he accompanied the soldier
to the officer's quarters. He was ushered into a large and well-
furnished apartment. . . .

"The captain . . . greeted my operative pleasantly and informed
him that he regretted the necessity of detaining him, but orders
had to be obeyed. Lewis related in substance what he had already
stated to the guard, which statement the captain unhesitatingly
received; and after a pleasant conversation he invited the detective to accept the hospitality of the camp. . . . A soldier was dispatched to bring [in] the horses and carriage and their impatient
driver. . . .

"Supper was ordered. . . . During the meal, Sam stood behind
the chair of Lewis and awaited upon him in the most approved
fashion, replying invariably with a deferential, 'Yes, my lord.'

"After full justice had been done to the repast, Price directed

Bridgeman and Lewis with Confederate captain

Bridgeman to bring in from the carriage a couple of bottles of champagne. . . . Lewis, being an Englishman by birth, was very well posted about English affairs, and he entertained his host with several very well invented anecdotes of the Crimea, in which he was supposed to have taken an active part; and his intimacy with Lord Raglan, the commander of the British army, gained for him the unbounded admiration and respect of the doughty captain.

"From this officer Lewis learned that there were a number of troops in Charleston, but a few miles distant, and that General Wise [the ex-governor] . . . had arrived there that day. [Wise, in truth, was still in the process of transferring from Richmond.]

"After a refreshing sleep and a bounteous breakfast, Lewis informed the captain that he would continue his journey toward Charleston and endeavor to obtain an interview with General Wise. The captain cordially recommended him to do so, and furnished him with passports which would carry him without question or delay upon the road.

"As they were about taking their leave, the captain put into Lewis' hands an unsealed letter, at the same time remarking with great earnestness: 'My lord, I beg of you to accept the enclosed letter of introduction to General Wise. As I am personally acquainted with him, this letter may be of some service to you. . . .'

" 'Thank you,' replied Lewis, '. . . Believe me, I shall always recall my entertainment at your hands with pleasure.'

"The valiant captain was not aware that he had been furnishing very valuable information to his gentlemanly visitor, and that . . . his servant, the quiet Sam Bridgeman, was unobservedly making notes of all that he heard in relation to the situation of affairs and with regard to the probable movements of the rebel troops. . . .

"They had proceeded but a short distance upon their way when one of the horses . . . cast a shoe, which made it necessary for them to stop at a little village and secure the services of a blacksmith. Driving up to the hotel, Lewis alighted from the wagon, while Bridgeman drove to the blacksmith shop. . . . As Lewis ascended the steps of the hotel he noticed a tall, rather commanding-looking gentleman seated upon the porch, who was evidently scrutinizing his appearance very carefully. . . . There was an air of seeming importance about him. . . . Lewis, in order to pave the way to his acquaintance, invited him to partake of a drink [from the hotel bar]. . . . In a few minutes, under its influence, the two men were conversing with all the freedom of old friends.

"Lewis ascertained that his companion was a justice of the peace, an office of some importance in that locality, and that the old gentleman was disposed to give to his judicial position all the dignity which a personal appreciation of his standing demanded. In a quiet manner, Lewis at once gave the justice to understand his appreciating the honor he had received in meeting him. . . .

"Their pleasant conversation was progressing with very favorable success when Sam Bridgeman drove up with the team, having succeeded in finding a smithy and in having the lost shoe replaced. With a deferential semi-military salute, he addressed Lewis, 'We are all ready, my lord.'

"At the mention of the title the old fellow jumped to his feet in blank amazement, and in the most obsequious manner, and with an air of humility that, compared with his bombastic tone of a few moments before, was perfectly ridiculous.

"Jerking off his hat and placing it under his left arm, he advanced and said, 'If my lord would do me the honor to accept my poor hospitality, I would only be too happy to have the pleasure of his company for dinner. My house is only a short distance off, on the road to Charleston. . . .'

"Lewis hesitated a moment, and then remembering that he had represented himself as traveling purely for pleasure, he did not see how he could avoid accepting his kind invitation. . . .

"They remained overnight with the old gentleman, and on the following morning . . . they started on their journey . . . towards Charleston, traveling but slowly, as the roads were heavy from the recent rains. About noon they arrived at a farmhouse, to which they had been recommended by their host of the night before. Here they stopped for dinner, and, after refreshing themselves, they again went on.

"The afternoon was warm and pleasant, and their journey lay through a beautiful stretch of country. . . . Their enjoyment was, however, suddenly interrupted by the sound of loud voices and the clattering of horses' hoofs immediately behind them. Quickly turning around, the cause of this unusual excitement was at once apparent. A fine black horse, covered with foam, was tearing down the turnpike at breakneck speed and evidently running away. Upon his back was seated a young lady who bravely held her seat, and who was vainly attempting to restrain the unmanageable animal. Some distance behind were a party of ladies and gentlemen on horseback, all spurring their horses to the utmost, as if with the intention of overtaking the flying steed. . . .

"Quick as a flash, my operatives realized the situation of affairs and the necessity for prompt action. Without uttering a word, Sam Bridgeman turned his horses directly across the road, intending by that means to stop the mad course of the fiery charger approaching them. As he did so, Lewis sprang from the wagon, and with the utmost coolness advanced to meet the approaching horse.

"On came the frightened animal at a speed that threatened every moment to hurl the brave girl from her seat, until he approached nearly to the point at which my operatives had stationed themselves; and then, evidently perceiving the obstructions in his path, he momentarily slackened pace. In that instant Lewis sprang forward and, grasping the bridle firmly with a strong hand, he forced the frightened animal back upon his haunches.

"The danger was passed. The horse, feeling the iron grip upon the bridle and recognizing the voice of authority, stood still and trembling in every joint, his reeking sides heaving and his eyes flashing fire. The young lady, with a sudden revulsion of feeling, fell back in the saddle, and would have fallen but that Sam Bridgeman, hastening to the relief of his companion, was fortunately in time to catch the fainting figure in his arms. Extricating her quickly from the saddle, he set her gently on the ground, and as he did so the fair head fell forward on his shoulder, and she lost consciousness.

"By this time Lewis had succeeded in quieting the excited animal and had fastened him to a tree by the wayside, and, as he turned to the assistance of Bridgeman, the companions of the unconscious girl rode up. Hastily dismounting, they rushed to her aid, and in a few minutes, under their ministrations, the dark eyes were opened and the girl gazed wonderingly around. After being assisted to her feet, she gratefully expressed her thankfulness to the men who had probably saved her life, in which she was warmly joined by the remainder of the party.

"Sam Bridgeman received these grateful expressions with an air of modest confusion . . . and then said, 'It ain't no use thanking me, Miss. It was my lord here that stopped the animal.'

"At the words 'my lord,' a look of curiosity came over the faces of the newcomers, and Lewis stepped gracefully forward. . . .

" 'I am glad, ladies and gentlemen, to have been of service to this young lady; and permit me to introduce myself as Henry Tracy, of Oxford, England, now traveling in America.'

"The three gentlemen who were of the riding party grasped the hand of their new-made English acquaintance, and in a few words introduced him to the ladies who accompanied them, all of whom were seemingly delighted to make the acquaintance of a gentleman who had been addressed by his servant as 'my lord.'

"This adventure proved to be a most fortunate one for my two operatives. The gentlemen, upon introducing themselves, were discovered to be connected with the rebel army and to be recruiting officers sent [from Richmond] by Governor Letcher to organize such rebel volunteers as were to be gathered in western Virginia.

"By them Lewis was cordially invited to join their company to Charleston, which he as cordially accepted. Suggesting that as the young lady, who had scarcely recovered from the accident, might not feel able to ride her horse into town, he politely offered her a seat in his carriage, which offer was gratefully accepted; and, attaching the runaway horse to the rear of the vehicle, the party proceeded on their way to Charleston, at which point they arrived without further event or accident.

"The young lady whom Lewis had so providentially rescued was the only daughter of Judge Beveridge, one of the wealthiest and most influential men in the State; and, upon conducting her to her home, the detective was received with the warmest emotions by the overjoyed father. Lewis was pressed to make the house of the judge his home during his stay, but, gratefully declining the invitation, he took up his quarters at the hotel, where he could more readily extend his acquaintance, and where his movements would be more free.

"The young officers whom he had met upon the road had their quarters at the hotel at which Lewis had stopped, and, under their friendly guidance, no one thought of questioning his truthfulness or impeaching his professions. By this means he was enabled to acquire a wonderful amount of information, both of value and importance to the cause of the North. . . .

"Recognizing the importance of holding West Virginia and of preventing the Union forces from penetrating through the mountains in the direction of Staunton [in the Shenandoah Valley], the rebel authorities had sent two new commanders into that region. Ex-Governor Wise was dispatched to the Kanawha Valley, and General [Robert S.] Garnett, formerly a major in the Federal army, was sent to Beverly. . . .

"General Wise . . . was expected to arrive at Charleston on the day following the appearance of my operatives, and the city was in a state of subdued excitement in anticipation of his coming.

"In the evening, Lewis, in company with the officers whom he had met in the morning, proceeded to the residence of Judge Beveridge, where he was cordially received by that gentleman and his charming daughter, who had now thoroughly recovered from the effects of her dangerous ride. With rare grace she greeted my operative, and her expressions of thankfulness were couched in such delicate language that the pretended Englishman felt a strange fluttering in his breast. . . . He passed a very delightful evening, and by his knowledge of English affairs and his unqualified approval of the cause of the South—added to the fact that he was believed to be a gentleman of rank and fortune—he succeeded in materially increasing the high opinion which had previously been entertained regarding him.

"The next morning General Wise arrived, and his appearance was hailed with delight by the disunion element of the city, while those whose sympathies were with the North looked with apprehension and disfavor upon the demonstrations that were being made in his honor.

"At the first opportune moment, Price Lewis, with the assistance of his new-found friends, the rebel officers, succeeded in obtaining an introduction to the ancient-looking individual whose career had been marked by such exciting events, and who was so prominent a figure in the tragedy that was now being enacted. He was a small, intelligent-looking man . . . whose emaciated appearance gave every token that he had not long to live. [He was only fifty-four and was good for another fifteen years.] His eyes shone with the brilliancy of youth, and the fires of ambition seemed to be burning brightly in his breast. . . .

"The general had been previously informed of the presence of Lewis in the hotel and of his adventure of the day previous; consequently, when he was presented to the new commander he was received with warm cordiality. The general inquired particularly into his history and his present movements, all of which were replied to by Lewis in a dignified and satisfactory manner. Under the influence of Lewis' good nature, the general became social and familiar and invited him to dine with him in his apartments.

"Leaving no opportunity that offered, the detective took advantage of every available suggestion, and the result was he became fully posted upon everything that was of importance. . . . Sam Bridgeman, too, had not been idle, but, mingling freely with the soldiers, he had succeeded in learning much. . . . They remained in Charleston about eight days, and then, taking leave of the many friends they had made, they made their way safely back to Cincinnati and reported.

"The other two men whom I dispatched upon the same mission [actually, a mission north of Charleston designed to carry them eastward through the Allegheny Mountains] traveled by rail across the State of Ohio and reached the West Virginia line at Point Pleasant. Here they began their investigations. . . . It is enough to say that they performed their duty in a manner creditable to themselves and valuable to the cause they represented, and I will simply summarize the situation [as they found it].

"General Garnett had posted himself in the pass at Laurel Hill [also called Laurel Mountain], with an additional force at Beverly, while another detachment, under Col. [John] Pegram, had established itself in the pass at Rich Mountain. . . . [Garnett] found affairs upon his arrival in a miserable condition. The troops were disorganized and without discipline, arms, or ammunition; and General Lee immediately sent him reinforcements.

"This was the condition of affairs when . . . General McClellan resolved to take the offensive and drive the rebels from West Virginia."

20

Rich Mountain and Carrick's Ford

McCLELLAN NOW HAD some twenty thousand troops at his disposal, whereas the Confederates in western Virginia numbered only about six thousand. The general decided to make his principal effort against the concentration in the northeast, that of Garnett in the Beverly region. For the present, only a containing force was to be stationed before the westerly concentration, that of Wise in the Charleston area of the Kanawha Valley. Once Garnett was bested, Wise might be taken from the rear.

McClellan's journey from his headquarters in Cincinnati to take personal charge of the Beverly operation was a matter for civilian celebration. Regarding his railway trip across Ohio to the border of western Virginia, he wrote his wife (née Ellen Marcy):

"We . . . had a continual ovation all along the road. At every station where we stopped, crowds had assembled to see the 'young general': gray-headed old men and women, mothers holding up their children to take my hand, girls, boys, all sorts, cheering and crying, 'God bless you!' I never went through such a scene in my life. . . . You would have been surprised at the excitement. At Chillicothe the ladies had prepared a dinner, and I had to be trotted through. They gave me about twenty beautiful bouquets and almost killed me with kindness. The trouble will be to fill their expectations, they seem to be so high. I could hear them say, 'He is our own general'; 'Look at him, how young he is'; '*He* will thrash them'; 'He'll do,' etc., etc., *ad infinitum*."

Reaching his army's staging area in western Virginia (some forty miles northwest of Garnett's positions), McClellan issued a proc-

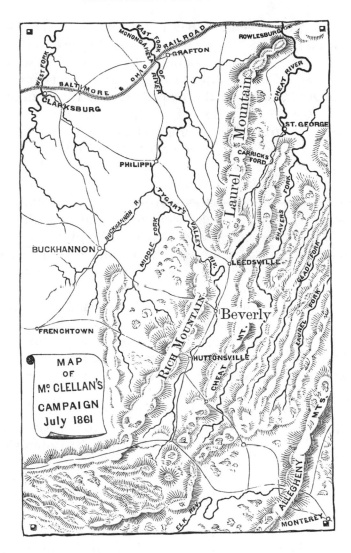

lamation that exhorted the troops to fight courageously but humanely, and to give full respect to the rights of private property. He closed with the lines:

"Soldiers, I have heard that there was danger here. I have come to place myself at your head and share it with you. I fear now but one thing, that you will not find foemen worthy of your steel. I know that I can rely upon you."

While making his final preparations for action, McClellan included the following lines in a series of letters to Ellen:

"Everything here needs the hand of the master and is getting it fast. . . . I am detained . . . by want of supplies now on the way, and which I hope to receive soon. . . . I never worked so hard in my life before. . . . Unless where I am in person, everything seems to go wrong. . . . Look on the maps and find Buckhannon and Beverly; that is the direction of my [planned] march. . . . One thing takes up a great deal of time, yet I cannot avoid it: crowds of the country people who have heard of me and read my proclamations come in from all directions to thank me, shake me by the hand, and look at their 'liberator, the general.' Of course I have to see them and talk to them. Well, it is a proud and glorious thing to see a whole people here, simple and unsophisticated, looking up to me as their deliverer from tyranny."

A letter from Buckhannon written on July 5 informed Ellen: "Yesterday was a very busy day with me, reviewing troops all the morning and giving orders all day and pretty much all night. . . . I realize now the dreadful responsibility on me—the lives of my men, the reputation of the country, and the success of our cause. The enemy are in front, and I shall probably move forward tomorrow. . . . I shall feel my way and be very cautious, for I recognize the fact that everything requires success in first operations."

It was July 10 before McClellan, his army divided, got into position just west of Garnett's two defense sectors. Facing Garnett himself, who held Laurel Hill in the north, was Brigadier General Thomas A. Morris, a volunteer from Indiana. McClellan was in personal command of the southern force, that facing Pegram at Rich Mountain. Morris had orders to keep Garnett occupied with a demonstration while McClellan attacked Pegram. McClellan wanted to break through to the towns of Beverly and Huttonsville, which lay on the main road through the Alleghenies to the Shenandoah Valley. The seizure of these towns would sever Garnett's line of retreat, forcing him either to surrender or try to make his way eastward to safety by means of difficult mountain passes.

One of the brigadiers with McClellan was William S. Rosecrans of the regular army (and destined for fame in the war), who suggested that Pegram be flanked. McClellan agreed, making another division of his forces. He himself was to hold fast in front of Pegram while Rosecrans made a southerly swing to the Confederate's rear. Pegram, as it happened, was posted below the hilltop farmlands owned by a Unionist family named Hart, who had fled the Confederate occupation. A son of the family, David Hart, was now accorded a moment of glory:

"I was with General Rosecrans as guide at the Battle of Rich Mountain. The enemy . . . were strongly entrenched at the foot of the mountain on the west side. They had rolled whole trees from the mountainside and lapped them together, filling in with stones and earth from a trench outside. General McClellan . . . sent General Rosecrans with the 8th, 10th, and 15th Indiana Regiments, the 19th Ohio, and the Cincinnati Cavalry, to get in their rear. . . .

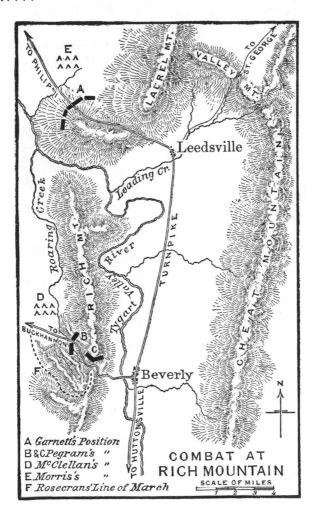

A *Garnett's Position*
B & C *Pegram's "*
D *McClellan's "*
E *Morris's "*
F *Rosecrans'Line of March*

COMBAT AT
RICH MOUNTAIN
SCALE OF MILES

"We started about daylight [on July 11] . . . and turned into the woods on our right. I led . . . through a pathless route. . . . We pushed along through the bush, laurel, and rocks . . . in perfect silence. The bushes wetted us thoroughly, and it was very cold. Our circuit was about five miles. About noon we reached the top of the mountain, near my father's farm. It was not intended that the enemy should know of our movements."

But something had gone wrong. As explained by Virginia's Jedediah Hotchkiss, then serving as an engineer in Garnett's army:

"A cavalry sergeant following after Rosecrans missed his way and was captured. Pegram gathered from him some information about the flank movement, which induced him to send Major J. A. De Lagnel, of the Confederate States Artillery, with a section of artillery [a single piece], a company of cavalry, and two companies of infantry . . . to meet this Federal advance."

Returning to David Hart:

"They entrenched themselves with earthworks on my father's farm, just where we were to come [out of the bushes] into the road. We did not know they were there until we came on their pickets, and their cannon opened fire upon us. We were then about a quarter of a mile from the house, and skirmishing began. . . . The rain began pouring down in torrents, while the enemy fired his cannon, cutting off the treetops over our heads quite lively. . . . We had no cannon with us."

The Federals soon fell back. According to Confederate narrator Jed Hotchkiss:

"A second advance . . . came on again in about twenty minutes. Moving his gun a little higher up the slope, De Lagnel again opened at short range . . . and again forced the enemy to a hasty retreat, which was followed by shouts from the Confederates, who confidently believed that they had gained the day.

"Rosecrans soon reformed his men, lengthening his lines, and renewed the attack, his sharpshooters firing on the artillery horses so that they ran away down the mountain with the drivers and caissons, leaving the gunners only a little ammunition. . . . De Lagnel moved his gun near a small log stable, a little farther to the right, but by that time the enemy's fire became so heavy that it rapidly disabled the artillerists, leaving but few to the gun, when De Lagnel, who had had his horse shot under him, gallantly volunteered in person and helped to load and fire the gun three or

The final Union charge

four times, at last with only the help of a boy, all his artillerists having been killed or wounded.

"Finally, receiving a severe wound and finding his command outflanked on both sides, he ordered his men to retreat . . . to the northward . . . having sustained a brave fight, from 3 P.M. to 6 P.M., with his staunch 310 men of all arms, against over six times his own number, and suffered a loss of nearly one-third of [his strength]."

Again in the words of Unionist David Hart:

"The enemy broke from their entrenchments in every way they could. The Indiana boys had previously been ordered to 'fix bayonets.' We could hear the rattle of the iron very plainly as the order was obeyed. 'Charge bayonets' was then ordered, and away went our boys after the enemy. . . . A general race for about three hundred yards followed through the bush, when our men were recalled and re-formed in line of battle to receive the enemy from the entrenchments at the foot of the mountains, as we supposed they would certainly attack us from that point."

Jed Hotchkiss says that such an attempt was made:

"Moved by the noise of furious battle in his rear, Pegram, late in the day, took six companies . . . and hurried up the mountain . . . ordering [a] gun . . . to follow. . . . He found De Lagnel's men in retreat, their gun abandoned and the Federals in possession. The runaway horses of De Lagnel's caisson rushed down the mountain just in time to meet and overturn the second piece of artillery on its way up."

With his infantry units, Pegram advanced only far enough to learn that Rosecrans was too strong for him, then gave up his effort and returned to his lines at the western base of the mountain. McClellan was still facing these lines, having remained inactive throughout the day. He had planned to attack as soon as he could be certain that Rosecrans was succeeding, but no such indication had reached him, so he had postponed his attack until the following day. Pegram, however, evacuated during the night, and at 9 A.M. McClellan wired Washington:

"I have taken all his guns, a very large amount of wagons, tents, etc.—everything he had—a large number of prisoners, many of whom were wounded. . . . They lost many killed. We have lost, in all, perhaps twenty killed and fifty wounded, of whom all but two or three were in the column under Rosecrans, which turned the position. The mass of the enemy escaped through the woods, entirely disorganized. . . . I had a position ready for twelve guns near the main camp, and, as the guns were moving up, I ascertained that the enemy had retreated. I am now pushing on to Beverly."

The general took the time to pay a visit to the battlefield atop the mountain, where the residual scene was a grim one. In the words of an unidentified Union newsman:

"Our own and the rebel wounded lay strewn together in blankets on the floor of Hart's house. Every available space was covered with their convulsive and quivering bodies. Down under the porch there was another line of wounded. There was no difference in the treatment of the sufferers. The severely wounded of

the enemy were attended to before the slightly wounded of our
own army.

"Most of them suffered in silence; a few slept soundly; but some
moaned with intense agony. One poor fellow, an Indiana man
shot through the head, who could even yet stand on his feet with
assistance, suffered great agony. Now and then a rebel would
stare sullenly at our people, but the majority appeared gratefully
surprised at the kindness with which they were treated. . . .

"General McClellan . . . visited the hospital and spoke cheerfully to the sufferers, making many kind inquiries. When he came
out . . . a rough soldier exclaimed to a comrade, 'Why, the General is crying!' "

That afternoon (July 12) McClellan wired Washington:

"I occupied Beverly by a rapid march. Garnett abandoned his

Capture of a Confederate gun

camp [on Laurel Mountain] early in the morning, leaving much of his equipage. He came with a few miles of Beverly, but our rapid march turned him back . . . and he is now retreating on the road to St. George [to the northeast]. I have ordered General Morris to follow him up closely."

On the ensuing day (July 13), McClellan was visited by a courier from Colonel Pegram. The man had been without food for two days. "I at once," explains McClellan, "gave him some breakfast, and shortly after gave him a drink of whiskey. As he drank it, he said, 'I thank you, general. I drink that I may never again be in rebellion against the general government.' "

The courier gave McClellan a note from Pegram:

"I have, in consequence of the retreat of General Garnett and the jaded and reduced condition of my command . . . concluded, with the concurrence of the majority of my captains and field officers, to surrender my command to you tomorrow *as prisoners of war.*"

McClellan said in his answering note:

"As commander of this department, I will receive you and [your troops] with the kindness due to prisoners of war, but it is not in my power to relieve you, or them, from any liabilities incurred by taking arms against the United States."

Pegram's surrender, though a good number of his troops eluded it by disappearing into the woods, gave McClellan the opportunity to send another glowing report to Washington.

Little mention was made of the occupation of Huttonsville, south of Beverly, for its importance was secondary, but a correspondent of the *New York Times* found the march to the town worthy of recording:

"Many of the houses were vacated entirely by men, women, and children, all having been put in mortal fear by the terrible stories of our atrocities. In many cases the men—secessionists—fled, leaving their families . . . locked up in their houses [with] closed . . . curtains, except . . . when woman's irrepressible curiosity overcame them, and a slightly-drawn corner of the curtain revealed the gazing eye.

"A few who were Union people stood in their front doors and yards and waved their handkerchiefs in the highest joy. . . . The slaves, who were told that we should cut off their hands to disable them from working for their masters, are delighted with the army pageant, and come about in great freedom and tell with joy how they had been frightened and humbugged."

The northeasterly pursuit of Garnett (over rough mountain roads) had been launched late in the day on July 12. As related by an unidentified correspondent of the Cincinnati *Commercial:*

"The rebels . . . were moving in the direction of St. George. . . . Every few rods we found stacks of tent poles, tents, blankets, and other camp equipage which they had thrown out of their wagons and off their shoulders to lighten their burdens and facilitate their retreat. Several wagons had got off the track and were found upside down in the gorges of the mountains. . . .

"Our column . . . [soon] halted for the night. The rear came up in a couple of hours with only four provision wagons. In the haste of starting, most of our troops had left their haversacks behind. The supply of crackers averaged about one to each man. A little salt pork was served out, the men generally cutting it in thin slices, distributing it as far as it would go, and eating it raw with their crackers. Hundreds, however, went supperless to their bivouac in the bushes. . . .

"We were under way in the morning by three o'clock. The sky was overcast and the weather cold. A drizzling mist commenced falling, which, in an hour or two, turned into a steady, chilling rain. . . . We forded Leading Creek twice, and by the time we reached the miserable little village of New Interest . . . there was not a dry thread in our clothing. . . .

"Passing the village a few miles, we struck directly over the mountains for Cheat River by a byroad which the rebels had taken. It was of the worst description. At every step, the mud grew deeper and the way more difficult, and one felt as though some-body were tugging at his heels to pull off his shoes. Now slipping down in the mud, now plunging into a pool knee-deep, staggering about in the mire like drunken men, the soldiers—elated with the prospect of a fight—pushed steadily and bravely on. So thoroughly was the mire kneaded by the feet of the thousands—pursued and pursuing—that it flowed down the mountain road like thick tar. Every rivulet, too, became a torrent, while the creeks, swollen with the burden of the rains, became dashing and foaming rivers.

"In the Laurel Mountains [an easterly extension of this range], we found more evidences of the disorderly flight of the rebels. For miles, tents, tent poles, knapsacks—everything, indeed, even to personal apparel—was strewn in an indiscriminate litter and trodden down under their flying feet. Here were more wagons upset—and kept from plunging over gorges down which it made me dizzy to look, only by the dense thickets of chaparral and the trunks of trees. Everywhere it was disaster following after disaster.

"Occasionally we halted, and those so fortunate as to have them, munched their wet crackers with as much satisfaction as you would sit down to a banquet. . . . Others stretched themselves out along the roadside, and some were so weary that they [simply] sat down in the middle of the road to rest. A few gave out entirely.

"At last we emerged from the Laurel Mountains and came out on the Cheat River at Kahler's Ford, about twelve miles . . . due south of St. George. It was then noon.

"Our advance [troops] consisted of the Ohio 14th . . . 9th Indiana . . . 7th Indiana . . . and two pieces of artillery with 40 men— the total being 1,840. The reserve was an hour or more behind, their march being doubly wearisome because of the . . . roads made worse by those who had preceded them.

"The boys were glad to plunge into the ford, as the swift flowing waters of the Main Cheat purged them of heavy loads of mud, with which most were plastered to their waistbands. Emerging from the ford [of the winding river], our advance came in sight of the rear of the fugitive army at the second ford . . . where their baggage train was at rest and their infantry drawn up. . . . [But] the unlucky firing of a gun by one of our men [a premature shot] set the whole body in motion.

Robert S. Garnett

"The chase now became highly exciting. The enemy pitched the rest of their camp equipment into the bushes. The officers threw their trunks, containing their personal effects, into the gulleys and ravines, and the privates gave up their blankets, knapsacks, and canteens. . . .

"Our advance pushed them so hard that they formed in line and commenced a scattering fire, when our artillery opened on them, and they instantly renewed their stampede. . . .

"Within a mile of the next ford, the mountains recede on both sides from the river. The most of this comparatively level bottom land is comprised in the farm of Mr. James Carrick, and the fords are known by his name. In crossing the first of these fords . . . one of their wagons mired, and those in the rear had to halt. . . . The rebels meantime drew up in line [on the far bank] on the opposite side of an oat field, and were concealed by a rail fence and the trees and bushes fringing that bank of the river. The bluff is from fifty to eighty feet higher than the land . . . down which the Ohio 14th was advancing. . . . As [the regiment] came opposite the bank where the rebels were drawn up, General Garnett cried, 'Three cheers for Jeff Davis!' And at that instant the whole line was a blaze of light as they poured a destructive fire upon the 14th.

"The men came to an instant halt, and returned the compliment . . . and then advanced nearer the river, taking position behind a worn-out fence. The rebel battery then opened fire, and [our] artillery was ordered up. The action became general. . . . [Soon outflanked,] the rebels ceased firing along the entire line and stampeded through a wheat field down to the second ford [which they crossed, coming to a halt a distance down the road]. . . .

"General Garnett was the last to cross the ford, which he did on foot, and stood by the river shore waving his handkerchief and [apparently] calling them to come back and dispute the passage of the ford. . . . [A] Sergeant Burlingame drew a deliberate sight on the general and fired. He was seen to throw up his hands and fall back on the sand. At the same instant, almost the only man who had the pluck to stand by the general, a Georgian . . . fell dead by his side.

"[Colonel Ebenezer] Dumont's regiment had come up . . . and poured a raking fire into the enemy, who made a stand of some ten minutes, during which the fire was sharp on both sides; and then they ran, crowding upon each other in the wildest confusion.

Dumont's regiment crossed the ford and chased them two miles up the St. George Road, where they gave out from absolute exhaustion. . . . The action was over."

Most of Garnett's three or four thousand men made a clean escape (even eluding troops of an outpost to the north that McClellan had activated by telegraph). But the Federals at Carrick's Ford were pleased with themselves. It had been necessary for them to employ only a few regiments to effect the rout of many. Moreover, the trophies of the battle included the body of Garnett himself.

This was a special fascination for a news correspondent named Whitelaw Reid, of the Cincinnati *Gazette,* destined to achieve fame under the pen name "Agate."

"Not a Virginian stood by him when he fell. . . . Of all the army . . . but one was with his general—a slight, boyish figure with scarcely the dawn of approaching manhood on his face, and wearing the Georgian uniform and button. . . . There they lay, in that wild region, on the banks of the Cheat. . . . The one was the representative of Virginia aristocracy . . . the other . . . evidently from the lower walks of life, and with only a brave heart and stern

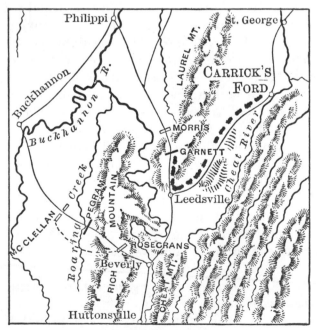

Garnett's line of retreat

determination to stand by the cause he had espoused to the bitter end. . . .

"Returning from the bank where Garnett lay, I went up to the bluff on which the enemy had been posted. The first object that caught the eye was a large iron rifled cannon, a six-pounder, which they had left in their precipitate flight. The star-spangled banner of one of our regiments floated over. Around was a sickening sight. Along the brink of that bluff lay ten bodies, stiffening in their own gore, in every contortion which their death anguish had produced. Others were gasping in the last agonies, and still others were writhing with horrible but not mortal wounds. . . .

"Never before had I so ghastly a realization of the horrid nature of this fraternal struggle. These men were all Americans. . . .

"One poor fellow was shot through the bowels. The ground was soaked with his blood. I stooped and asked him if anything could be done to make him more comfortable. He only whispered, '*I'm so cold!*' He lingered for nearly an hour, in terrible agony.

"Another—young and just developing into vigorous manhood—had been shot through the head by a large Minié ball. The skull was shockingly fractured. His brains were protruding from the bullet hole and lay spread on the grass by his head. And he was still living! I knelt by his side and moistened his lips with water from my canteen, and an officer who came up a moment afterward poured a few drops of brandy from his pocket-flask into his mouth. God help us! What more could we do? A surgeon rapidly examined the wound, sadly shook his head, saying it were better for him if he were dead already, and passed on to the next. And there that poor Georgian lay, gasping in the untold and unimaginable agonies of that fearful death for more than an hour!

"Near him lay a Virginian, shot through the mouth and already stiffening. He appeared to have been stooping when he was shot. The ball struck the tip of his nose, cutting that off, cut his upper lip, knocked out his teeth, passed through the head, and came out at the back of the neck. The expression of his ghastly face was awful beyond description.

"And near him lay another, with a ball through the right eye which had passed out through the back of the head. . . .

"All around the field lay men with wounds in the leg, or arm, or face, groaning with pain, and trembling lest the barbarous foes they expected to find in our troops should commence mangling and torturing them at once. Words can hardly express their astonishment when our men gently removed them to a little knoll, laid them all together, and formed a circle of bayonets around them to keep off the curious crowd till they could be removed to the hospital and cared for by our surgeons. . . .

"Every attention was shown the enemy's wounded. . . . Limbs were amputated, wounds were dressed with the same care with which our own brave volunteers were treated. The wound on the battlefield removed all differences. In the hospital all were alike, the objects of a common humanity that left none beyond its limits."

Now that both Pegram and Garnett had been bested, McClellan issued an address that thrilled the troops, with no one taking exception to its overblown style.

"*Soldiers of the Army of the West:* I am more than satisfied with you. You have annihilated two armies, commanded by educated and experienced soldiers, entrenched in mountain fastnesses and fortified at their leisure. You have taken five guns, twelve colors, fifteen hundred stand of arms, one thousand prisoners, including more than forty officers. One of the . . . commanders of the rebels is a prisoner, the other lost his life on the field of battle. You have killed more than two hundred and fifty of the enemy, who has lost all his baggage and camp equipage. All this has been accomplished with the loss of twenty brave men killed and sixty wounded on your part. . . .

"Soldiers! I have confidence in you, and I trust you have learned to confide in me. . . . I am proud to say that you have gained the highest reward that American troops can receive—the thanks of Congress and the applause of your fellow-citizens."

The public applause included articles in the newspapers, such as this one in the Louisville *Journal:*

"We can say most cordially . . . that, in perusing the narrative of General McClellan's triumphant career in western Virginia the uppermost impression left in the mind is that it is a thing completely done. . . . It stands before us perfect and entire, wanting nothing. . . .

"McClellan set out to accomplish a certain definite object. . . . Onward he moves, and neither wood, mountain, nor stream checks his march. . . . Nothing decoys or diverts or forces him from the trail of the enemy. Outpost after outpost, camp after camp, gives way. The main body falls back, and is at last put to an ignominious and disgraceful retreat. He remains master of the field, and reports that he has accomplished his mission.

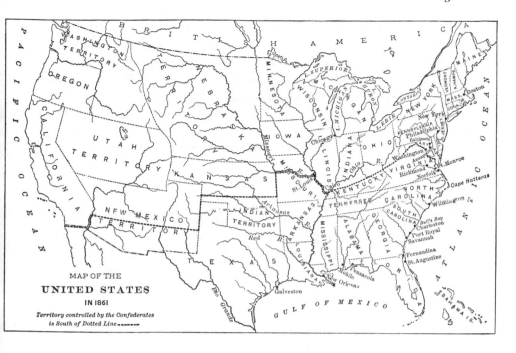

MAP OF THE
UNITED STATES
IN 1861
*Territory controlled by the Confederates
is South of Dotted Line* -------

"There is something extremely satisfactory in contemplating what might be called a piece of finished military workmanship by a master hand."

The fight for western Virginia was actually far from over. The lesser problem of Henry Wise at Charleston was only now being addressed, and Richmond had already decided to make new efforts against the conquest. But it would turn out that McClellan had won nearly as much glory as he accepted for himself.

After the war, one of his western Virginia opponents, Jed Hotchkiss the engineer, would write:

"McClellan . . . compelled the Confederates to retreat from the banks of the Ohio to near the Allegheny range of the Appalachians, and abandon to Federal control—which thenceforward during the war was well-nigh continuous—most of Trans-Allegheny Virginia, nearly one-third of the State. These results were not only of present but of great future importance to the Federal Government in the conduct of the war. They not only gave it control of the navigable waters of the Ohio along and within the borders of Virginia . . . but also gave it . . . control of the important coal mines and salt works on the Big Kanawha, and the newly discovered petroleum wells in the Little Kanawha basin . . . and enabled it to establish camps of observation . . . far within the borders of Virginia, from which raiding parties were constantly threatening Virginia's interior lines of communication through the Great Valley [the Shenandoah] and the lead mines, salt works, coal mines, blast furnaces, foundries, and other important industrial establishments in and near that grand source of military supplies—thus requiring the detaching of large numbers of troops to watch these Federal movements and to guard these important and indispensable sinews of war.

"They deprived Virginia of a large portion of her annual revenues, of a most important recruiting ground for troops; and enabled the *bogus* government of Virginia to establish and maintain itself at Wheeling, and, under the protection of Federal armies, strengthen the disloyal element in that part of the State, and organize numerous regiments of infantry and companies of cavalry and artillery to swell the numbers of the Federal army.

"McClellan had good reason to exult at his success, no matter if it had been easily won."

21

The March to Fairfax

THE NEWS of McClellan's conquest was followed at once by the breaking of another story, a major one in the war's eastern theater.

On July 14 (the day after the action at Carrick's Ford), a correspondent of the *New York Times* wrote from Washington:

"The whole country is impatient for a vigorous prosecution of the war. This impatience finds vent in all the leading public journals, and is fully shared by Congress. In some quarters it takes the shape of direct and bitter censure of the Administration, or some influential member of it, who is supposed to be responsible for the tardy progress of events. . . .

"The Administration . . . assert[s] that the movement of the main army [that of Irvin McDowell] is quite as rapid as consists with its safety; and that it is much better to advance slowly . . . than to push on recklessly. . . . Probably this is true. But it must be borne in mind that public sentiment is a powerful element of strength in this war—that it must be secured and kept in full vigor even at some expense of scientific routine, and that the present temper of our people demands swift and sudden blows, a bold and dashing policy. . . . Delay and apparent inaction discourages and disgusts them. . . .

"[But] much of this criticism . . . is the result of entire ignorance of the nature and wants of an army. Men who fight must be fed; and they must not be taken into any place or position where they cannot have food, shelter, and the means of fighting. In going into an enemy's country, they must take with them all their tents,

provisions, spades and other tools for throwing up entrenchments, cannon, ammunition, and whatever else they expect to
use. To arrive without these is simply to insure their starvation or
swift destruction by the enemy. And to carry them requires wagons, horses, teamsters, time and space. . . .

"When reduced to the lowest point, fifteen wagons with four
horses each, to each full regiment of infantry, is a fair allow-
ance. . . . All these wagons had to be made, and all these horses
purchased before any considerable movement in advance was possible. . . . Many were [also] wanted for General Patterson's column
[facing Joe Johnston in the Shenandoah Valley]. . . . This makes
no account of the horses needed for the artillery and the cavalry. . . .

"General McClellan's splendid successes in western Virginia are
quoted to show that movements may be made without all this
preparation. But it must be remembered that he has a comparatively small body of men to care for, that he is moving in a friendly
country where supplies are easy of access, that there is no difficulty in keeping his communications open. . . . This is not the case
with either of the other columns. . . .

"But all these difficulties have been surmounted; and the causes
of past delays, whether valid or not, are rapidly disappearing.
Horses, mules, and wagons are coming into the city in great numbers, and everything is ready for an advance. . . .

"General Patterson will move his forces down from Martinsburg toward Winchester. . . . General McDowell will push forward his forces gradually, each regiment feeling its way as it moves
along. . . . Thus it may be several days before any collision takes
place between the opposing forces, although the advance may
begin at once. . . .

"According to present appearances, the main body of our forces
across the Potomac [about thirty-five thousand men] will move
forward on Tuesday . . . the 16th. . . . They will probably go on, if
not sooner resisted, to Manassas Junction; and, unless all our
advices hitherto have deceived us, we may expect there to meet
the rebels in considerable force [the number was about twenty-
two thousand] and thoroughly entrenched. I doubt whether an
attack will be made upon them directly in front. . . . This is mainly
speculation. . . . But the Government will certainly move forward
immediately in the prosecution of the war.

"The capture of Richmond has undoubtedly become a matter

Segment of fortifications at Manassas

of necessity, since that city has been made the capital of the Confederate States. . . . While it was merely the capital of a State, it was a matter of little consequence who should hold it. . . . The rebels, however, saw fit to make Virginia the seat of war and to establish their capital within reach of Washington. . . . They will unquestionably see reason, ere long, to repent their temerity."

Right now the Confederates, repenting nothing, were thinking chiefly in terms of improving their Manassas defenses.

"By nature," wrote a correspondent of the New Orleans *Picayune*, "the position is one of the strongest that could have been found. . . . The right wing stretches off toward the headwaters of the Occoquan through a wooded country which is easily made impassable by the felling of trees. The left is a rolling table-land, easily commanded from the successive elevations. . . . The key to the whole position . . . is precisely the point which General Beauregard chose for his center. . . . It is a succession of hills, nearly equidistant from each other, in front of which is a ravine . . . deep and thickly wooded [and cradling the stream called Bull Run]. . . .

"Of the fortifications super-added here by General Beauregard to those of nature it is, of course, not proper for me to speak. The general reader . . . will have a sufficiently precise idea of them by conceiving a line of forts . . . zig-zag in form, with angles, salients, bastions, casemates, and everything that properly belongs to works of this kind. . . .

"Water is good and abundant. Forage . . . is everywhere found . . . and the communication with all parts of the country easy.

"Here, overlooking an extensive plain . . . divided into verdant fields of wheat and oats and corn, pasture and meadow, are the headquarters of the advanced forces of the army. . . . They are South Carolinians, Louisianians, Alabamians, Mississippians, and Virginians. . . . Never have I seen a finer body of men—men who were more obedient to discipline, or breathed a more self-sacrificing patriotism.

"As might be expected, from the skill with which he has chosen his positions, and the system with which he encamps and moves his men, General Beauregard is very popular here. I doubt if Napoleon himself had more the undivided confidence of his army."

The country fanning out before Beauregard's lines was covered both by cavalry patrols and infantry outposts, with the most advanced outpost being at Fairfax Courthouse, about ten miles from Manassas. The post's commander was Brigadier General Milledge L. Bonham, a tall, well-born South Carolinian in his late forties who wore a broad-brimmed hat with a large plume extending behind. Combining a knightly bearing with democratic ways, Bonham enjoyed both the admiration and affection of his troops. He had made them aware that their post was an important one.

Among the men in Bonham's command was D. Augustus Dickert, the fifteen-year-old who had taken an active part in the affair at Fort Sumter three months earlier. Dickert relates:

"Our main duties, outside of our regular drills, consisted in picketing the highways and blockading all roads by felling the timber across for more than a hundred yards on either side. . . . Large details armed with axes were sent out to blockade the thoroughfares leading to Washington and points across the Potomac. For miles out, in all directions, wherever the road led through wooded lands, large trees, chestnut, hickory, oak, and pine were cut pell-mell, creating a perfect abatis across the road—so much so as to cause our troops, in their verdant ignorance, to think it almost an impossibility for such obstructions to be cleared away in many days; whereas, in fact, the pioneer corps of the Federal Army [would clear] it away as fast as the army marched, not causing as much as one hour's halt. . . .

"On our outposts we could plainly hear the sound of the drums of the Federalists in their preparation for the 'On to Richmond' move. General Bonham had also some fearless scouts at this time. Even some of the boldest of the women dared to cross the Potomac in search of information. . . . It was here that . . . Miss Belle Boyd made herself famous by her daring rides, her many escapades and hairbreadth escapes, her bold acts of crossing the Potomac sometimes disguised and at other times not, even entering the City of Washington itself. In this way she gathered much valuable information. . . .

"The duties of picketing were the first features of our army life that looked really like war. . . . There was an uncanny feeling in

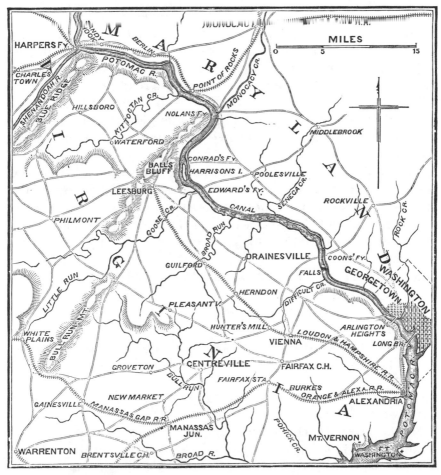

Potomac regions of McDowell's campaign

standing alone in the still hours of the night, in a strange country, waiting for an enemy to crawl up and shoot you unawares. This feeling was heightened . . . in my company by an amusing incident that happened [in the daytime] while on picket duty on the Annandale road. . . .

"A large pine thicket was to our right, while on the left was an old field with here and there a few wild-cherry trees. The cherries being ripe, some of the men had gone up in the trees. . . . The other part of the company lay indolently about, sheltering themselves as best they could from the hot July sun. . . . All felt a perfect security, for . . . the pickets in front, the cavalry scouring the country, and the almost impassable barricades of the roads seemed to render it impossible for an enemy to approach unobserved. . . .

"While the men were thus pleasantly engaged, and the officers taking an afternoon nap, from out in the thicket on the right came 'bang, bang,' and a hail of bullets came whizzing over our heads.

"What a scramble! What an excitement! What terror depicted on the men's faces! . . . Some started up the road, some down. . . . The whole Yankee army was thought to be over the hills.

"At last the officer commanding got the men halted some little distance up the road. A semblance of a line formed, men cocked their guns. . . .

"The amusing part of it was [that] the parties who fired the shots . . . were running for dear life's sake across the fields—worse scared, if possible, than we ourselves. They were three of a scouting party who had eluded our pickets, and, seeing our good, easy, and indifferent condition, took it into their heads to have a little amusement at our expense. But the sound of their guns in the quiet surrounding no doubt excited the Yankees as much as it did the Confederates. . . .

"Picket duty after this incident was much more stringent."

Union General McDowell gave his army its marching orders on Monday, July 15. Nurse Emma Edmonds says that the men realized that "a great battle was to be fought. Oh, what excitement and enthusiasm that order produced! Nothing could be heard but the wild cheering of the men, as regiment after regiment received their orders."

Mingled with the cheers were cries of "On to Richmond! On to Richmond!" Bands struck up, and one of the tunes they played was that of an old revival hymn, later to be modified by Julia Ward

Howe into the mighty "Battle Hymn of the Republic" but presently provided with stanzas that began:

> *John Brown's body lies a-mouldering in the grave;*
> *John Brown's body lies a-mouldering in the grave;*
> *John Brown's body lies a-mouldering in the grave;*
>   *His soul is marching on!*
> *Glory, glory, hallelujah!*
> *Glory, glory, hallelujah!*
> *Glory, glory, hallelujah!*
>   *His soul is marching on!*

These words had won their first public notice only a few weeks earlier when they were sung by a Massachusetts regiment passing through New York City on its way to Washington. As reported in the New York *Independent:*

"Who would have dreamed, a year and a half since, that a thousand men in the streets of New York would be heard singing reverently and enthusiastically in praise of John Brown! . . . Seldom, if ever, has New York witnessed such a sight or heard such a strain. No military hero of the present war has been thus honored. No statesman has thus loosed the tongues of a thousand men to chant his patriotism. . . .

"It is a notable fact that, while the regiment united as with one voice singing this song, thousands of private citizens, young and old, on the sidewalks and in crowded doorways and windows, joined in the chorus. The music was in itself impressive, and many an eye was wet with tears. Few who witnessed the triumphal tread of that noble band of men arrayed for the war for freedom will ever forget the thrilling tones of that song."

While preparing for the march to Manassas, according to one observer, McDowell's army presented "a glorious spectacle. The various regiments were brilliantly uniformed according to the aesthetic taste of peace, and the silken banners they flung to the breeze were unsoiled and untorn." Many of the regiments were made up of "ninety-day-men" whose term was about to expire, and more than a few of these men had every intention of starting for home the moment their time was up; but they expected to play a role in ending the war before they left.

A novel part of the preparations was that they extended to parties of civilians who were going along to enjoy the pageantry of

Federal uniforms of First Bull Run

the anticipated triumph. Included were senators, congressmen, other Washingtonians, and even citizens who had assembled from various parts of the North. Well represented were portly gentlemen garnished with golden watch chains, and fashionably dressed women carrying parasols against the ravages of the sun. Many of the parties were going in splendid carriages drawn by richly trapped horses. Stored in the carriages were not only gourmet picnic lunches but also bottles of champagne for the victory celebration. Ultimate in the optimism was that someone had distributed tickets for a grand ball in Richmond.

These people had no idea they were to end up a laughingstock, even in the North—that a Boston newspaper would make them the topic of a ballad that began:

> *Have you heard of the story, so lacking in glory,*
>   *About the civilians who went to the fight*
> *With everything handy, from sandwich to brandy,*
>   *To fill their broad stomachs and make them all tight?*

Among the military professionals, of course, there were examples of more realistic views. Colonel William T. Sherman, now in command of a brigade, wrote home: "I . . . regard this as but the beginning of a long war; but I hope my judgment therein is wrong, and that the people of the South may yet see the folly of their unjust rebellion against the most mild and paternal government ever designed for men."

Although a few of McDowell's regiments set forth on the planned date of July 16, the great part of the army was then still maturing its readiness. In the words of a correspondent of the Boston *Transcript,* who spent much of the day in Washington:

"The evening of Tuesday, July 16th, 1861, will long be remembered by all who were in this region on that day as one of the finest in the whole season—warm, but clear and delightfully pleasant. During the morning, our little party (of newsmen, legislators, and private citizens) secured the necessary passes to carry them across the river; and at three P.M. we reached the base of Arlington Heights on horseback. . . . Our animals were fresh, and we spent an hour or two moving around among the camps, where all was bustle and stir. . . .

"Horses were saddled, baggage was stored, rations for three or four days were got in readiness, forty rounds of ball cartridges were distributed, the evening parade was dispensed with, the sunset gun boomed forth its thunder upon the still warm air, night fell upon the scene, and the soldiers slept upon their arms, in readiness to start at the sound of the drum or bugle. . . .

"Our men were in most excellent spirits, and only evinced a

general anxiety to *get started*. So general was this feeling among the troops, and so universal was the desire to get a sight at the enemy, about whom they had heard so much—as being at Fairfax in force, etc.—that few slept soundly . . . your humble servant [included]. . . .

"At daybreak, after staying overnight each in a blanket upon the tent floor in one of the camps, we rose with the lark—or earlier—at the sound of the 'long roll,' and in a few minutes' time everybody was out. Horses were brought up, a hasty breakfast was swallowed, a little parading was done, orders rang forward from tent to tent and from regiment to regiment, and it was soon ascertained that the word had gone forth to move forthwith.

"At eight o'clock the column was being rapidly formed, the regiments and detachments of cavalry and artillery were forming into line; and at the signal we moved briskly forward toward Fairfax Court House, simultaneously from Arlington, from Alexandria, and from the space between these two points—leaving behind a sufficient force to protect and to operate the fortified works at all points along the line.

"The sun shone brilliantly and the fresh morning air was highly invigorating. The troops on foot started off as joyfully as if they were bound upon a New England picnic or a clambake; and not the slightest exhibition of fear or uneasiness . . . seemed for an instant to occupy any part of their thoughts. . . .

"The huge column fell into line at last, along the road. From an occasional elevation which we mounted, for the sake of enjoying the grand *coup d'oeil*, we could see this immense body of men, in uniform dress, with stately tread and glistening arms, move steadily forward . . . all marching on—on to Fairfax."

Adds a correspondent of the New York *Herald:*

"The seemingly endless forest of . . . bayonets, undulating with the ascents and descents of the road; the dark mass of humanity rolling on . . . irresistably [*sic*], like a black stream forcing its way through a narrow channel; the waving banners, the inspiring strains of the numerous bands, the shouts and songs of the men, formed a most inspiring and animated scene which was contemplated with both amazement and terror by the unprepared country people along the road. Some of these rustics . . . looked . . . with hostile sullenness, while again some made off for the woods as soon as they caught sight of the head of the army."

The march soon slowed, according to General McDowell, because many of the troops forsook their adherence to discipline:

"They stopped every moment to pick blackberries or get water. They would not keep in the ranks, order as much as you pleased. When they came where water was fresh, they would pour the old water out of their canteens and fill them with fresh water. They were not used to denying themselves much. They were not used to journeys on foot."

There was little regard for civilian property. "One of the citizens . . . had a bee-house well stocked with hives," says the Boston *Journal*'s Charles Carleton Coffin. "A soldier espied them. He seized a hive and ran. Out came the bees, buzzing about his ears. Another soldier, thinking to do better, upset *his* hive and seized the comb, dripping with honey. Being also hotly besieged, he dropped it . . . slapped his face, swung his arms, and fought manfully. Other soldiers, seeing what was going on, and anxious to secure a portion of the coveted sweets, came up, and over went the half-dozen hives. The air was full of enraged insects, which

Asking directions along the way

A forager in consultation

stung men and horses indiscriminately, and which finally put a whole regiment to flight."

The same narrator, Charles Carleton Coffin, was with the van of the first troops to approach the army's initial objective:

"The column . . . passed through a narrow belt of woods and reached a hill from which Fairfax Court House was in full view. A Rebel flag was waving over the town. There were two pieces of Rebel artillery in a field, a dozen wagons in park, squads of soldiers in sight, horsemen galloping in all directions. Nearer, in a meadow, was a squadron of cavalry on picket. I stood beside [the captain] . . . commanding the skirmishers.

" 'Let me take your Sharpe's rifle,' said he to a soldier. He rested it on the fence, ran his eye along the barrel, and fired. The nearest Rebel horseman, half a mile distant, slipped from his horse in an instant and fell upon the ground. . . . The other troopers put spurs to their horses and fled towards Fairfax, where a sudden commotion was visible. . . .

" 'First and second pieces into position,' said [the captain] commanding a New York battery.

"The horses leaped ahead, and in a moment the two pieces were pointing toward Fairfax. . . .

" 'Load with shell,' was the order, and the cartridges went home in an instant.

"Standing behind the pieces and looking directly along the road . . . I could see the Rebels in a hollow beyond a farmhouse. The shells went screaming towards them, and in an instant they disappeared, running into the woods."

The next target for the long-range fire was Bonham's main array of tents. In the words of Confederate narrator D. Augustus Dickert:

"It is needless to say excitement and consternation overwhelmed the camp. While all were expecting and anxiously awaiting it, still the idea of being now in the face of a real live enemy, on the eve of a great battle . . . came upon them with no little feelings of dread and emotion. . . .

"Tents were hurriedly struck, baggage rolled and thrown into wagons, with which the excited teamsters were not long in getting into the pike road. Drums beat the assembly, troops formed in line and took position behind the breastwork, while the artillery galloped up to the front and unlimbered, ready for action.

"The enemy threw twenty-pound shells repeatedly over the camp that did no further damage than add to the consternation of the already excited teamsters, who seemed to think the safety of the army depended on their getting out of the way. It was an exciting scene to see four-horse teams galloping down the pike at break-neck speed, urged forward by the frantic drivers.

"It was [apparently] the intention of McDowell, the Federal chief, to surprise the advance at Fairfax Court House and cut off their retreat. Already a column was being hurried along the Germantown road . . . in our rear. . . . But soon General Bonham had his forces, according to preconcerted arrangements, following the retreating trains along the pike towards Bull Run.

"Men overloaded with baggage, weighted down with excitement, went at double-quick down the road, panting and sweating . . . while one of the field officers in the rear accelerated the pace by a continual shouting, 'Hurry up, men; they are firing on our rear.' . . .

"The Negro servants, evincing no disposition to be left behind, rushed along with the wagon train like men beset. . . . We were none too precipitate in our movement, for as we were passing through Germantown we could see the long rows of glistening bayonets of the enemy crowning the hills to our right."

According to the correspondent of the Boston *Transcript:*

"Our troops entered Fairfax—ten thousand of them—at early noon, the bands ringing out with cheerful tones the 'Star-Spangled Banner,' and the boys cheering lustily for the Union and the Stars and Stripes. Six or seven thousand infantry blocked up the main street for a time. The Court House building was taken possession of by the New Hampshire 2nd. . . . A secession flag was hauled down and the banner of the regiment run up in its place; and then the foot soldiers opened right and left, or gave way, for the entrance of the cavalry and artillery. These dashed through the town at a gallop, and down the road out into the country beyond, in search of the fugitives. After going four miles beyond Fairfax, and finding that the legs of the rebels were evidently the longest . . . our troopers returned, with the cannon, and joined the van again."

Adds the Boston *Journal's* Charles Carleton Coffin:

"Camp equipage, barrels of flour, clothing, entrenching tools, were left behind, and we made ourselves merry over their running. . . . War was a pastime, a picnic, an agreeable diversion.

"A gray-haired old Negro came out from his cabin, rolling his eyes and gazing at the Yankees.

Fairfax Courthouse

" 'Have you seen any Rebels this morning?' we asked.

" 'Gosh a'mighty, massa! Dey was here as thick as bees, ges 'fore you cum. But when dat ar bumshell cum screaming among 'em, dey ran as if de Ole Harry was after 'em!'

"All of this, the flight of the Rebels, the Negro's story, was exhilarating to the troops, who more than ever felt that the march to Richmond was going to be a nice affair."

Union nurse Emma Edmonds takes up:

"The main column reached Fairfax toward evening and encamped for the night. Col. R.'s wife . . . Mrs. B., and myself were, I think, the only three females who reached Fairfax that night. . . . Not being accustomed to ride all day beneath a burning sun, we felt its effects very sensibly, and consequently hailed with joy the order to encamp for the night.

"Notwithstanding the heat and fatigue of the day's march, the troops were in high spirits, and immediately began preparing supper. Some built fires while others went in search of, and appropriated, every available article which might in any way add to the comfort of hungry and fatigued men.

"The whole neighborhood was ransacked for milk, butter, eggs, poultry, etc., which were found insufficient in quantity to supply the wants of such a multitude. There might have been heard some stray shots fired in the direction of a field where a drove of cattle were quietly grazing; and, soon after, the odor of fresh steak was issuing from every part of the camp.

"I wish to state, however, that all raids made upon hen-coops, etc., were contrary to the orders of the General in command, for during the day I had seen men put under arrest for shooting chickens by the roadside.

"I was amused to hear the answer of a hopeful young darkey cook when interrogated with regard to the broiled chickens and beefsteak which he brought on for [our] supper.

"Col. R. demanded in a very stern voice, 'Jack, where did you get that beefsteak and those chickens?'

" 'Massa, I'se carried dem cl'ar from Washington. Thought I'd cook 'em 'fore dey sp'ild.' . . .

"The colonel told us how he had seen Jack running out of a house as he rode along, and a woman ran out calling after him with all her might; but Jack never looked behind him, but escaped as fast as he could and was soon out of sight. . . . 'I thought the young rascal had been up to some mischief, so I rode up and asked the woman what was the matter, and found he had stolen all her chickens. I asked her now much they were worth. She reckoned about two dollars. I think she made a pretty good hit, for after I paid her she told me she had had only two chickens.' "

According to a New York journalist named George Wilkes, the Federal depredations went far beyond the seizure of edibles:

"The soldiers, unrestrained by duty, entered every dwelling that had been abandoned, and, taking its desertion as a confession of [anti-Union] judgment on the part of its proprietor, sacked it as mercilessly as if it had been condemned to plunder by a lawful process. In some instances they set houses on fire, in some insulted women; and terror took possession of the town. . . .

"When the rage of acquisition had subsided, the place wore the softened aspect of a carnival; and soldiers, apparelled in crinoline and female sheen, walked with their bearded gallants up and down, replying with affected gab to the rather racy compliments tendered them from every side.

"This, to the superficial looker-on, gave the scene a merry show; but I noticed that the shuddering inhabitants regarded it with fear and undisguised abhorrence.

"One female, hearing me condemn the conduct of the soldiers as a fellow passed by with a pair of ladies' ruffled drawers hauled up over his pantaloons, said she thought it was really too bad that the clothes of Mr. Smith's poor dead mother, which had been packed away for several years untouched, should be desecrated in that coarse, vulgar way.

"I myself half shuddered as she made this remark on the fellow's conduct. . . . I have been desirous all along to conceal whatever was discreditable to our soldiers, but I now perceive that this is the worst way to treat the evil. Public condemnation must be turned upon their outrages in its fullest tide."

General McDowell himself decided that strong measures had to be taken against such offenses. While at Fairfax he published an order that included the following paragraphs:

"It is with the deepest mortification that the General commanding finds it necessary to reiterate his orders for the preservation of the property of the inhabitants of the district occupied by the troops under his command. . . .

"Commanders of regiments will select a commissioned officer as a provost marshal, and ten men as a police force under him, whose special and sole duty it shall be to preserve the property from depredations, and to arrest all wrongdoers. . . . The least that will be done to them will be to send them to Alexandria jail. . . .

"The troops must behave themselves with as much forbearance and propriety as if they were at their own homes. They are here to fight the enemies of the country, not to judge and punish the unarmed and defenseless, however guilty they may be. When necessary, that will be done by the proper person."

It would have been a fortunate thing for General McDowell if the only shadow on his campaign that day (July 17) had been the conduct of his men. But the day saw the development of a situation that posed a critical threat to his plans against Beauregard at Manassas. General Patterson, with his orders from Washington still indefinite, had moved from Martinsburg in a way that was of no help to the campaign. Under the remarkable apprehension that Joe Johnston had him fearfully outnumbered and might be laying a trap for him, Patterson, instead of attacking toward Winchester, had sidestepped eastward to Charlestown (famous as the scene of John Brown's trial and hanging) to get farther from Johnston's reach.

Pennsylvania's Chaplain A. M. Stewart had expected to report to his newspaper that he'd been involved in a battle that day, but his report, written in the evening, had the sound of one made by a tourist:

"Shades of Old John Brown! Here sits your correspondent on the identical spot where, less than two years since, the Chivalry of Virginia, with Henry A. Wise as its head and governor, aided by a large military force, hung a strange, enigmatical, unyielding old fanatic. Wise and Virginia understood, at the time, John Brown's raid better far than did we of the North. Their terror—at which we laughed—was not so much misplaced. . . . They beheld visions of armed men . . . crowding down from the North . . . into the Old Dominion . . . to overturn her debasing and growingly effete institution. . . .

"Wise . . . was the true seer, and we the ignorant and unobservant. Had all the prophets, from Enoch down to John and Jude, arisen from the dead and prophesied, on the day that Brown was hung, that within two years the realities on which my eyes now look would take place, I, with all others, would have looked upon them as messengers sent . . . to deceive.

"In the beautiful, undulating fields and woodlands around the spot where Brown and his confederates were hung is now encamping a Northern army. . . . Regiments from Wisconsin and Maine; Indiana and New Hampshire; Ohio and Massachusetts; Pennsylvania and New York, are now quietly pitching their tents around this poor, guilty secession town. . . .

"And for what has this Northern array of battle come? . . . Substantially, to carry out the great design of John Brown's insignificant raid. True, it may be that multitudes of soldiers in this Northern army may now little understand, or even believe this. But when the true history of the present great Revolution shall be correctly written, some future Macaulay will chronicle that Old John Brown threw the first bomb, discharged the first cannon, and thrust the first bayonet. . . .

"Our troops had orders last night [they were then camped at Bunker Hill, on the road between Martinsburg and Winchester] to be ready for marching by daybreak this morning. In the eager expectation of meeting the enemy at Winchester early in the day, little sleeping was done. . . .

"However, through some military ruse or blunder, early in the morning the head of the column, instead of marching direct to Winchester, took the road leading to this place, Charlestown. . . . From Bunker Hill . . . to this place is thirteen miles. From here to Winchester is twenty miles—while in the morning we were only twelve miles distant from it. Whatever may be the intent or result of this movement, the Lord has evidently designed that this great Northern army should encamp around this spot. . . .

"The people are rabid secessionists. Men and women looked savagely at me as I walked through the streets [of the town]. . . . Approaching a group of gentlemen and ladies who occupied a piazza of the best-looking house on main street, I introduced myself with the query, 'Can you point out to me the precise spot where Old John Brown was hung?'

"Blood and daggers, revenge and hatred, scorn and *fear,* were all concentrated in the look which was centered on me. What their tongues might have uttered deponent saith not, as at this moment a company of Uncle Sam's dragoons galloped along the street. Having a seeming prudential conception as to how matters were now conditioned, an elderly gentleman, pointing with his finger in a certain direction, said, 'It was out there.'

"Not content, however, with vagaries, the question was pressed until a guide was furnished and the identical spot pointed out. A fine growth of corn now covers the place of execution.

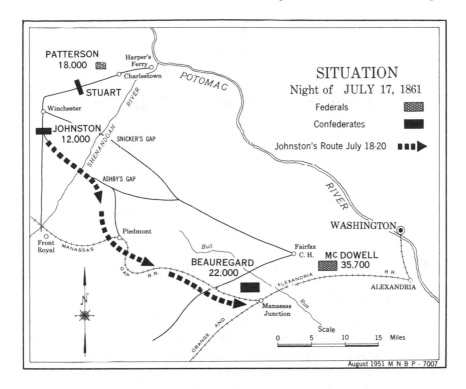

PATTERSON
18.000

Harper's
Ferry
Charlestown

STUART

Winchester

JOHNSTON
12.000

SNICKER'S GAP

POTOMAC

RIVER

SITUATION
Night of JULY 17, 1861

Federals

Confederates

Johnston's Route July 18-20

SHENANDOAH RIVER

ASHBY'S GAP

Piedmont

Front
Royal

MANASSAS

GAP

R.R.

Bull

BEAUREGARD
22.000

Manassas
Junction

ORANGE AND

Run

ALEXANDRIA

Fairfax
C. H.

WASHINGTON

MC DOWELL
35.700

R.R.

ALEXANDRIA

N

Scale

0   5   10   15   Miles

August 1951 M N B P · 7007

"Returning to the town, I made inquiry for the jailer and asked permission to take a look in the old prison. No prisoner at present occupies the dingy cell where Old John was confined. A broken stool, a rickety table, an old bed-quilt with plenty of dust, are the only furniture. Traces of the old man's pencil . . . are yet . . . on the walls, in the texts of scripture and quaint sentences.

"Within this long, narrow, dirty cell, with its double row of grated windows, was confined for weeks a spirit as true to its convictions of right as the world has ever witnessed. . . .

"Charlestown has, from appearance, about fifteen hundred inhabitants. . . . It is located in the midst of a fair agricultural and most picturesque country, eight miles west of Harpers Ferry."

Patterson's move to this spot was nothing less than a retreat. He had, in effect, withdrawn himself from the campaign. From the Confederate point of view, Patterson's timing was perfect. That night Johnston received word from Beauregard that he was needed at Manassas.

22

Events Approach a Climax

According to Virginia minister Robert Dabney, who was, during this period, a frequent visitor to the camps of Brigadier General Thomas Jackson:

"On the forenoon of Thursday the 18th, the Army of the Valley, numbering about eleven thousand men, was ordered under arms at its camp north of Winchester, and the tents were struck. No man knew the intent, save that it was supposed they were about to attack Patterson, who lay to the north of them . . . with twenty thousand men; and joy and alacrity glowed on every face. But at midday they were ordered to march in the opposite direction. . . .

"As they passed through the streets of Winchester, the citizens, whose hospitality the soldiers had so often enjoyed, asked, with sad and astonished faces, if they were deserting them and handing them over to the Vandal enemy. They answered, with equal sadness, that they knew no more than others whither they were going.

"The 1st Virginia Brigade, led by General Jackson, headed the march. The cavalry of Stuart guarded every pathway between the line of defense which Johnston had just held and the Federalists, and kept up an audacious front, as though they were about to advance upon them, supported by the whole army. The mystified commander of the Federalists stood anxiously on the defensive. . . .

"As soon as the troops had gone three miles from Winchester, General Johnston commanded the whole column to halt, and an order was read explaining their destination. . . . Every countenance brightened with joy, and the army rent the air with their shouts. They hurried forward."

This pace, however, was not long maintained. Says Joe Johnston: "The discouragement of that day's march to one accustomed, like myself, to the steady gait of regular soldiers, is indescribable. . . . Frequent and unreasonable delays caused so slow a rate of marching as to make me despair of joining Beauregard in time to aid him. Major [W. H. C.] Whiting was therefore dispatched to the nearest station of the Manassas Gap Railroad, Piedmont, to ascertain if trains, capable of transporting the troops to their destination more quickly than they were likely to reach it on foot, could be provided there; and, if so, to make the necessary arrangements."

In Washington, General Winfield Scott had begun to suspect that things were going awry in the Valley. He wired Patterson:

"I have certainly been expecting you to beat the enemy. If not, to hear that you have felt him strongly, or, at least, had occupied him by threats and demonstrations. You have been at least his equal, and, I suppose, superior in numbers. Has he not stolen a march and sent reinforcements toward Manassas Junction?"

Patterson, some of whose men were then skirmishing with Jeb Stuart's thin line of troopers, wired back indignantly:

The march grows tedious

"The enemy has stolen no march upon me. I have kept him actively employed. . . . I have accomplished more in this respect than the General-in-Chief asked, or could well be expected in the face of an enemy far superior in numbers."

The dawn of this day, July 18, found General McDowell's army still at Fairfax. However, according to nurse Emma Edmonds, "reveille beat, the whole camp was soon in motion, and, after a slight breakfast from our haversacks, the march was resumed. The day was very hot, and we found great difficulty in obtaining water, the want of which caused the troops much suffering. Many of the men were sun-struck, and others began to drop out of the ranks from exhaustion. All such as were not able to march were put into ambulances and sent back to Washington. . . .

"The tedium of the march began to be enlivened by sharp volleys of musketry in the direction of the advance guard; but those alarms were only occasioned by our skirmishers pouring a volley into everything which looked as if it might contain a masked battery or a band of the enemy's sharpshooters.

"Considerable excitement prevailed . . . as we were every hour in expectation of meeting the enemy. Carefully feeling its way, however, the army moved steadily on, investigating every field, building, and ravine . . . in front and to the right and left, until it reached Centreville, where we halted. . . .

"There was . . . a lack of that picnic hilarity which had characterized . . . the day before. Several regiments had been supplied with new shoes . . . before leaving camp, and they found by sad experience that they were not the most comfortable things to march in, as their poor blistered feet testified. In many cases, their feet were literally raw, the thick woolen stockings having chafed the skin off.

"Mrs. B. and I, having provided ourselves, before leaving camp, with a quantity of linen, bandages, lint, ointment, etc., found it very convenient now, even before a shot had been fired by the enemy.

"Our surgeons began to prepare for the coming battle by appropriating several buildings and fitting them up for the wounded—among others the stone church in Centreville."

These preparations were launched none too soon. A round of action was already beginning. Early that morning Daniel Tyler's division of McDowell's army had gone ahead to probe the right wing of Beauregard's lines lying just across Bull Run. McDowell

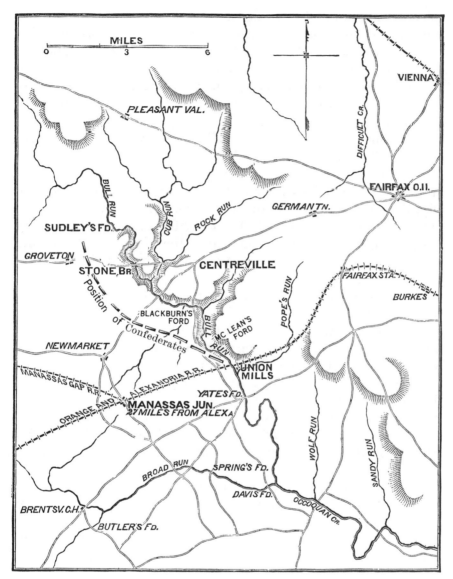

Scene of Tyler's reconnaissance

was contemplating a move (to his own left) that would flank the Confederate right.

An important part of Beauregard's right-wing defenses was the Washington Artillery of New Orleans. The battalion's main camp was at McLean's Ford, where Beauregard had his headquarters, having established himself in Wilmer McLean's farmhouse. (Mc-

Lean did not appreciate being caught up in the war like this, and after the second Battle of Bull Run in 1862 he decided that enough was enough. He moved to the quiet village of Appomattox Courthouse. In 1865, of course, the war caught up with him again. Lee surrendered to Grant in his living room. It was a coincidence of fantastic dimensions that the first and last scenes of the war in Virginia were enacted on McLean's property.)

Adjutant of the Washington Artillery of New Orleans was Lieutenant William Miller Owen, who relates:

"On the 18th we were up and stirring at the peep of dawn, and, after a hasty breakfast of fried bacon and crackers, mounted, and with the four howitzers under Lieutenant [T. L.] Rosser, moved in the direction of Union Mills Ford, further down the Run, where it is crossed by a railroad bridge. The other guns of the command were left at Blackburn's and McLean's Fords. . . . Union Mills Ford was the extreme right of our line, which extended for eight miles up the stream to the Stone Bridge at the Warrenton Turnpike, where our left rested.

"From our elevated position at the Mills we could see the enemy's Zouaves coming out of the patch of woods opposite, drawing water from the tank beside the railroad. They were evidently there in force, and Rosser wants to shell them out. But General [Richard S.] Ewell said, 'Wait awhile.'

"While lounging under the trees we were surprised to see riding towards us a little lady with the rebel colors pinned upon her dress. We sprang to our feet, and, with our kepis doffed, greeted her.

"What a strange sight! So young and gentle a girl here, among a thousand soldiers and frowning cannon awaiting battle. To our inquiries where she was from, and how she came, she replied, 'Oh, I'm from Fairfax Court House. I came around the Yankees, and have information for your commander. Who is he?'

"We told her General Ewell was in command, and, at her request, escorted her to his headquarters. What news she brought we never knew."

General Ewell (a forty-four-year-old man of nervous movements, a bald head, and a pointed nose—a curiously bird-like combination) was not so much impressed with the girl's news as he was perturbed by her rashness. Pointing out the Yankees on the bank across the stream, he snapped at her, "You'll be a dead damsel in less than a minute! Get away from here! Get away!" But

Richard S. Ewell

the girl, taking only the merest glance at the Yankees, continued with her discourse.

Observing the scowling and fidgeting general with secret amusement was Major John B. Gordon, who wrote later:

"General Ewell, who afterward became a corps commander, had, in many respects, the most unique personality I have ever known. He was . . . the oddest, most eccentric genius in the Confederate army. . . . No man had a better heart nor a worse manner of showing it. He was in truth as tender and sympathetic as a woman, but, even under slight provocation, he became externally as rough as a polar bear. . . .

"When he was first assigned to command at the beginning of the war, he had recently returned from fighting Indians on the Western frontier. . . . His experience in that wild border life, away from churches, civilization, and the refining influences of woman's society, were not particularly conducive to the development of the softer and better side of his nature. . . .

"This Virginia girl, who appeared to be seventeen or eighteen years of age, was in a flutter of martial excitement. She was profoundly impressed with the belief that she really had something of importance to tell. . . . General Ewell . . . was astounded at this exhibition of feminine courage. He gazed at her in mute wonder for a few minutes [as she kept talking], and then turned to me suddenly and, with a sort of jerk in his words, said:

" 'Women! I tell you, sir, women would make a grand brigade—if it was not for snakes and spiders. . . . They don't mind bullets. Women are not afraid of bullets. But one big black snake would put a whole army to flight!' "

The Virginia girl, it must be noted, was in no real danger at this time. The Federal Zouaves who had come to Union Mills had no orders to test this rightward extremity of the Confederate line, and they did nothing of an aggressive nature. The real probe, made by Israel B. Richardson's brigade of Tyler's division, was aimed at a spot about two miles farther up the run. Some of the Confederates in this area were stationed on the north bank.

One of the Union newsman who covered the action was Charles Carleton Coffin:

"It was a little past 11 o'clock when Richardson's brigade . . . moved toward Blackburn's Ford. Passing through a woods, the brigade came into a field looking down a gentle slope. The skirmishers soon encountered the Confederates. There was a rattling of musketry, and then General Tyler directed Captain [R. B.] Ayres to wheel his guns into position and open fire. I saw a puff of smoke and then heard a strange noise in the air. The next moment there was an explosion a few rods distant from where I was standing. The shell had burst among a company of dragoons. . . .

"Three companies of the Massachusetts 1st, with two cannon, were sent down the slope. General Tyler took his position under some peach trees near a deserted house. Wishing to see what was going on, I followed the advancing line, when suddenly the air was filled with bullets. The troops had come in contact with [James] Longstreet's Confederate brigade, holding Blackburn's Ford.

"Louder, wilder, and more startling than the volley which they had fired was the rebel yell. A thousand Confederates were howling like wolves. . . . There are times when discretion is better than boldness, and, as the bullets were striking the ground in the immediate vicinity, I made a quick retreat to General Tyler's position, to receive a reprimand.

" 'You have no business down there,' he said sternly.

"I agreed with him, and, finding a position somewhat sheltered

Charles Carleton Coffin in the field

in the road, could see all that took place without being very much exposed.

"The Ambulance Corps was called for to bring back the wounded. I recall the first wounded man brought back on a stretcher, his thigh torn to pieces by a cannon shot. . . . The reflection came that this was war. All its glamor was gone in an instant.

"The strain upon my nerves was a little relieved at seeing Captain Brackett, commanding the cavalry, an old army officer who had served in Mexico, deliberately fill his pipe, strike a match, and begin smoking, unmindful of the shells which were flying through the air."

Adds a correspondent of the Washington *Star:*

"More of our artillery came up, and when that opened upon the enemy's position in the woods along the creek . . . a second masked battery of theirs, surrounded by their infantry . . . replied. That did us considerable damage. I saw four or five of our killed or wounded carried past me to the rear on litters.

"Dr. Pullston of Pennsylvania, Mr. McCormick of the New York *Evening Post,* Mr. Hill of the New York *Tribune,* Mr. Raymond of the *New York Times,* myself, and a few other civilians were at that time standing surrounded by a few straggling soldiers, quietly looking on from the top of the hill . . . where General Tyler had taken his station. One of the first shells from that second battery of the enemy passed between the shoulders of Dr. Pullston and Mr. McCormick . . . and burst against a small building . . . in the rear of them. It grazed Mr. McCormick's shoulder.

"Just then the enemy's infantry fired a volley of Minié balls which took effect in our group, wounding half a dozen, all slightly. . . . We noncombatants quickly sought different and safer positions."

"Their artillery," says a correspondent of the Baltimore *Exchange,* "was of the best kind. A shot from one of their batteries severed a bough from a tree quite two miles distant, and but a few feet from where the vehicles of two Congressmen were standing. One ball fell directly in the midst of a group of Congressmen, among whom was Owen Lovejoy [a well-known abolitionist], but injured no one, the members scampering in different directions, sheltering among trees, etc."

The Massachusetts regiments fighting in the woods had some odd company—two brilliantly clad Fire Zouaves who did not belong there. As explained by Hill, the *Tribune* correspondent:

"These Zouaves had inexplicably appeared at the van a little while before the period of the conflict. Their regiment was far behind. . . . They declared that they had missed it . . . and were now looking for it. . . . I privately believe that they scented the battle afar off, and could not control the temptation to step on and share the danger. At any rate, they were with us, and they pushed themselves into a fighting position at the first opportunity that opened. . . .

"They fought in those woods with daring intrepidity, wholly on their own account, and conscious of no other authority beside their own. They were perpetually in the advance. . . . Their manner of treating the rebel soldiers was eccentric. They waited until one showed himself tolerably near, and then ran forward, chased him down, and killed him. . . . One of them actually penetrated a small battery . . . bayoneted one of the gunners, and escaped unharmed. In this way they occupied themselves . . . [until] they got separated, and consequently became uneasy on each other's account. They both [however] came out without a wound."

The Confederates on the north bank of the run soon withdrew to the south bank. Although the fighting never grew to involve more than a few regiments on either side, it spread, with much confusion, up and down the woods and fields of the stream for nearly a mile.

A conspicuous figure among the Southern troops was tall, broad-chested, blue-eyed, and brown-bearded James Longstreet, who rode about in the coolest manner, giving judicious orders and tendering words of encouragement.

He was soon obliged to do something more:

"Part of my line broke and started [to the rear] at a run. To stop the alarm I rode with saber in hand for the leading files, determined to . . . stop the break. They seemed to see as much danger in their rear as in front, and soon turned and marched back to their places."

To General Beauregard, Longstreet seemed to have a special talent for being "in the right place at the right moment."

Another officer who caught the commanding general's attention was the brusque, tobacco-chewing Colonel Jubal Early. While

James Longstreet

bringing up and deploying his brigade as a reinforcement, Early displayed both a "capacity for command and personal gallantry."

In general, the inexperienced volunteers on the Southern side reacted to the ordeal somewhat better than those of the North, since their work was mainly defensive. It was a more difficult task to attack.

As related by the correspondent of the New York *Tribune:*

"The New York 12th Regiment . . . marched down to the woods at the extreme left of our line. . . . A perfect hail of shot came flying among them, which seemed to throw them into a panic before their start. It was difficult to drive some of them . . . into the woods. At length, however, it was done, and the regiment disappeared. For about one minute they were absent, at the end of which came a volley [from the enemy] more tremendous than any that had yet been heard, and the men were seen breaking and running back in disorder.

"Their officers vainly endeavored to rally them, and they flew irregularly up the hill, passing by the General and his staff and taking refuge in the grove far behind. I suspect they fancied they were pursued, for I saw one fellow turn suddenly about and hurriedly fire at one of his own party, who fell instantly to the ground."

By this time William T. Sherman's infantry had moved up from Centreville (having started soon after Ayres's battery, which belonged to Sherman's brigade), but these troops were not committed to an active role in the fight. They stood for half an hour, however, under Confederate artillery fire. This was a new experience not only for Sherman's volunteers but also for the colonel himself. Although he had graduated from West Point as early as 1840, he had never seen combat. "For the first time in my life I saw cannon balls strike men and crash through the trees and saplings above and around us." The brigade lost several men killed or wounded.

With each side having suffered, in all, less than a hundred casualties, General Tyler's probe was now ending. He had actually exceeded his orders. McDowell hadn't wanted him to initiate so strong an engagement. It seems that Tyler had been impelled by the notion he could raise himself to glory by breaking Beauregard's line and putting him to flight.

In Beauregard's words:

"The Federals . . . met a final repulse. . . . After their infantry attack had ceased, about one o'clock, the contest lapsed into an artillery duel [of about an hour], in which the Washington Artillery of New Orleans won credit against the renowned batteries of the United States regular army.

"A comical effect of this artillery fight [which added a few casualties to both lists] was the destruction of the dinner of myself and staff by a Federal shell that fell into the fireplace of my headquarters at the McLean House.

"Our success in this first limited collision was of special prestige to my army of new troops."

Northern morale, on the other hand, had been dealt a setback. There was much discouragement among Tyler's troops as they withdrew to Centreville, and the dismal news soon spread through the entire army. Some of the "ninety-day men," utterly demoralized, began preparing to go home.

"The repulse," says Charles Carleton Coffin, "served to dissipate in some degree the confidence manifest at the beginning of the movement [from Washington]. We began to see that we were not going straight on to Richmond."

The day of the fight at Blackburn's had been an anxious one for the Virginia citizens within hearing of its rumble. As related by

Beauregard's headquarters: the McLean House

Listening to the guns

Constance Cary (a cousin to the Cary sisters of Baltimore), originally of Fairfax County but now living at Bristow Station, just southwest of Manassas:

"There was, for us, no way of knowing the progress of events during the long, long day of waiting, of watching, of weeping, of praying, of rushing out upon the railway track to walk as far as we dared in the direction whence came that intolerable booming of artillery. The cloud of dun smoke arising over Manassas became heavier in volume as the day progressed.

"Still, not a word of tidings, till toward afternoon there came limping up a single, very dirty soldier with his arm in a sling. What a heaven-send he was, if only as an escape valve for our pent-up sympathies!

"We seized him, we washed him, we cried over him, we glorified him until the man was fairly bewildered. Our best endeavors could only develop a pin-scratch of a wound on his right hand; but when our hero had laid in a substantial meal of bread and meat, we plied him with trembling questions, each asking news of some staff or regiment or company. . . .

"He was a humorist in disguise. His invariable reply, as he looked from one to the other of his satellites, was: 'The ——

Virginia, marm? They warn't no two ways 'o thinkin' 'bout that ar reg'ment. They just *kivered* tharselves with glory!'

"A little later two wagon-loads of slightly wounded claimed our care, and with them came authentic news of the day."

General McDowell, of course, was most unhappy about Tyler's overzealousness and the resultant fiasco. The only positive note was that Beauregard's show of strength convinced McDowell he was right in his belief that the line would have to be flanked. On the day of the fight, however, the commander had made a personal investigation of the terrain on Beauregard's right, only to learn that its roads, mostly narrow and tortuous, were unsuited to his purposes. He would have to switch his attention to the Confederate left (to his own right), where he knew the route was feasible. But he was apprehensive about the delay that new preparations would entail. He was already struggling with inhibitory supply problems.

As for General Beauregard, he, too, spent the evening of the eighteenth thinking in terms of offensive action. But his plans could not be finalized until he could be sure of Joe Johnston's cooperation, and as yet Johnston's role in the proceedings was not fully defined.

The Valley army, with Jackson in the van, had been on the march through the entire day. Jackson's aide, Dr. Dabney, says that the troops "waded the Shenandoah River, which was waist-deep . . . ascended the Blue Ridge at Ashby's Gap, and, two hours after midnight, paused for a few hours' rest at the little village of Paris, upon the eastern slope of the mountain. Here General Jackson turned his brigade into an enclosure occupied by a beautiful grove, and the wearied men fell prostrate upon the earth without food.

"In a little time an officer came to Jackson, reminded him that there were no sentries posted around his bivouac while the men were all wrapped in sleep, and asked if some should be aroused and a guard set.

" 'No,' replied Jackson, 'let the poor fellows sleep. I will guard the camp myself.'

"All the remainder of the night he paced around it, or sat upon the fence watching the slumbers of his men."

This incident was to become the subject of a poem, widely published in the South, entitled "The Lone Sentry." These lines were included:

Athwart the shadows of the vale
Slumbered the men of might—
And one lone sentry paced his rounds
To watch the camp that night.
A grave and solemn man was he,
With deep and somber brow,
Whose dreamful eyes seemed hoarding up
Some unaccomplished vow.
His wistful glance peered o'er the plains
Beneath the starry light,
And with the murmured name of God
He watched the camp that night.

Returning to Dr. Dabney:

"An hour before daybreak, he yielded to the repeated requests of a member of his staff, and relinquished the task to him. Descending from his seat upon the fence, he rolled himself upon the leaves in a corner, and in a moment was sleeping like an infant. But at the first streak of the dawn, he aroused his men and resumed the march.

"From Winchester to Manassas Junction the distance is about sixty miles. The forced march of thirty miles brought the army to the Piedmont Station, at the eastern base of the Blue Ridge, whence they hoped to reach their destination more easily by railroad."

Adds one of Jackson's private soldiers, a Virginian named John O. Casler:

"When we arrived at the station, the citizens for miles around came flocking in to see us, bringing us eatables of all kinds, and we fared sumptuously. There were not trains enough to transport all at once, and our regiment had to remain there until trains returned. . . .

"We had a regular picnic; plenty to eat, lemonade to drink, and beautiful young ladies to chat with. We finally got aboard, bade the ladies a long farewell, and went flying down the road, arriving at the Junction in the night.

"The next day, the 20th of July, we marched about four miles down Bull Run to where General Beauregard had engaged the enemy on the 18th and repulsed their advance. There we joined the brigade."

According to D. B. Conrad, a staff officer in one of Jackson's regiments, this location was not a pleasant one. "A line of fresh

graves was rather depressing. The trees were lopped and mangled by shot, and perforated by Minié balls, the short, dry grass
showing in very many spots a dark chocolate hue."

Joe Johnston, now at Bull Run in person, had expected to have
his entire army with him, but several thousand men were still in
transit. Trouble had developed with the trains. Approaching the
field without help from the railway were the army's artillery batteries and Jeb Stuart with about three hundred troopers withdrawn from the outposts facing the static Patterson. (It was about
this time that Patterson realized he'd lost his contest with
Johnston—and suspected, correctly, that his own career was
ruined.) Even though Johnston's army was still short of the anticipated numbers, the Bull Run army as a whole had risen to a
strength of over thirty thousand, which placed it respectably close
to being a match for the foe. Now top commander at Bull Run,
Johnston agreed with Beauregard on the desirability of an offensive operation, but they were denied time to get one under way.

On the evening of July 20, General McDowell issued orders for
his army to be ready to move by two A.M. the next day, Sunday,
July 21, and a three-day supply of rations was given each man.
After packing the rations, the troops turned to personal pursuits
by their campfires: writing letters, reading pocket-sized Bibles,
holding prayer meetings, singing hymns, conversing in low and
earnest tones.

Says a Michigan soldier named D. G. Crotty:

"We sit around and smoke our pipes. Not a shot is fired by
either party, and all is still; but it is the ominous stillness before a
great struggle, and each has his own peculiar thoughts. What are
the loved ones at home thinking of? Probably everyone is . . .
thinking of the loved ones in danger, and many a prayer goes up
to the throne of Grace . . . but, alas, the fortunes of war require
some sacrifice."

Adds Edwin S. Barrett, a civilian from New England who had
won permission to accompany the 5th Massachusetts as an observer:

"Wrapping my blanket around me at ten o'clock, I stretched
myself upon the bare ground to sleep. The night was cool, and at
twelve o'clock I awoke, feeling very cold; and, unable to sleep
more, I anxiously waited to hear the signal to prepare."

Switching to the Confederate side and to the private in Jackson's brigade, John Casler:

"We lay on our arms all night. We tore all the feathers out of our hats because we heard the Yanks had feathers in theirs, and we might be fired on by mistake. . . .

"My particular friend and messmate, William I. Blue, and myself lay down together, throwing a blanket over us, and talked concerning our probable fate the next day. We had been in line of battle several times [in the Shenandoah Valley], and had heard many false alarms; but we all knew there was no false alarm this time; that the two armies lay facing each other, and that a big battle would be fought the next day; that we were on the eve of experiencing the realities of war in its most horrible form— brother against brother, father against son, kindred against kindred. . . .

"While lying thus, being nearly asleep, he roused me up and said he wanted to make a bargain with me, which was, if either of us got killed the next day the one who survived should see the other buried, if we kept possession of the battlefield.

"I told him I would certainly do that, and we pledged ourselves accordingly. I then remarked that perhaps we would escape unhurt or wounded. He said, 'No, I don't want to be wounded. If I am shot at all, I want to be shot right through the heart.'

"During the night we heard a gun fired on the left of the regiment, and I got up and walked down the line to see what had happened. I found one of the men had shot himself through the foot, supposed to have been done intentionally, to keep out of the fight; but the poor fellow made a miscalculation as to where his toes were, and held the muzzle of the gun too far up and blew off about half of his foot, so it had to be amputated."

23

The Fateful Battle Is Joined

McDOWELL'S ATTACK PLAN was well conceived. His army, in four divisions, was concentrated at Centreville. (Another division, guarding the road to Washington, played no part in the battle.) One of the divisions at Centreville, that of Dixon S. Miles—with Richardson's brigade of Tyler's division attached—was to stay at the village in reserve, a part of it thrusting toward Blackburn's Ford, not to make an attack but to demonstrate as though preparing to do so. McDowell's other three divisions, with Tyler's remaining brigades in the lead, were to begin their role by marching toward Bull Run on the Warrenton Turnpike.

Tyler's brigades (those of William T. Sherman, Erasmus D. Keyes, and Robert C. Schenck) were to go all the way to the banks of the Stone Bridge, there to stop and demonstrate strongly while McDowell himself, with the divisions of David Hunter and Samuel P. Heintzelman, slued right from the turnpike for a wide north-westerly march to Sudley Ford, which was guarded by pickets alone. McDowell hoped to launch an unexpected attack on the Confederate left, destroying the entire line by rolling it up. Tyler, coming across Bull Run at the Stone Bridge when the time was right, was to help with the drive.

The plan was enhanced by the fact that the Confederate left was weak. Johnston and Beauregard, while trying to develop their own attack plan, had been strengthening their right. They had hoped to hit McDowell's left before he advanced from Centreville. Their plan against McDowell, indeed, was much like his against them.

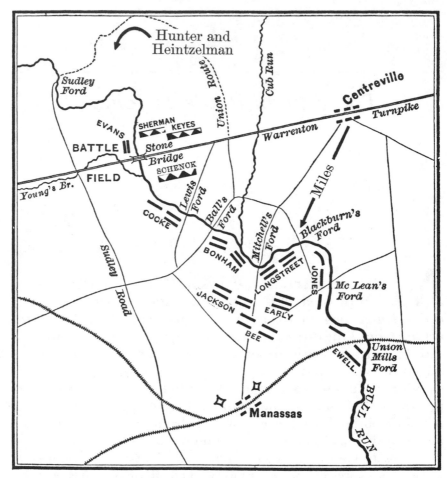

First Bull Run. Situation just prior to the battle. The Confederates (shown as black bars) are in their positions along the stream. McDowell's flanking column (broken line at upper left) is making its way from the Warrenton Turnpike to Sudley Ford. Sherman, Keyes, and Schenck have reached the Stone Bridge. Miles, in reserve at Centreville, has launched a demonstration against Blackburn's Ford.

It was soon after one A.M. on Sunday, July 21, that the federal camps around Centreville were called to life by a low roll of drums. In truth, a great many of the troops had been up and doing before the drums sounded. As pictured by a correspondent of the New York *World:*

"There was moonlight. . . . Through the hazy valleys and on hill slopes, miles apart, were burning the fires at which forty regiments had prepared their midnight meal. In the vistas opening along a dozen lines of view, thousands of men were moving among the fitful beacons. Horses were harnessing to artillery; white army wagons were in motion with the ambulances—whose black coverings . . . seemed as appropriate as that of the coffin which accompanies a condemned man to the death before him.

"All was silent confusion and intermingling of moving horses and men. But forty thousand soldiers stir as quickly as a dozen, and in fifteen minutes from the commencement of the bustle every regiment had taken its place, ready to fall into the division to which it was assigned. . . .

"At 2½ A.M. the last soldier had left the extended encampments, except those remaining behind on guard. . . . Here were thousands of comrades-in-arms going forward . . . in a common cause. Here was all—and *more* than one had read of the solemn paraphernalia of war. . . .

"As I followed along that [moonlit] procession of rumbling cannon-carriages and caissons, standards and banners, the gleaming infantry with their thousands of shining bayonets, and the mounted officers of every staff, what fine excitement was added to the occasion by the salutations and . . . assurances. . . .

"The spirit of the soldiery was magnificent. They were all smarting under the reproach of Thursday [the defeat at Blackburn's] and longing for the opportunity to wipe it out. There was glowing rivalry between the men of different States.

" 'Old Massachusetts will not be ashamed of us tonight!'

" 'Wait till the Ohio boys get at them!'

" 'We'll fight for New York today!'

"And a hundred similar utterances were shouted from the different ranks."

It must be noted here that McDowell had made a mistake in the order of his advance. Tyler's division, detailed to march straight for the Stone Bridge at Bull Run (located about four miles from Centreville), had been put on the turnpike first, and it took the division more than two hours to clear the road junction, just past Cub Run, where the divisions of Hunter and Heintzelman planned to turn right. These divisions might just as well have remained in camp for an extra two hours. McDowell, to be sure, did not expect Tyler to move so slowly. After the disapproval he had received for his rashness at Blackburn's Ford, the division commander seemed now to be moving with a calculated deliber-

ateness. Since both the cover of darkness and speed were important to the operation, McDowell considered the two-hour delay to
be "a great misfortune."

All of McDowell's troops, as they crossed the bridge over Cub
Run, were treated to a novel sight. Says Captain Henry N. Blake
of the 11th Massachusetts volunteers: "I noticed about twenty
barouches and carriages that contained members of Congress and
their friends, who had left Washington for the purpose of witnessing the approaching conflict."

Adds James Tinkham, another volunteer from Massachusetts:
"We thought it wasn't a bad idea to have the great men from
Washington come out to see us thrash the Rebs."

It was about five A.M. when Tyler's column reached a point
overlooking Bull Run and the hilly fields and woodlands beyond.
This was the extreme left of the eight miles of Confederate lines,
and it was held by hardly more than a thousand men. Their
commander was Colonel Nathan G. Evans, a sturdy, stern-faced
South Carolinian who had graduated from West Point and who
was known in the old United States Army as "Shanks" Evans. He
had been an officer of dragoons on the frontier. "In 1850 to
1853," a period sketch explains, "he served in New Mexico and
began a famous career as an Indian fighter, which was continued
in Texas and Indian Territory after his promotion to captain in
1856, in various combats with the hostile Comanches. At the Battle of Wachita Village, October 1, 1858, his command defeated a
large body of the Comanches, and he killed two of their noted
chieftains in a hand-to-hand fight. For this he was voted a handsome sword by the Legislature of South Carolina."

Right now—although he didn't know it yet—Shanks Evans was
in another position of critical danger.

On the Union side of the stream, William T. Sherman was
among the forward observers.

"We saw in the gray light of morning men moving about, but no
signs of batteries. I rode well down to the stone bridge which
crosses the stream, saw plenty of trees cut down, some bush huts
such as soldiers use on picket guard, but none of the evidences of
strong fortifications we had been led to believe [were there].

"Our business was simply to threaten, and give time for Hunter
and Heintzelman to make their circuit. We arranged our troops to
this end, Schenck to the left of the road, and I to the right, Keyes
behind in reserve."

"The sun," says the correspondent of the New York *World,* who watched the deployment, "had risen as splendid as the sun of Austerlitz [where Napoleon had achieved one of his victories]. Was it an auspicious omen for us, or for the foe? Who could foretell?

"The scenery was too beautiful and full of nature's own peace for one to believe in the possibility of the tumult and carnage just at hand. . . . Then, too, it was Sunday morning. Even in the wilderness the sacred day seems purer and more hushed than any other."

Down the run, on the Confederate side, a correspondent of the Charleston *Mercury* was watching the development of Miles's demonstration (led by Richardson's brigade) from Centreville toward Blackburn's Ford.

"We see the columns moving, and, as they deploy through the forests, we see the cloud of dust floating over them, to mark their course. When the dust ceases, we are sure that they have taken their position."

For the moment, Richardson's troops remained quiet.

Returning to the Union correspondent at the Stone Bridge:

"It was ours to first jar upon the stillness of the morning. . . . A great 32-pound rifled Parrott gun . . . was brought forward, made to bear on the point where we had just seen the enemy—for the bayonets suddenly disappeared in the woods behind—and a shell was fired at fifteen minutes past 6 A.M., which burst in the air. . . . The report of the piece awoke the country, for leagues around, to a sense of what was to be the order of the day. The reverberation was tremendous. . . .

"We waited a moment for an answering salute, but, receiving none, sent the second shell at a hilltop two miles off, where we suspected that a battery had been planted by the rebels. The bomb burst like an echo close at the intended point, but still no answer came."

The shell had struck a Confederate signal station, tearing through the tent of Captain E. P. Alexander, the army's chief signal officer.

Now a new sound was heard. Says the Boston *Journal's* Charles Carleton Coffin, who was with Miles and his reserves at Centreville:

"The Union cannon at Blackburn's Ford began to thunder. I hastened toward Blackburn's Ford. . . . Learning that Richardson was to stand on the defensive, I returned to Centreville, where I discovered a battery without any gunners, and learned that the term for which the men had been serving had expired that morning and they were on their way to Washington."

Across Bull Run, Johnston and Beauregard were trying to fathom McDowell's intentions. They were concerned about the weakness of their left. Drums sounded everywhere as men were rushed to arms. Officers galloped about, shouting orders. Horses were harnessed and hitched to artillery pieces and caissons.

The brigades of Barnard E. Bee and Francis S. Bartow, with Bee in top command, were ordered to march from the right wing toward the Stone Bridge. Six hundred unattached troops under wealthy South Carolina planter Wade Hampton formed to follow. Thomas Jackson, in a spot just below the center of the Bull Run lines, was also alerted to move.

As related by Private John Opie of Jackson's brigade:

"The regiments having formed into line, great bolts of white cotton were brought out, which the officers tore into strips, and we tied a piece around our hats and another to our left arms [as a means of identification]. . . .

"The men looked at each other, then up and down the line, and raised one loud and general shout of laughter. Comments were numerous. One fellow said, 'I feel like a fool,' whereupon a comrade observed, 'I suppose, then, you feel quite natural.' Another swore that we would frighten the Yankees to death before we could get a shot at them. . . .

"After we were thus decorated, we were given the watchword in a whisper, for fear the enemy, who was two miles off, might hear it. It was 'Our Homes.'

"The next thing was the signal. When you met anyone and were in doubt as to who he was, you were to throw your right hand across your left breast and shout, 'Our Homes,' holding your gun in your left hand.

"They, however, failed to tell us that, while we were going through this Masonic performance, we thus gave the other fellow an opportunity to blow our brains out—if we had any!

"Now you laugh and look incredulous. . . . The fact is, our generals were as green as gourds in June. We destroyed on that morning cotton enough to make shirts for half the army."

At the Stone Bridge, Union General Tyler's demonstration was languishing under small response from Shanks Evans, who had opted for watching and waiting. William T. Sherman had a curi-

Barnard E. Bee

ous experience with a Southern civilian on the Union side of Bull Run.

"Early in the morning I saw a flag flying behind some trees [across the stream]. Some of the soldiers, seeing it, called out, 'Colonel, there's a flag—a flag of truce!' A man in the field with his dog and gun called out, 'No, it is no flag of truce, but a flag of defiance!' I was at the time studying the ground, and paid no attention to him."

Sherman goes on to tell of something that happened while he was looking across Bull Run a little later:

"I . . . observed two men on horseback ride along a hill, descend, cross the stream, and ride . . . towards us. [One] had a gun in his hand which he waved over his head, and called out to us,

'You damned black abolitionists, come on,' etc. I permitted some of the men to fire on him, but no damage was done."

On the Confederate side, a party of newsmen that included one writing for the Richmond *Dispatch* had been looking for a good spot from which to observe.

"At about 8 o'clock we reached a hill above Mitchell's Ford, almost entirely bare of trees and sufficiently high to afford an unobstructed view of the opposite heights. After taking a leisurely survey of the beautiful landscape . . . and listening with watchful intent to the booming of the heavy cannon on our right [at Blackburn's Ford], and anxiously examining the locations where the guns of the enemy on the opposite hills were plainly to be seen with the naked eye . . . we each sought the shade of a tree, where we drew forth our memorandum books and pencils. . . .

"An interesting meeting took place between our party and the venerable Edmund Ruffin, who had against the walls of Fort Sumter fired the first defiant gun [or, at least, one of the first]. He had come to this conflict with his . . . years weighing upon him, and his flowing white locks, to take part in this fight, encouraging our young men by his presence and example. Agile as a youth of sixteen, with rifle on his shoulder, his eyes glistened with excitement as he burned to engage the Yankee invader.

"Shortly afterwards Generals Beauregard, Johnston, and Bonham, accompanied by their aides, came galloping up the hill and dismounted on the summit. The generals held an earnest conversation for a few minutes, while taking a survey of the field and watching the excessive challenges from the enemy's batteries. . . .

"Just at this time, by the aid of our glass, we could see their guns brought to bear on the hill where we stood. . . . In a few moments the smoke was discovered issuing from their batteries of rifled cannon; and, before scarcely a word could be said, the peculiar whiz and hissing of the balls notified us that their aim had been well taken. Several balls fell in a field immediately behind us and not a hundred yards from the spot where the generals stood.

"An officer of General Beauregard's staff requested us to leave the hill, and, as we moved away, a shell burst not twenty feet off. . . . The enemy no doubt discovered the horses of the generals, and thought it a good opportunity to display their marksmanship."

By this time the Union divisions of Hunter and Heintzelman were well advanced in their roundabout journey to Sudley Ford.

They were raising a cloud of dust that was spotted by the Confederates, but its meaning wasn't divined. The supposition was that Patterson had come down from Charlestown—that McDowell was being reinforced.

According to Union Captain Henry Blake, who marched with Heintzelman, the divisions were accompanied by a guide, and "followed a narrow pathway which was not often used, and led in its tortuous course through a dry territory that was well-shaded by the forest. An open space . . . sometimes intervened. . . . The day was one of the hottest of the year . . . and it was impossible for the

Federals going into action

army to march a long distance with unusual speed. Nevertheless, for twelve miles the men were pushed forward . . . generally walking as rapidly as possible. . . . Some of them sank upon the ground, wholly overcome by faintness.

"There was a very small number, if any, in the Union host that wished to evade the unknown perils of combat; and many, throwing away their blankets and rations to facilitate their progress, merely retained their muskets and ammunition. . . . The artillery upon the left continued to fire at regular intervals in the vicinity of the fords. . . . The scarcity of water to allay . . . thirst . . . was another impediment; but the cannonading inspired the men with patriotism, and gave them a physical strength which they could not have possessed . . . in the avocations of a peaceful life."

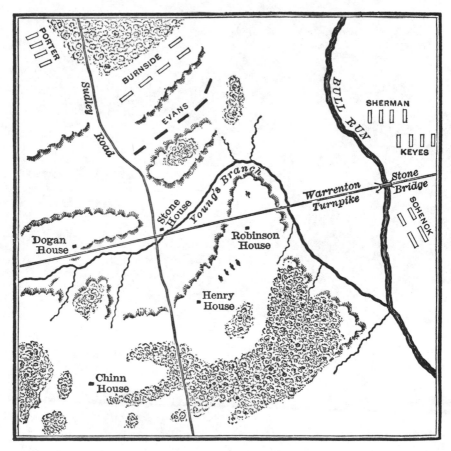

Battle of Bull Run begins. Left-flank Confederates who have hurried from the Stone Bridge are shown (as black bars) facing McDowell's attack.

The Confederates, thanks to E. P. Alexander's observation system, had begun to realize what was happening. Joe Johnston explains:

"At nine o'clock, Captain Alexander . . . reported that large bodies of Federal troops could be seen . . . about two miles above our extreme left. . . . This movement was reported to Colonel Evans [at the Stone Bridge]. . . . He moved rapidly to the left and rear with eleven companies and two field-pieces to endeavor to check or delay the progress of the enemy, having left three companies and two field-pieces to prevent the passage of the bridge by the body of troops he had been observing in front of it.

"Following the base of the hill on the north of Young's Branch, he threw himself in the enemy's way [unobserved, since the enemy was still some distance from Sudley Ford] a little in advance of the intersection of the turnpike and Sudley Road, and formed his small force under cover of a detached wood."

McDowell had been marching with Hunter's division in front, and Hunter was leading with the brigade of Ambrose E. Burnside. This man with the sweeping side-whiskers was destined for a long and varied career in the war, much of it worthy but some of it blameworthy. All in all, he'd survive with honor. Burnside's prewar military experience had involved West Point, service in Mexico, and several peacetime appointments. Resigning from the army in 1853, he became a manufacturer of self-designed breech-loading rifles; and he was a railway executive when the war began. He was now a colonel of volunteers.

Burnside relates:

"Nothing of moment occurred till the arrival of the division at the crossing of Bull Run at half-past nine o'clock, when intelligence was received that the enemy was in front. . . . The brigade was ordered to halt for a supply of water and a temporary rest. Afterwards, an advance movement was made."

The men at the head of the brigade splashed across the ford. As pictured by Union newsman Charles Carleton Coffin:

"The 2nd Rhode Island Infantry is thrown out, deployed as skirmishers. The men are five paces apart. They move slowly, cautiously, and nervously through the fields and thickets.

"Suddenly, from bushes, trees, and fences there is a rattle of musketry. . . . Evans's skirmishers are firing. There are jets of flame and smoke, and a strange humming in the air. There is another rattle, a roll, a volley. The cannon join.

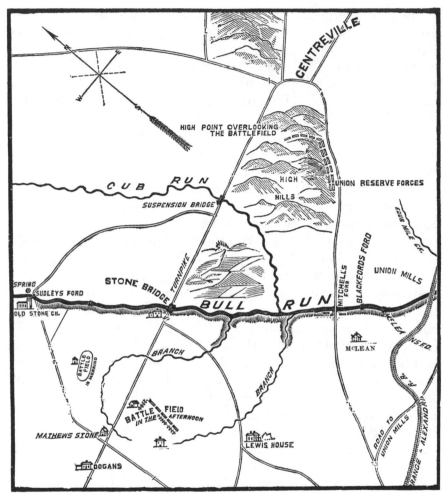

Morning and afternoon battlefields as seen from Centreville. Some of the observers ventured as far forward as the Stone Bridge, and a few even crossed Bull Run.

"The first great battle has begun."

These sounds were heard from afar by an internationally known British war correspondent who was approaching the field from Washington. He and a friend were traveling in a rented carriage. During the past ten years, William Howard Russell of the London *Times* had covered events in four hot spots, including the Crimea, and he was known for his vivid depictions and his shrewd, outspoken observations. These had won him awards, and he'd eventually be knighted. But right now Russell was about to earn himself the animosity of American Northerners. They already considered him to be pro-Southern, and his manner of reporting the Bull Run debacle would clinch their disapproval. He was to be dubbed, in derisive tones, "Bull Run Russell."

The correspondent relates:

"The long and weary way was varied by different pickets along the road, and by the examination of our papers and passes at different points. But the country looked vacant, in spite of crops of Indian corn, for the houses were shut up, and the few indigenous people whom we met looked most blackly under their brows at the supposed abolitionists. . . . The specimens of the [Negro] race I saw were well-dressed and not ill-looking.

"On turning into one of the roads which leads to Fairfax Court House and to Centreville beyond it, the distant sound of cannon reached us. That must have been about 9½ A.M. . . .

"In a few minutes afterward, a body of men appeared on the road, with their backs toward Centreville and their faces toward Alexandria. Their march was so disorderly that I could not have believed they were soldiers in an enemy's country . . . but for their arms and uniform. It soon appeared that there was no less than an entire regiment marching away, singly or in small knots of two or three, extending for some three or four miles along the road. A Babel of tongues rose from them, and they were all in good spirits, but with an air about them I could not understand.

"Dismounting at a stream where a group of thirsty men were drinking and halting in the shade, I asked an officer, 'Where are your men going, sir?'

" 'Well, we're going home, sir, I reckon—to Pennsylvania.'

"It was the 4th Pennsylvania Regiment . . . as I learned from the men.

" 'I suppose there is severe work going on behind you, judging from the firing?'

" 'Well, I reckon, sir, there is. We're going home . . . because the men's time is up. We have had three months of this work.'

"I proceeded on my way ruminating on the feelings of a general who sees half a brigade walk quietly away on the very morning of an action—and on the frame of mind of the men, who would have shouted till they were hoarse about their beloved Union . . . coolly turning their backs on it when in its utmost peril, because the letter of their engagement bound them no further. . . . Let us hear no more of the excellence of the three months service volunteers.

"And so we left them. The road was devious and difficult. . . .

Some few commissariat wagons were overtaken at intervals. Wherever there was a house by the roadside, the Negroes were listening to the firing.

"All at once a terrific object appeared in the wood above the trees. . . . In much doubt, we approached as well as the horses' minds would let us, and discovered that the strange thing was an inflated balloon attached to a car [on a] wagon, which was on its way to enable General McDowell to reconnoiter the position he was then engaged in attacking—just a day too late. The operators and attendants swore . . . horribly . . . but they could not curse down the trees [that obstructed their forward movement]. . . .

"At last Centreville appeared in sight—a few houses . . . beyond which rose a bald hill, the slopes covered with bivouac huts, commissary carts and horses, and the top crested with spectators of the fight. . . . There were carriages and [other] vehicles drawn up as if they were attending a small country race. . . . In one was a lady with an opera-glass. In and around . . . others were legislators and politicians. There were also a few civilians on horseback, and on the slope of the hill a regiment [of Miles's reserves] had stacked arms and was engaged in looking at and commenting on the battle below."

24

Massing for a Decision

THE OUTSET of the battle found Generals Johnston and Beauregard on the commanding height near Mitchell's Ford, five miles down the run. In Johnston's words:

"The noise and smoke of the fight were distinctly heard and seen by General Beauregard and myself . . . but . . . in its earlier stages, they indicated no force of the enemy that the troops on the ground [those of Shanks Evans] and those of Bee, Hampton, and Jackson—that we could see hastening toward the firing in the order given—were not competent to cope with.

"Bee, who was much in advance of the others, saw the strength and dispositions of the combatants . . . from the summit of the hill south of Young's Branch; and, seeing the advantage given to this position by its greater elevation than that of the opposite ridge, on which the enemy stood . . . he formed his brigade, including Bartow's two regiments . . . there.

"But, being appealed to for aid by Evans, then fully engaged, and seeing that his troops—that had suffered much in the unequal contest—were about to be overwhelmed, he moved forward . . . and, crossing the valley under the fire of the Federal artillery, formed on the right, and in advance of his line."

Bee, according to Union newsman Charles Carleton Coffin, "is in such a position that he can pour a fire upon the flank of the Rhode Island boys, who are pushing Evans. It is a galling fire, and the brave fellows are cut down. . . . They are almost overwhelmed.

"But help is at hand. The 71st New York, the 2nd New Hamp-

353

Behind the Union front

shire, and the 1st Rhode Island, all belonging to Burnside's brigade, move toward [Bee]. . . . They bring their guns to a level, and
the rattle and roll begin. There are jets of flame, long lines of
light, white clouds unfolding and expanding, rolling over and
over and rising above the treetops.

"Wilder the uproar. Men fall, tossing their arms. Some leap into
the air, some plunge headlong, falling like logs of wood or lumps
of lead. Some reel, stagger, and tumble. Others lie down gently as
to a night's repose, unheeding the din, commotion, and uproar.
They are bleeding, torn, and mangled. . . .

"The air is full of fearful noises. . . . The trees are splintered,
crushed, and broken as if smitten by thunderbolts. Twigs and
leaves fall to the ground. There is smoke, dust, wild talking, shouting, hissings, howlings, explosions. It is a new, strange, unantici-
pated experience to the soldiers of both armies, far different from
what they thought it would be.

"Far away, church bells are tolling the hour of Sabbath worship,
and children are singing sweet songs in many a Sunday school.

Strange and terrible the contrast! You cannot bear to look upon the dreadful scene. How horrible those wounds! The ground is crimson with blood. You are ready to turn away, and shut the scene forever from your sight. But the battle must go on. . . .

"It is terrible to see, but there are worse things than war. It is worse to have the rights of men trampled in the dust; worse to have your country destroyed, to have justice, truth, and honor violated. You had better be killed, torn to pieces by cannon shot, than lose your manhood, or yield that which makes you a man. It is better to die than give up that rich inheritance bequeathed us by our fathers, and purchased by their blood."

The Union artillery battery commanded by Captain Charles Griffin was at this time dueling, at a distance of two-thirds of a mile, with a battery under Captain John Imboden of Bee's brigade. Imboden was located where Bee had first formed—on the broad, undulating plateau atop a set of hills whose northerly slopes fell toward Young's Branch, on the far side of which the Confederate foot troops were fighting. This hilltop plateau, which held two small houses, those of Mrs. Judith Henry and a free Negro named James Robinson, was to figure strongly in the battle. Right now, however, Imboden and his crews and their guns, caissons, and horses were alone there. Jackson and Hampton were still on the march up the run. Bee, before going down the hill and across Young's Branch to join Shanks Evans, had ordered Imboden to hold his position until ordered to leave it.

Imboden tells of his duel with the federal guns:

"The firing of both batteries now became very rapid. They at first overshot us and burst their shells in our rear, but at every round improved their aim and shortened their fuse. In about fifteen minutes we received our first injury. A shell passed between two of our guns and exploded amongst the caissons, mangling the arm of Private J. J. Points with a fragment in a most shocking manner. I ordered him to be carried off the field to the surgeon at once. He was scarcely gone when another shell exploded at the same place and killed a horse.

"About this time the enemy began to fire too low, striking the knoll in our front . . . from which the ricochet was sufficient to carry the projectiles over us. They discovered this, and again began to fire, [but] over us.

"After we had been engaged for perhaps a half hour, the enemy brought another battery [that of Captain James B. Ricketts] . . . into position about 400 yards south of the first, and a little nearer to us, and commenced a very brisk fire upon us. A shell from this last battery soon plunged into our midst, instantly killing a horse and nearly cutting off the leg of Private W. A. Siders, just below the knee. He was immediately taken to the surgeon.

"A few minutes afterwards, another shell did its work by wounding 2nd Lieutenant A. W. Garber so severely in the wrist that I ordered him off the field for surgical aid.

"We now had ten guns at work upon us. . . . During this time the enemy's infantry [across the valley of Young's Branch] was assembling . . . in immense numbers."

The numbers at the front, however, were not so heavy, and Union leadership had suffered with the early wounding of General Hunter. Burnside, whose brigade had been carrying the burden of the assault, was obliged to send to Andrew Porter's brigade for help.

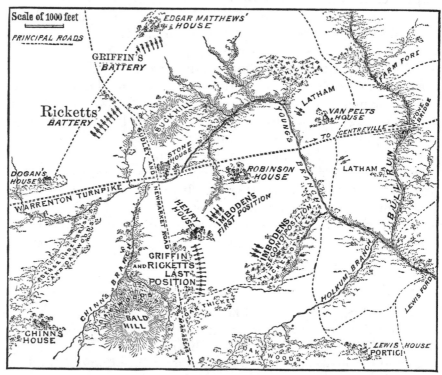

Lower center of map shows Imboden's first and second positions on the Henry-Robinson plateau. Also shown are Griffin's and Ricketts's original positions (upper left) and their fatal forward position on the plateau.

"He asks," says Charles Carleton Coffin, "for the brave old soldiers, the regulars who have been true to the flag of their country. . . . They have been long in the service, and have had many fierce contests with the Indians on the Western plains. They are as true as steel. [Major George] Sykes commands them. He leads the way.

"You see them, with steady ranks, in the edge of the woods east of Dogan's house. . . . They pass through the grove of pines and enter the open field. They are cut through and through with solid shot, shells burst around them, men drop from the ranks, but the battalion does not falter. It sweeps on close up to the cloud of flame and smoke rolling from the hill north of the turnpike.

"Their muskets come to a level. There is a click, click, click, along the line. A broad sheet of flame, a white, sulphurous cloud, a deep roll like the angry growl of thunder. There is a sudden staggering in the Rebel ranks. Men whirl round and drop upon the ground. The line wavers and breaks. They run down the hill, across the hollows, to another knoll. There they rally, and hold their ground awhile. . . .

"General Heintzelman's division was in rear of General Hunter's on the march. When the battle began, the troops were several miles from Sudley Church. They were parched with thirst, and when they reached the stream they, too, stopped and filled their canteens. Burnside's and Porter's brigades were engaged two hours before Heintzelman's division reached the field."

It was now nearly noon. With elements of Heintzelman's division entering the fight, and with William T. Sherman and Erasmus Keyes of Tyler's division starting across Bull Run by way of a ford above the Stone Bridge, Evans, Bee, and Bartow were in a position fast becoming untenable.

Hampton and Jackson were drawing near. As related by D. B. Conrad of Jackson's brigade:

"For two long, hot hours did we move toward the rattling of musketry, which at first was very faint, then became more and more audible. At last we halted under a long ridge covered with small pines. Here were the wounded of that corps who had been first engaged; men limping on gun or stick; men carried off in blankets, bleeding their life away; men supported on each side by soldiers. And they gave us no very encouraging news. . . .

"Up the narrow lane our brigade started, directly to where the musketry seemed the loudest, our regiment, the 2nd, bringing up the rear. Reaching the top, a wide clearing was discovered. A broad table-land spread out, the pine thicket ceased, and far away over the hill in front was the smoke of musketry. At the bottom of the long declivity was the famous turnpike, and on the hills beyond could be seen clearly Griffin's and Ricketts' batteries. In their front, to their rear, and supported on each side, were long lines of blue. To our right, about one hundred yards off, was a small building, the . . . Henry House [and Mrs. Henry, aged and bedridden, was in it].

"The infantry was engaged on the [forward] side of the long, gradual slope of the hill on which we stood and in the bottom below. . . . We could hear the sound and see the white smoke."

Jackson began setting up a line in a rearward position on the plateau. At this time Confederate artillery commander John Imboden was still on the plateau, in his perilous forward position. He had been waiting anxiously for Bee to send him word to draw back. As it happened, an aide that Bee had sent with just such a message had fallen badly wounded along the way.

In Imboden's words:

"Infantry was now massing near the Stone House on the turnpike, not five hundred yards away. . . . On making this discovery, and learning from the sergeants of pieces that our ammunition was almost entirely exhausted, there remained but one way to save our guns, and that was to run them off the field. More than half of our horses had been killed, only one or two being left in several of my six-horse teams. Those that we had were quickly divided among the guns and caissons, and we limbered up and fled.

"Then it was that the Henry House was riddled, and the old lady, Mrs. Henry, was mortally wounded; for our line of retreat was so chosen that for 200 or 300 yards the house would conceal us from [Ricketts's] battery. . . . Several . . . shot passed through the house, scattering shingles, boards, and splinters all around us. A rifle shot from [Griffin] broke the axle of one of our guns and dropped the gun in the field, but we saved the limber. . . .

"We crossed the summit [to] the edge of the pines . . . and there met . . . Jackson. . . . I felt very angry at what I then regarded as bad treatment from General Bee in leaving us so long exposed . . . and I expressed myself with some profanity, which I could see was displeasing to Jackson.

"He remarked, 'I'll support your battery. Unlimber right here.'

"We did so."

While Jackson was completing his deployment along the edge of the pines, D. B. Conrad was looking toward the opposite rim of the plateau, from beneath which issued the smoke and din of the battle.

"There rode up fast toward us from the front a horse and rider, gradually rising to our view from the bottom of the hill. He was an officer, all alone; and as he came closer, erect and full of fire, his jet-black eyes and long hair and . . . uniform of a general officer made him the cynosure of all [eyes]. In a strong, decided tone he inquired of the nearest aide what troops we were and who commanded. He was told that . . . Jackson, with five Virginia regiments, had just arrived, pointing to where the [general] stood at the same time.

"The strange officer then advanced, and we of the regimental staff crowded to where he was, to hear the news from the front. He announced himself as General B. E. Bee, commanding South Carolina troops.

" 'We have been heavily engaged all the morning, and, being overpowered, we are now being slowly pushed back. We will fall back on you as a support. The enemy will make their appearance in a short time over the crest of that hill.'

" 'Then, sir, we will give them the bayonet,' was the only reply of . . . Jackson.

"With a salute, General Bee wheeled his horse and disappeared down the hill."

The general did not go far, for the first of his retreating men were climbing to the plateau's rim. By this time Wade Hampton's legion had advanced across the plateau past the Robinson House on the right, but these troops could do nothing more than cover the retreat, and they were badly cut up in the process.

The mounted Bee, swept over the rim as he tried to slow the rolling tide, pointed with his sword and shouted, "There is Jackson, standing like a stone wall! Rally behind the Virginians! Let us determine to die here, and we will conquer!"

Bee himself was soon mortally wounded. His reference to Jackson, however, had earned him enduring fame. From that time on, Jackson would be known to the world as "Stonewall," and the unit he commanded at First Bull Run would be called the "Stonewall Brigade."

But at least one of Jackson's soldiers, Private John Opie, would

Bee's meeting with Jackson

always consider the image of the brigade's "standing like a stone wall" to be something of a delusion. "Instead of standing, we were lying flat upon the ground, by order of General Jackson."

Continuing in Opie's words:

"We lost several of our men while lying in this position, and . . . the firing drew nearer and nearer. At first a few wounded men appeared, then squads of stragglers, and, finally, crowds of men without order or organization. Some of them . . . rushed head-long through our ranks to the rear. . . . Very few of Bee's men fell into our ranks."

The greater part of the retreating troops, with the pursuit ending and the Yankees falling back to regroup, swung around Jackson's right flank to a position in his right rear. Here they were spotted by Generals Johnston and Beauregard, who—now fully aware that their left was in mortal danger—had come galloping up the run.

Beauregard relates:

"We found the commanders resolutely stemming the further flight of the routed forces, but vainly endeavoring to restore order; and our own efforts were as futile. Every segment of line we succeeded in forming was again dissolved while another was being formed. More than two thousand men were shouting, each some suggestion to his neighbor, their voices mingling with the noise of the shells hurtling through the trees overhead, and all word of command drowned in the confusion and uproar. . . .

"The disorder seemed irretrievable, but happily the thought came to me that if their colors were planted out to the front [on Jackson's right] the men might rally on them, and I gave the order to carry the standards forward some forty yards, which was promptly executed by the regimental officers, thus drawing the common eye of the troops. . . . And as General Johnston and myself rode forward . . . with the colors of the 4th Alabama [which had lost all its field officers] . . . the [entire] line that had fought all morning and had fled, routed and disordered, now advanced again into position as steadily as veterans. . . .

"As soon as order was restored, I requested General Johnston to go back to Portici (the Lewis House), and from that point—which I considered most favorable for the purpose—forward me the reinforcements as they would arrive from the Bull Run lines below [Jubal Early's brigade had been ordered up], and those that were expected to arrive from Manassas [some of the Shenandoah Valley troops were still on the way by rail], while I should direct the field. . . . He considerately yielded to my urgency. . . .

"As General Johnston departed for Portici, I hastened to form our line of battle. . . . I ordered up the 49th and 8th Virginia regiments from [Philip St. George] Cooke's neighboring brigade in the Bull Run lines. . . .

"As the 49th Virginia rapidly came up, its colonel . . . indicated to them the immediate presence of [myself on the field]. . . . As the regiment raised a loud cheer, [my] name was caught by some of the troops of Jackson's brigade in the immediate wood, who rushed out calling for General Beauregard. Hastily acknowledging these happy signs of sympathy and confidence . . . I paused to say a few words to Jackson; [and,] while hurrying back to the right, my horse was killed under me by a bursting shell, a fragment of which carried away part of the heel of my boot."

The general appropriated a government-owned horse that was standing nearby. As Beauregard galloped away, the man who had been using the horse was left to lament that a bag attached to the saddle contained his toilet articles and other personal effects.

It was during these moments that artillery captain John Imboden, whose battery had fallen back upon Jackson after taking a beating in the morning's fighting, informed the general that this fighting had left him with only three rounds of ammunition.

"I . . . suggested that the caissons be sent to the rear for a supply. He said, 'No, not now—wait till other guns get here, and then you can withdraw your battery, as it has been so torn to pieces, and let your men rest.'

"During the lull in front, my men lay about, exhausted from want of water and food, and black with powder, smoke, and dust. Lieutenant [Thomas] Harman and I . . . amused ourselves training one of the guns on a heavy column of the enemy . . . 1200 to 1500 yards away. While we were thus engaged, General Jackson rode up and said that three or four batteries were approaching rapidly, and that we might soon retire. I asked permission to fire the three rounds of shrapnel left to us, and he said, 'Go ahead.'

"I picked up a charge—the fuse was cut and ready—and rammed it home myself, remarking to Harman, 'Tom, put in the primer and pull her off.'

"I forgot to step back far enough from the muzzle, and, as I wanted to see the shell strike, I squatted to be under the [screen of] smoke, and gave the word 'Fire!'

"Heavens! What a report! Finding myself [thrown] full twenty feet away, I thought the gun had burst. But it was only the pent-up gas that, escaping sideways as the shot cleared the muzzle, had struck my side and head with great violence. I recovered in time to see the shell explode in the enemy's ranks. The blood gushed out of my left ear . . . [in which I was] totally deaf.

"The men fired the other two rounds and limbered up and

Confederates rallying on Jackson's line

moved away, just as the Rockbridge Artillery . . . came into position, followed a moment later by the Leesburg Artillery. . . . Several other batteries soon came into line."

Not all of the Confederate batteries of the lower Bull Run lines could be called up. Union General Miles and his Centreville reserves continued to demonstrate in the region of Blackburn's Ford. (Miles, it seems, was drinking heavily that day, but his troops performed adequately.) Not only Confederate guns, but also Confederate troops were held in their original positions. James Longstreet's brigade, for one, would see nothing of the main battle.

Beauregard now had about sixty-five hundred men on his Jackson line. Before him, in the valley of Young's Branch, McDowell was making an expansive deployment of some ten thousand men:

the brigades of Andrew Porter, Orlando B. Willcox, William T. Sherman, William B. Franklin, Oliver O. Howard, and Erasmus Keyes. Burnside's men had dropped back to rest. Schenck remained in his position on the other side of Bull Run, below the Stone Bridge. The batteries of Griffin and Ricketts continued to serve as McDowell's chief artillery supports.

The success of the morning attack had filled the Federals with exultation. Heard everywhere during the deployment were such cries as these:

"We've whipped them!"

"We'll hang Jeff Davis to a sour apple tree!"

"The war is over!"

One of Sherman's junior officers, Lieutenant William Thompson Lusk, tells of his regiment's rapid trip to its designated position:

"On we rushed by the flank, over fields, through woods, down into ravines, plunging into streams, up again onto rising meadows, eager, excited, thrilled with hot desire to bear our share in routing the enemy. We cheered, and yelled, pressing onward, regardless of shells now and then falling among us, thinking only of a sharp fight and certain victory. . . .

"From many a point not long since covered by secession forces, the American banner now floated. What wonder we felt our hearts swelling with pride, and saw, hardly noticing, [a] horse and rider lying stiff, cold, and bloody together! What, though we stepped unthinking over the pale body of many a brave fellow still grasping convulsively his gun, with the shadows of death closing around him! We . . . were dreaming only of victory.

"So we were marched to the edge of a slope which sheltered us partially from the aim of the enemy's artillery. Here, lying prostrate, shell after shell flew over our heads or tore up the ground around. Now we could feel the hot breath of a cannon ball fan our cheeks. Now we could see one, fairly aimed, falling among our horses and rolling them prostrate. And now again one of these messengers would come swift into the ranks of one of our columns, and, without a thought or a groan, a soul was hurried into eternity."

The civilian spectators on the hill at Centreville, according to British journalist William Howard Russell, "were all excited, and a lady with an opera glass who was near me was quite beside herself when an unusually heavy discharge roused the current of her blood. 'That is splendid! Oh, my! Is not that first-rate? I guess we will be in Richmond this time tomorrow.' . . .

"Loud cheers suddenly burst from the spectators as a man dressed in the uniform of an officer, whom I had seen riding violently across the plain in an open space below, galloped along the front, waving his cap and shouting at the top of his voice. He was brought up, by the press of people round his horse, close to where I stood.

" 'We've whipped them on all points!' he cried. 'We have taken all their batteries! They are retreating as fast as they can, and we are after them!'

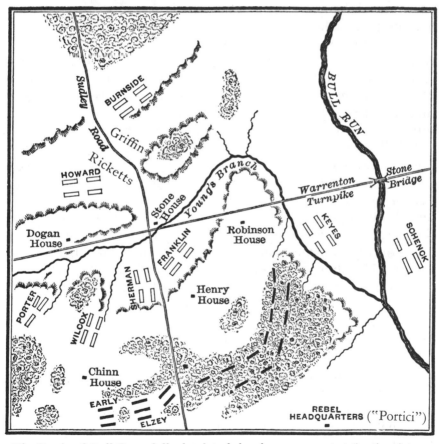

The Battle of Bull Run, fully developed, has become a contest for the plateau holding the Henry and Robinson houses. Confederate lines are at bottom of map. Federal units are shown as white bars. Griffin and Ricketts are in their original positions.

"Such cheers as rent the welkin! The congressmen shook hands with each other and cried out, 'Bully for us! Bravo! Didn't I tell you so?' "

Turning to Union newsman Charles Carleton Coffin:

"It is two o'clock Sunday afternoon. . . . I stand upon the roof of a house overlooking the field, and see the brigades of Sherman, Franklin, Willcox, and Porter advancing towards the houses of Mr. Robinson and [Mrs.] Henry. . . . Howard's brigade is moving towards the turnpike by Dogan's house. Keyes's brigade is near the Stone Bridge. There are parts of fourteen Union regiments advancing to assail the Confederate line. . . .

"There are twenty-two Confederate cannon pouring a heavy fire upon the advancing men in blue, and twelve regiments delivering their volleys. . . .

"The batteries of Griffin and Ricketts are on the plateau east of Dogan's. . . . General McDowell at this moment commits another error: he orders the batteries to go across the stream in advance of the infantry. [Several regiments, however, were assigned to join him in support.] Ricketts does not like the order, but he is a soldier in the regular army and believes in obeying commands.

"The battery moves down the road, crosses the stream, ascends the hill towards the Henry House, and opens fire at close range. The Confederate sharpshooters behind the picket fence and under the peach trees [on the Henry property] begin to pick off his horses, but he rains canister on them and riddles the house with shells. . . . [Some accounts claim it was at this time that Mrs. Henry was mortally wounded, and not when the house was fired upon earlier.] The sharpshooters are compelled to retreat.

"Griffin comes, with his horses upon the gallop, across the stream and takes position to the [right] of Ricketts. Major [William F.] Barry, chief of artillery, [had] brought him the order to take this position. He, too, [had] objected. . . .

" 'The Zouaves will support you,' says Barry.

" 'Why not let them go in advance until I get into position? Then they can fall back.'

" 'It is McDowell's order for you to go.'

" 'That settles it. But, mark my words, the Zouaves will not support me.' "

These troops, however, were presently advancing up the hill in fine order, four ranks deep, their red knickers especially bright in the strong sunlight. Marching on their right, heading for a patch

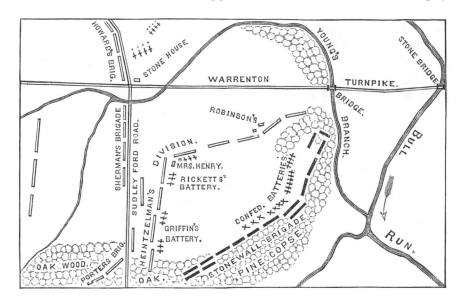

Ricketts's and Griffin's batteries facing Jackson's "stone wall" position.

of woods, was another support regiment, but one in ordinary uniform.

Griffin's guns were now roaring in unison with those of Ricketts, and Beauregard's guns were responding. Confederate artilleryman John Imboden, who had retired his own battery a little earlier, was presently back at the front, having come to ask Jackson's permission to take his tattered command to a safer spot farther down the run. To the captain's surprise, he was put to work.

"Jackson ordered me to go from battery to battery to see that the guns were properly aimed and the fuses cut the right length. This was the work of but a few minutes. On returning to the left of the line of guns, I stopped to ask General Jackson's permission to rejoin my battery.

"The fight was just then hot enough to make him feel well. His eyes fairly blazed. He had a way of throwing up his left hand with the open palm toward the person he was addressing. And, as he told me to go, he made this gesture. The air was full of flying missiles, and, as he spoke, he jerked down his hand, and I saw that blood was streaming from it. I exclaimed, 'General, you are wounded!'

"He replied, as he drew a handkerchief from his breastpocket and began to bind it up, 'Only a scratch—a mere scratch,' and galloped away along his line."

By this time Jackson's left-flank regiment, the 33rd Virginia, was hurrying through the woods, unobserved by the Federals, on a swing toward the right flank of Griffin and Ricketts.

Again in the words of Union newsman Charles Carleton Coffin:

"From my position I can see a dust-cloud in the west, rising above the treetops. A little later, a regiment comes out of the woods . . . west of the road leading to Manassas. The men are in gray, as are several of the Union regiments. They climb over a rail fence. The colonel walks along the ranks as if saying something to them.

Griffin and Barry in disagreement

"Griffin sees them, believes them to be Confederates, and wheels his guns to mow them down with canister. The cannon are loaded, and the gunners stand ready to send the double-shotted charges into the line. . . .

" 'Don't fire!' It is Major Barry, commanding the artillery, who shouts it.

" 'They are rebels,' Griffin replies.

" 'No, they are your supports.'

"The 14th New York Regiment has gone up into the woods to the right of Griffin's battery, and Major Barry makes a mistake in supposing that the men in gray, which have just come out of the wood, are those who a few moments ago entered it.

" 'Sure as the world, they are rebels!' Griffin shouts again.

" 'I know that they are your supports.'

"Griffin wheels his guns in the other direction . . . and opens fire once more. The officer addressing the men in gray has finished his speech, and now faces them to the left, marches a few rods, faces them to the right as deliberately as if at drill in camp, advances steadily towards Griffin, then comes to a halt. The men bring their guns to a level, and take aim.

"There is a flash, a white cloud, a roll of musketry. The air is filled with leaden hail. Men and horses go down. Hardly one of the gunners that is not killed, wounded, or taken prisoner. The horses plunge madly down the ravine. The Zouaves in rear of Griffin behold the spectacle in amazement, then break, and stream over the field towards Dogan's house, a few only remaining to fire parting shots. In vain the efforts of the officers to rally them."

A Unionist who witnessed the entire incident from the rim of the plateau was Captain Henry Blake of the 11th Massachusetts.

"The regiment was not actively engaged at that moment, and most of the men were watching the section of Griffin's battery which was planted near them. . . . I never saw . . . work of destruction more sudden or complete. The battery of Ricketts, which was in line of that of Griffin, had been annihilated in the same decisive manner. . . .

"The few cannoneers that survived this fatal volley immediately rushed to the rear. Wounded horses, in their agony, galloped through the ranks of the infantry and trampled upon the dead and helpless who were lying upon the field. Three animals which were harnessed and attached to a caisson dashed through [our] regiment at a furious rate of speed, and dragged one that was severely injured. A soldier whose leg had been shattered by a solid shot sat upon the carriage, clinging to it with his hands, and a stream of blood sprinkled the earth and made a trail by which the course of the caisson could be traced. . . .

"A squadron of their cavalry [led by Jeb Stuart] attempted to make a charge, but . . . they were easily repulsed by a body of men who belonged to different regiments."

It was probably at this time that a captured Union Zouave caught the special attention of a correspondent of the Charleston *Courier*.

"I saw him on the field, just after he was taken. While passing a group of our men, one of the latter called him some hard name.

" 'Sir,' said the Zouave, turning on his heel and looking the Virginian full in the eye, 'I have heard that yours was a nation of gentlemen, but your insult comes from a coward and a knave. I am your prisoner, but you have no right to fling your curses upon me. . . . Of the two, sir, I consider *myself* the gentleman.'

"I need not add that the Virginian slunk away under this merited rebuke, or that a dozen soldiers generously gathered around the prisoner and assured him of protection from further insult."

On the Union side, the fate of the two batteries had been witnessed by the civilian from Massachusetts, Edwin Barrett, from a unique position—high in a persimmon tree behind the lines. Although the development shocked him, Barrett was hardly less disturbed by things occurring in his immediate vicinity.

"I had now been in the tree some two hours, and all this time a continuous stream of wounded were being carried past me to the rear. The soldiers would cross their muskets, place their wounded companions across, and slowly carry them past. Another soldier would have a wounded man with his arm around his neck, slowly walking back. And then two men would be bearing a mortally wounded comrade in their arms, who was in convulsions and writhing in his last agonies. . . . I could hardly keep back the tears. . . .

"Picking a couple of persimmons as a remembrance, I descended the tree, startling two soldiers leaning against it, by requesting them to move their guns so that I could get down. . . .

"Leaving the tree, I went along over the field to the left, the bullets whistling about me, and the cannon balls plowing up the ground in every direction. . . . [He was on the battlefield of the morning, which was now a background for Confederate fire from the Henry-Robinson plateau.] I came across two of our men with

Destruction of the Union batteries

a prisoner, who said he belonged to a South Carolina regiment. I
asked him some questions, but he was dogged and silent. . . .

"The shot fell so thick; and, shells bursting around me, I hardly
knew which way to turn. A musket ball whizzed past my ear, so
near that I felt the heat, and for a moment thought I was hit. The
ground was strewed with broken guns, swords, cartridge-boxes,
blankets, haversacks, gun-carriages, together with all the [other]
paraphernalia of warfare, mingled with the dead and wounded
men. . . .

"Seeing a small white house still towards the left, with a well
near it, I started for some water; and, getting over a wall, I discovered lying beside it a number of our dead with their haversacks drawn over their faces. I lifted the cover from [each] . . .
thinking perhaps I might come across some of my friends; but
they were all strangers, or so disfigured that I could not recognize
them.

"I went to the well for a drink, and, as I drew near the house,
I heard loud groans. And such a scene as was there presented, in

that little house of two rooms and on the grass around it, was
enough to appall the stoutest heart.

"The rooms were crowded, and I could not get in; but all
around on the grass were men mortally wounded. I should think
there were at least forty on that greensward. . . . And such
wounds! Some with both legs shot off; some with a thigh shot
away; some with both legs broken; others with horrid flesh
wounds. . . . I saw one man with a wound in his back large enough
to put in my fist. He was fast bleeding to death.

"They lay so thick around me that I could hardly step between
them, and every step was in blood. As I walked among them, some
besought me to kill them and put an end to their agony. Some
were just gasping, and some had died since they had been brought
here; and the dying convulsions of these strong men were ago-
nizing in the extreme. Some were calling for the surgeon, but the
hospital was more than a mile off [back at the old stone church at
Sudley Ford], and there were but two surgeons here.

"I left the house and bore off to the right, towards some low
pine woods . . . and scattered along were the dead bodies of our
men. On reaching the wood [which had figured strongly in the
morning phase of the battle], I found the ground literally covered
with the corpses of the enemy, and I counted, in the space of
about ten rods square, forty-seven dead rebels, and ten mortally
wounded; and scattered all through the woods, still farther back,
were any number more.

"I talked with several of the wounded, and they told me they
belonged to the 8th Georgia Regiment, Colonel Bartow, and had
arrived at Manassas from Winchester the day before. . . . They
told me their whole regiment was posted in this pine wood. One
young man told me he was from Macon, and that his father was
a merchant.

"I asked another where he was from. He replied, defiantly, 'I
am for disunion—opposed to you.' This man had both thighs
broken.

"I heard one of our soldiers ask a wounded Georgian if their
orders were to kill our wounded. He answered, 'No.' Our soldiers
carried water to these wounded men. . . .

"The convulsions of one of these was awful to look upon. He
appeared to have been shot in the lungs . . . as he vomited blood
in large quantities, and in his struggles for breath, would throw
himself clear from the ground.

"I noticed among this heap of bodies an officer dressed in light blue uniform, with green stripes on his pants—a fine-looking man whom I took to be a captain.

"I also saw one of our soldiers take sixty dollars from the body of a dead Georgian. And their knives, revolvers, etc., were appropriated in the same way. This I looked upon as legitimate plunder for the soldiers; but, as a citizen, I forbore to take anything from the field. . . .

"Passing through these pine woods, I still bore to the right, towards our center, and crossed a cleared space and came to some heavy wood, on the edge of which I perceived a number of dead scattered about; and, seeing several wounded men, I went up to one of them and found he was a rebel belonging to an Alabama regiment. . . . He pointed to a dead horse close to us and said, 'There is my colonel's horse, and I suppose you have taken him prisoner.'

"Most of these rebels had gray suits with black trimmings—very similar to the uniforms of some of our men. Scattered all through this wood were our men and the Alabamians, dead and wounded mingled together.

"I noticed a splendid bay horse nibbling the leaves from a tree, and was thinking what a fine animal he was, when I saw that one foreleg was shot off, clean as though cut by a knife, and bleeding a stream."

The narrator's wanderings ended at this point. His attention was called back to the afternoon battle involving the Henry-Robinson plateau. A lot had been happening up there.

25

The Great Retreat

THE UNION RESPONSE to the quashing of Griffin and Ricketts is described by Stonewall Jackson's biographer, John Esten Cooke, who was on the battlefield that afternoon:

"Their infantry, swarming upon the face of the plateau, was massed in the vicinity of the Henry House, and all at once the bristling lines were thrown forward and hurled with fury [toward] the Confederate center. . . . They . . . were almost in contact with Jackson when he ordered his men to charge. They responded with wild cheers, and, firing a heavy volley, rushed forward. . . .

"The enemy met them with determination; and, with one mad yell arising from both adversaries and mingling its savage echoes, the surging masses came together. The scene which followed is indescribable. The thunder of artillery and the sustained crash of musketry rolled like some diabolical concert across the hills, and the opposing lines were lost in a dense cloud of smoke, from which rose shouts, yells, cheers, and the groans of the dying.

"Jackson had charged without orders, from the necessity of the situation. But General Beauregard, it seems, had at nearly the same moment ordered his whole front to advance. . . . The men seemed inspired with a species of fury, almost, which made them careless of wounds and death. One who was carried dying from the field exclaimed with clenched hands, 'They've done for me now, but my father's there yet! Our army's there yet! Our cause is there yet! And liberty's there yet!'

"The officers set a chivalric example to the troops, and suffered

heavily. Hampton was shot while bravely leading on his men. . . .
General Bartow, who had said, 'I shall go into that fight with a
determination never to leave the field alive but in victory,' was
shot through the heart while rallying the 7th Georgia, and fell,
exclaiming to the men around him, 'They've killed *me*, but never
give up the field!'

"In the midst of this hot struggle Jackson's equanimity remained unshaken. He does not seem, during any portion of the
battle, to have contemplated disaster or defeat, and [presented] to
the agitation and flurry of many around him a demeanor entirely
unmoved.

"When an officer rode up to him and exclaimed with great
excitement, 'General, I think the day is going against us,' Jackson
replied, with entire coolness in his brief, curt, tone, 'If you think
so, sir, you had better not say anything about it.'

"His bayonet charge had pierced the Federal center, separating
the two wings; but . . . this advantage . . . became of doubtful
value. . . . The Confederate line was in danger of being enveloped
by the heavy masses closing in upon its flanks.

"Jackson put forth all his strength to retain his vantage ground,
and the enemy made corresponding exertions to drive him from
the plateau. At this stage the struggle reached its utmost intensity.
In portions of the field, especially near the Henry House, the
opposing lines fought almost breast to breast; and, though repeatedly repulsed, the Federal infantry constantly returned with new
vigor to the charge."

The lost Union batteries were regained, then lost again; and the
process was repeated. At one point General McDowell himself was
so far forward that he was able, for a brief time, to use the second
floor of the Henry House as an observation post.

William T. Sherman was also in the thick of things.

"My horse was shot through the foreleg. My knee was cut round
by a ball, and another . . . hit my collar and did not penetrate. . . .
I sat on my horse on the ground where Ricketts' battery had been
shattered to fragments, and saw the havoc done."

There was one Union leader who caught the special attention of
Confederate staff officer D. B. Conrad.

"A gray-haired man, sitting sideways on horseback, whom I
understood to be General Heintzelman . . . directed the movements of each regiment as it came up the hill, and his coolness and
gallantry won our admiration."

Federals assaulting Henry Hill

These regiments were soon fragmented by Confederate fire. One regiment contained many United States Marines that Conrad had known while he was serving in the old United States Navy, and several of his former friends fell helplessly wounded near the spot where he was fighting.

"They called on me by name to help them. . . . 'Water! Water!' 'Turn me over!' 'Raise my head!' and 'Pull me out of this fire!' "

Because he himself was under heavy fire, there was little that Conrad could do.

Confederate Private John Opie says of the men around him:

"O'Donnell, Scanlan, and Steinbuck fall. A boy from Bee's brigade is shot in the forehead, and dies without a groan. . . . One fellow fell, shot on the eyebrow by a spent ball [which made] a slight wound. . . . He, kicking and tossing his arms about him, yelled, 'O Lordy, I am killed! I am killed! O Lordy, I am dead!'

"I saw the fellow was not hurt much—only alarmed—and I said . . . 'Are you really killed?'

" 'Yes, O Lordy, I am killed!'

" 'Well,' said I, 'if you are really killed, why in the devil don't you stop hallooing?' "

Union General McDowell believed he was wearing Beauregard down, and he was right.

A correspondent of the Charleston *Mercury* (he signed himself "L.W.S.") who approached the field from the rear during this period did not like the look of things. Demoralized men were streaming back, many without wounds. And men *with* wounds were much in evidence.

"At the first trench I came to, which was just beyond the range of bullets, lay one hundred, at least, in every stage of suffering. . . . One had his leg shot off with a cannon ball, another had his arm broken, another had his jaw shot away.

"Colonel Hampton met us with the appearance of having had a ball in his temple, and he said he had been insensible from the effects, but he hoped soon to be upon the field again. . . . I met . . . an ambulance which . . . contained . . . General Bee. The general lay prostrate and . . . expiring from the wound in his abdomen. . . .

"Others were there—aged men, whose gray hairs proclaimed them sixty and more; boys whose young hearts yearned, I know, for softer hands and sweeter faces than were around them there."

From the wounded, the correspondent learned that the battle remained undecided. "The chances seemed against us."

According to John Esten Cooke, however, "the Confederate front remained unbroken. . . . Jackson had held his position for about an hour; and this had enabled General Beauregard to hurry forward [additional] troops from the lines along Bull Run. These were at last in position, and, taking command of them in person, General Beauregard . . . ordered the whole line to advance and make a decisive assault. Jackson still held the center. . . . At the word, his brigade rushed forward . . . and, supported by the reserves, drove the enemy from the plateau."

Tactically, the Union lines were still strong. They comprised a wide arc around Beauregard's position. But the morale of the troops was fast declining. As explained by Henry Blake, the captain from Massachusetts:

"It was three o'clock, and the soldiers had been engaged upon the march or in action during the long period of thirteen hours. A large number, from various causes, had left their commands and escaped to the rear. . . . The exhausting march, the terrible heat, the lack of water, the horrors of the battle, and, above all, the loss of the artillery, had affected those who remained to such an extent that they became every minute more unfitted to resist the onset of the enemy, who maintained an irregular fire from the forest [on the plateau].

"Some officers [had] behaved in a most cowardly manner; and certain companies were commanded by sergeants because the captains and lieutenants absented themselves during the engagement. An uninjured colonel who pretended to be severely wounded and declared that he was unable to walk, was borne from the field by four members of his regiment.

"There was no general demoralization in the army, although many of the troops acted like *all* novices in the dreadful art of war, and executed some movements with great confusion. Two men [of our regiment] placed their hands upon their ears to exclude the noise of the musketry and artillery, and rushed to the woods in the rear. . . .

"The ghastly faces of the dead and the sufferings of the wounded, who were begging for water or imploring aid to be carried to the hospital, moved the hearts of men who had not, by long experience, become callous to the sight of human agony."

Precious few of the troops were pleased when McDowell decided to make another attack. As the units formed, however, their lack of spirit was not evident to the Confederates.

"It was a grand spectacle," says Edward Pollard of the Richmond *Examiner*, "as this crescent outline of battle developed itself and [moved] forward on the broad, gentle slopes of the ridge occupied by its clouds of skirmishers. . . . As far as the eye could reach, masses of infantry and carefully preserved cavalry stretched through the woods and fields. . . .

"While the Federals . . . prepared for the renewal of the struggle, telegraph signals from the hills warned General Beauregard to 'look out for the enemy's advance on the left.' At the distance of more than a mile [from the federal right], a column of men was approaching. At their head was a flag which could not be distinguished; and, even with the aid of a strong glass, General Beauregard was unable to determine whether it was the Federal flag or the Confederate flag—that of the stripes or that of the bars.

" 'At this moment,' said General Beauregard in speaking afterwards of the occurrence, 'I must confess my heart failed me. I came, reluctantly, to the conclusion that, after all our efforts, we should at last be compelled to leave to the enemy the hard-fought and bloody field. I again took the glass to examine the flag of the approaching column; but my anxious inquiry was unproductive of result—I could not tell to which army the waving banner belonged. At this time all the members of my staff were absent, having been dispatched with orders to various points. The only person with me was the gallant . . . Colonel Evans ["Shanks"]. . . . I told him that I feared the approaching force was in reality Patterson's division [from the Shenandoah Valley]; that, if such was the case, I would be compelled to fall back upon our reserves and postpone, until the next day, a continuation of the engagement.'

"Turning to Colonel Evans, the anxious commander directed him to proceed to General Johnston and request him to have his reserves collected in readiness to support and protect a retreat. Colonel Evans had proceeded but a little way. Both officers fixed one final, intense gaze upon the advancing flag. A happy gust of wind shook out its folds, and General Beauregard recognized the Stars and Bars of the Confederate banner! . . .

" 'Colonel Evans,' exclaimed Beauregard, his face lighting up, 'ride forward and order General Kirby Smith to hurry up his command, and strike them on the flank and rear!'

E. Kirby Smith

"It was the arrival of Kirby Smith with a portion of Johnston's army left in the Shenandoah Valley, which had been anxiously expected during the day. And now cheer after cheer from regiment to regiment announced his welcome. As the train approached Manassas with some two thousand infantry, mainly of [Arnold] Elzey's brigade, General Smith knew, by the sounds of firing, that a great struggle was in progress; and, having stopped the engine, he had formed his men and was advancing rapidly through the fields. . . .

"At the same time, Early's brigade . . . had just come up [from the lower Bull Run lines, guided to McDowell's right by Jeb Stuart, who had been doing some significant harassment work there]. . . . The two movements were made almost simultaneously, while General Beauregard himself led the charge in front.

"The combined attack was too much for the enemy."

As confirmed by General McDowell:

"They . . . opened a fire of musketry on our men which caused them to break and retire down the hillside. This soon degenerated into disorder for which there was no remedy."

Adds Colonel Andrew Porter of Hunter's division:

"Soon the slopes . . . were swarming with our retreating and disorganized forces, while riderless horses and artillery teams ran furiously through the flying crowd. All further efforts were futile. The words, gestures, and threats of our officers were thrown away upon men who had lost all presence of mind, and only longed for absence of body."

Still in his position behind the lines, on the battlefield of the morning, Massachusetts civilian Edwin Barrett was incredulous at the turn of events.

"To my utter astonishment, [I] saw our whole body retreating in utter confusion and disorder—no lines, no companies, no regiments could be distinguished. . . . The whole line was drifting back through the valley. I fell in with them . . . occasionally halting and looking back. I stopped on the brow of a hill while the volume drifted by, and I can compare it to nothing more than a drove of cattle. . . .

"The enemy had nearly ceased firing from the batteries on their right and center, but still, on our extreme right, beyond a patch of woods, the fighting was going on. . . . [Union Major George Sykes, with his battalion of regulars, made a temporary stand there.]

"I did not leave the hill until the enemy's infantry came out from their entrenchments and slowly moved forward, their guns glistening in the sun. . . . They showed no disposition to charge. . . . Had they precipitated their columns upon our panic-stricken army, the slaughter would have been dreadful, for so thorough was the panic that no power on earth could have stopped the retreat and made our men turn and fight."

Switching to the Confederate side and to Private John Casler:

"We did not follow them far, for . . . we had lost severely and were considerably demoralized. I . . . took a stroll over the battle-field to see who of my comrades were dead or wounded, and saw my friend, William I. Blue, lying on his face dead. [This was the man with whom the narrator had made a burial pact.] I turned him over to see where he was shot. He must have been shot through the heart, the place where he wanted to be shot, if shot at all. He must have been killed instantly, for he was in the act of loading his gun. . . .

"I sat down by him and took a hearty cry, and then, thinks I, 'It does not look well for a soldier to cry,' but I could not help it. I then stuck his gun in the ground by his side, marked his name, company, and regiment on a piece of paper, pinned it to his breast, and went off."

He would return the next day and make the burial he had promised.

Confederate Private John Opie's movements on the field took him through the debris of Ricketts's battery.

"It is deserted by all save the dead and wounded. There, shot through the thigh, between two of his guns, the gallant old hero lay, dead men and horses piled around him.

"Our lieutenant-colonel, William H. Harman, said, 'Why, Ricketts, is this you?'

" 'Yes,' said he, 'but I do not know you, sir.'

" 'We were in the Mexican War together. Harman is my name.'

"Ricketts then recognized him, and they shook hands, literally across the bloody chasm."

Ricketts was taken prisoner. His wound was a very serious one and might have proved fatal, except that his wife, Fanny, came down from the North, wangled her way through the Confederate lines, and won permission to nurse him. Upon his recovery, he was exchanged.

President Jefferson Davis, who arrived from Richmond by train during the final phase of the battle, came riding up to the rear of

Fanny Ricketts

the Confederate lines without any knowledge of what had happened. Stonewall Jackson was then in the rear, seated on a stool at a field hospital and accepting attention for his wounded hand from his brigade's medical director, Dr. Hunter McGuire.

The doctor relates:

"I saw President Davis ride up. . . . He had been told by stragglers that our army had been defeated. He stopped his horse in the middle of [a] little stream, stood up in his stirrups—the palest, sternest face I ever saw—and cried to the great crowd of soldiers, 'I am President Davis. Follow me back to the field!'

"General Jackson did not hear [him] distinctly. I told him who it was and what he said. He stood up, took off his cap, and cried, 'We have whipped them! They ran like sheep! Give me 10,000 men, and I will take Washington City tomorrow!' "

Davis rode on toward the front, passing groups of dusty and weary soldiers, some of them bloody with wounds, who cheered and shouted as they learned his identity. He reached a forward position at about the time the last of the Yankees departed the field. In the president's words:

"The signs of an utter rout . . . were unmistakable, and justified the conclusion that the watchword of 'On to Richmond!' had been changed to 'Off for Washington!' "

There were at least a few Federals who were not yet thinking in terms of making for the capital. The more levelheaded men

counted on finding safety amid the reserves at Centreville, where
the whole army might regroup. Somewhat curiously, the troops
who had come to the field that morning by way of Sudley Ford
retreated along the same detour. This stream of fugitives was
followed by a joyous Jeb Stuart and his troopers, who gathered
prisoners in such numbers that they soon had to desist because
they could handle no more.

The Unionists who retreated across the Stone Bridge and the
fords in its vicinity were not at first molested, but their route
toward Centreville on the Warrenton Turnpike was fairly blocked
with supply wagons. It was, indeed, among these wagons themselves that the first heavy confusion developed.

As related by British journalist William Howard Russell, who,
unaware of McDowell's defeat, was at this time coming forward,
on horseback, from Centreville toward the bridge over Cub Run:

"I was threading my way when my attention was attracted by
loud shouts in advance, and I perceived several wagons coming
from the direction of the battlefield, the drivers of which were
endeavoring to force their horses past the ammunition carts going
in the contrary direction near the bridge. A thick cloud of dust
rose behind them, and running by the side of the wagons were a
number of men in uniform whom I supposed to be the guard. My
first impression was that the wagons were returning for fresh
supplies of ammunition.

"But every moment the crowd increased. Drivers and men cried
out with the most vehement gestures, 'Turn back! Turn back! We
are whipped!' They seized the heads of the horses and swore at
the opposing drivers.

"Emerging from the crowd, a breathless man in the uniform of
an officer, with an empty scabbard dangling by his side, was cut
off by getting between my horse and a cart for a moment. 'What
is the matter, sir? What is all this about?'

" 'Why, it means we are pretty badly whipped—that's the truth,'
he gasped, and continued.

"By this time the confusion had been communicating itself
through the line of wagons toward the rear, and the drivers endeavored to turn round their vehicles in the narrow road, which
caused the usual amount of imprecations from the men, and
plunging and kicking from the horses.

"The crowd from the front continually increased."

And now the civilian carriages—their occupants pale-faced and wide-eyed, the men shouting and the women shrieking—came rolling down the hillsides to gain the turnpike and push their way into the thickening stream.

On the Confederate side, a battery planted near the Stone Bridge began firing (with old Edmund Ruffin serving as a volunteer gunner!), and it soon dropped a shell on the Cub Run Bridge. The result was an impossible jam of wagons and artillery pieces, and some of the guns were abandoned.

Additional trouble was caused by a regiment of Confederate cavalry—the 30th Virginia under Colonel R. C. W. Radford—that now went into action. In the words of a trooper named McFarland:

"Taking a rapid gallop, we crossed Bull Run about three-quarters of a mile below the Stone Bridge and made for the rear of the now-flying enemy. On we dashed, with the speed of the wind, our horses wild with excitement, leaping fences, ditches,

Stampede of the baggage wagons

and fallen trees, until we came opposite to the house of Mrs. Spindle, which was used by the enemy as a hospital . . . and found ourselves on the flank of the enemy. . . . Our onslaught was terrific. . . .

"With several others, I rode up to the door of the hospital, in which a number of terrified Yankees had crowded for safety, and as they came out we shot them down with our pistols. Happening at this moment to turn round, I saw a Yankee soldier in the act of discharging his musket at the group stationed around the door. Just as he fired, I wheeled my horse and endeavored to ride him down, but he rolled over a fence which crossed the yard.

"This I forced my horse to leap, and, drawing my revolver, I shouted to him to stop. As he turned, I aimed to fire into his face; but, my horse being restive, the ball intended for his brain only passed through his arm, which he held over his head. . . .

"I was about to finish him with another shot (for I had vowed to spare no prisoners that day), when I chanced to look into his face. He was a beardless boy, evidently not more than seventeen years old. I could not find it in my heart to kill him, for he pled piteously. So, seizing him by the collar . . . I dragged him to our rear guard."

As it happened, these Confederate troopers were repelled by fresh federal infantry. At McDowell's order, Miles had sent Louis Blenker's brigade forward from Centreville.

Blenker relates:

"This order was executed with great difficulty, as the road was nearly choked up by retreating baggage wagons of several divisions and by the vast number of flying soldiers belonging to various regiments. Nevertheless, owing to the coolness of the commanding officers and the good discipline of the men, the passage . . . was successfully executed. . . . I was thus enabled to take a position which would prevent the advance of the enemy and protect the retreat of the army."

The army did not *feel* protected. Word flew around that the enemy's troopers were attacking, and the panic increased. As reported by the correspondent of the New York *World:*

"I saw officers with leaves and eagles on their shoulder-straps—majors and colonels who had deserted their commands—pass me galloping as if for dear life. . . . Only one field officer, so far as my observation extended, seemed to have remembered his duty . . . [and] strove against the current. . . .

Blenker's brigade covering the retreat

"I saw a man in citizen's dress, who had thrown off his coat, seized a musket, and was trying to rally the soldiers who came by, at the point of the bayonet. In a reply to a request for his name, he said it was Washburne, and I learned he was the member [of Congress] by that name from Illinois. The Hon. Mr. Kellogg made a similar effort. Both these Congressmen bravely stood their ground till the last moment. . . . And other civilians did what they could.

"But what a scene! And how terrific the onset of that tumultuous retreat. For three miles, hosts of Federal troops—all detached from their regiments, all mingled in one disorderly rout—were fleeing along the road, but mostly through the lots on either side. Army wagons, sutlers' teams, and private carriages choked the passage, tumbling against each other amid clouds of dust and sickening sights and sounds.

"Hacks containing unlucky spectators of the late affray were smashed like glass, and the occupants were lost sight of in the debris. Horses flying wildly from the battlefield, many of them in death agony, galloped at random forward, joining in the stampede. Those on foot who could catch them rode them bareback, as much to save themselves from being run over as to make quicker time.

"Wounded men lying along the banks . . . appealed with raised hands to those who rode horses, begging to be lifted behind, but few regarded such petitions. Then the artillery, such as was saved, came thundering along, smashing and overpowering everything. The regular cavalry, I record it to their shame, joined in the meleé, adding to its terrors, for they rode down footmen without mercy.

"One of the great guns was overturned and lay amid the ruins of a caisson as I passed it. I saw an artilleryman running between the ponderous fore-and-after wheels of his gun carriage, hanging on with both hands and vainly striving to jump upon the ordnance. The drivers were spurring the horses. He could not cling much longer, and a more agonized expression never fixed the features of a drowning man. The carriage bounded from the roughness of a steep hill leading to a creek. He lost his hold, fell, and in an instant the great wheels had crushed the life out of him.

"Who ever saw such a flight? . . . It did not slack in the least until Centreville was reached. There the sight of the reserve . . . formed in order on the hill, seemed somewhat to reassure the van. But still the teams and foot-soldiers pushed on, passing their own camps and heading swiftly for the distant Potomac. . . .

"From the branch route [coming in from Sudley Ford] the trains [in advance of the detouring troops] . . . had caught the contagion of the flight, and poured into its already swollen current another turbid freshet of confusion and dismay.

"Who ever saw a more shameful abandonment of munitions gathered at such vast expense? The teamsters—many of them— cut the traces of their horses and galloped from the wagons. Others threw out their loads to accelerate their flight; and grain, picks and shovels, and provisions of every kind lay trampled in the dust for leagues. Thousands of muskets strewed the route. . . . Enough was left behind to tell the story of the panic.

"The rout of the Federal army seemed complete."

It *was* complete. Unable to rebuild his army around the Centreville reserve, McDowell had no choice but to allow the retreat to continue.

In Washington, according to Lincoln's private secretary, John

Nicolay, "the loyal people . . . were rejoicing over a victory steadily reported during the greater part of the day, when suddenly, at about five o'clock, came the startling telegram: 'General McDowell's army in full retreat through Centreville. The day is lost. . . .'

"By midnight, officers and civilians who were lucky enough to have retained horses began to arrive, and the apparent proportions of the defeat to increase. It was a gloomy night. . . . Next day, Monday, the rain commenced falling in torrents. . . . Through this rain the disbanded soldiers began to pour into Washington City, fagged out, hungry, and dejected, and having literally nowhere to turn their feet or lay their head.

"History owes a page of honorable mention to the Federal capital for its unselfish generosity on this occasion. The rich and poor, the high and low of her loyal people, with one quick and entirely unprompted impulse opened their doors and dealt out food and refreshment to the footsore, haggard, and half-starved men . . . so unexpectedly reduced to tramps and fugitives. . . .

"By Monday noon the full extent of the disaster . . . could be reasonably estimated, since indications began to show that the enemy had not pressed their pursuit in force. But, in due preparation for the worst . . . General McClellan was called to Washington [from western Virginia] to take command, McDowell being continued in charge of the defenses on the Virginia side of the Potomac."

At Manassas on that rainy Monday, July 22, 1861, plans for making a quick thrust against the Union capital were seriously considered, but the idea was soon abandoned. The Confederate army was woefully disorganized, and Washington, it was realized, was not wholly defenseless. The Potomac River itself was a barrier to easy access, and the Federals, it was concluded, still had enough organized troops to meet an attack.

The Confederates spent the day in celebrating their victory, in collecting the vast amount of valuable military goods left in the Union wake, and in dealing with the many dead and wounded of both armies scattered about the area. Since the weather was warm, the dead—Confederates and Federals alike—were buried quickly and with little ceremony, mostly grouped in long, shallow trenches, and only thinly covered.

"Sometimes," says Private John Opie, "a hand or foot of some poor fellow served as a head or foot board."

More shocking to Opie were the field hospitals. "I visited one, located outside of a farmhouse. . . . There were two huge piles of

Back in Washington after the battle

legs, feet, hands, and arms, all thrown together. . . . Many of the feet still retained the boot or shoe. Wounded men were lying upon tables; and surgeons, some of whom . . . were very unskillful, were carving away like farmers in butchering season, while the poor devils under the knife fairly yelled with pain."

In aggregate, the Battle of Bull Run (or Manassas, as the Confederates called it) cost about five thousand in killed, wounded, captured, and missing—about three thousand for the Federals and two thousand for the Confederates.

Richmond and the entire Confederacy, of course, rejoiced over the great triumph. Later, however, its value had to be reassessed.

"The victory of Manassas," explains Southerner Edward Pollard, "proved the greatest misfortune that could have befallen the Confederacy. It was taken by the Southern public as the end of the war, or at least as its decisive event. . . . President Davis, after the battle, assured his intimate friends that the recognition of the Confederate States by the European powers was now certain.

"The newspapers declared that the question of manhood between North and South was settled forever; and the phrase of 'one Southerner equal to five Yankees' was adopted in all speeches about the war—although the origin, or rule, of the precise proportion was never clearly stated.

"An elaborate article in *De Bow's Review* compared Manassas with the decisive battles of the world, and considered that the war would now degenerate into mere desultory affairs, preliminary to a peace.

"On the whole, the unfortunate victory of Manassas was followed by a period of fancied security and of relaxed exertions on the part of the Southern people [that was] highly dangerous and inauspicious."

To be sure, there were Southerners who had reservations about the situation. Judith McGuire said in her dairy: "It is true that we have slaughtered them and whipped them and driven them from our land, but they are people of such indomitable perseverance that I am afraid that they will come again, perhaps in greater force."

Mrs. Louis T. Wigfall fretted that the North might be "exasperated to frenzy at such a defeat."

Robert E. Lee anticipated a rigorous continuation of the war, writing his wife that he expected to be kept very busy. "All my thoughts and strength are given to the cause to which my life, be it long or short, will be devoted."

The Union reaction to Bull Run is given by John Nicolay:

"To say that the hope and enthusiasm of the North received a painful shock of humiliation and disappointment is to use but a mild description of the popular feeling. This first experience of defeat—or recognition of even the possibility of defeat—was inexpressibly bitter. Stifling the sharp sorrow, however, the great public of the Free States sent up its prompt and united demand that the contest should be continued and the disgrace wiped out.

"Impatience and overeagerness were chastened and repressed;

and the North reconciled itself to the painful prospect of a tedious civil war . . . [and] the necessity of bending every energy to immediate preparation on a widely extended scale. . . .

"An important event . . . now became the pivot and controlling force of military operations. This was the disbandment of the three-months volunteers. Within a few weeks almost the whole seventy-five thousand men were mustered out and returned to their homes. . . . But out of the whole number of troops thus suddenly dissolved, a considerable proportion immediately entered the three-years service as individuals, and in many instances their drill and experience secured them election or appointment as officers in the new regiments. . . .

"The three-years quota, and the increase of the regular army called by President Lincoln—in advance of strict authority of law at the beginning of May—had so far progressed that garrisons and camps suffered no serious diminution.

"Congress, being convened in special session, now legalized their enlistment, perfected their organization, and made liberal provisions for their equipment and supply. It authorized an army of five hundred thousand men, and a national loan of two hundred and fifty millions of dollars. It provided an increase of the navy to render the blockade vigilant and rigorous. . . .

"Washington City . . . and the fortified strip of territory held by the Union armies on the Virginia side of the Potomac, once more became a great military camp.

"Here, under McClellan's personal supervision, grew up that famous Army of the Potomac."

At the outset of his new career, McClellan, characteristically, made the boast: "I shall carry this thing *en grand* and crush the rebels in one campaign."

Many of the more practical-minded military professionals saw things differently. " 'Tis folly," said William Tecumseh Sherman, "to underestimate the task." Sherman expected the war to be one of such a length and ferocity that he would not survive it.

One of the sagest Northern responses to Bull Run was voiced by Pennsylvania's Chaplain A. M. Stewart:

"The Constitution of the United States—what is it? A mere compact between the States, or a document constituting us a combined whole? . . . The sword is now the arbiter and must decide the character of our government—or rather, perhaps, whether we have a government. . . .

"When this war is ended, the rebellion crushed out, and the nation's power vindicated, the government for the whole American people will rest upon a basis more solid and compact than heretofore. . . . Ropes of sand will be replaced by wire cables strong enough to sustain the whole Union arch."

Quotation Sources

Abbott, John S. C. *The History of the Civil War in America.* 2 vols. Springfield, MA: Gurdon Bill, 1863–1866.

Annals of the War. Philadelphia: Times Publishing, 1879.

Appleman, Roy Edgar, ed. *Abraham Lincoln, from His Own Words and Contemporary Accounts* (National Park Service Source Book Series No. 2). Washington, DC: 1942.

Beers, Mrs. Fannie A. *Memories: A Record of Personal Experience and Adventure During Four Years of War.* Philadelphia: Lippincott, 1891.

Billings, John D. *Hardtack and Coffee.* Boston: George M. Smith, 1889.

Blake, Henry N. *Three Years in the Army of the Potomac.* Boston: Lee and Shepard, 1865.

Botts, John Minor. *The Great Rebellion.* New York: Harper & Brothers, 1866.

Casler, John O. *Four Years in the Stonewall Brigade.* James I. Robertson, Jr., ed. Dayton, OH: Morningside Bookshop, 1971. Facsimile of 1906 edition.

Coffin, Charles Carleton. *The Boys of '61.* Boston: Estes and Lauriat, 1884.

———. *Drum-Beat of the Nation.* New York: Harper & Brothers, 1888.

———. *My Days and Nights on the Battlefield.* Boston: Ticknor and Fields, 1866.

———. *Stories of Our Soldiers.* Boston: Journal Newspaper Company, 1893.

Cooke, John Esten. *Stonewall Jackson: A Military Biography.* New York: D. Appleton, 1866.

———. *Wearing of the Gray.* New York: E. B. Treat, 1867.

Crafts, William A. *The Southern Rebellion.* Paperbound set; 50 parts. Boston: Samuel Walker, 1864–1867.

Crotty, D. G. *Four Years Campaigning in the Army of the Potomac.* Grand Rapids, MI: Dygert Brothers, 1874.

Dabney, R. L. *Life and Campaigns of Lieut.-Gen. Thomas J. Jackson.* New York: Blelock, 1866.

Davis, Jefferson. *The Rise and Fall of the Confederate Government*. 2 vols. South Brunswick, NJ: Thomas Yoseloff, 1958. Reprint of edition by D. Appleton, 1881.

Davis, Varina Howell. *Jefferson Davis: A Memoir by His Wife*. 2 vols. New York: Belford, 1890.

Dickert, D. Augustus. *History of Kershaw's Brigade*. Dayton, OH: Morningside Bookshop, 1976. Facsimile of 1899 edition.

Duyckinck, Evert A. *National History of the War for the Union*. 3 vols. New York: Johnson, Fry, 1868.

Edmonds, S. Emma E. *Nurse and Spy in the Union Army*. Hartford, CT: W. S. Williams, 1865.

Eggleston, George Cary. *A Rebel's Recollections*. New York: Putnam's, 1905.

Evans, Clement A., ed. *Confederate Military History*. 12 vols. New York, London, Toronto: Thomas Yoseloff, 1962. Facsimile publication of 1899 edition by Confederate Publishing of Atlanta.

Gordon, John G. *Reminiscences of the Civil War*. New York: Scribner's, 1904.

Goss, Warren Lee. *Recollections of a Private*. New York: Thomas Y. Crowell, 1890.

Grant, U. S. *Personal Memoirs*. New York: Charles L. Webster, 1894.

Greeley, Horace. *The American Conflict*. 2 vols. Hartford, CT: O. D. Case, 1864, 1867.

Hart, Albert Bushnell, ed. *American History Told by Contemporaries*. Vol. 4. New York: Macmillan, 1910.

Hill, A. F. *Our Boys: The Personal Experiences of a Soldier in the Army of the Potomac*. Philadelphia: Keystone, 1890.

Holland, J. G. *The Life of Abraham Lincoln*. Springfield, MA: Gurdon Bill, 1866.

Howe, M. A. DeWolfe, ed. *Home Letters of General Sherman*. New York: Scribner's, 1909.

Jackson, Mary Anna. *Memoirs of Stonewall Jackson*. Louisville, KY: Prentice Press, 1895.

Johnson, Robert Underwood, and Clarence Clough Buel, eds. *Battles and Leaders of the Civil War*. 4 vols. New York: Century, 1884–1888.

Johnston, Joseph E. *Narrative of Military Operations*. New York: D. Appleton, 1874.

Keyes, E. D. *Fifty Years' Observation of Men and Events, Civil and Military*. New York: Scribner's, 1884.

King, W. C., and W. P. Derby. *Campfire Sketches and Battlefield Echoes*. Springfield, MA: W. C. King, 1887.

Lee, Fitzhugh. *General Lee of the Confederate Army*. London: Chapman and Hall, 1895.

Lee, Captain Robert E. *Recollections and Letters of General Robert E. Lee*. New York: Doubleday, Page, 1904.

Livermore, Mary A. *My Story of the War.* Hartford, CT: A. D. Worthington, 1889.

Longstreet, James. *From Manassas to Appomattox.* Philadelphia: J. B. Lippincott, 1903.

Lossing, Benson J. *Pictorial Field Book of the Civil War.* 3 vols. New York: T. Belknap, 1868.

Lusk, William Thompson. *War Letters.* New York: Privately printed, 1911.

McClellan, George B. *McClellan's Own Story.* New York: Charles L. Webster, 1887.

McClure, A. K. *Abraham Lincoln and Men of War Times.* Philadelphia: Times Publishing, 1892.

McGuire, Hunter. *Address Delivered on 23d Day of June, 1897, at the Virginia Military Institute.* Lynchburg, VA: J. P. Bell, 1897.

[McGuire, Judith W.]. *Diary of a Southern Refugee During the War.* New York: E. J. Hale, 1867.

Moore, Frank, ed. *The Civil War in Song and Story.* New York: P. F. Collier, 1889.

———. *The Rebellion Record.* Vols. 1 and 2. New York: Putnam, 1861, 1862.

Nicolay, John G. *The Outbreak of Rebellion.* Vol. 1, *Campaigns of the Civil War.* New York: Scribner's, 1881.

Opie, John N. *A Rebel Cavalryman with Lee, Stuart, and Jackson.* Dayton, OH: Morningside Bookshop, 1972. Facsimile of 1899 edition.

Our Women in the War. Charleston, SC: News and Courier Book Presses, 1885.

Owen, William Miller. *In Camp and Battle with the Washington Artillery.* Boston: Ticknor and Company, 1885. Second edition by Pelican Publishing Company, New Orleans, 1964.

Piatt, Donn. *Memories of the Men Who Saved the Union.* New York and Chicago: Belford, Clarke, 1887.

Pinkerton, Allan. *The Spy of the Rebellion.* New York: G. W. Carleton, 1883.

Pollard, Edward A. *The First Year of the War.* Richmond, VA: West & Johnston, 1862.

———. *The Lost Cause.* New York: E. B. Treat, 1866.

Porter, David D. *The Naval History of the Civil War.* New York: Sherman Publishing, 1886.

Pryor, Mrs. Roger A. *Reminiscences of Peace and War.* New York: Macmillan, 1904.

[Putnam, Sarah A.]. *Richmond During the War.* New York: G. W. Carleton, 1867.

Ratchford, J. W. *Some Reminiscences of Persons and Incidents of the Civil War.* Facsimile reproduction of the 1909 edition. Austin, TX: Shoal Creek, 1971.

Russell, William Howard. *My Diary North and South.* London: Bradbury & Evans, 1863.

Sherman, John. *Recollections of Forty Years in the House, Senate, and Cabinet.* 2 vols. Chicago, New York, London, Berlin: Werner, 1895.

Sherman, W. T. *Memoirs of Gen. W. T. Sherman Written by Himself.* 2 vols. New York: Charles L. Webster, 1891.

Stewart, A. M. *Camp, March and Battle-Field.* Philadelphia: Jas. B. Rodgers, 1865.

Tarbell, Ida M. *The Life of Abraham Lincoln.* 2 vols. New York: McClure, Phillips, 1902.

Tenney, W. J. *The Military and Naval History of the Rebellion.* New York: D. Appleton, 1865.

Tomes, Robert. *The Great Civil War.* 3 vols. New York: Virtue and Yorston, 1862.

Under Both Flags: A Panorama of the Great Civil War. Chicago: W. S. Reeve, 1896.

Wallace, Francis B. *Memorial of the Patriotism of Schuylkill County in the American Slaveholder's Rebellion.* Pottsville, PA: Benjamin Bannan, 1865.

The War of the Rebellion: A Compilation of the Official Records of the Union and Confederate Armies. Washington, DC: Government Printing Office, 1880–1901.

Wright, Mrs. D. Giraud. *A Southern Girl in '61: The Wartime Memories of a Confederate Senator's Daughter.* New York: Doubleday, Page, 1905.

Young, Jesse Bowman. *What a Boy Saw in the Army.* New York: Hunt & Eaton, 1894.

Supplementary References

Adams, F. Colburn. *The Story of a Trooper*. New York: Dick & Fitzgerald, 1865.

Angle, Paul M., and Earl Schenck Miers. *Tragic Years, 1860–1865*. 2 vols. New York: Simon & Schuster, 1960.

Arnold, Thomas Jackson. *Early Life and Letters of General Thomas J. Jackson*. New York: Fleming H. Revell, 1916.

Blackford, W. W. *War Years with Jeb Stuart*. New York: Scribner's, 1945.

Blay, John S. *The Civil War: A Pictorial Profile*. New York: Bonanza Books, 1958.

Butler, Benjamin F. *Butler's Book: A Review of His Legal, Political, and Military Career*. Boston: A. M. Thayer, 1892.

Caldwell, J. F. J. *The History of a Brigade of South Carolinians*. Philadelphia: King & Baird, 1866. Facsimile edition by Morningside Bookshop, Dayton, OH, 1974.

Carpenter, F. B. *The Inner Life of Abraham Lincoln*. New York: Hurd and Houghton, 1868.

Catton, Bruce. *The Coming Fury*. New York: Doubleday, 1961.

Century War Book: People's Pictorial Edition. New York: Century, 1894.

Commager, Henry Steele. *The Blue and the Gray*. Indianapolis and New York: Bobbs-Merrill, 1950.

Cooke, John Esten. *The Life of Stonewall Jackson*. Freeport, NY: Books for Libraries Press, 1971. First published in 1863.

——. *Robert E. Lee*. New York: G. W. Dillingham, 1899.

Curtis, Newton Martin. *From Bull Run to Chancellorsville*. New York: Putnam's, 1906.

Davis, Burke. *Jeb Stuart the Last Cavalier*. New York: Rinehart & Company, 1957.

De Trobriand, P. Regis. *Four Years With the Army of the Potomac*. Boston: Ticknor, 1889.

Doolady, M. *Jefferson Davis and Stonewall Jackson.* Philadelphia: John E. Potter, 1866.

Douglas, Henry Kyd. *I Rode With Stonewall.* Chapel Hill, NC: University of North Carolina Press, 1940.

Early, Jubal Anderson. *War Memoirs.* Frank E. Vandiver, ed. Bloomington, IN: Indiana University Press, 1960. First published in 1912.

Fiske, John. *The Mississippi Valley in the Civil War.* Boston and New York: Houghton Mifflin, 1900.

Frank Leslie's Illustrated History of the Civil War. New York: Mrs. Frank Leslie, 1895.

Gates, Theodore B. *The War of the Rebellion.* New York: P. F. McBreen, 1884.

Gay, Mary A. H. *Life in Dixie During the War.* Atlanta: Charles P. Byrd, 1897.

Gerrish, Theodore, and John S. Hutchinson. *The Blue and the Gray.* Portland, ME: Hoyt, Fogg & Donham, 1883.

Glazier, Willard. *Battles for the Union.* Hartford, CT: Dustin, Gilman, 1875.

Goode, John. *Recollections of a Lifetime.* New York and Washington: Neale Publishing, 1906.

Gragg, Rod. *The Illustrated Confederate Reader.* New York: Harper & Row, 1989.

Guernsey, Alfred H., and Henry M. Alden. *Harper's Pictorial History of the Great Rebellion.* 2 vols. Chicago: McDonnell Brothers, 1866, 1868.

Hansen, Harry. *The Civil War.* New York: Bonanza Books, 1962.

Harper's Encyclopaedia of United States History. 10 vols. New York: Harper & Brothers, 1915.

Headley, J. T. *The Great Rebellion.* 2 vols. Hartford, CT: Hurlbut, Williams, 1863, 1866.

Henderson, G. F. R. *Stonewall Jackson and the American Civil War.* 2 vols. London: Longman's, Green, 1913.

Johnson, Rossiter. *Campfires and Battlefields.* New York: Civil War Press, 1967. First published in 1894.

Jones, J. William. *Personal Reminiscences, Anecdotes, and Letters of Gen. Robert E. Lee.* New York: D. Appleton, 1874.

Jones, John B. *A Rebel War Clerk's Diary.* Edition condensed, edited, and annotated by Earl Schenck Miers. New York: Sagamore Press, 1958. First published in 1866.

Jones, Katharine M. *Ladies of Richmond.* Indianapolis and New York: Bobbs-Merrill, 1962.

Lewis, Lloyd. *Sherman, Fighting Prophet.* New York: Harcourt, Brace, 1932.

Loehr, Charles T. *War History of the Old First Virginia Infantry Regiment.* Dayton, OH: Morningside Bookshop, 1970. First published in 1884.

Logan, John A. *The Great Conspiracy.* New York: A. R. Hart, 1886.

Long, E. B., with Barbara Long. *The Civil War Day by Day.* Garden City, NY: Doubleday, 1971.

McCarthy, Carlton. *Detailed Minutiae of Soldier Life in the Army of Northern Virginia 1861–1865.* Richmond, VA: Carlton McCarthy, 1884.

Maclay, Edgar Stanton. *A History of the United States Navy.* Vol. 2. New York: D. Appleton, 1897.

McClellan, H. B. *The Life and Campaigns of Major-General J. E. B. Stuart.* Boston: Houghton Mifflin, 1885.

McClure, A. K. *Recollections of Half a Century.* Salem, MA: Salem Press, 1902.

Mitchell, Joseph B. *Decisive Battles of the Civil War.* New York: Putnam's, 1955.

Moore, Frank. *Women of the War.* Hartford, CT: S. S. Scranton, 1866.

Morton, Joseph W., Jr., ed. *Sparks from the Camp Fire.* Philadelphia: Keystone Publishing, 1892.

Paris, the Comte de (L. P. d'Orleans). *History of the Civil War in America.* 4 vols. Philadelphia: Jos. H. Coates, 1875–1888.

Pollard, Edward A. *The Early Life, Campaigns, and Public Services of Robert E. Lee; with a Record of the Campaigns and Heroic Deeds of His Companions in Arms.* New York: E. B. Treat, 1871.

Porter, David D. *Incidents and Anecdotes of the Civil War.* New York: D. Appleton, 1886.

Randall, Ruth Painter. *Mary Lincoln: Biography of a Marriage.* Boston: Little, Brown, 1953.

Richardson, Albert D. *A Personal History of Ulysses S. Grant.* Hartford, CT: American Publishing, 1868.

Selby, John. *Stonewall Jackson as Military Commander.* Princeton, NJ: D. Van Nostrand, 1968.

Smart, James G., ed. *A Radical View: The "Agate" Dispatches of Whitelaw Reid, 1861–1865.* 2 vols. Memphis, TN: Memphis State University Press, 1976.

Smith, James Power. *With Stonewall Jackson in the Army of Northern Virginia* (Southern Historical Society Papers). Richmond, VA: B. F. Johnson, 1920.

The Soldier in Our Civil War: A Pictorial History of the Conflict. New York: G. W. Carleton, 1886.

Spears, John R. *The History of Our Navy.* Vol. 4. New York: Scribner's, 1897.

Stephenson, Nathaniel W. *The Day of the Confederacy.* New Haven, CT: Yale University Press, 1920.

Stern, Philip Van Doren. *Robert E. Lee, the Man and the Soldier.* New York: Bonanza Books, 1963.

Stiles, Robert. *Four Years Under Marse Robert.* New York and Washington: Neale Publishing, 1903.

Stine, J. H. *History of the Army of the Potomac.* Philadelphia: J. B. Rodgers, 1892.

Stowe, Harriet Beecher. *Men of Our Times.* Hartford, CT: Hartford Publishing, 1868.

Swinton, William. *Campaigns of the Army of the Potomac.* New York: Scribner's, 1882.

————. *The Twelve Decisive Battles of the War.* New York: Dick & Fitzgerald, 1867.

Symonds, Craig L. *A Battlefield Atlas of the Civil War.* Baltimore: Nautical & Aviation Publishing, 1983.

Tate, Allen, *Stonewall Jackson the Good Soldier.* New York: Minton, Balch, 1928.

Thomas, Emory M. *Bold Dragoon: The Life of J. E. B. Stuart.* New York: Harper & Row, 1986.

Thomason, John W., Jr. *Jeb Stuart.* New York: Scribner's, 1930.

Urban, John W. *Battlefield and Prison Pen.* Edgewood Publishing, 1882.

Wheeler, Richard. *Sword Over Richmond.* New York: Harper & Row, 1986.

————. *Voices of the Civil War.* New York: Thomas Y. Crowell, 1977.

————. *We Knew Stonewall Jackson.* New York: Thomas Y. Crowell, 1977.

Williams, T. Harry. *Lincoln and His Generals.* New York: Knopf, 1952.

Wilshin, Francis F. *Manassas (Bull Run)* (National Park Service Historical Handbook Series No. 15). Washington, DC: 1953.

Wilson, John Laird. *Pictorial History of the Great Civil War.* Philadelphia: National Publishing, 1881.

Wittenmyer, Annie. *Under the Guns: A Woman's Reminiscences of the Civil War.* Boston: E. B. Stillings, 1895.

Wood, William. *Captains of the Civil War.* New Haven, CT: Yale University Press, 1921.

Worsham, John H. *One of Jackson's Foot Cavalry.* James I. Robertson, Jr., ed. Jackson, TN: McCowat-Mercer Press, 1964.

Index